ULTIMATE
AVENGERS

ULTIMATE AVENGERS

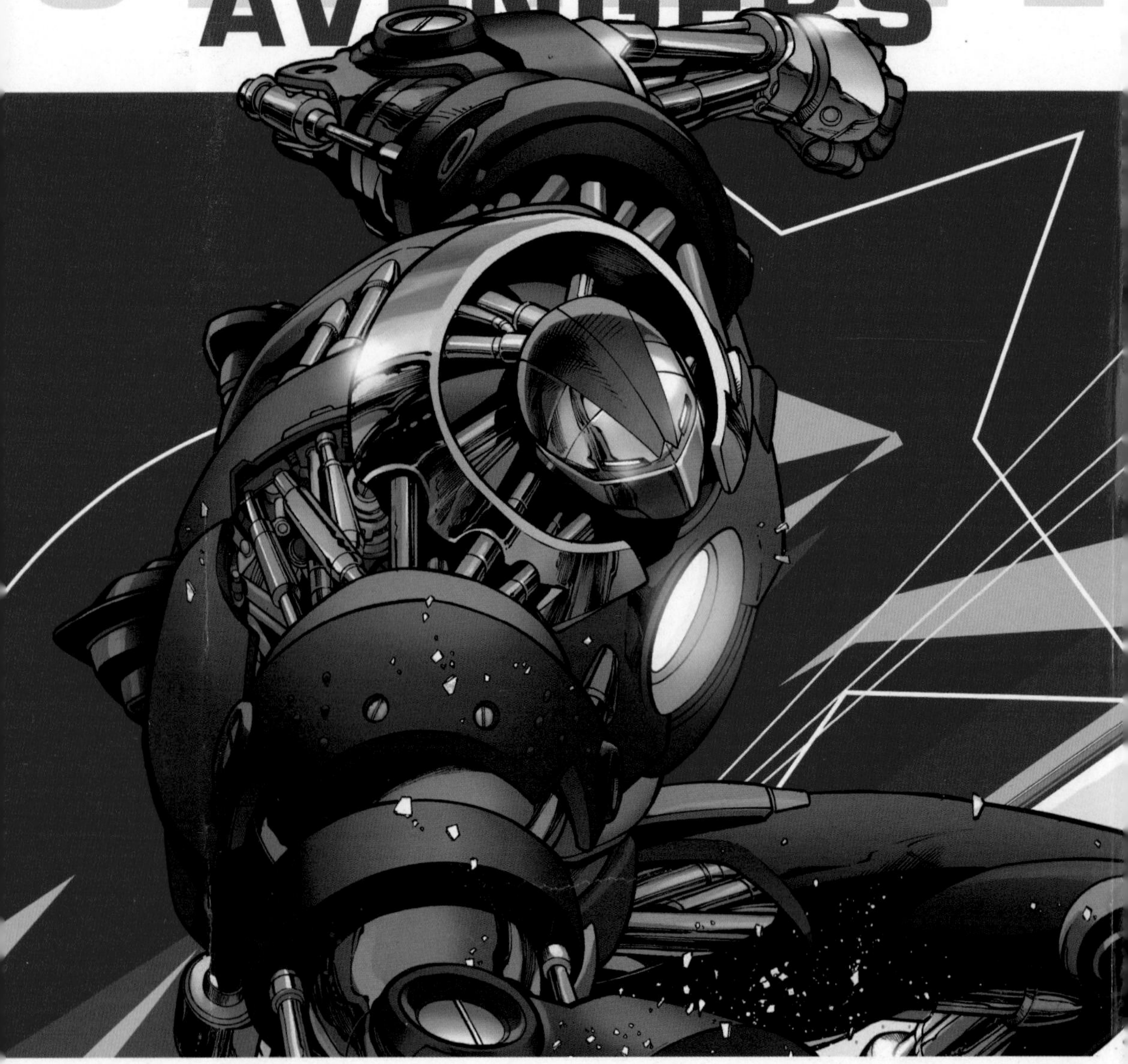

WRITER: **MARK MILLAR**

PENCILER: **CARLOS PACHECO**

INKERS: **DEXTER VINES** & **DANNY MIKI** WITH **ALLEN MARTINEZ, VICTOR OLAZABA** & **TOM PALMER**

COLORIST: **JUSTIN PONSOR** LETTERER: **VC'S CORY PETIT**

COVER ART: **CARLOS PACHECO, DANNY MIKI, DEXTER VINES, LAURA MARTIN** & **JUSTIN PONSOR**

ASSISTANT EDITOR: **SANA AMANAT**

ASSOCIATE EDITOR: **LAUREN SANKOVITCH**

SENIOR EDITOR: **MARK PANICCIA**

COLLECTION EDITOR: **JENNIFER GRÜNWALD**   ASSISTANT EDITOR: **ALEX STARBUCK**

ASSOCIATE EDITOR: **JOHN DENNING**   EDITOR, SPECIAL PROJECTS: **MARK D. BEAZLEY**

SENIOR EDITOR, SPECIAL PROJECTS: **JEFF YOUNGQUIST**

SENIOR VICE PRESIDENT OF SALES: **DAVID GABRIEL**

BOOK DESIGNER: **RODOLFO MURAGUCHI**

EDITOR IN CHIEF: **JOE QUESADA**   PUBLISHER: **DAN BUCKLEY**

EXECUTIVE PRODUCER: **ALAN FINE**

ULTIMATE COMICS AVENGERS: NEXT GENERATION. Contains material originally published in magazine form as ULTIMATE COMICS AVENGERS #1-6. First printing 2010. ISBN# 978-0-7851-4010-8. Published by MARVEL WORLDWIDE, INC., a subsidiary of MARVEL ENTERTAINMENT, LLC. OFFICE OF PUBLICATION: 417 5th Avenue, New York, NY 10016. Copyright © 2009 and 2010 Marvel Characters, Inc. All rights reserved. $24.99 per copy in the U.S. and $27.99 in Canada (GST #R127032852); Canadian Agreement #40668537. All characters featured in this issue and the distinctive names and likenesses thereof, and all related indicia are trademarks of Marvel Characters, Inc. No similarity between any of the names, characters, persons, and/or institutions in this magazine with those of any living or dead person or institution is intended, and any such similarity which may exist is purely coincidental. **Printed in the U.S.A.** ALAN FINE, EVP - Office of the President, Marvel Worldwide, Inc. and EVP & CMO Marvel Characters B.V.; DAN BUCKLEY, Chief Executive Officer and Publisher - Print, Animation & Digital Media; JIM SOKOLOWSKI, Chief Operating Officer; DAVID GABRIEL, SVP of Publishing Sales & Circulation; DAVID BOGART, SVP of Business Affairs & Talent Management; MICHAEL PASCIULLO, VP Merchandising & Communications; JIM O'KEEFE, VP of Operations & Logistics; DAN CARR, Executive Director of Publishing Technology; JUSTIN F. GABRIE, Director of Publishing & Editorial Operations; SUSAN CRESPI, Editorial Operations Manager; ALEX MORALES, Publishing Operations Manager; STAN LEE, Chairman Emeritus. For information regarding advertising in Marvel Comics or on Marvel.com, please contact Ron Stern, VP of Business Development, at rstern@marvel.com. For Marvel subscription inquiries, please call 800-217-9158. **Manufactured between 5/17/10 and 6/16/10 by R.R. DONNELLEY, INC., SALEM, VA, USA.**

10 9 8 7 6 5 4 3 2 1

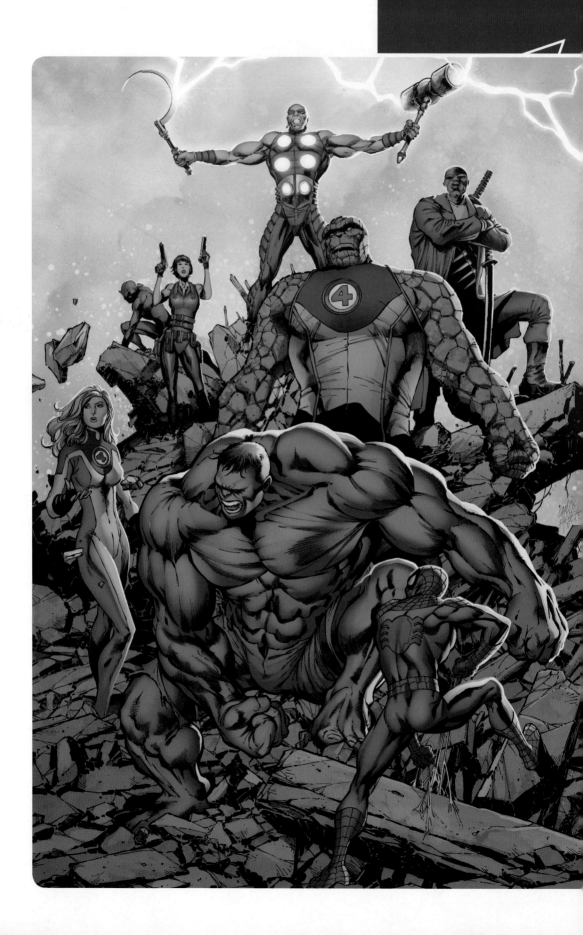

1

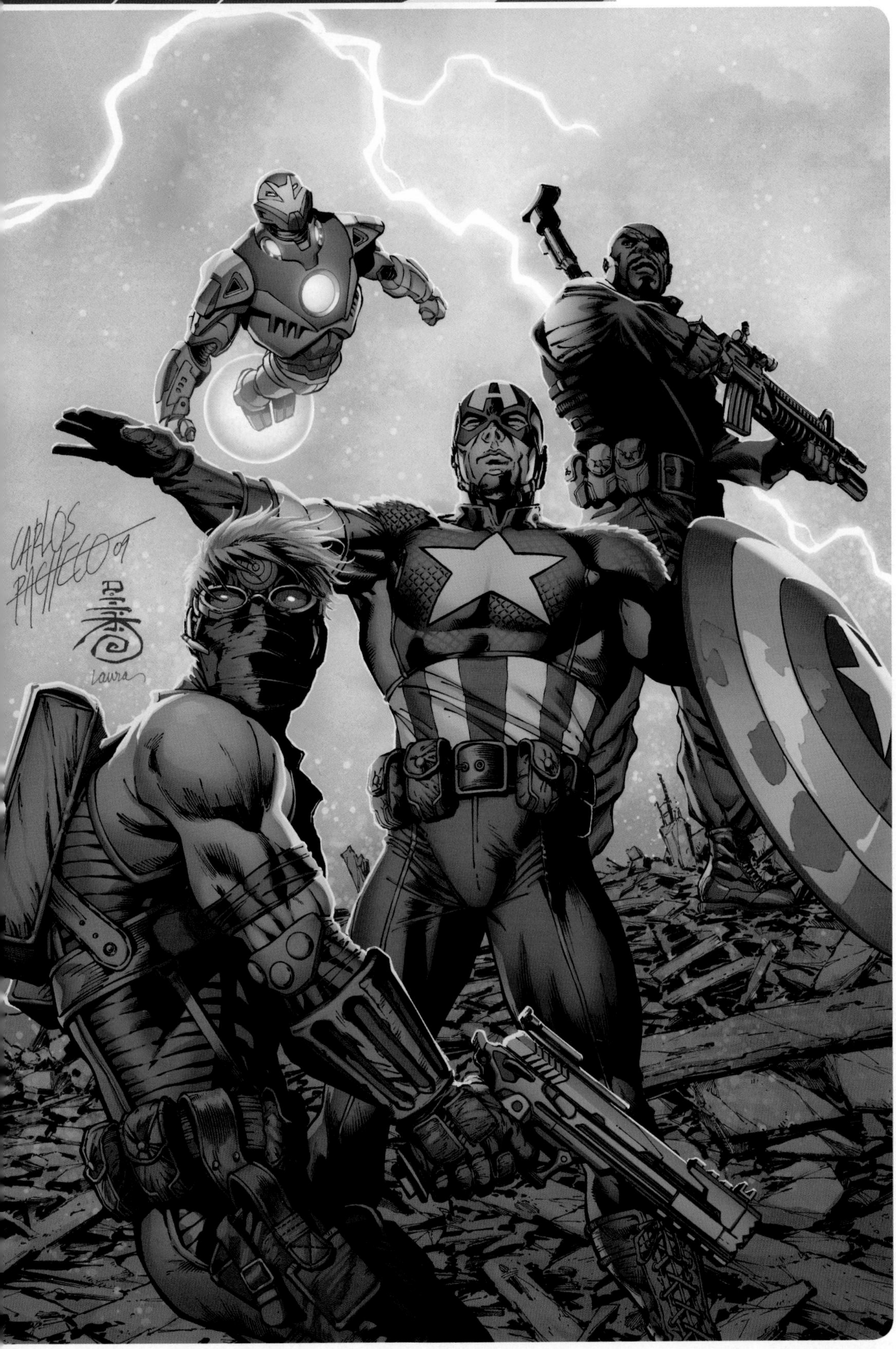
CARLOS PACHECO 09
Laura

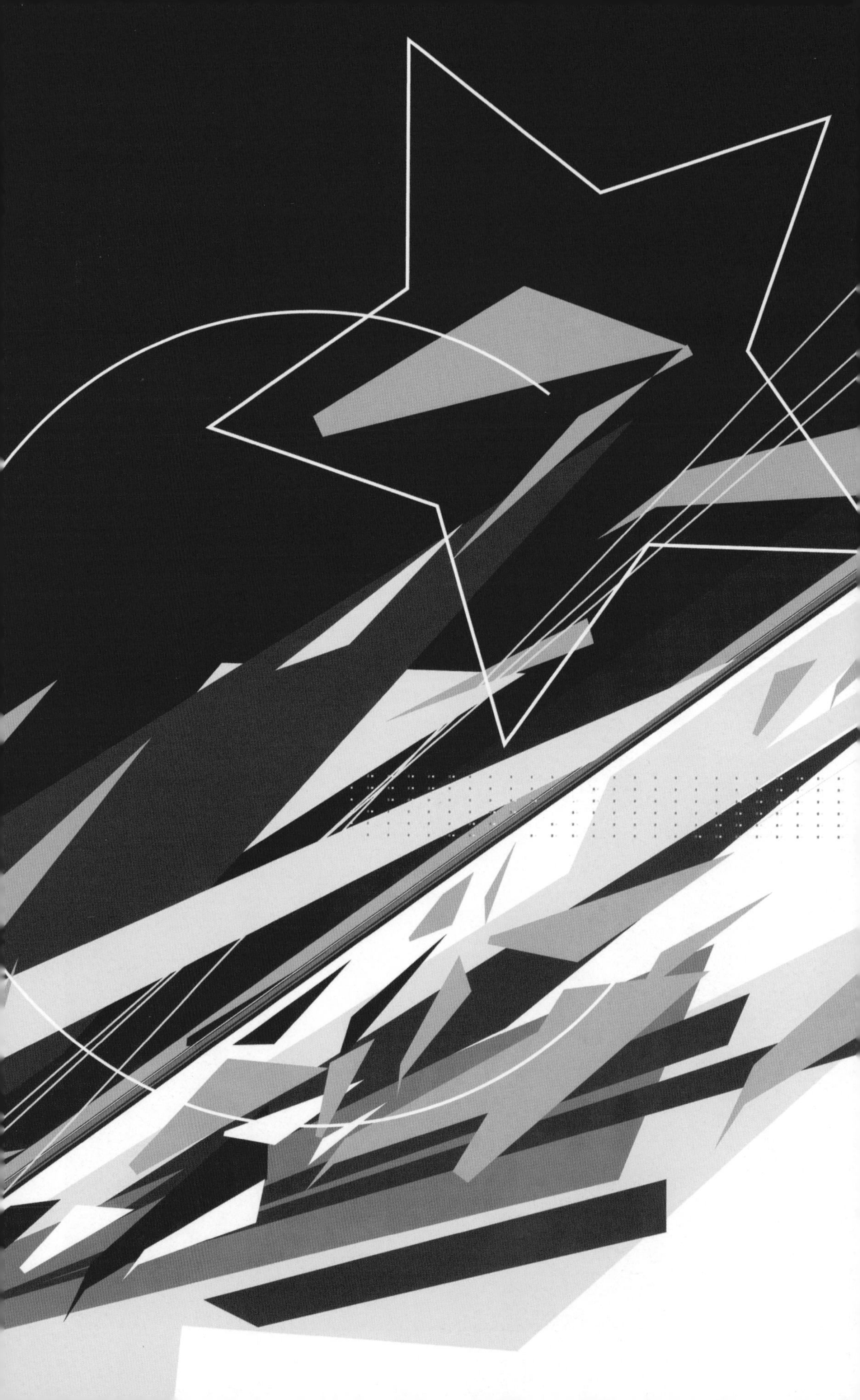

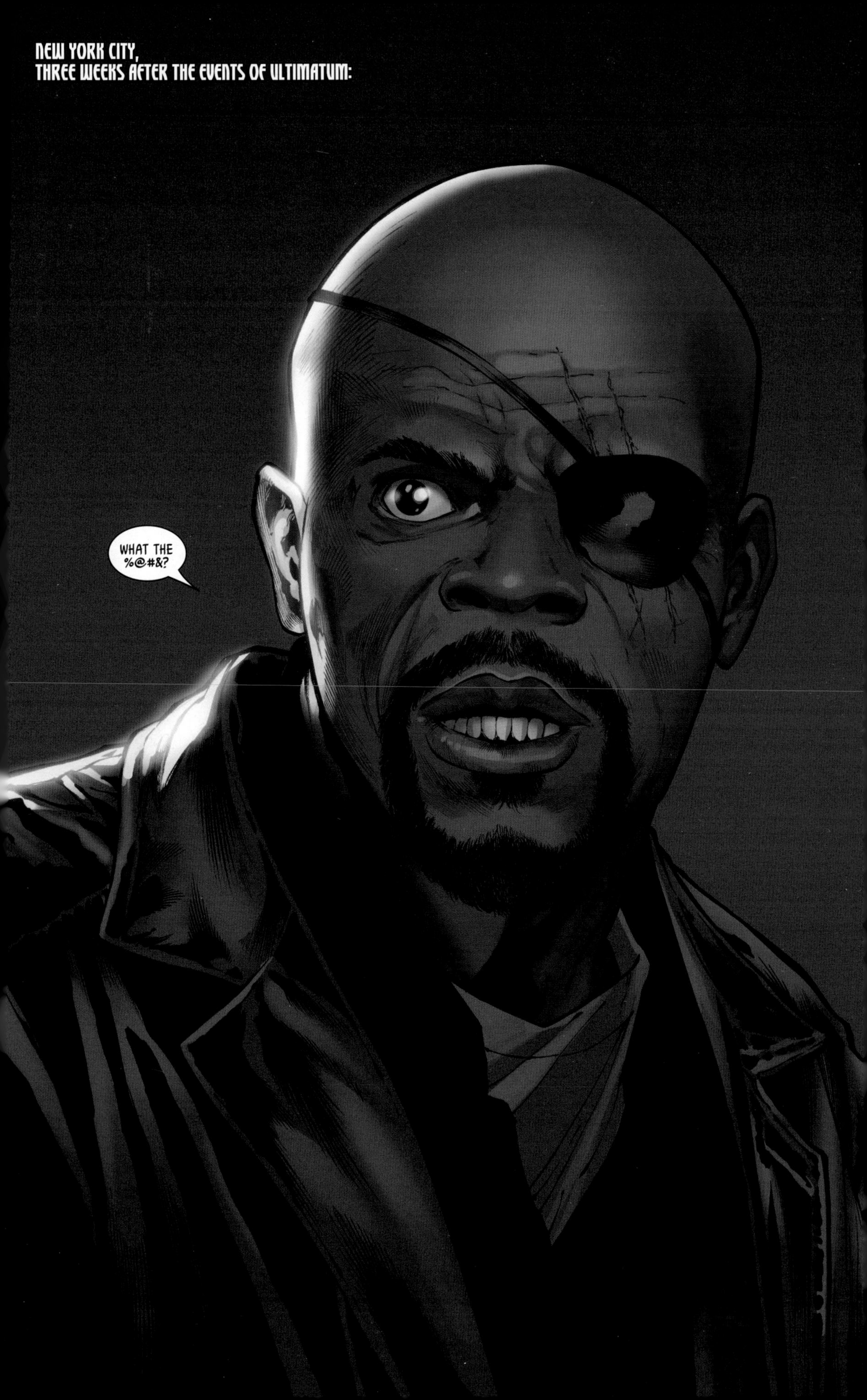
NEW YORK CITY,
THREE WEEKS AFTER THE EVENTS OF ULTIMATUM:
WHAT THE %@#&?

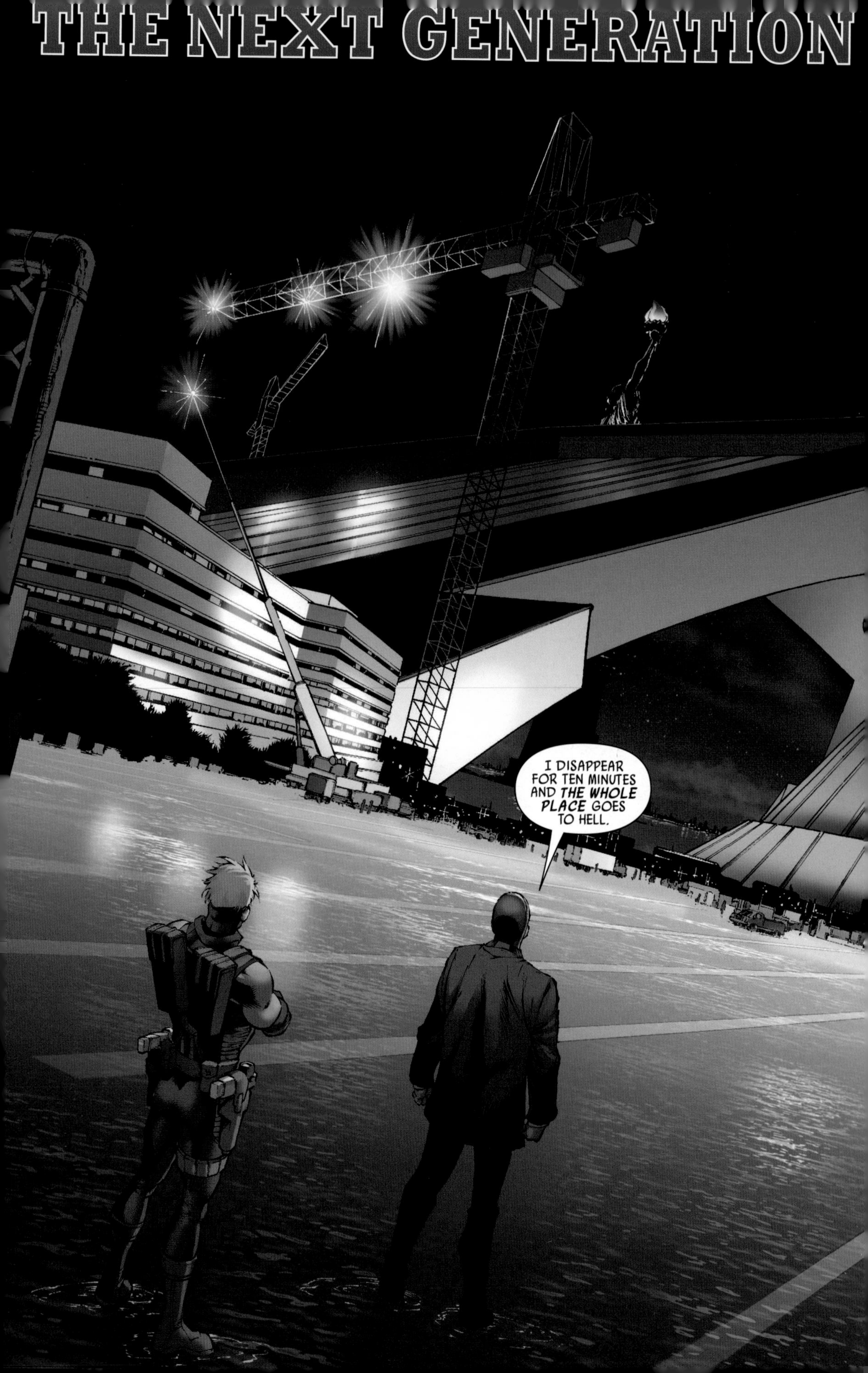
THE NEXT GENERATION
I DISAPPEAR FOR TEN MINUTES AND THE WHOLE PLACE GOES TO HELL.

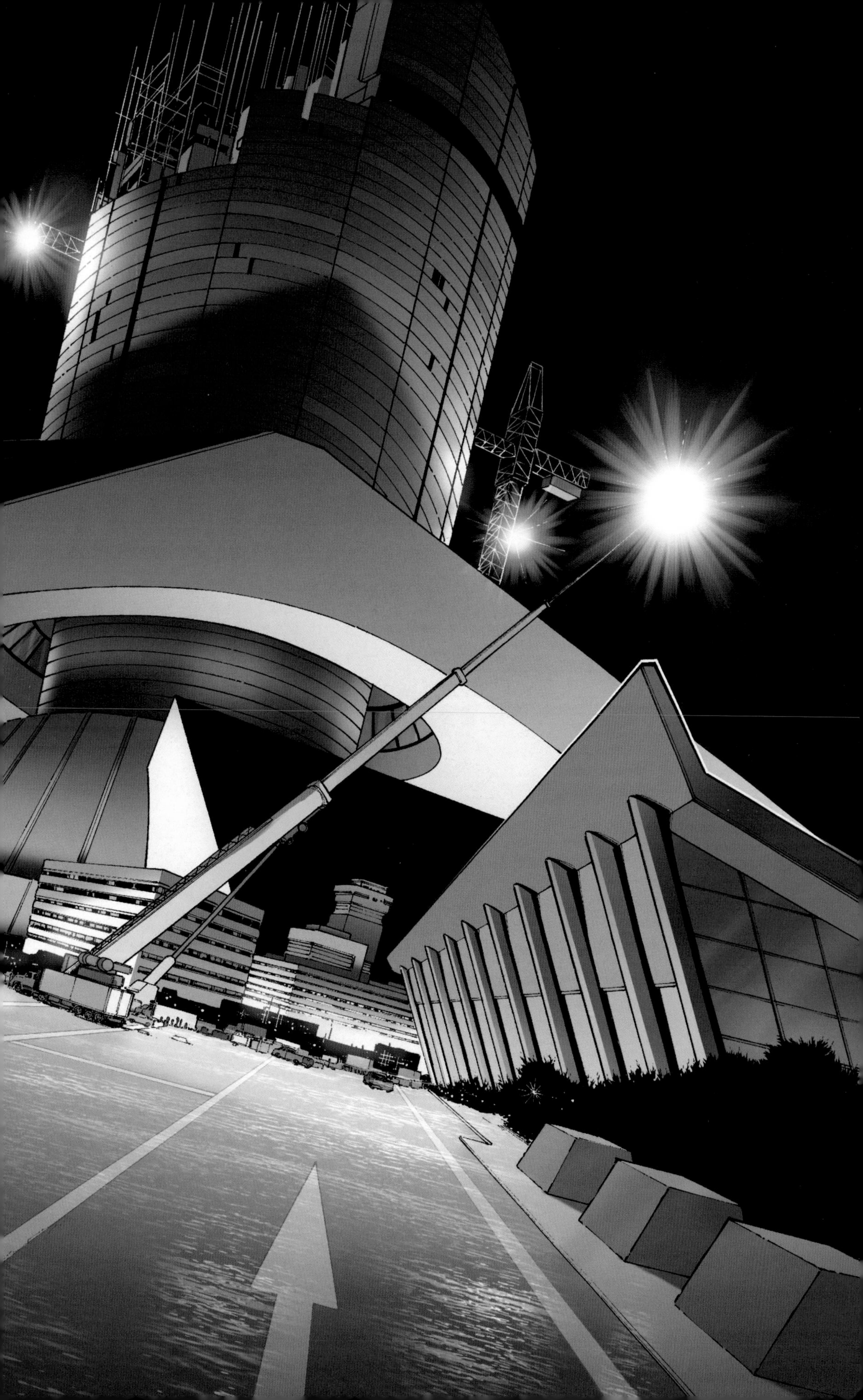

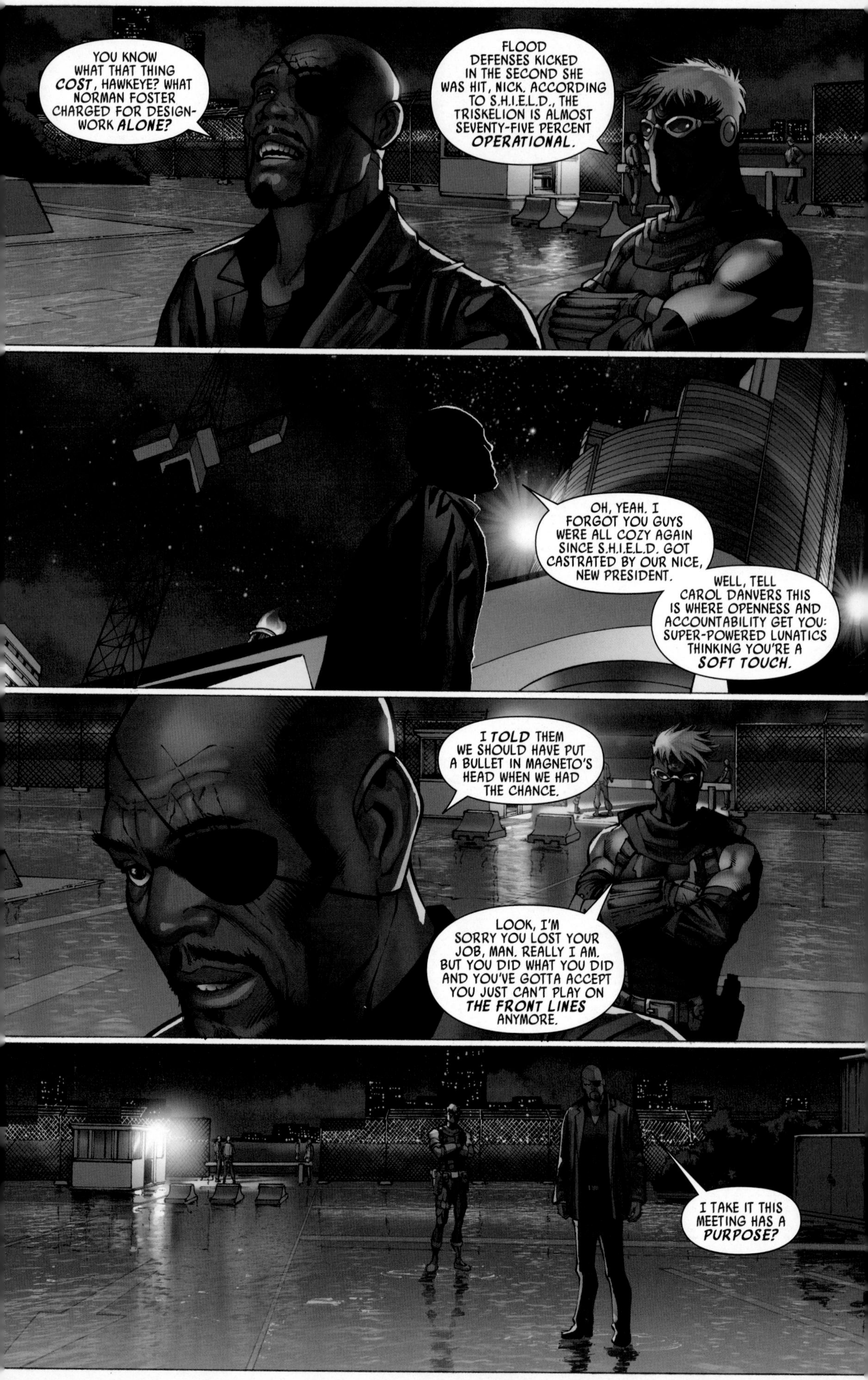
YOU KNOW WHAT THAT THING COST, HAWKEYE? WHAT NORMAN FOSTER CHARGED FOR DESIGN-WORK ALONE?
FLOOD DEFENSES KICKED IN THE SECOND SHE WAS HIT, NICK. ACCORDING TO S.H.I.E.L.D., THE TRISKELION IS ALMOST SEVENTY-FIVE PERCENT OPERATIONAL.
OH, YEAH. I FORGOT YOU GUYS WERE ALL COZY AGAIN SINCE S.H.I.E.L.D. GOT CASTRATED BY OUR NICE, NEW PRESIDENT.
WELL, TELL CAROL DANVERS THIS IS WHERE OPENNESS AND ACCOUNTABILITY GET YOU: SUPER-POWERED LUNATICS THINKING YOU'RE A SOFT TOUCH.
I TOLD THEM WE SHOULD HAVE PUT A BULLET IN MAGNETO'S HEAD WHEN WE HAD THE CHANCE.
LOOK, I'M SORRY YOU LOST YOUR JOB, MAN. REALLY I AM. BUT YOU DID WHAT YOU DID AND YOU'VE GOTTA ACCEPT YOU JUST CAN'T PLAY ON THE FRONT LINES ANYMORE.
I TAKE IT THIS MEETING HAS A PURPOSE?

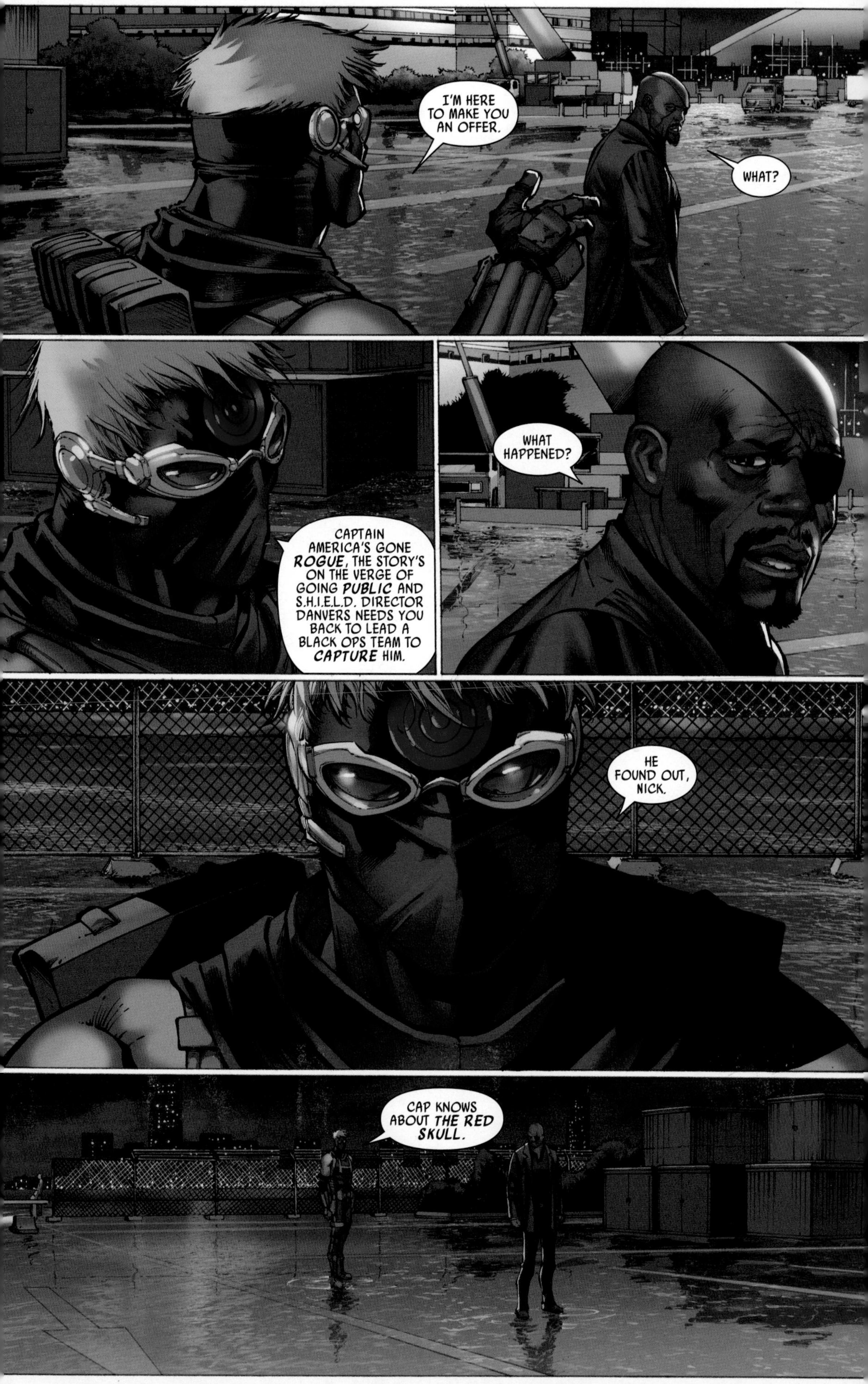
I'M HERE TO MAKE YOU AN OFFER.
WHAT?
WHAT HAPPENED?
CAPTAIN AMERICA'S GONE ROGUE, THE STORY'S ON THE VERGE OF GOING PUBLIC AND S.H.I.E.L.D. DIRECTOR DANVERS NEEDS YOU BACK TO LEAD A BLACK OPS TEAM TO CAPTURE HIM.
HE FOUND OUT, NICK.
CAP KNOWS ABOUT THE RED SKULL.

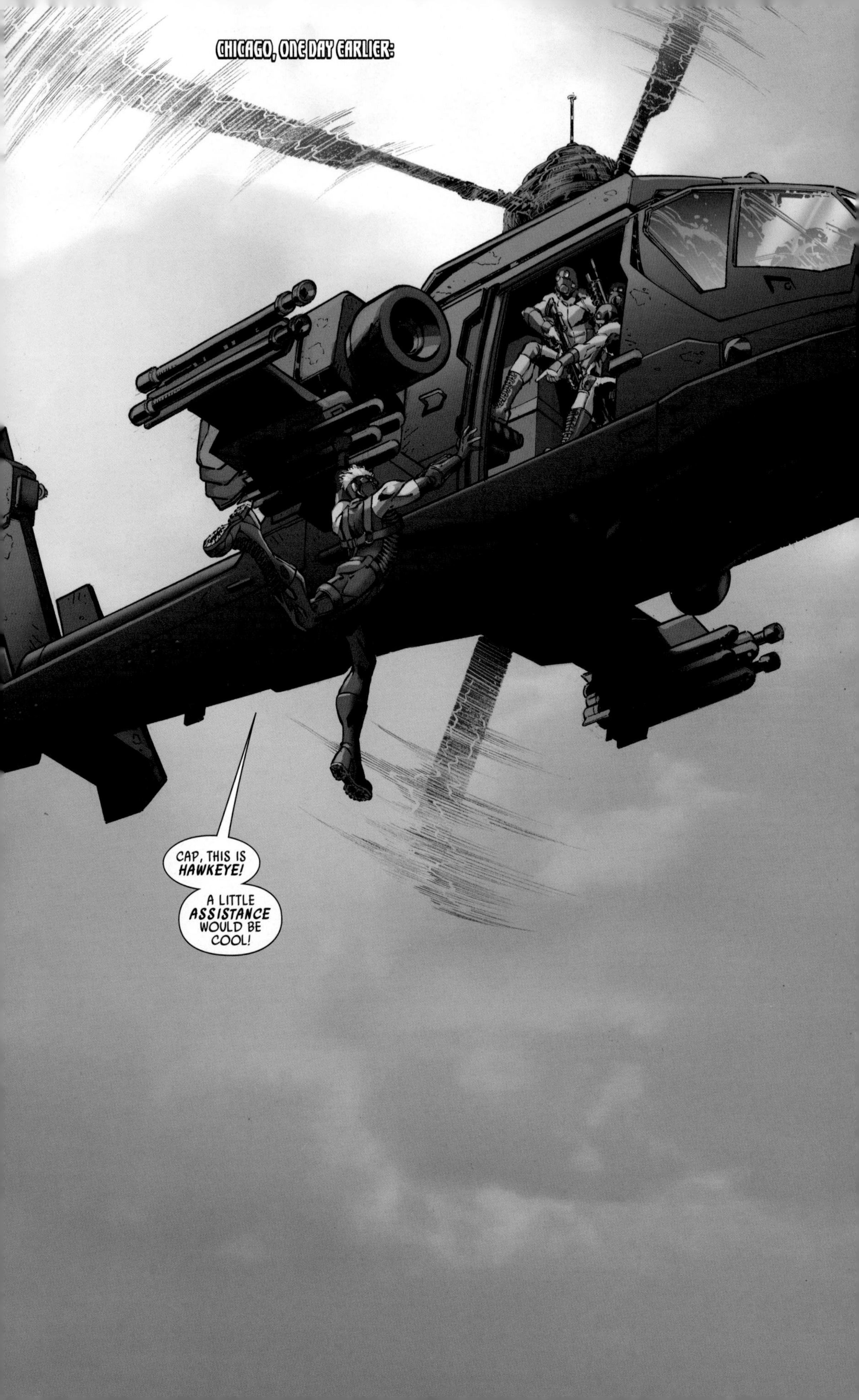
CHICAGO, ONE DAY EARLIER:
CAP, THIS IS HAWKEYE!
A LITTLE ASSISTANCE WOULD BE COOL!

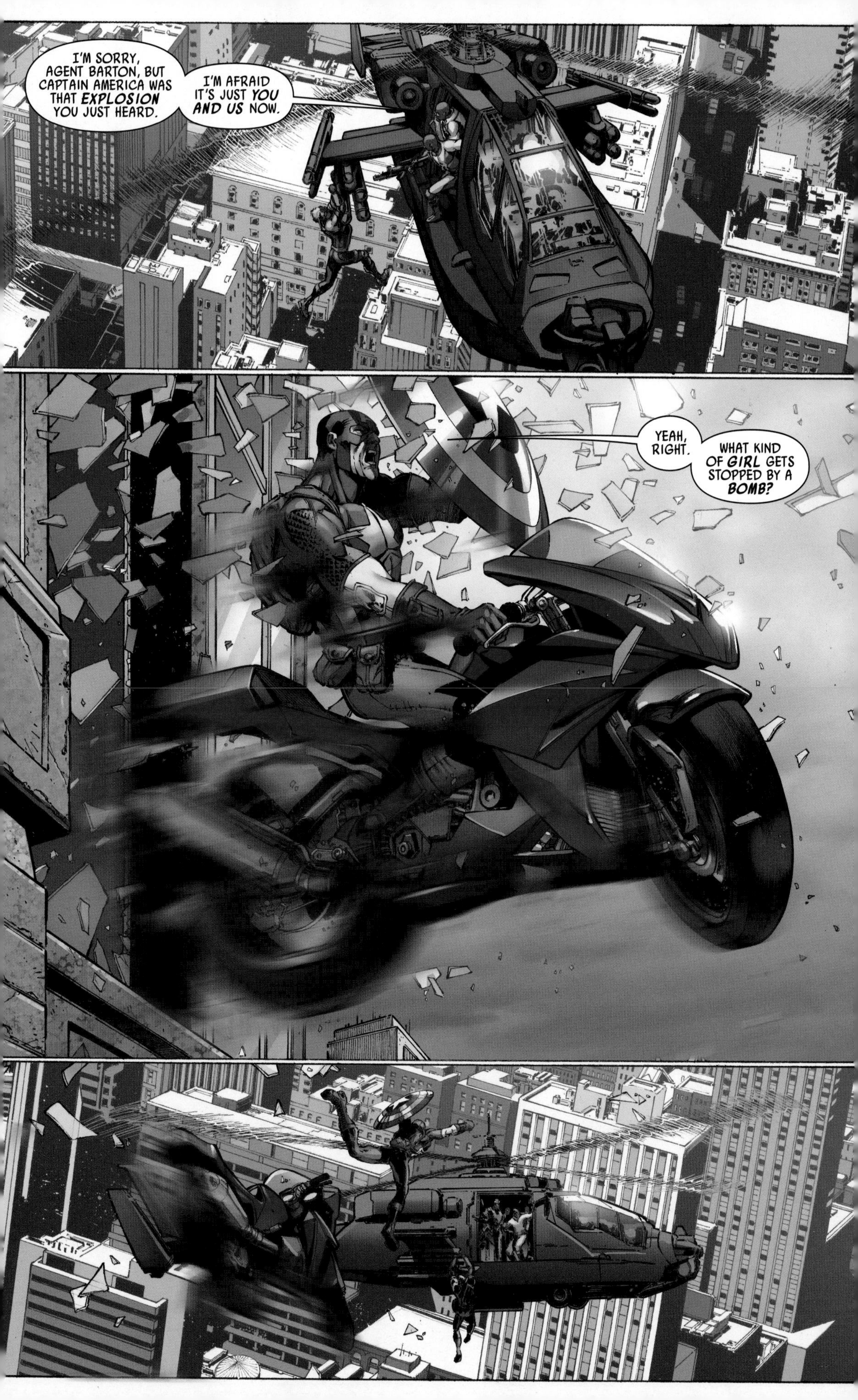
I'M SORRY, AGENT BARTON, BUT CAPTAIN AMERICA WAS THAT EXPLOSION YOU JUST HEARD.
I'M AFRAID IT'S JUST YOU AND US NOW.
YEAH, RIGHT.
WHAT KIND OF GIRL GETS STOPPED BY A BOMB?

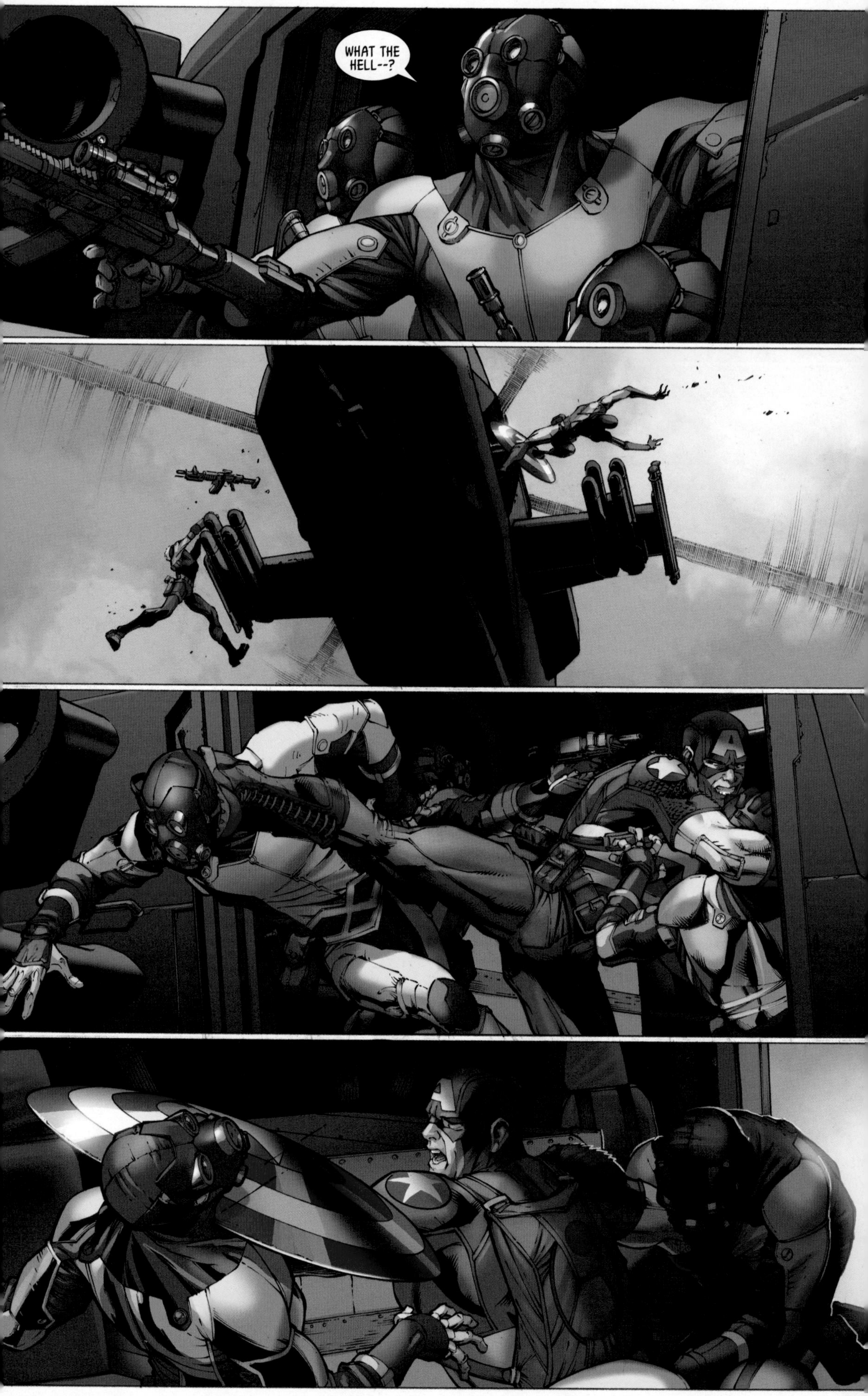
WHAT THE HELL--?

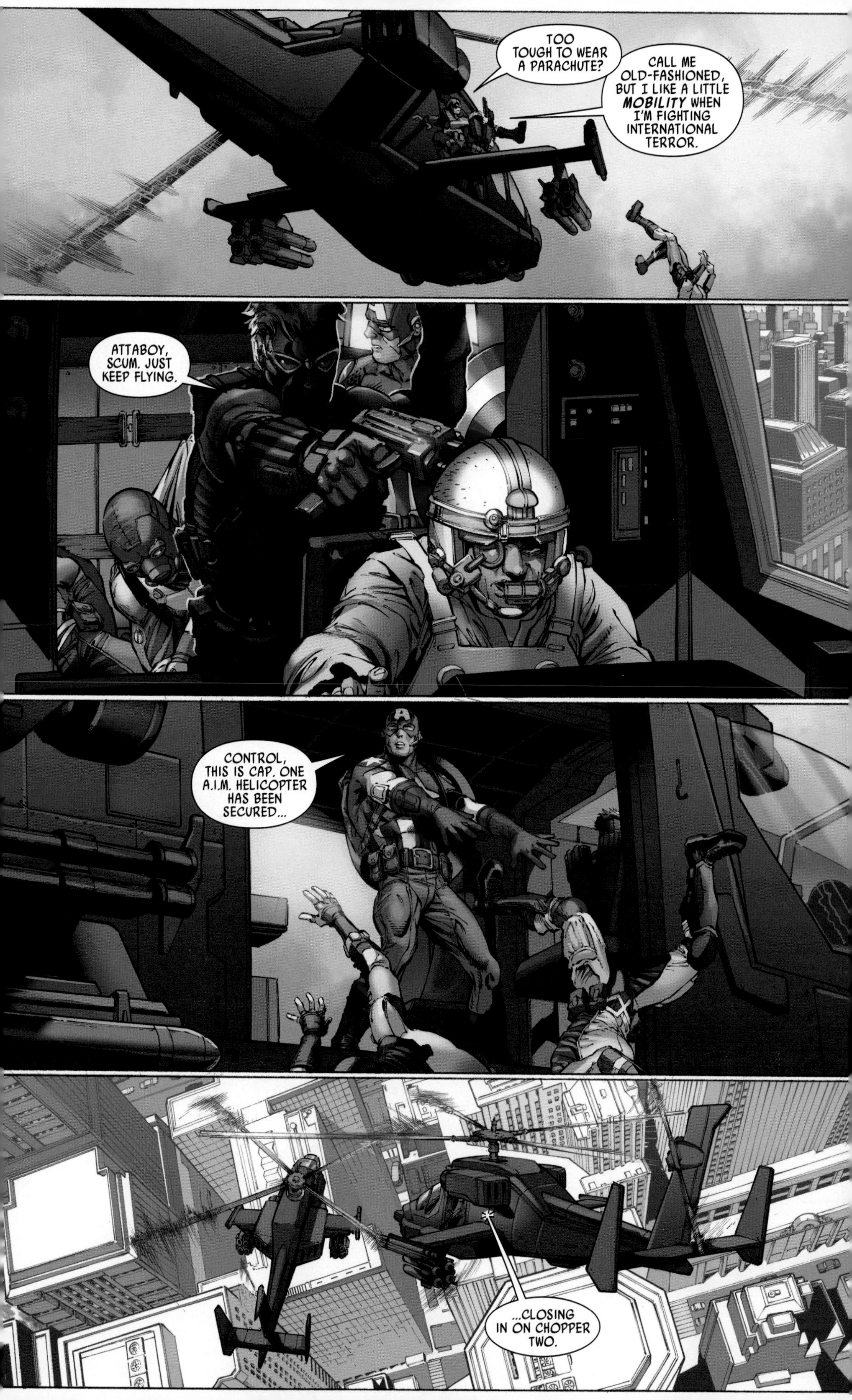
TOO TOUGH TO WEAR A PARACHUTE?
CALL ME OLD-FASHIONED, BUT I LIKE A LITTLE MOBILITY WHEN I'M FIGHTING INTERNATIONAL TERROR.
ATTABOY, SCUM. JUST KEEP FLYING.
CONTROL, THIS IS CAP. ONE A.I.M. HELICOPTER HAS BEEN SECURED...
...CLOSING IN ON CHOPPER TWO.

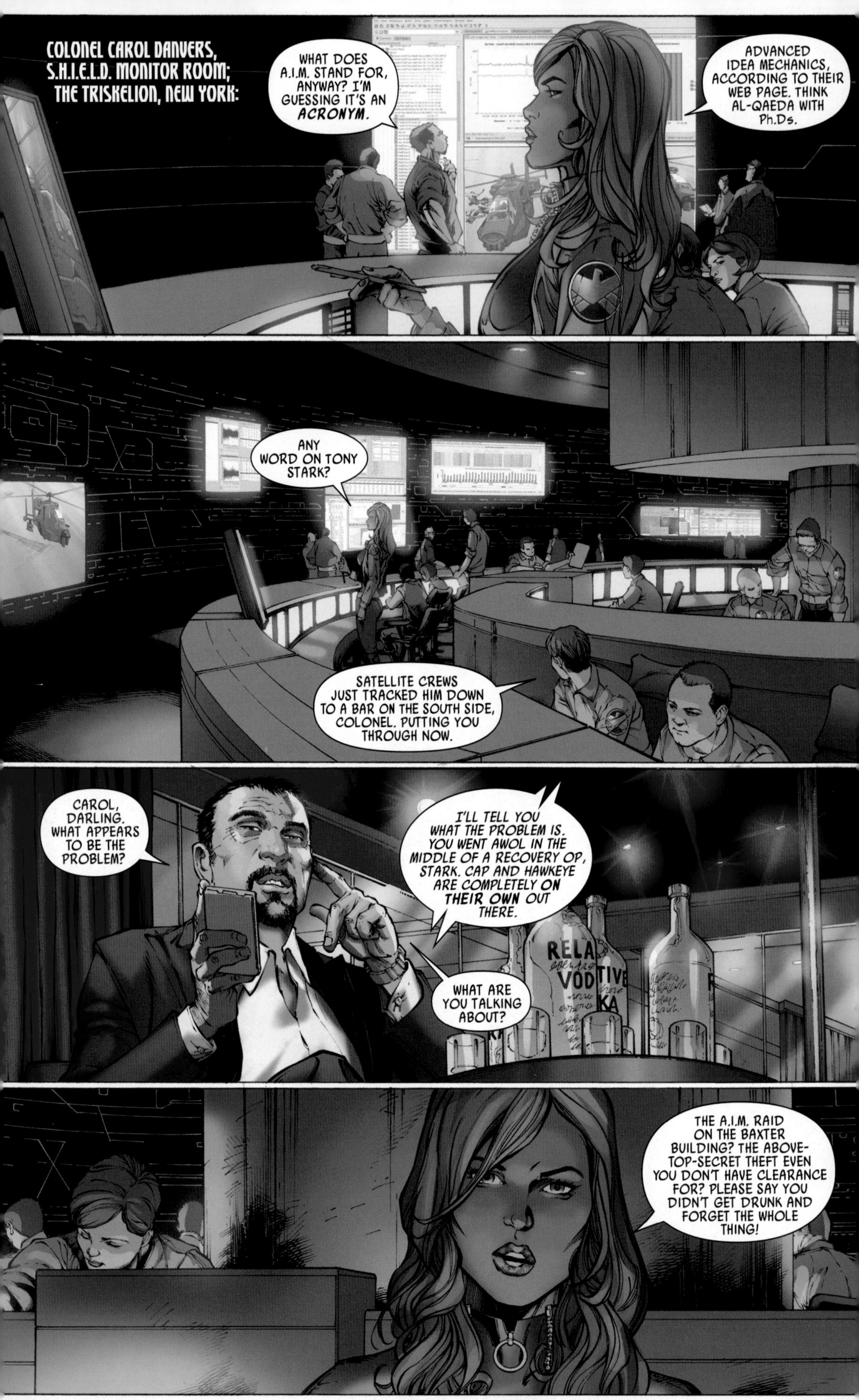
COLONEL CAROL DANVERS, S.H.I.E.L.D. MONITOR ROOM; THE TRISKELION, NEW YORK:
WHAT DOES A.I.M. STAND FOR, ANYWAY? I'M GUESSING IT'S AN ACRONYM.
ADVANCED IDEA MECHANICS, ACCORDING TO THEIR WEB PAGE. THINK AL-QAEDA WITH Ph.Ds.
ANY WORD ON TONY STARK?
SATELLITE CREWS JUST TRACKED HIM DOWN TO A BAR ON THE SOUTH SIDE, COLONEL. PUTTING YOU THROUGH NOW.
CAROL, DARLING. WHAT APPEARS TO BE THE PROBLEM?
I'LL TELL YOU WHAT THE PROBLEM IS. YOU WENT AWOL IN THE MIDDLE OF A RECOVERY OP, STARK. CAP AND HAWKEYE ARE COMPLETELY ON THEIR OWN OUT THERE.
WHAT ARE YOU TALKING ABOUT?
THE A.I.M. RAID ON THE BAXTER BUILDING? THE ABOVE-TOP-SECRET THEFT EVEN YOU DON'T HAVE CLEARANCE FOR? PLEASE SAY YOU DIDN'T GET DRUNK AND FORGET THE WHOLE THING!

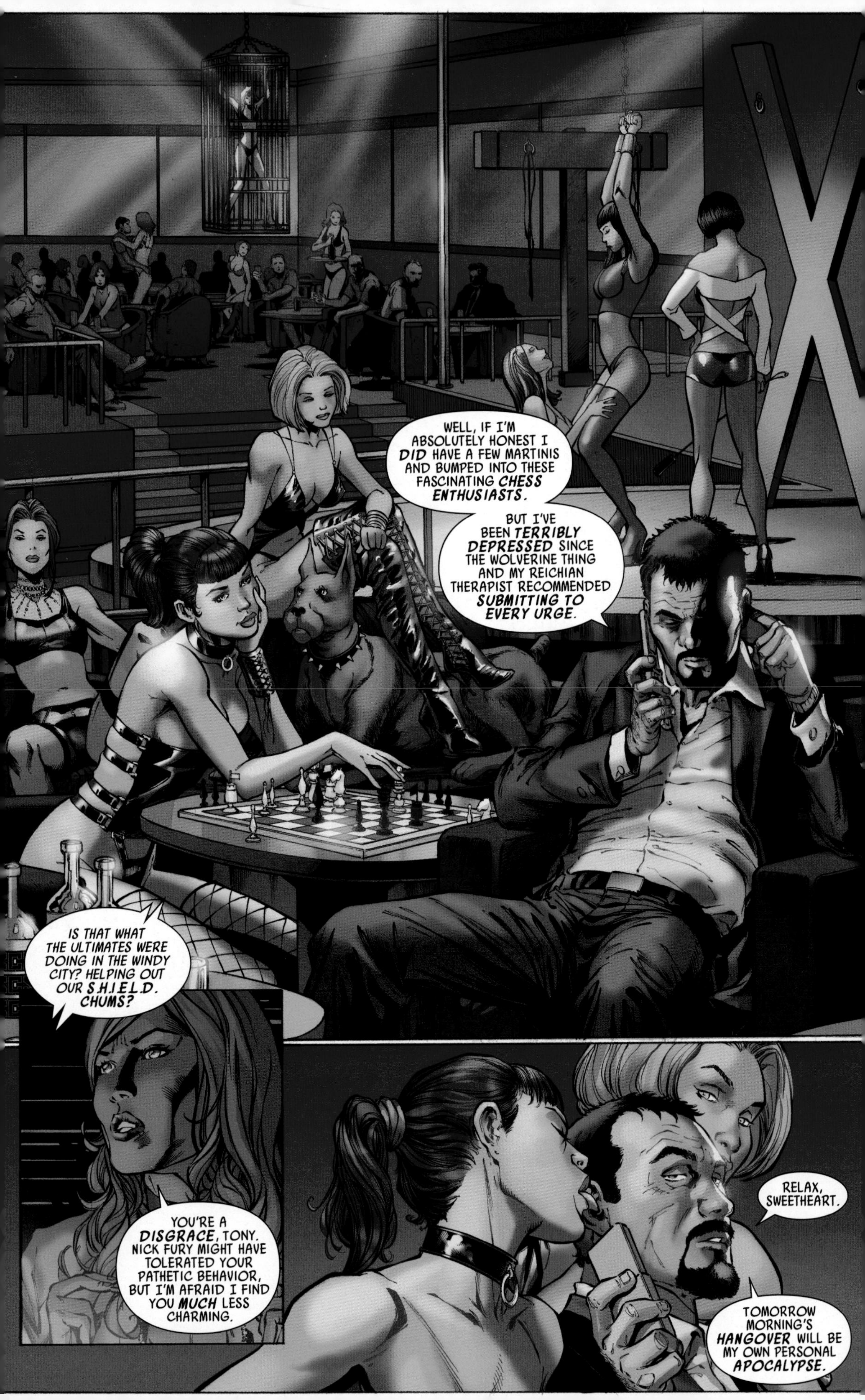
WELL, IF I'M ABSOLUTELY HONEST I DID HAVE A FEW MARTINIS AND BUMPED INTO THESE FASCINATING CHESS ENTHUSIASTS.
BUT I'VE BEEN TERRIBLY DEPRESSED SINCE THE WOLVERINE THING AND MY REICHIAN THERAPIST RECOMMENDED SUBMITTING TO EVERY URGE.
IS THAT WHAT THE ULTIMATES WERE DOING IN THE WINDY CITY? HELPING OUT OUR S.H.I.E.L.D. CHUMS?
YOU'RE A DISGRACE, TONY. NICK FURY MIGHT HAVE TOLERATED YOUR PATHETIC BEHAVIOR, BUT I'M AFRAID I FIND YOU MUCH LESS CHARMING.
RELAX, SWEETHEART.
TOMORROW MORNING'S HANGOVER WILL BE MY OWN PERSONAL APOCALYPSE.

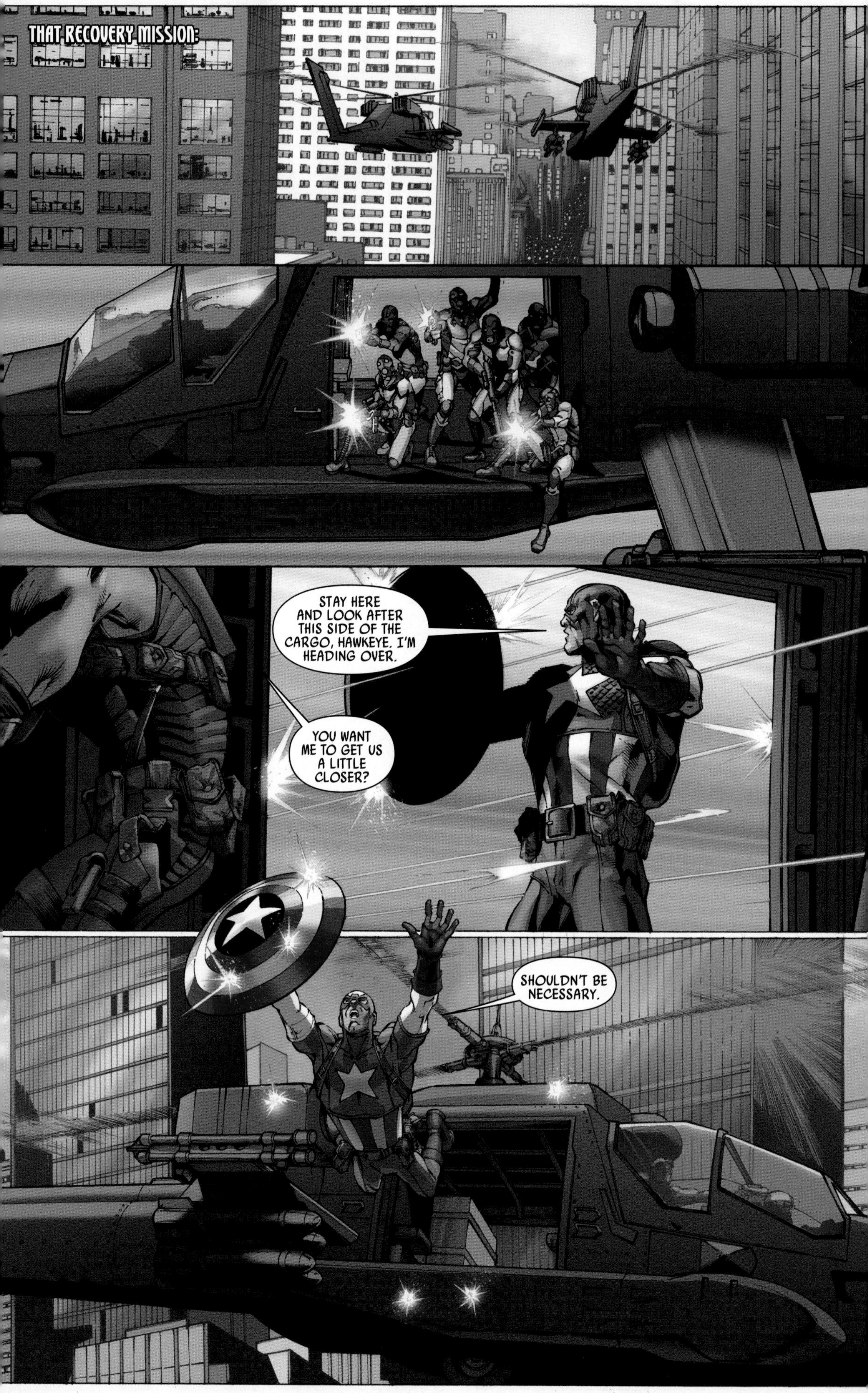
THAT RECOVERY MISSION:
STAY HERE AND LOOK AFTER THIS SIDE OF THE CARGO, HAWKEYE. I'M HEADING OVER.
YOU WANT ME TO GET US A LITTLE CLOSER?
SHOULDN'T BE NECESSARY.

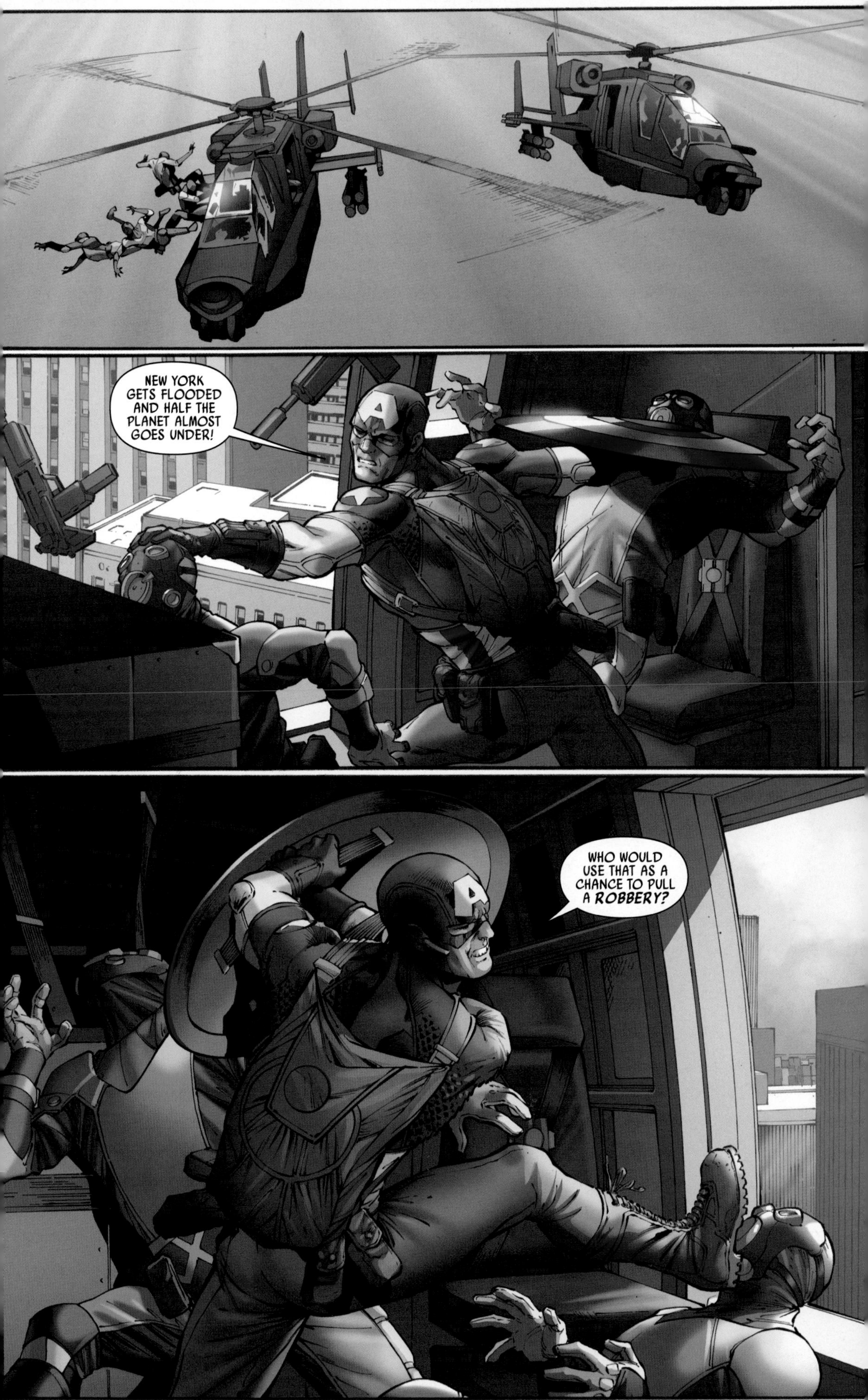
NEW YORK GETS FLOODED AND HALF THE PLANET ALMOST GOES UNDER!
WHO WOULD USE THAT AS A CHANCE TO PULL A *ROBBERY?*

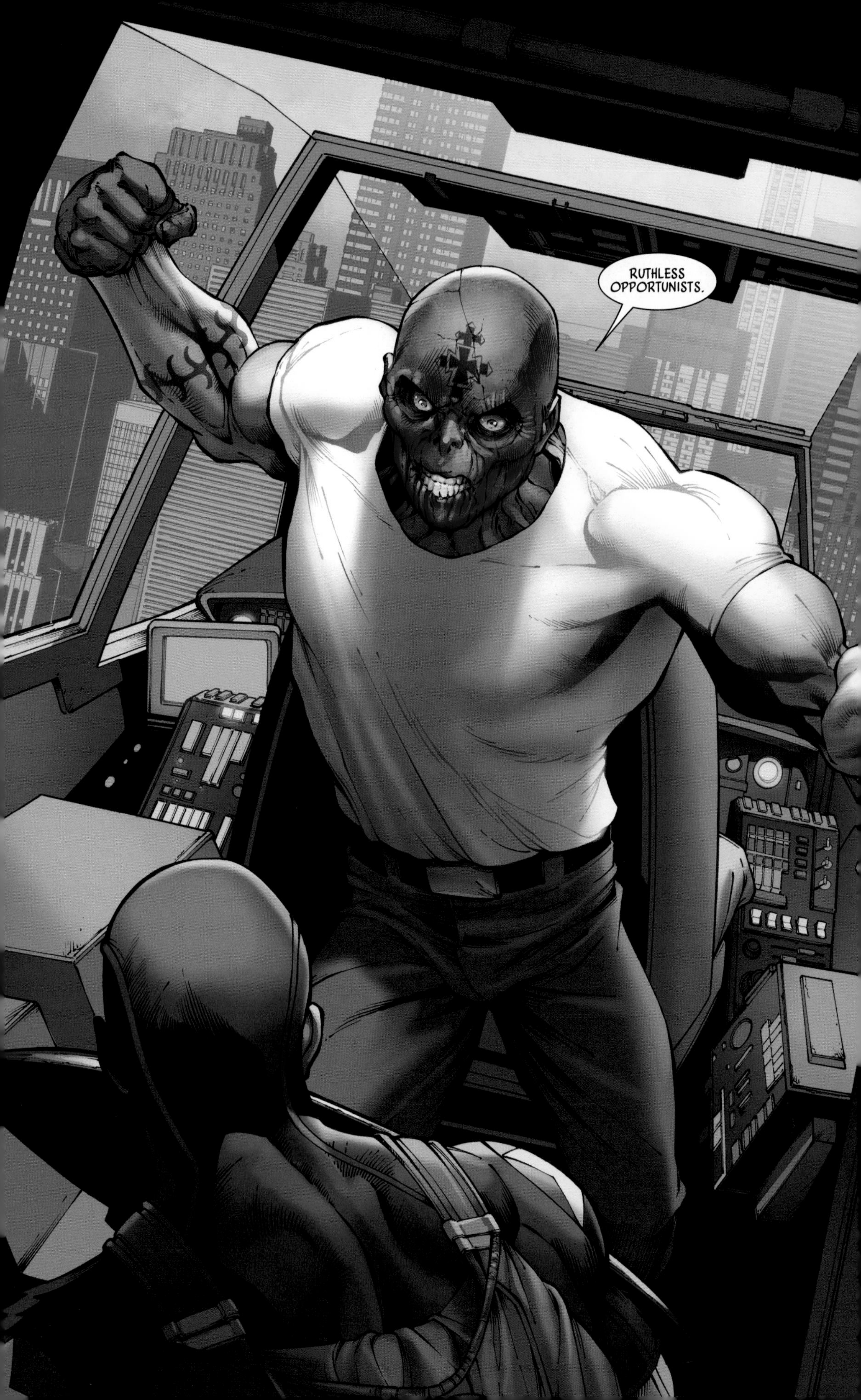
RUTHLESS OPPORTUNISTS.

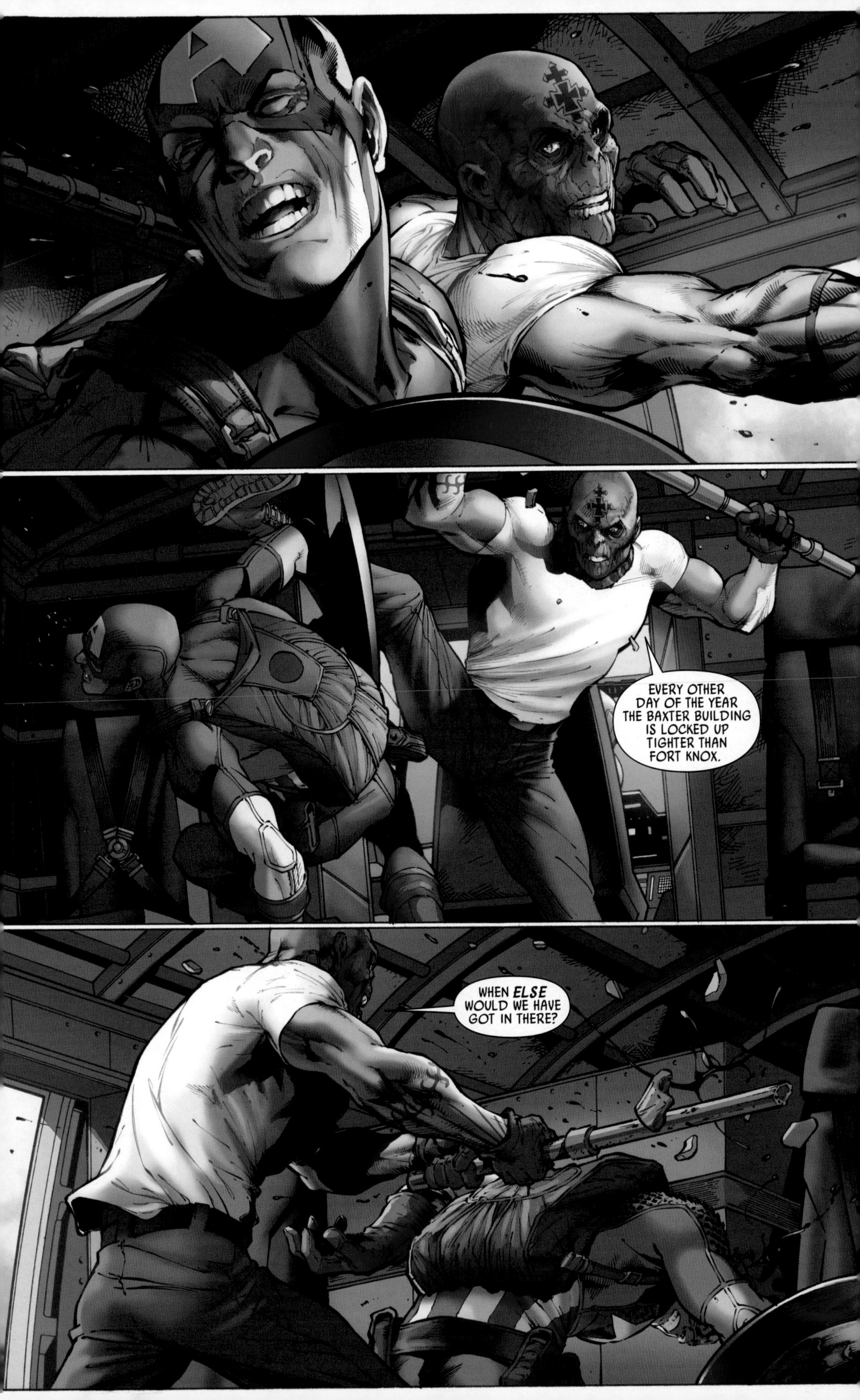
EVERY OTHER DAY OF THE YEAR THE BAXTER BUILDING IS LOCKED UP TIGHTER THAN FORT KNOX.
WHEN *ELSE* WOULD WE HAVE GOT IN THERE?

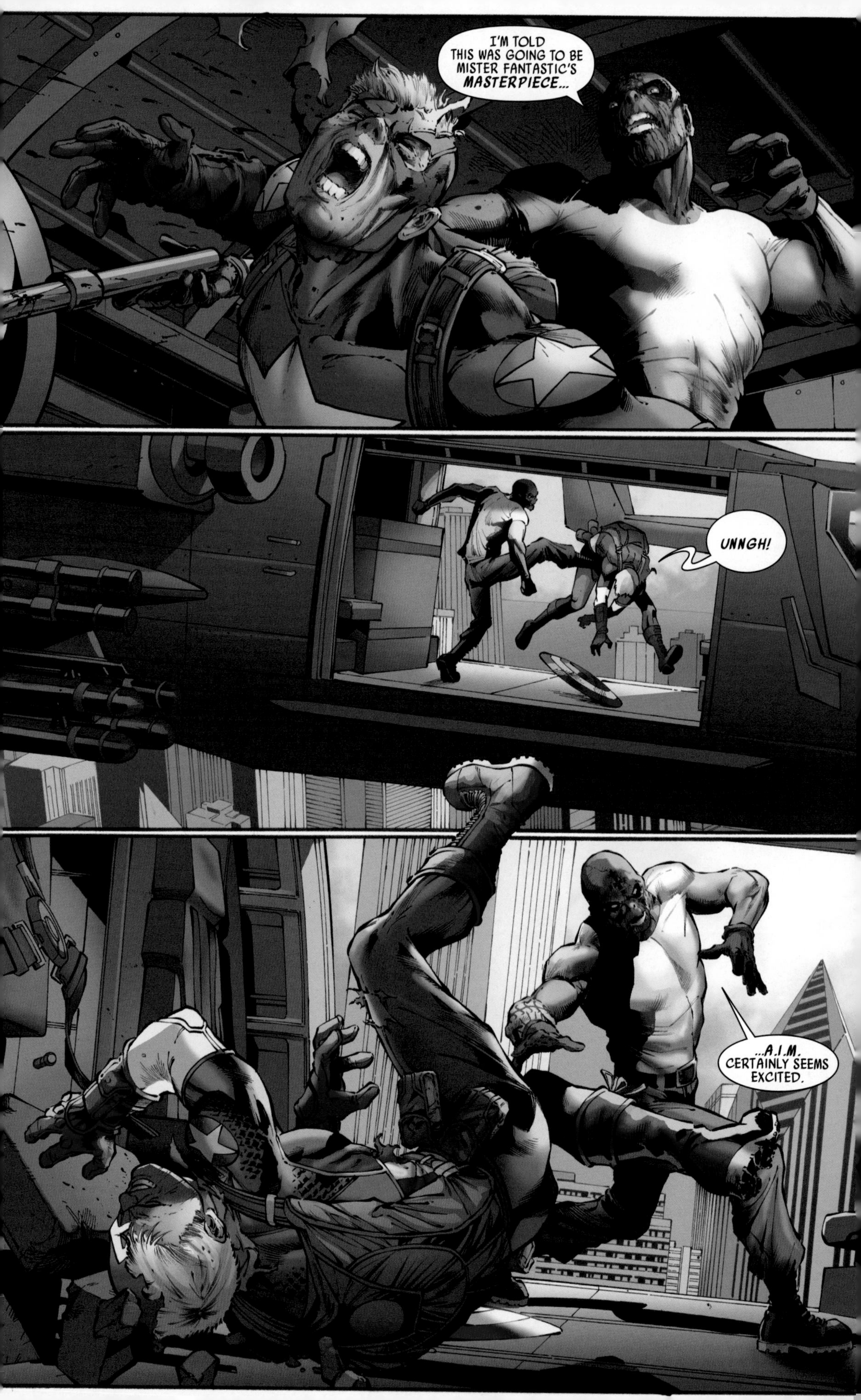
I'M TOLD THIS WAS GOING TO BE MISTER FANTASTIC'S MASTERPIECE...
UNNGH!
...A.I.M. CERTAINLY SEEMS EXCITED.

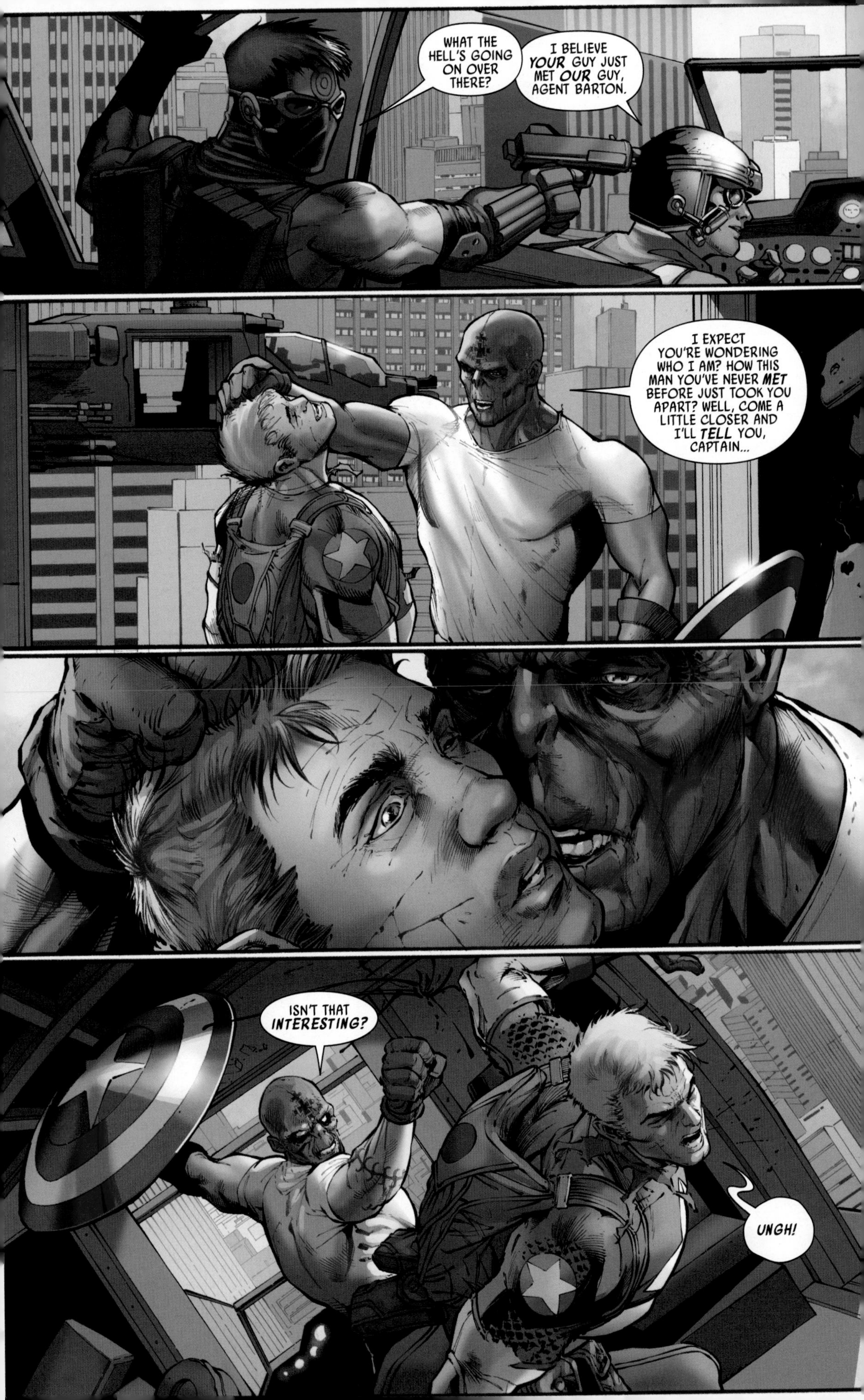
WHAT THE HELL'S GOING ON OVER THERE?
I BELIEVE *YOUR* GUY JUST MET *OUR* GUY, AGENT BARTON.
I EXPECT YOU'RE WONDERING WHO I AM? HOW THIS MAN YOU'VE NEVER *MET* BEFORE JUST TOOK YOU APART? WELL, COME A LITTLE CLOSER AND I'LL *TELL* YOU, CAPTAIN...
ISN'T THAT *INTERESTING?*
UNGH!

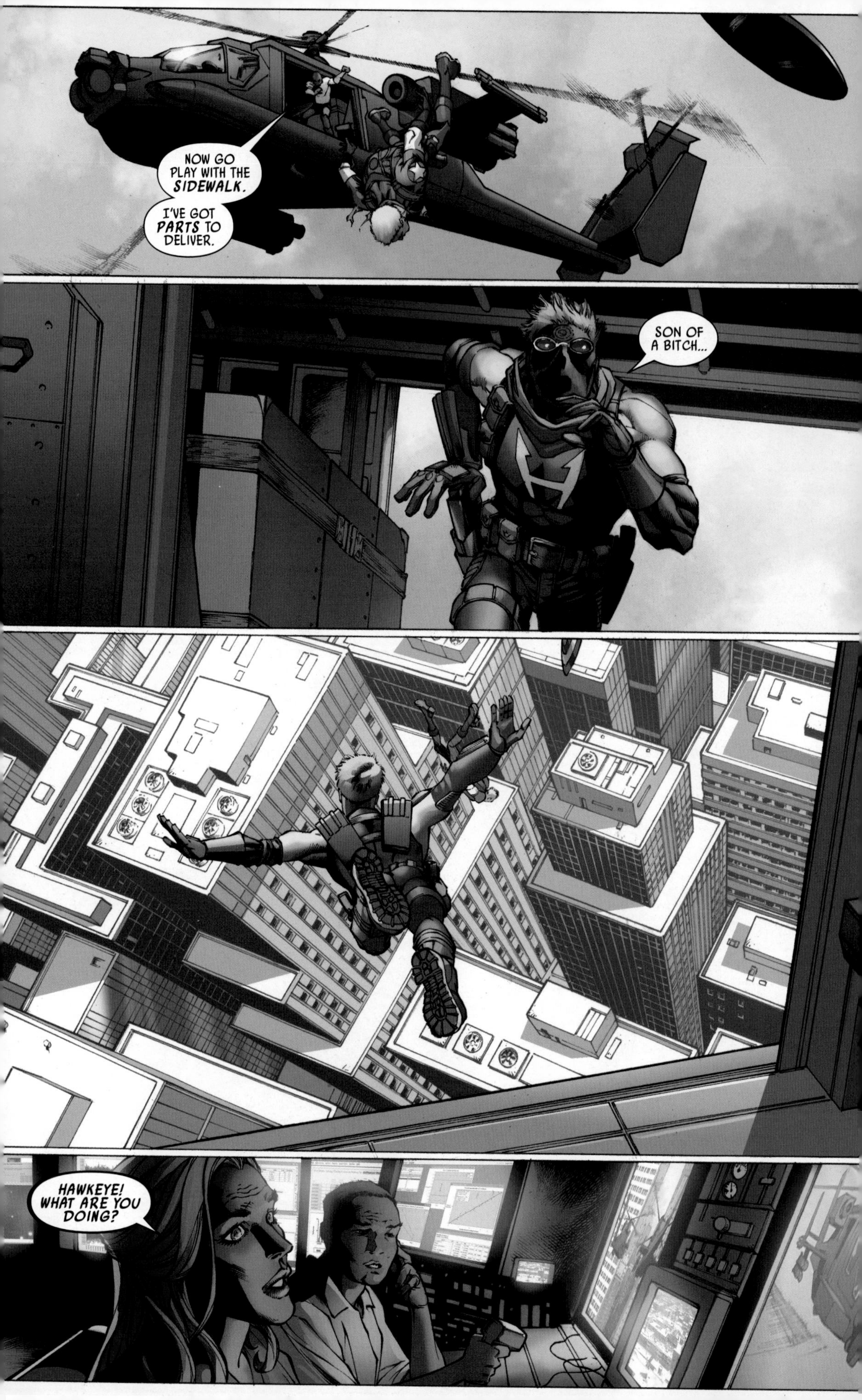
NOW GO PLAY WITH THE SIDEWALK.
I'VE GOT PARTS TO DELIVER.
SON OF A BITCH...
HAWKEYE! WHAT ARE YOU DOING?

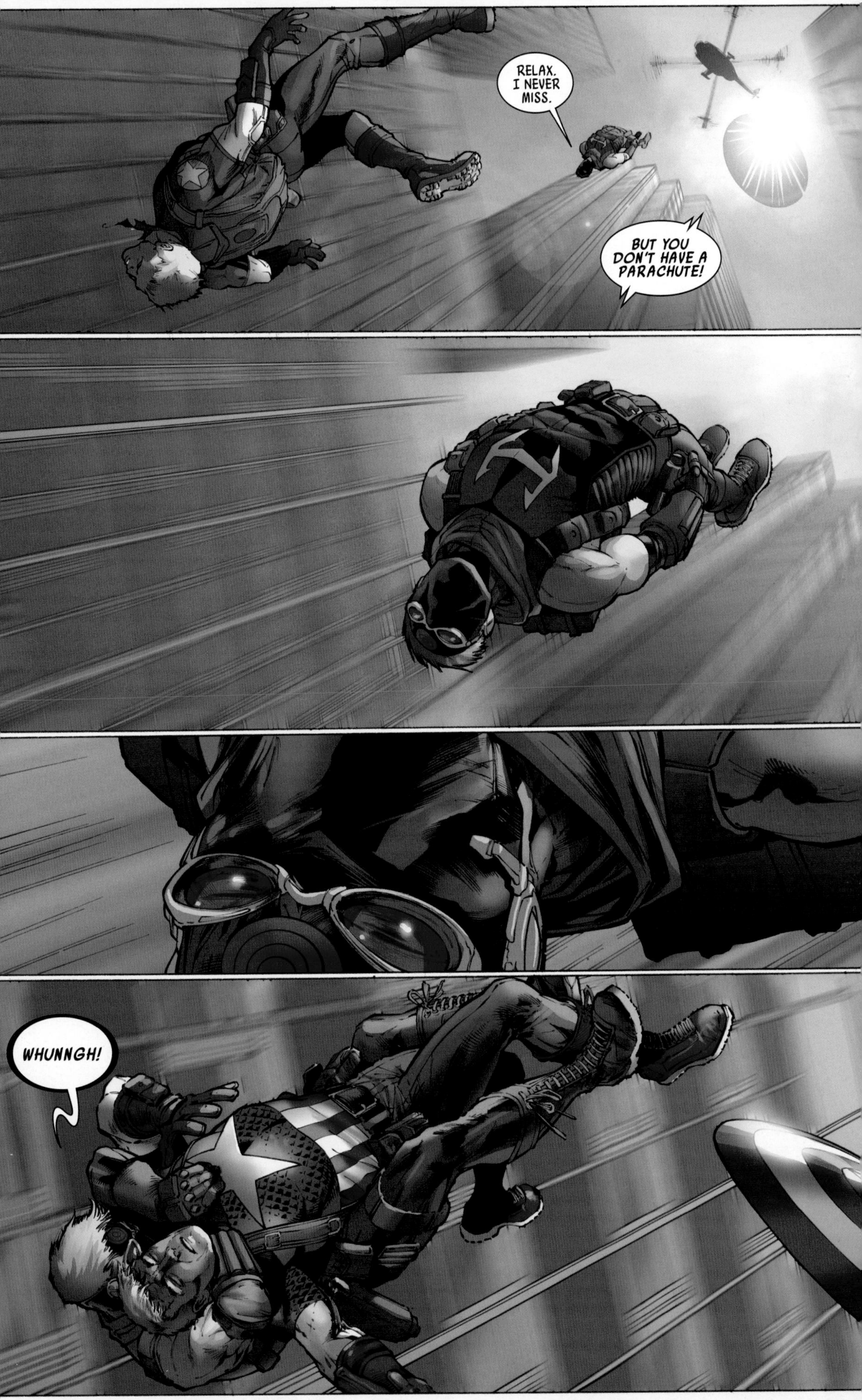
RELAX. I NEVER MISS.
BUT YOU DON'T HAVE A PARACHUTE!
WHUNNGH!

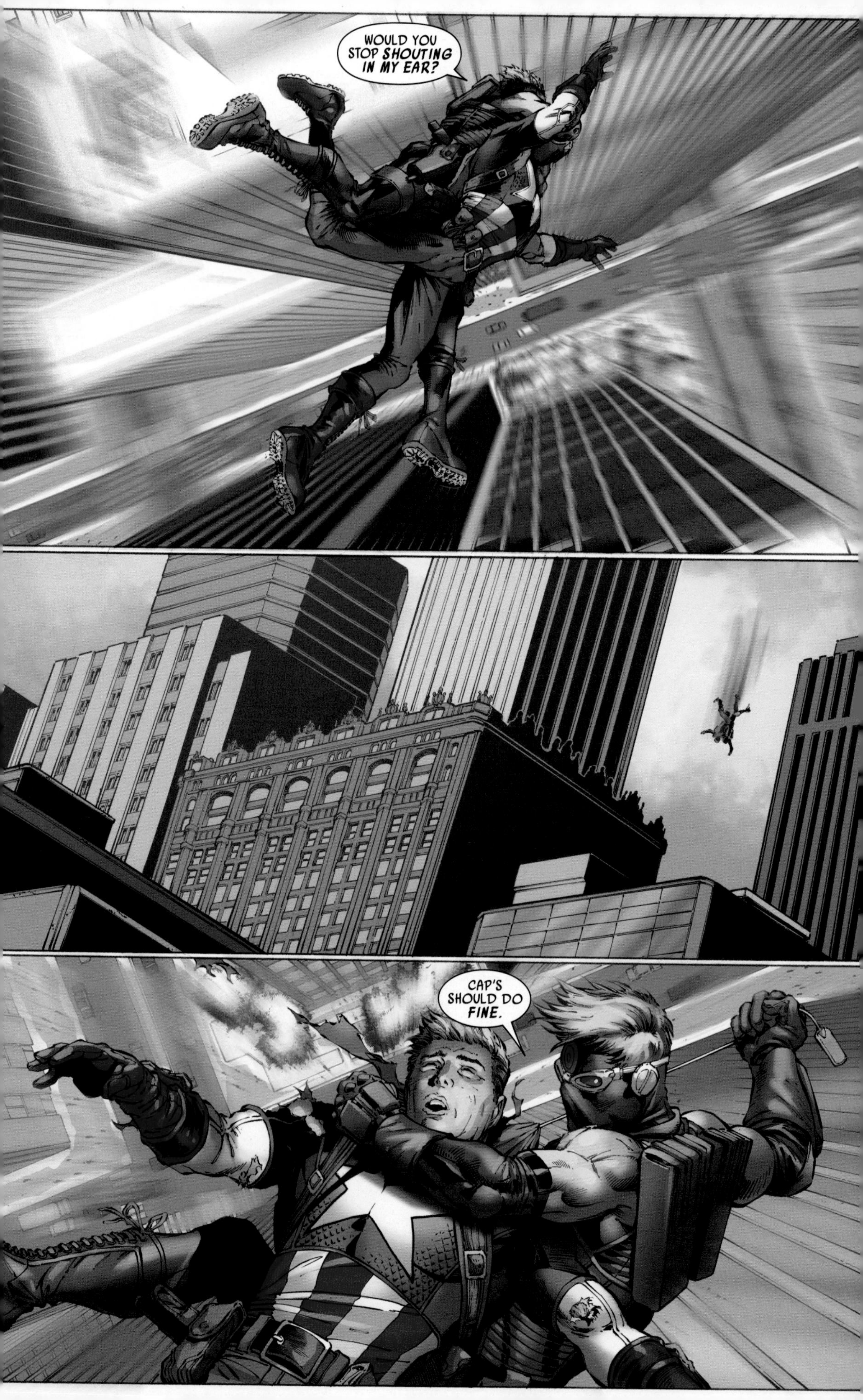
WOULD YOU STOP SHOUTING IN MY EAR?
CAP'S SHOULD DO FINE.

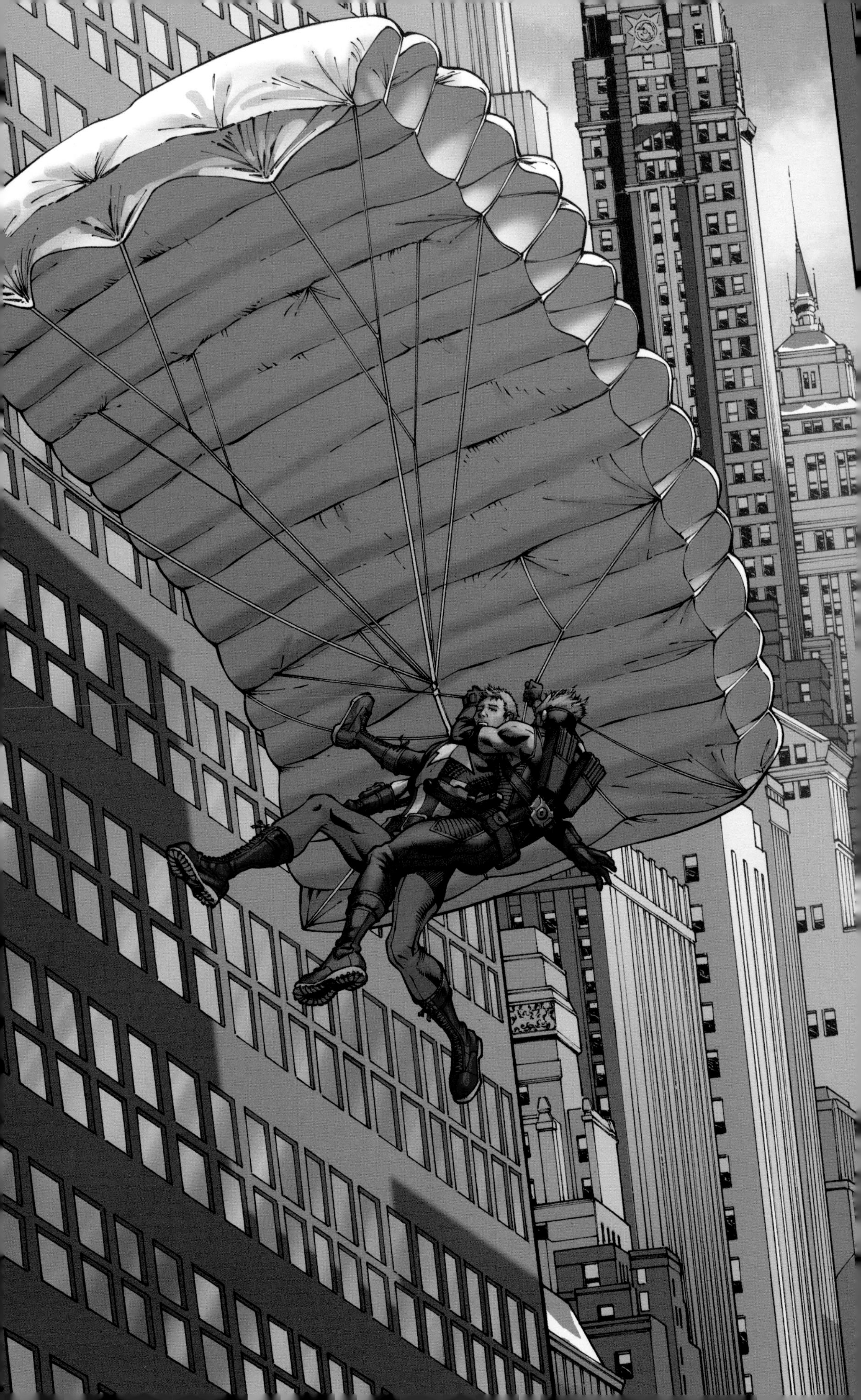

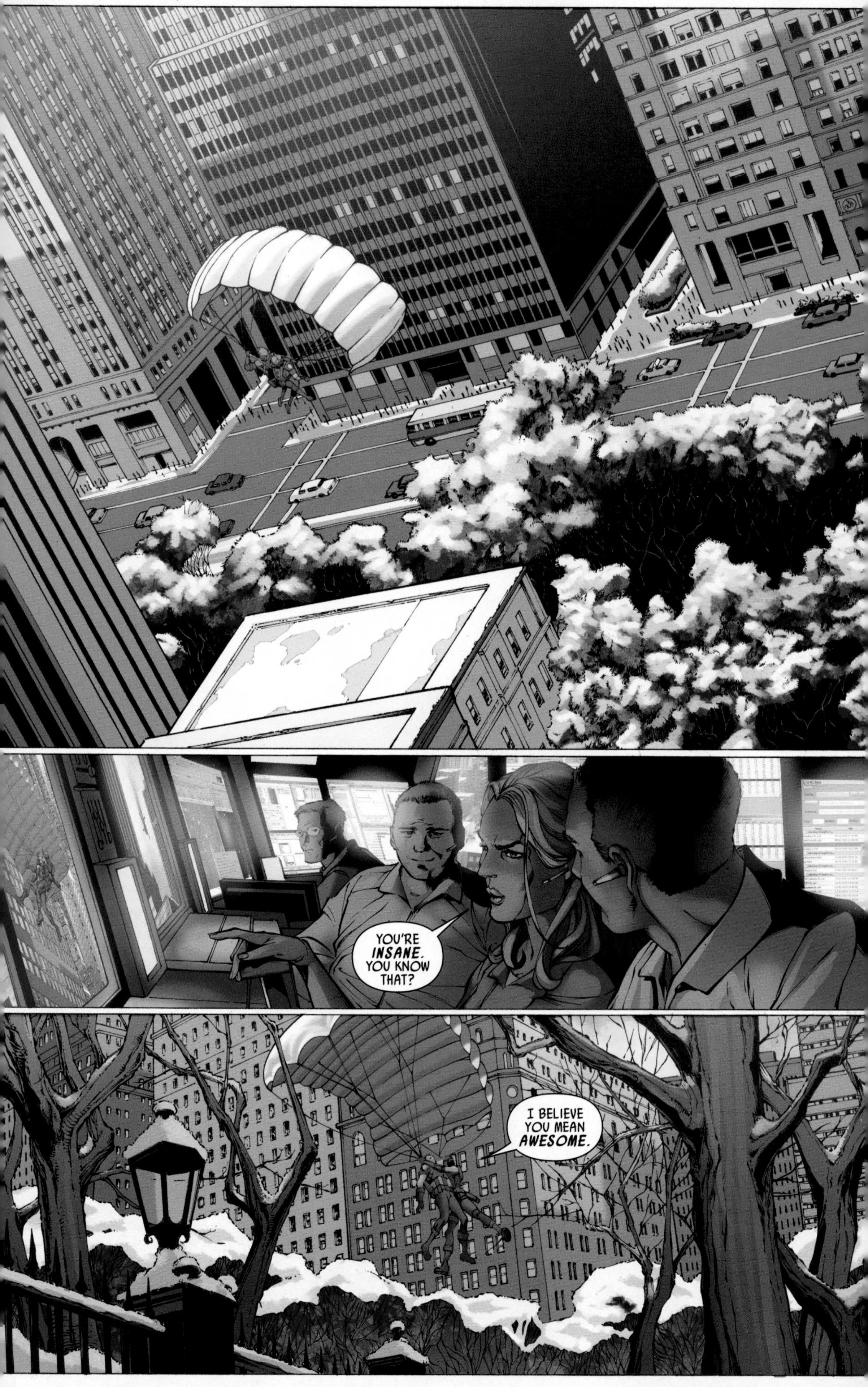
YOU'RE *INSANE*. YOU KNOW THAT?
I BELIEVE YOU MEAN *AWESOME*.

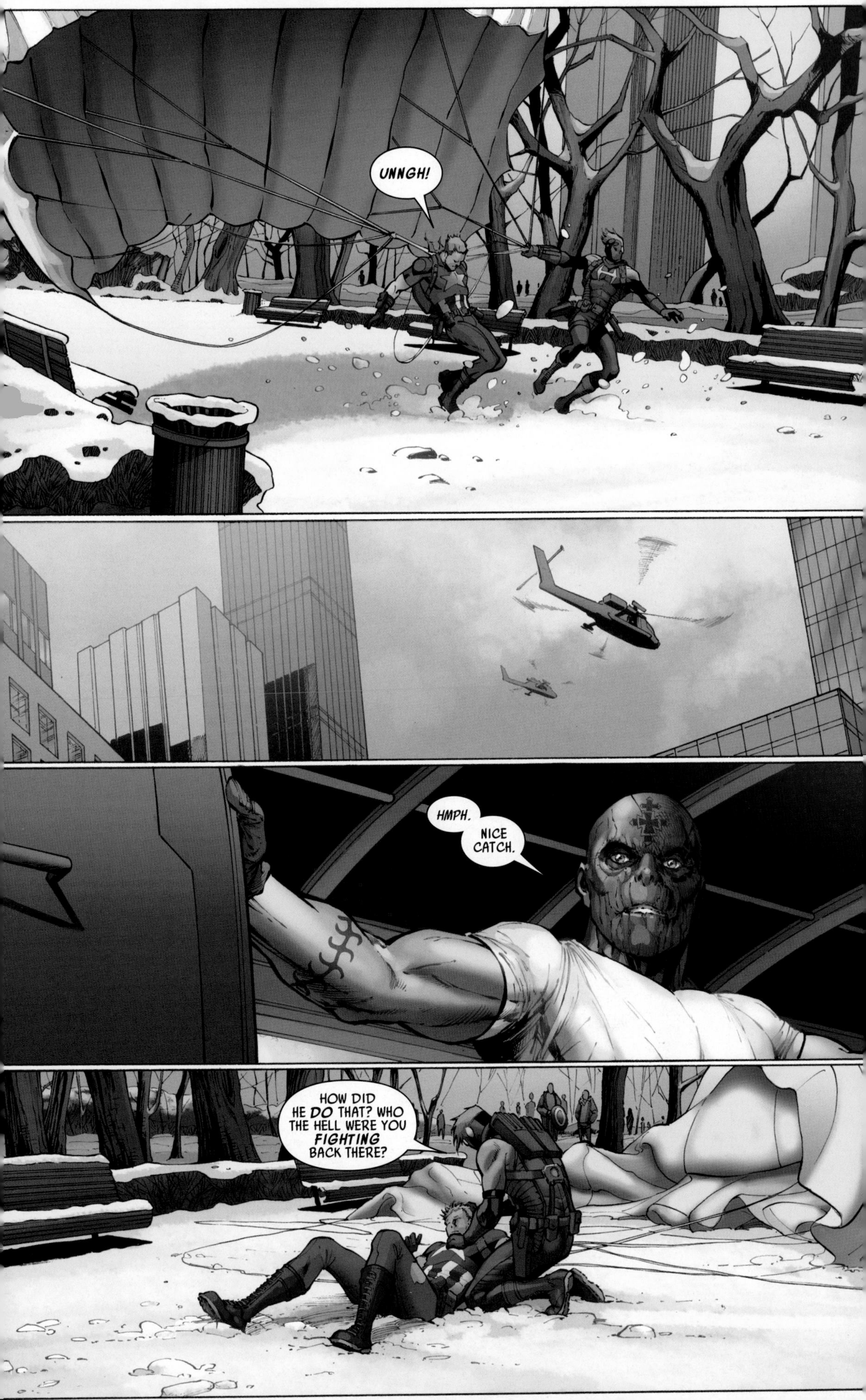
UNNGH!
HMPH.
NICE CATCH.
HOW DID HE DO THAT? WHO THE HELL WERE YOU FIGHTING BACK THERE?

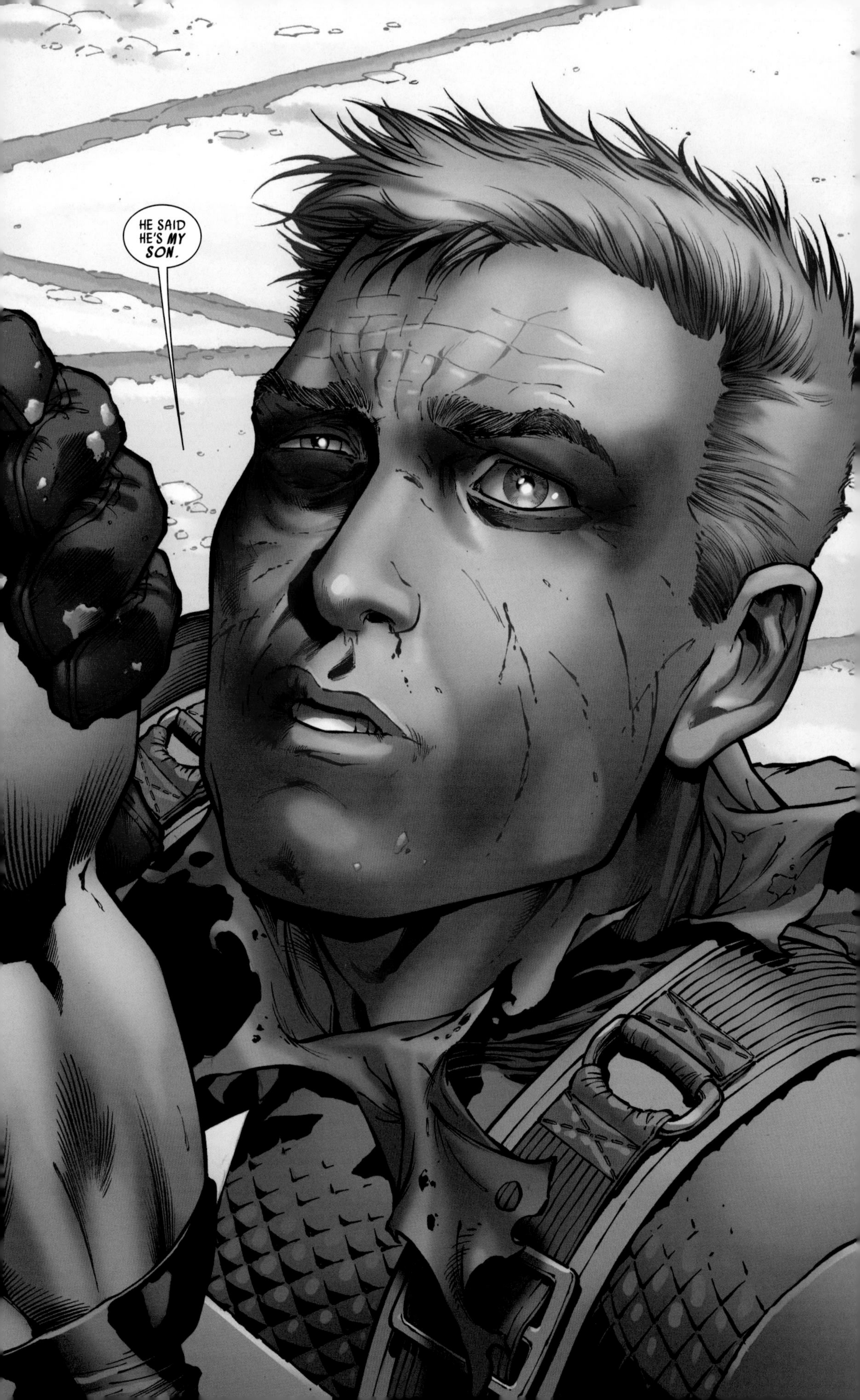
HE SAID HE'S MY SON.

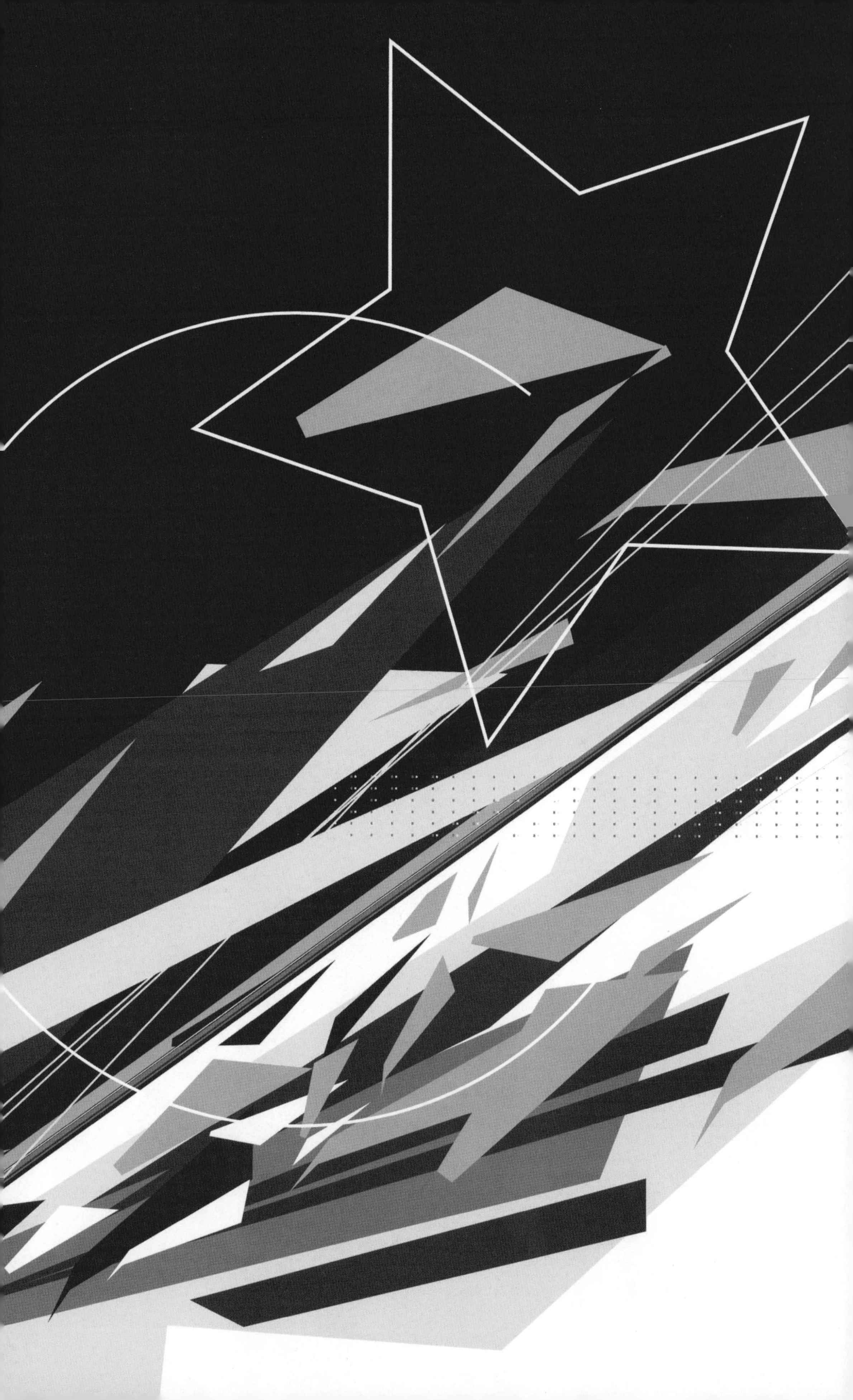

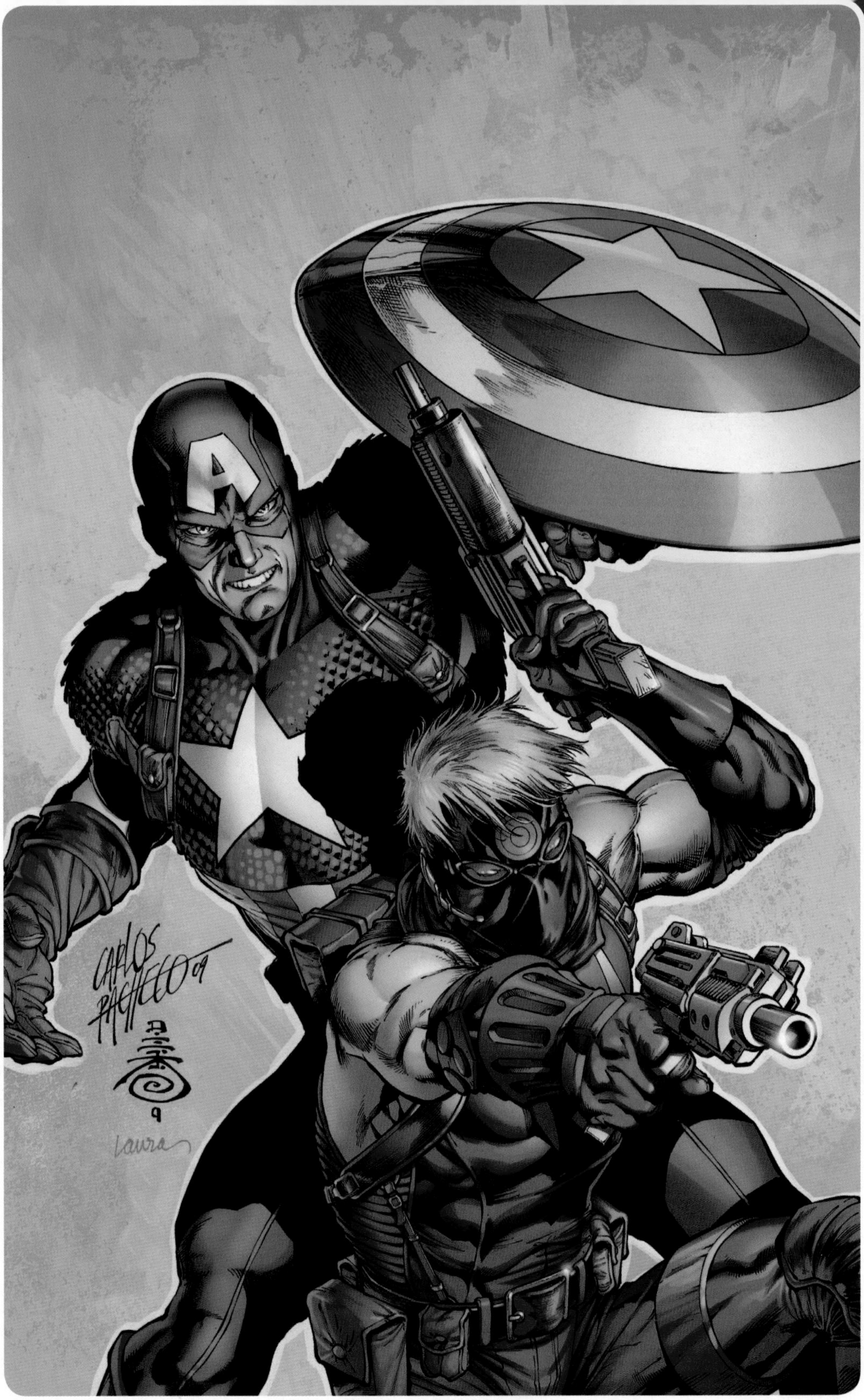
CARLOS PACHECO 09
Laura

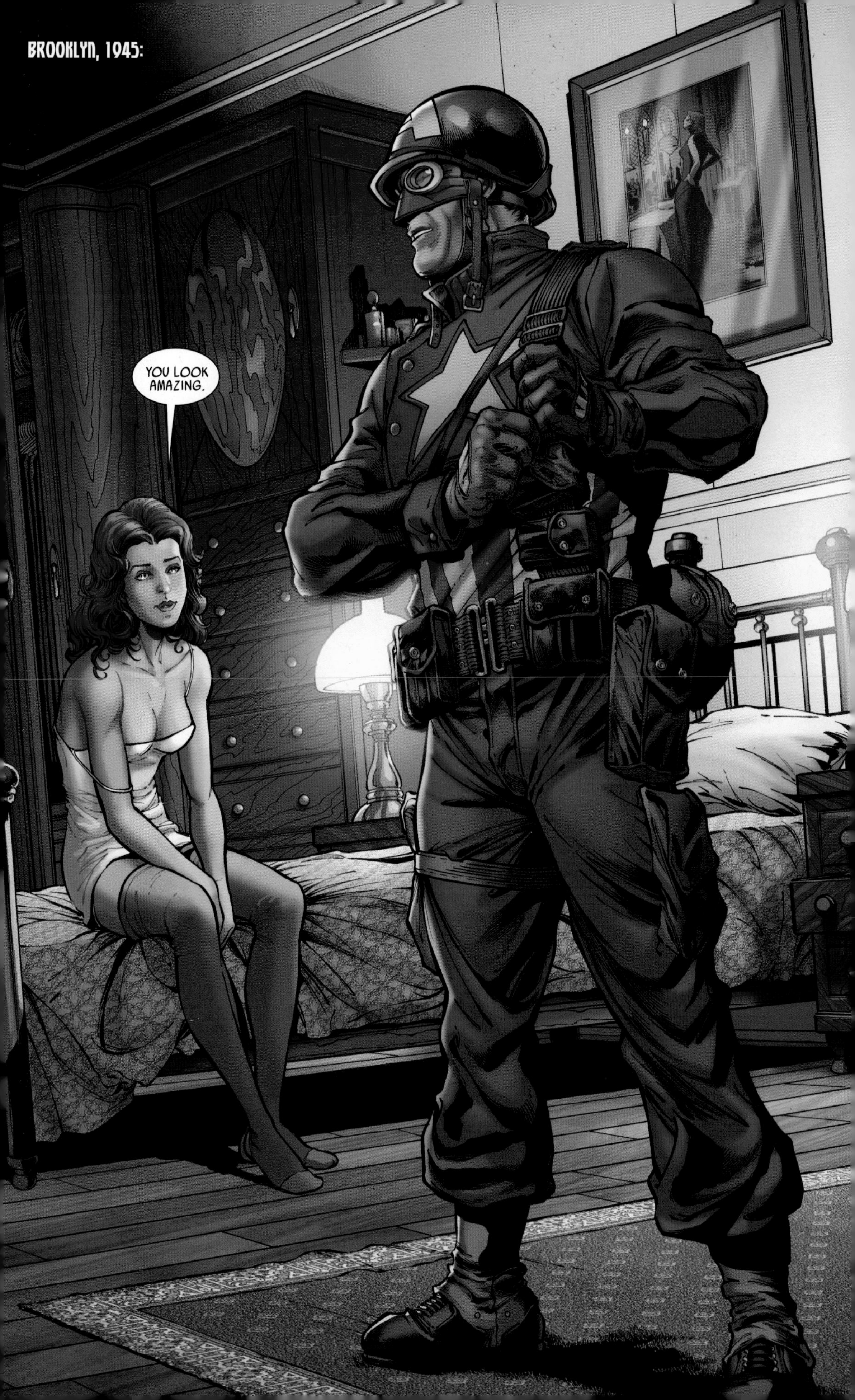
BROOKLYN, 1945:
YOU LOOK AMAZING.

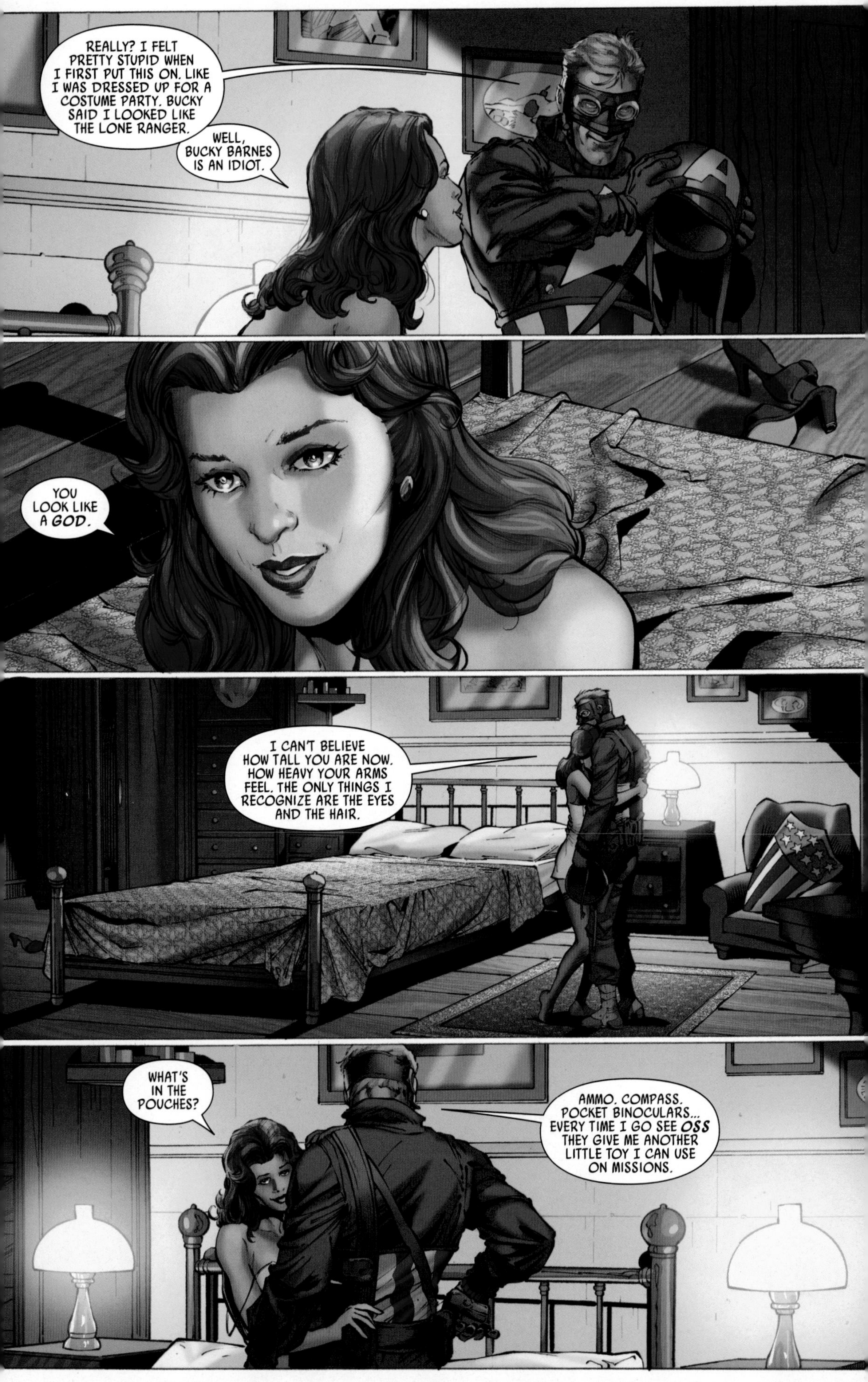
REALLY? I FELT PRETTY STUPID WHEN I FIRST PUT THIS ON. LIKE I WAS DRESSED UP FOR A COSTUME PARTY. BUCKY SAID I LOOKED LIKE THE LONE RANGER.
WELL, BUCKY BARNES IS AN IDIOT.
YOU LOOK LIKE A GOD.
I CAN'T BELIEVE HOW TALL YOU ARE NOW. HOW HEAVY YOUR ARMS FEEL. THE ONLY THINGS I RECOGNIZE ARE THE EYES AND THE HAIR.
WHAT'S IN THE POUCHES?
AMMO. COMPASS. POCKET BINOCULARS... EVERY TIME I GO SEE OSS THEY GIVE ME ANOTHER LITTLE TOY I CAN USE ON MISSIONS.

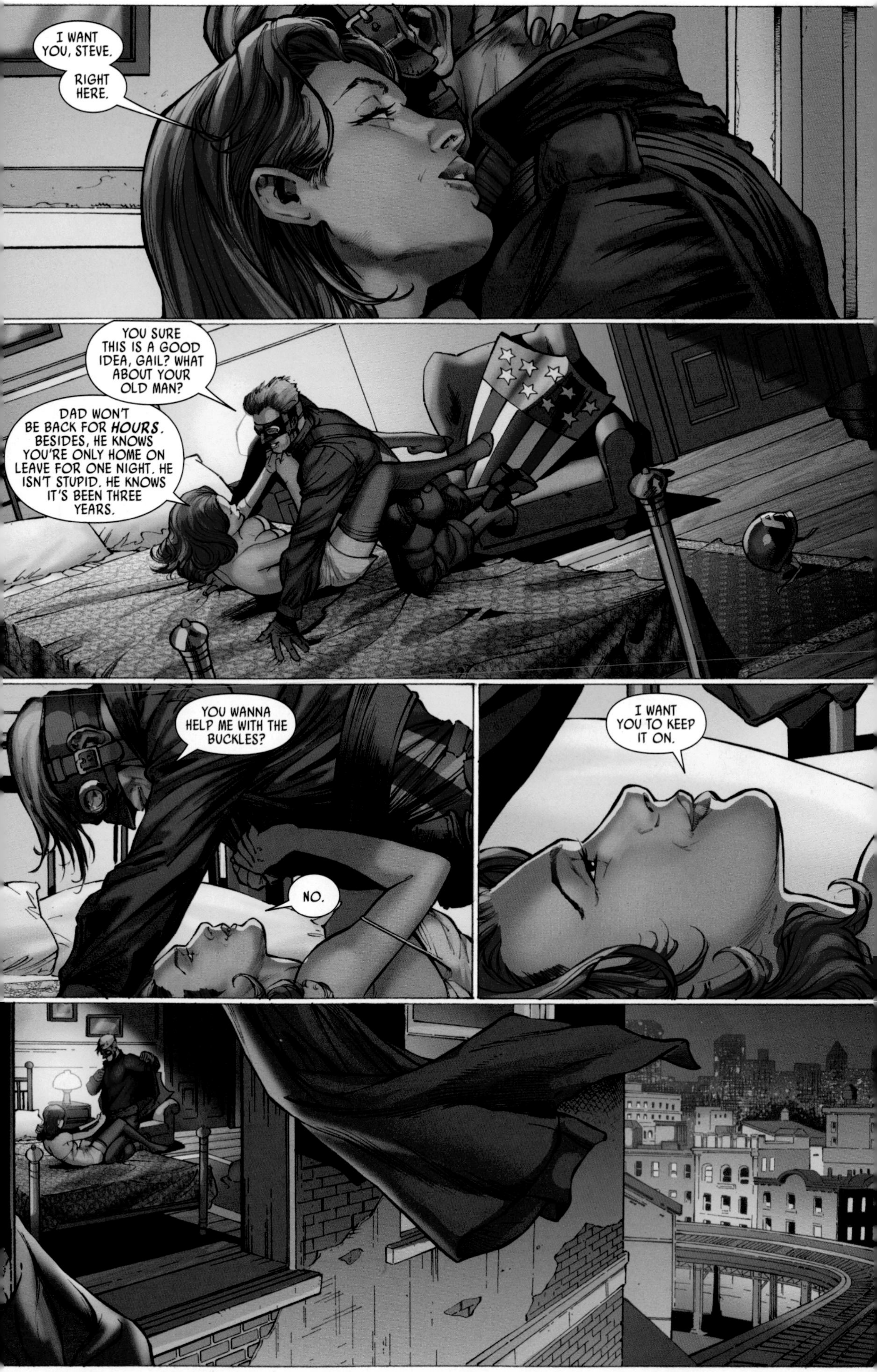

I WANT YOU, STEVE.
RIGHT HERE.
YOU SURE THIS IS A GOOD IDEA, GAIL? WHAT ABOUT YOUR OLD MAN?
DAD WON'T BE BACK FOR HOURS. BESIDES, HE KNOWS YOU'RE ONLY HOME ON LEAVE FOR ONE NIGHT. HE ISN'T STUPID. HE KNOWS IT'S BEEN THREE YEARS.
YOU WANNA HELP ME WITH THE BUCKLES?
NO.
I WANT YOU TO KEEP IT ON.

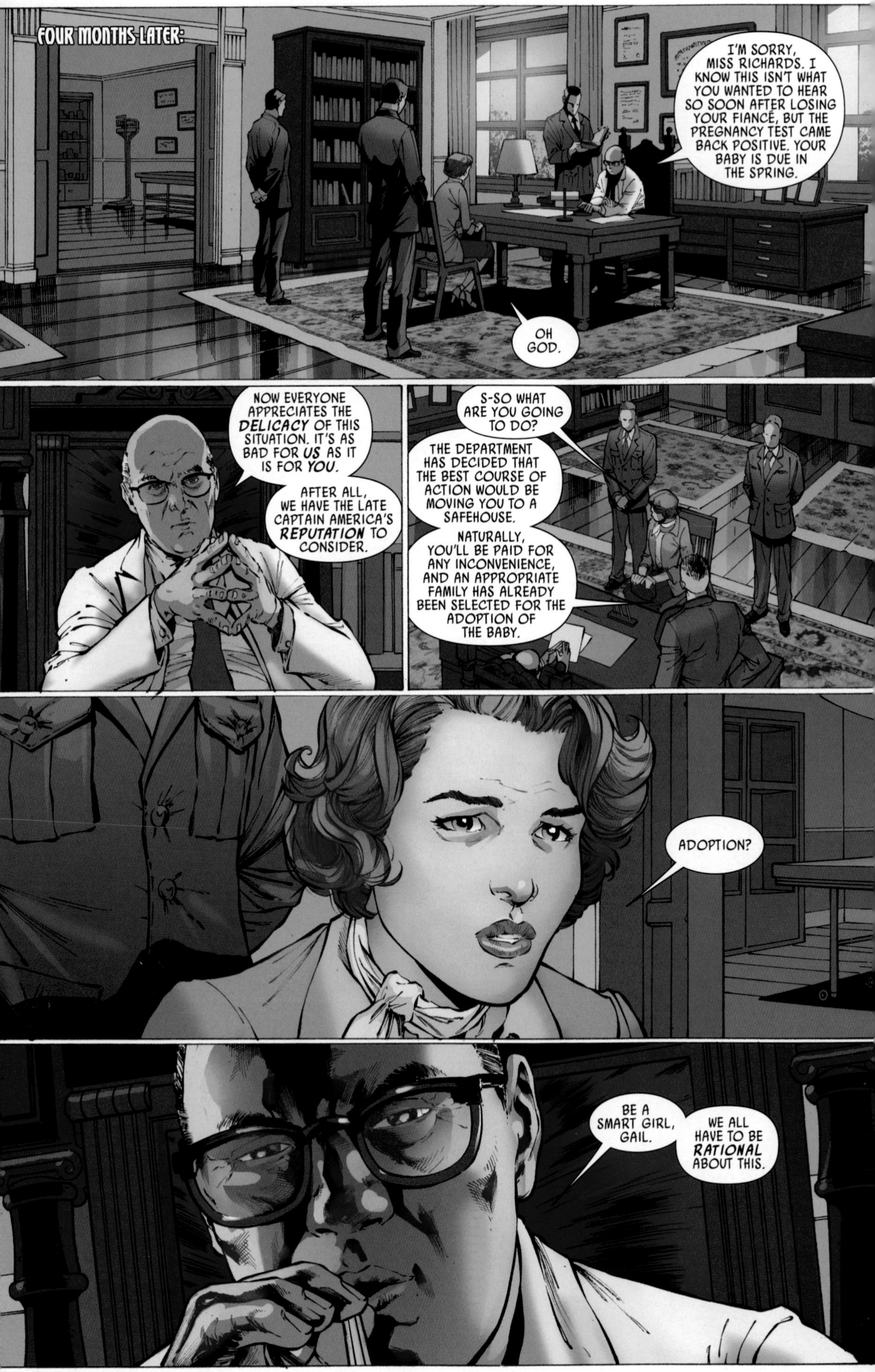
FOUR MONTHS LATER:
I'M SORRY, MISS RICHARDS. I KNOW THIS ISN'T WHAT YOU WANTED TO HEAR SO SOON AFTER LOSING YOUR FIANCÉ, BUT THE PREGNANCY TEST CAME BACK POSITIVE. YOUR BABY IS DUE IN THE SPRING.
OH GOD.
NOW EVERYONE APPRECIATES THE DELICACY OF THIS SITUATION. IT'S AS BAD FOR US AS IT IS FOR YOU.
AFTER ALL, WE HAVE THE LATE CAPTAIN AMERICA'S REPUTATION TO CONSIDER.
S-SO WHAT ARE YOU GOING TO DO?
THE DEPARTMENT HAS DECIDED THAT THE BEST COURSE OF ACTION WOULD BE MOVING YOU TO A SAFEHOUSE.
NATURALLY, YOU'LL BE PAID FOR ANY INCONVENIENCE, AND AN APPROPRIATE FAMILY HAS ALREADY BEEN SELECTED FOR THE ADOPTION OF THE BABY.
ADOPTION?
BE A SMART GIRL, GAIL.
WE ALL HAVE TO BE RATIONAL ABOUT THIS.

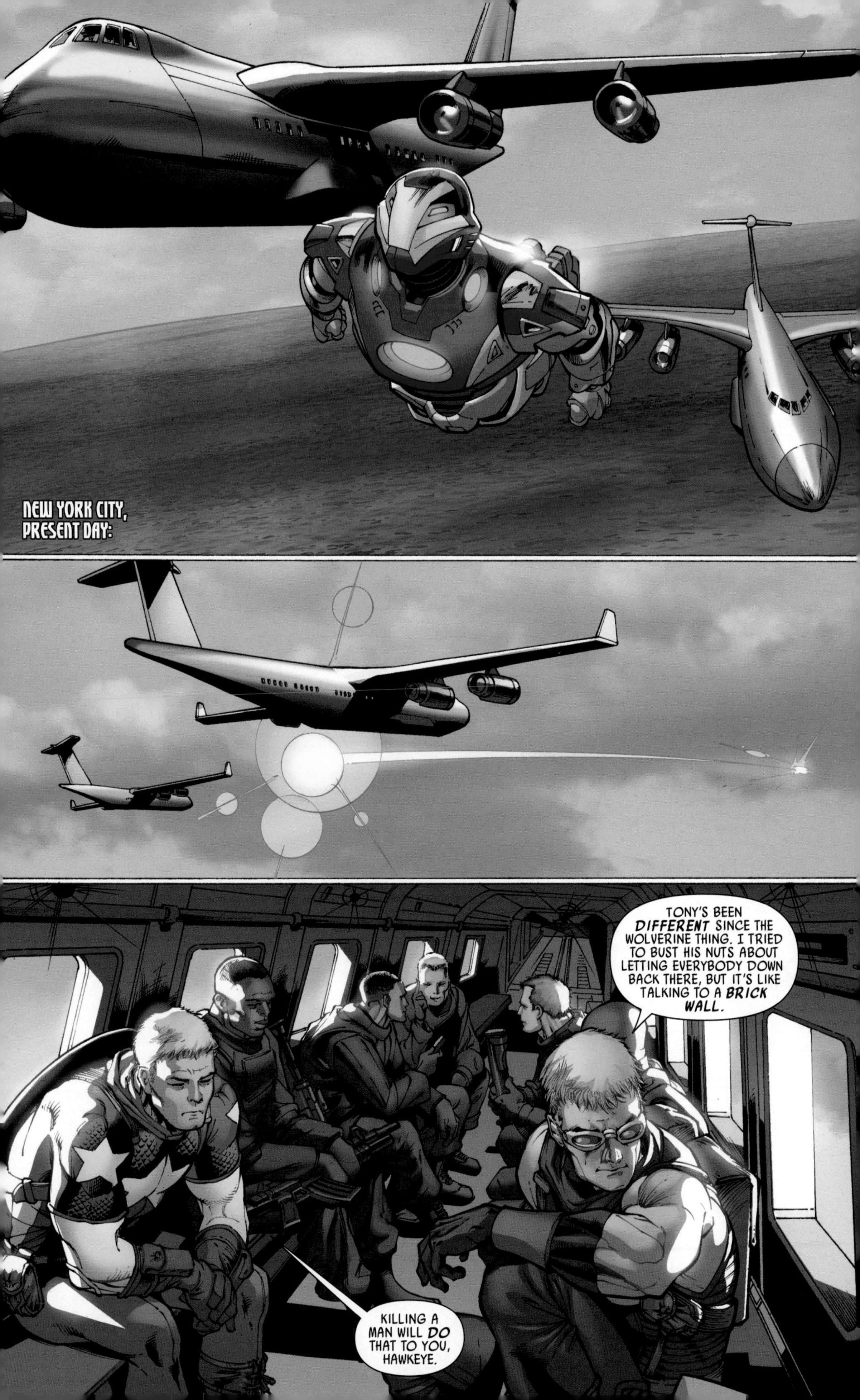
NEW YORK CITY, PRESENT DAY:
TONY'S BEEN DIFFERENT SINCE THE WOLVERINE THING. I TRIED TO BUST HIS NUTS ABOUT LETTING EVERYBODY DOWN BACK THERE, BUT IT'S LIKE TALKING TO A BRICK WALL.
KILLING A MAN WILL DO THAT TO YOU, HAWKEYE.

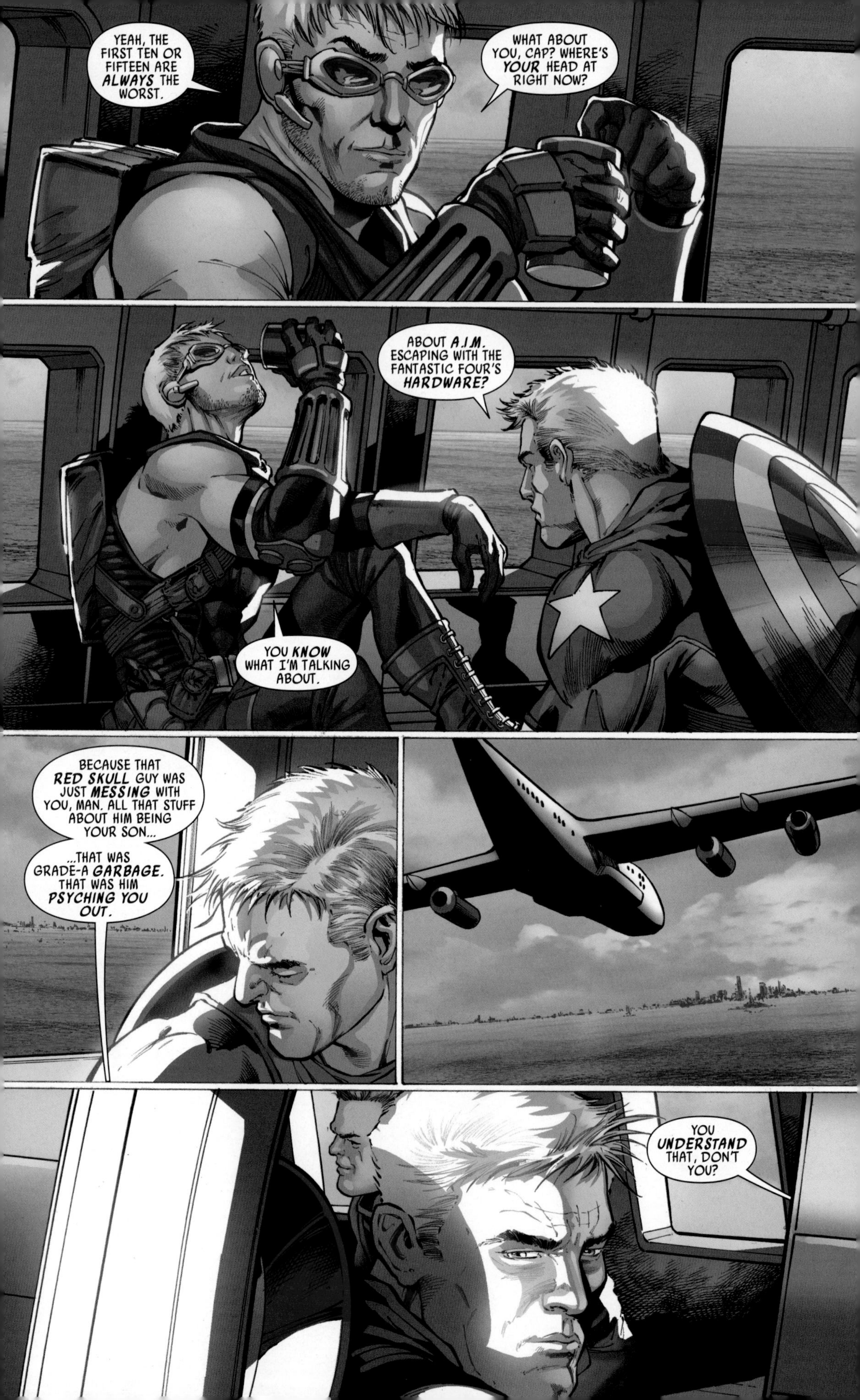
YEAH, THE FIRST TEN OR FIFTEEN ARE ALWAYS THE WORST.
WHAT ABOUT YOU, CAP? WHERE'S YOUR HEAD AT RIGHT NOW?
ABOUT A.I.M. ESCAPING WITH THE FANTASTIC FOUR'S HARDWARE?
YOU KNOW WHAT I'M TALKING ABOUT.
BECAUSE THAT RED SKULL GUY WAS JUST MESSING WITH YOU, MAN. ALL THAT STUFF ABOUT HIM BEING YOUR SON...
...THAT WAS GRADE-A GARBAGE. THAT WAS HIM PSYCHING YOU OUT.
YOU UNDERSTAND THAT, DON'T YOU?

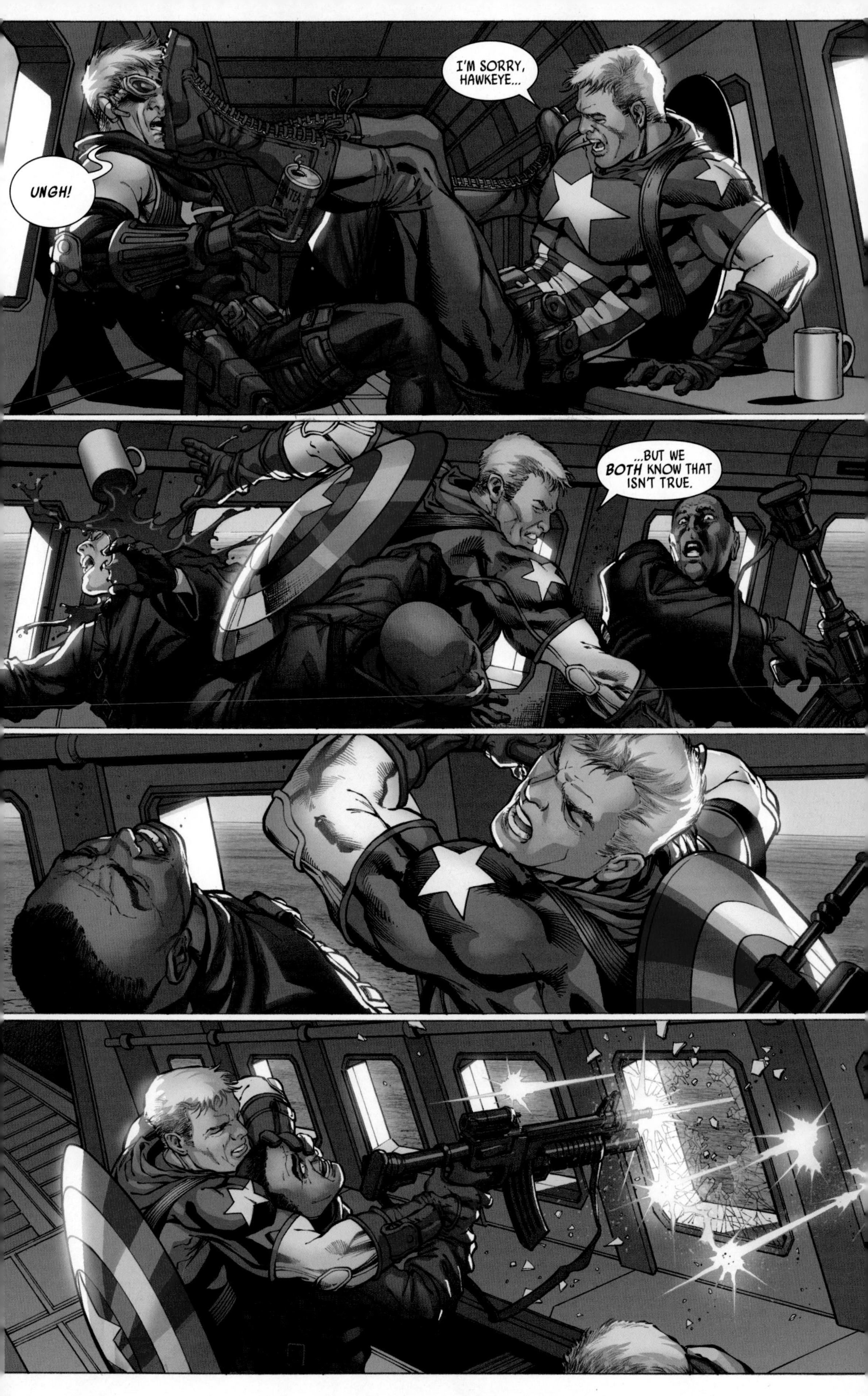
UNGH!
I'M SORRY, HAWKEYE...
...BUT WE BOTH KNOW THAT ISN'T TRUE.

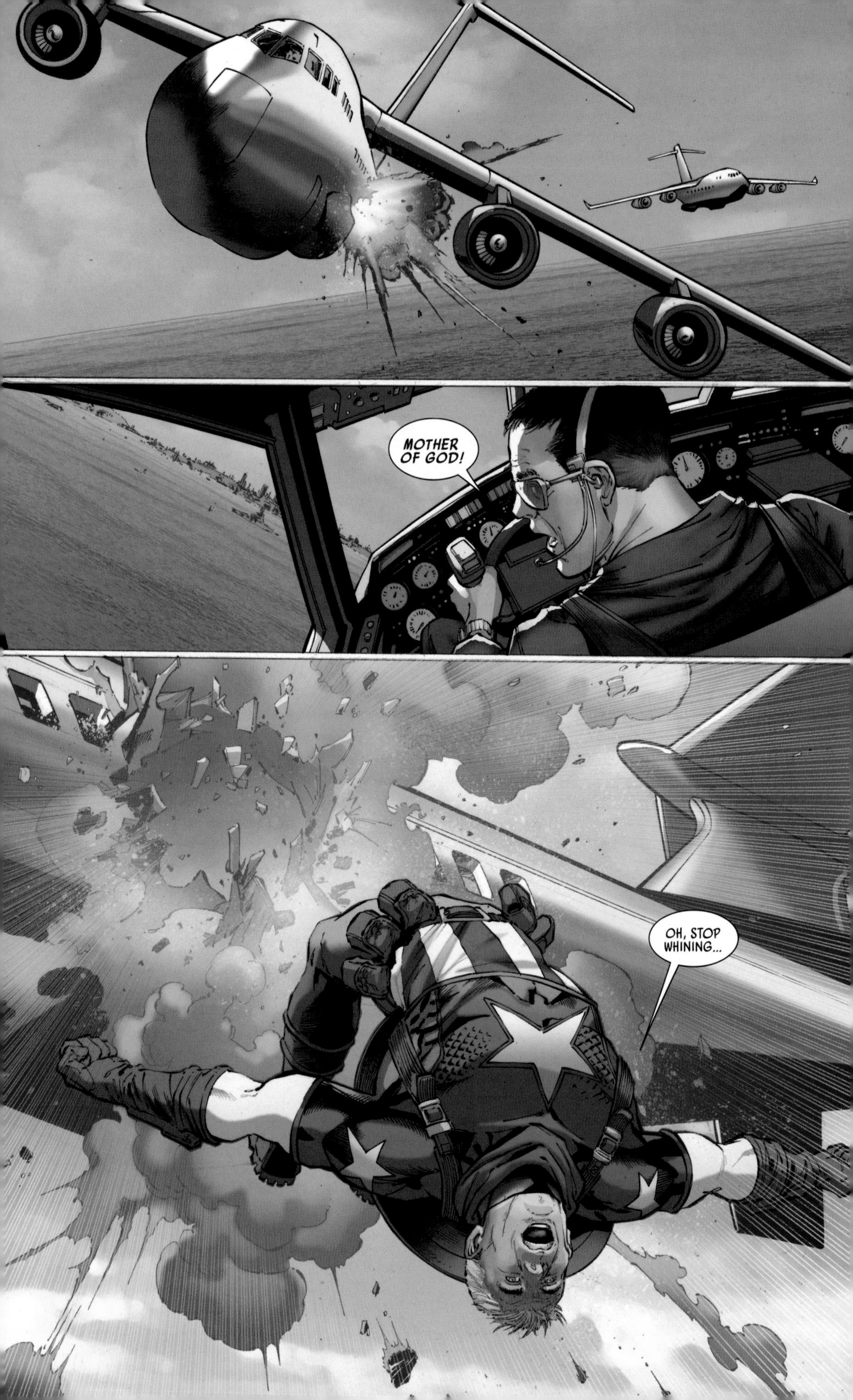
MOTHER OF GOD!
OH, STOP WHINING...

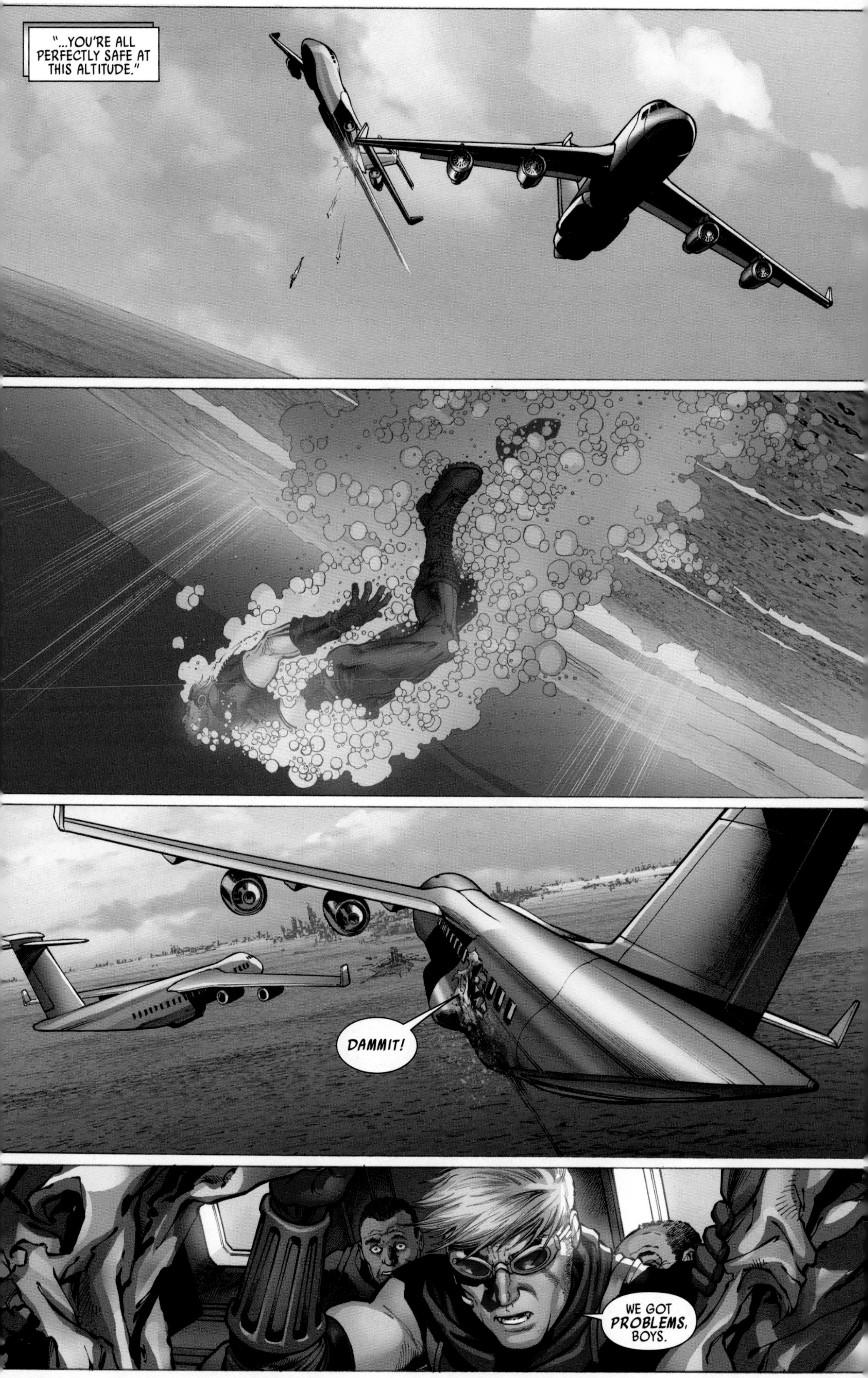
"...YOU'RE ALL PERFECTLY SAFE AT THIS ALTITUDE."
DAMMIT!
WE GOT PROBLEMS, BOYS.

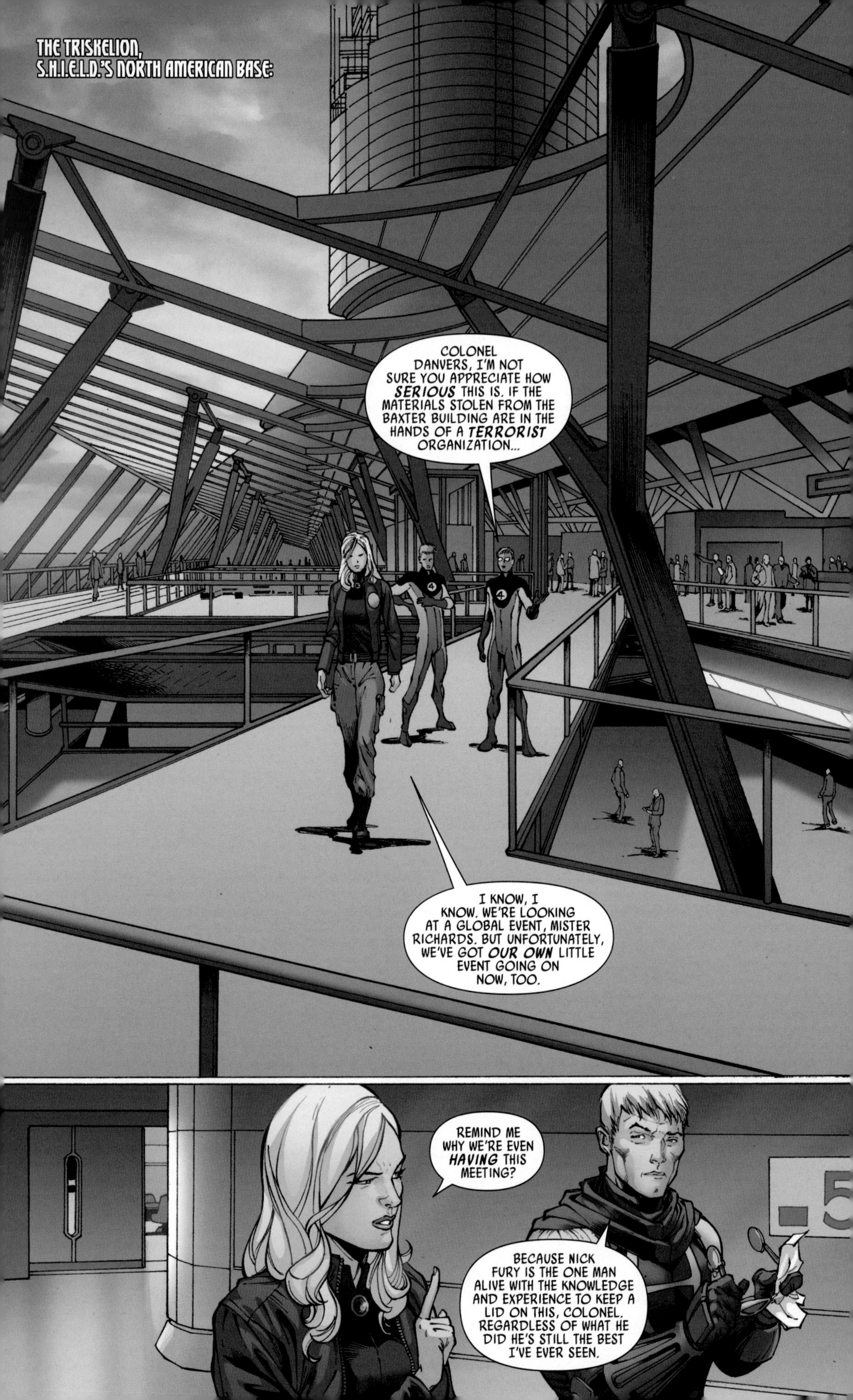
THE TRISKELION, S.H.I.E.L.D.'S NORTH AMERICAN BASE:
COLONEL DANVERS, I'M NOT SURE YOU APPRECIATE HOW SERIOUS THIS IS. IF THE MATERIALS STOLEN FROM THE BAXTER BUILDING ARE IN THE HANDS OF A TERRORIST ORGANIZATION...
I KNOW, I KNOW. WE'RE LOOKING AT A GLOBAL EVENT, MISTER RICHARDS. BUT UNFORTUNATELY, WE'VE GOT OUR OWN LITTLE EVENT GOING ON NOW, TOO.
REMIND ME WHY WE'RE EVEN HAVING THIS MEETING?
BECAUSE NICK FURY IS THE ONE MAN ALIVE WITH THE KNOWLEDGE AND EXPERIENCE TO KEEP A LID ON THIS, COLONEL. REGARDLESS OF WHAT HE DID HE'S STILL THE BEST I'VE EVER SEEN.

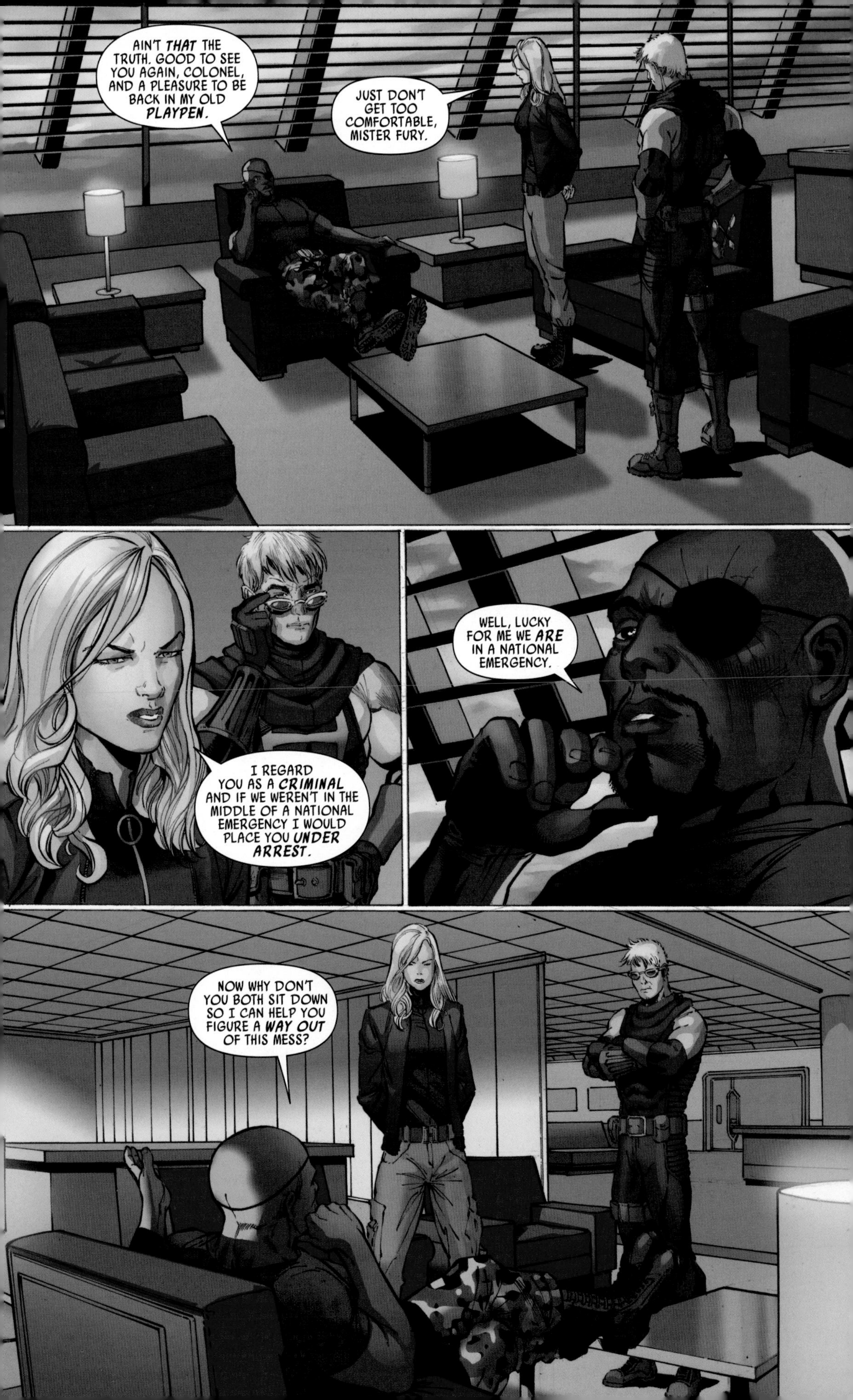
AIN'T THAT THE TRUTH. GOOD TO SEE YOU AGAIN, COLONEL, AND A PLEASURE TO BE BACK IN MY OLD PLAYPEN.
JUST DON'T GET TOO COMFORTABLE, MISTER FURY.
I REGARD YOU AS A CRIMINAL AND IF WE WEREN'T IN THE MIDDLE OF A NATIONAL EMERGENCY I WOULD PLACE YOU UNDER ARREST.
WELL, LUCKY FOR ME WE ARE IN A NATIONAL EMERGENCY.
NOW WHY DON'T YOU BOTH SIT DOWN SO I CAN HELP YOU FIGURE A WAY OUT OF THIS MESS?

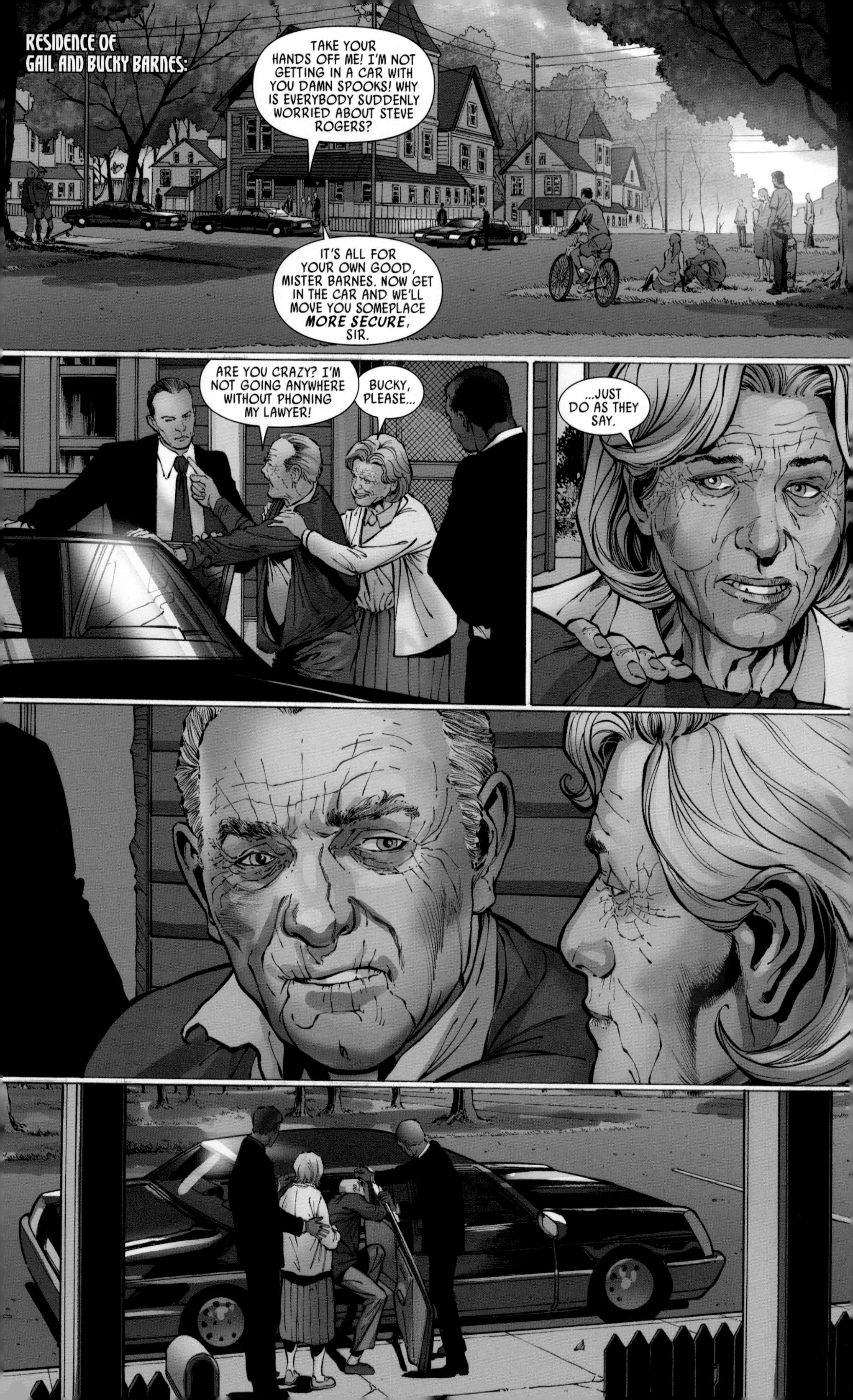
RESIDENCE OF GAIL AND BUCKY BARNES:
TAKE YOUR HANDS OFF ME! I'M NOT GETTING IN A CAR WITH YOU DAMN SPOOKS! WHY IS EVERYBODY SUDDENLY WORRIED ABOUT STEVE ROGERS?
IT'S ALL FOR YOUR OWN GOOD, MISTER BARNES. NOW GET IN THE CAR AND WE'LL MOVE YOU SOMEPLACE MORE SECURE, SIR.
ARE YOU CRAZY? I'M NOT GOING ANYWHERE WITHOUT PHONING MY LAWYER!
BUCKY, PLEASE...
...JUST DO AS THEY SAY.

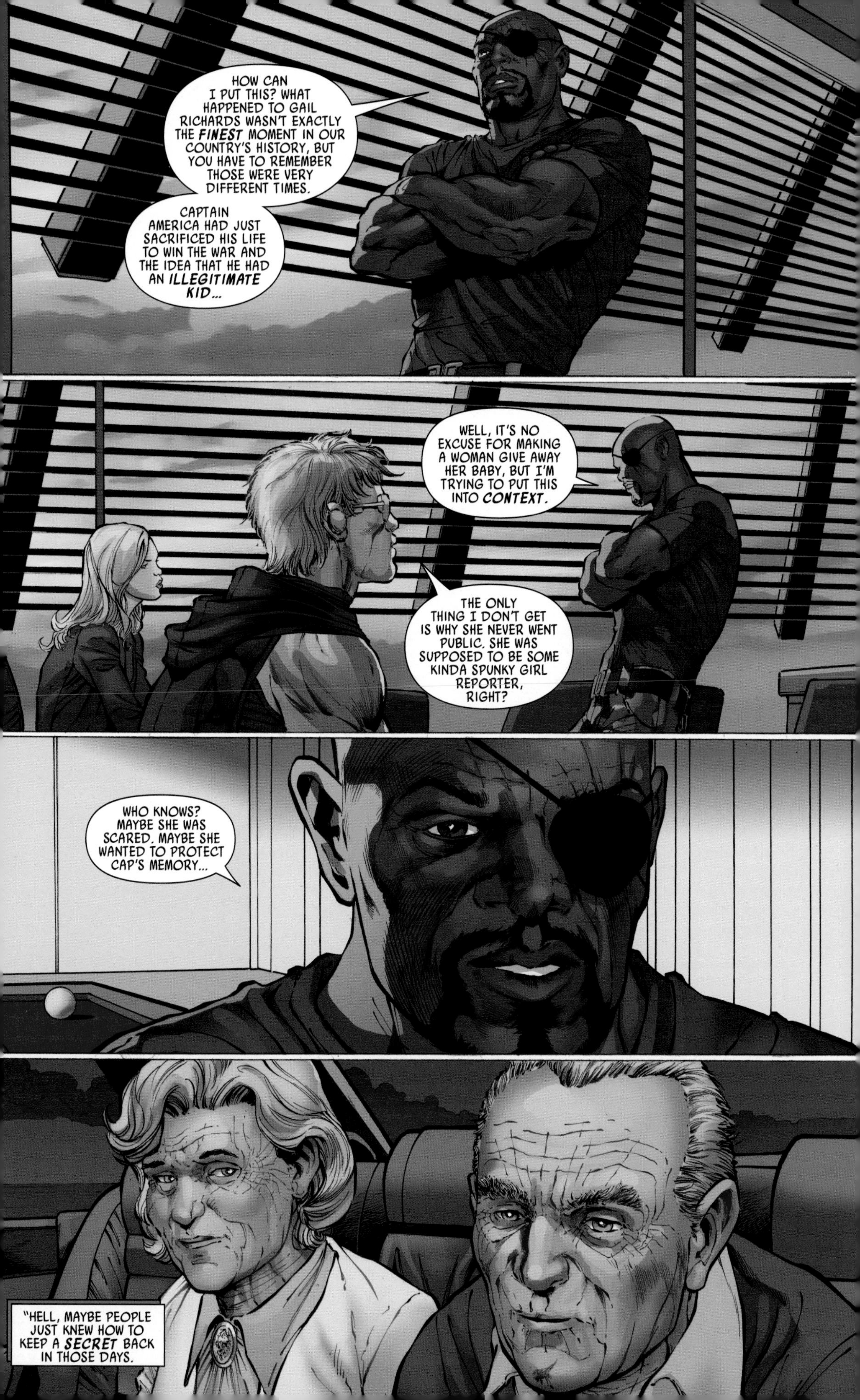
HOW CAN I PUT THIS? WHAT HAPPENED TO GAIL RICHARDS WASN'T EXACTLY THE FINEST MOMENT IN OUR COUNTRY'S HISTORY, BUT YOU HAVE TO REMEMBER THOSE WERE VERY DIFFERENT TIMES.
CAPTAIN AMERICA HAD JUST SACRIFICED HIS LIFE TO WIN THE WAR AND THE IDEA THAT HE HAD AN ILLEGITIMATE KID...
WELL, IT'S NO EXCUSE FOR MAKING A WOMAN GIVE AWAY HER BABY, BUT I'M TRYING TO PUT THIS INTO CONTEXT.
THE ONLY THING I DON'T GET IS WHY SHE NEVER WENT PUBLIC. SHE WAS SUPPOSED TO BE SOME KINDA SPUNKY GIRL REPORTER, RIGHT?
WHO KNOWS? MAYBE SHE WAS SCARED. MAYBE SHE WANTED TO PROTECT CAP'S MEMORY...
"HELL, MAYBE PEOPLE JUST KNEW HOW TO KEEP A SECRET BACK IN THOSE DAYS.

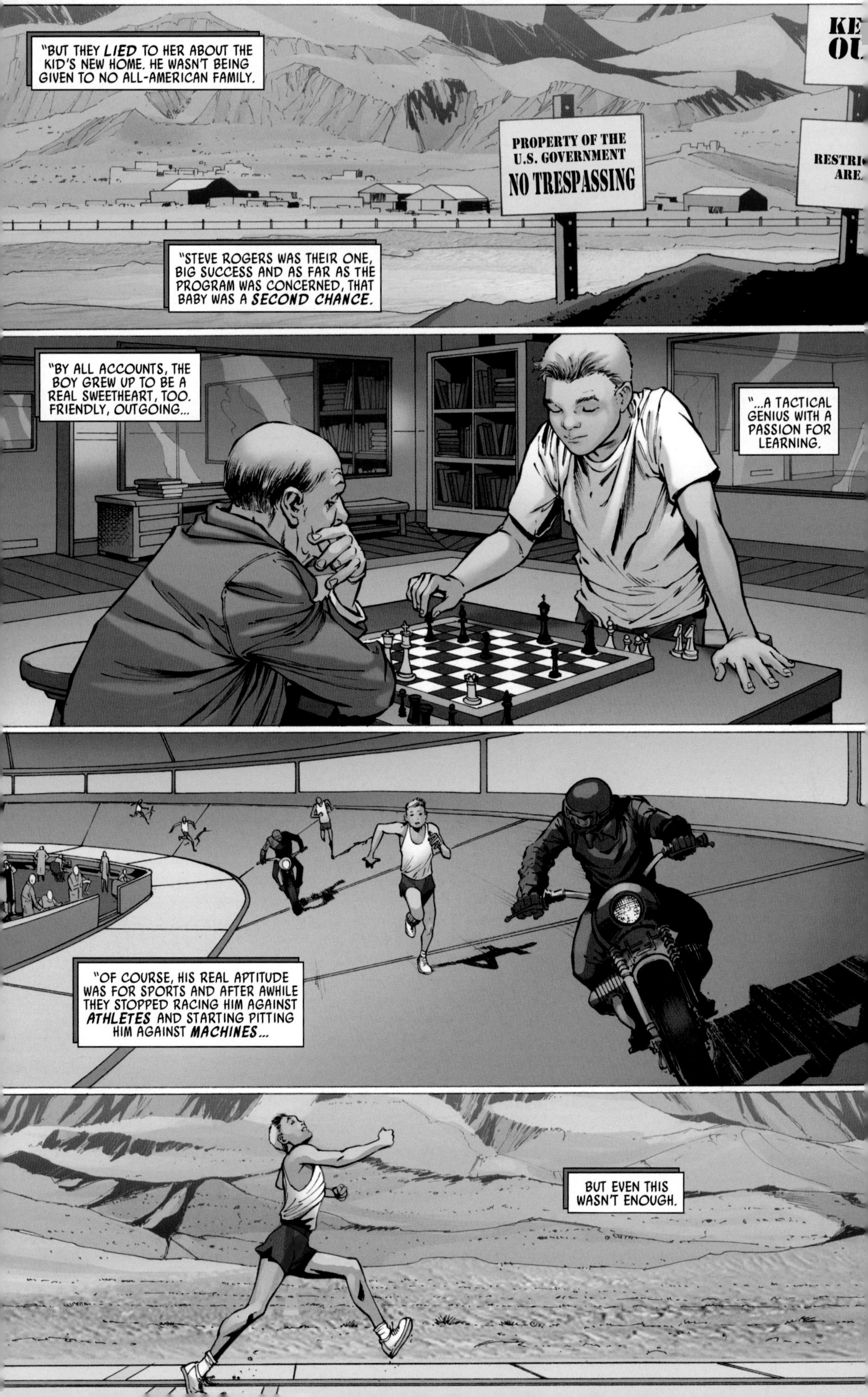
"BUT THEY LIED TO HER ABOUT THE KID'S NEW HOME. HE WASN'T BEING GIVEN TO NO ALL-AMERICAN FAMILY.
PROPERTY OF THE U.S. GOVERNMENT NO TRESPASSING
"STEVE ROGERS WAS THEIR ONE, BIG SUCCESS AND AS FAR AS THE PROGRAM WAS CONCERNED, THAT BABY WAS A SECOND CHANCE.
"BY ALL ACCOUNTS, THE BOY GREW UP TO BE A REAL SWEETHEART, TOO. FRIENDLY, OUTGOING...
"...A TACTICAL GENIUS WITH A PASSION FOR LEARNING.
"OF COURSE, HIS REAL APTITUDE WAS FOR SPORTS AND AFTER AWHILE THEY STOPPED RACING HIM AGAINST ATHLETES AND STARTING PITTING HIM AGAINST MACHINES...
BUT EVEN THIS WASN'T ENOUGH.

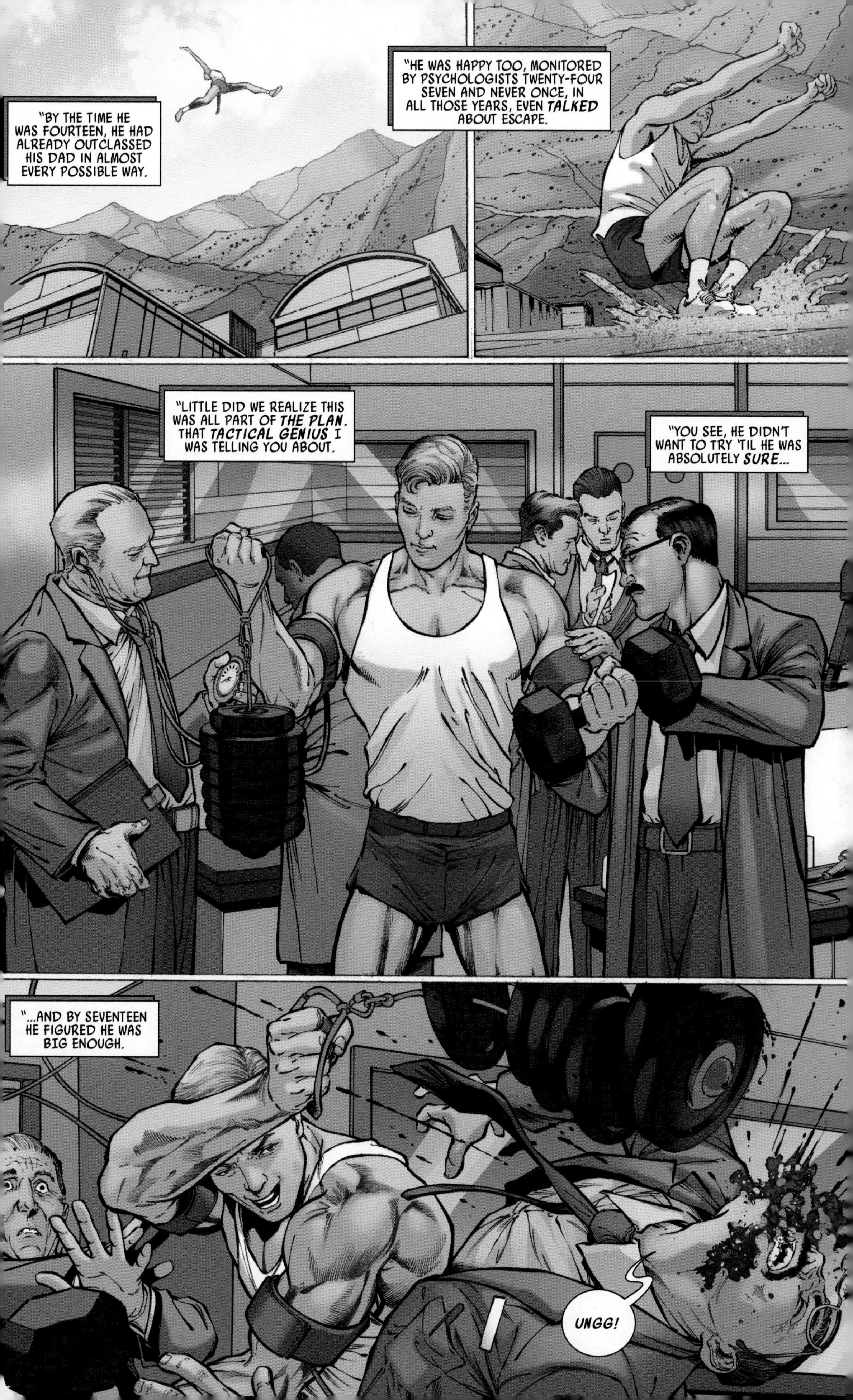
"BY THE TIME HE WAS FOURTEEN, HE HAD ALREADY OUTCLASSED HIS DAD IN ALMOST EVERY POSSIBLE WAY.
"HE WAS HAPPY TOO, MONITORED BY PSYCHOLOGISTS TWENTY-FOUR SEVEN AND NEVER ONCE, IN ALL THOSE YEARS, EVEN TALKED ABOUT ESCAPE.
"LITTLE DID WE REALIZE THIS WAS ALL PART OF THE PLAN. THAT TACTICAL GENIUS I WAS TELLING YOU ABOUT.
"YOU SEE, HE DIDN'T WANT TO TRY 'TIL HE WAS ABSOLUTELY SURE...
"...AND BY SEVENTEEN HE FIGURED HE WAS BIG ENOUGH.
UNGG!

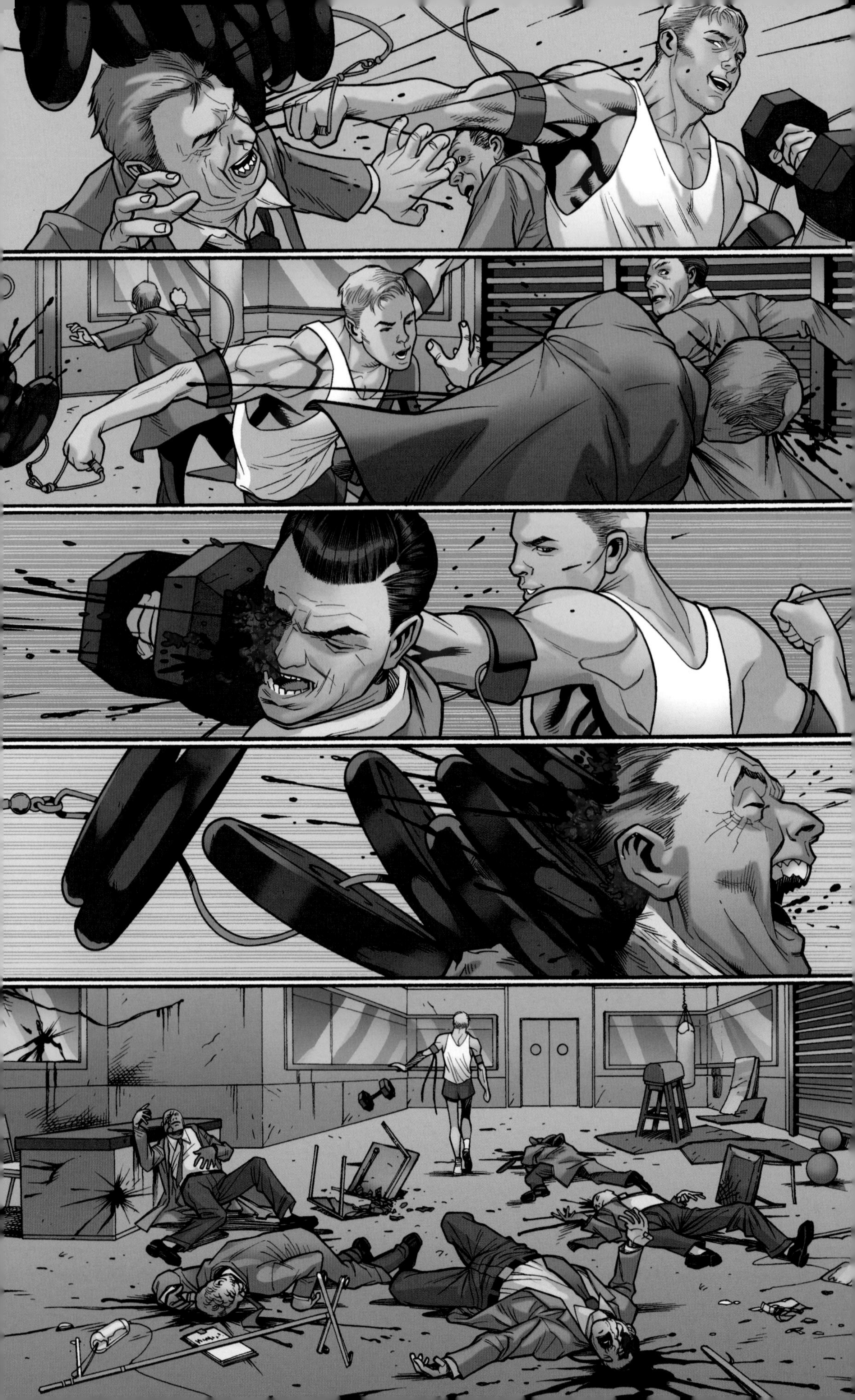

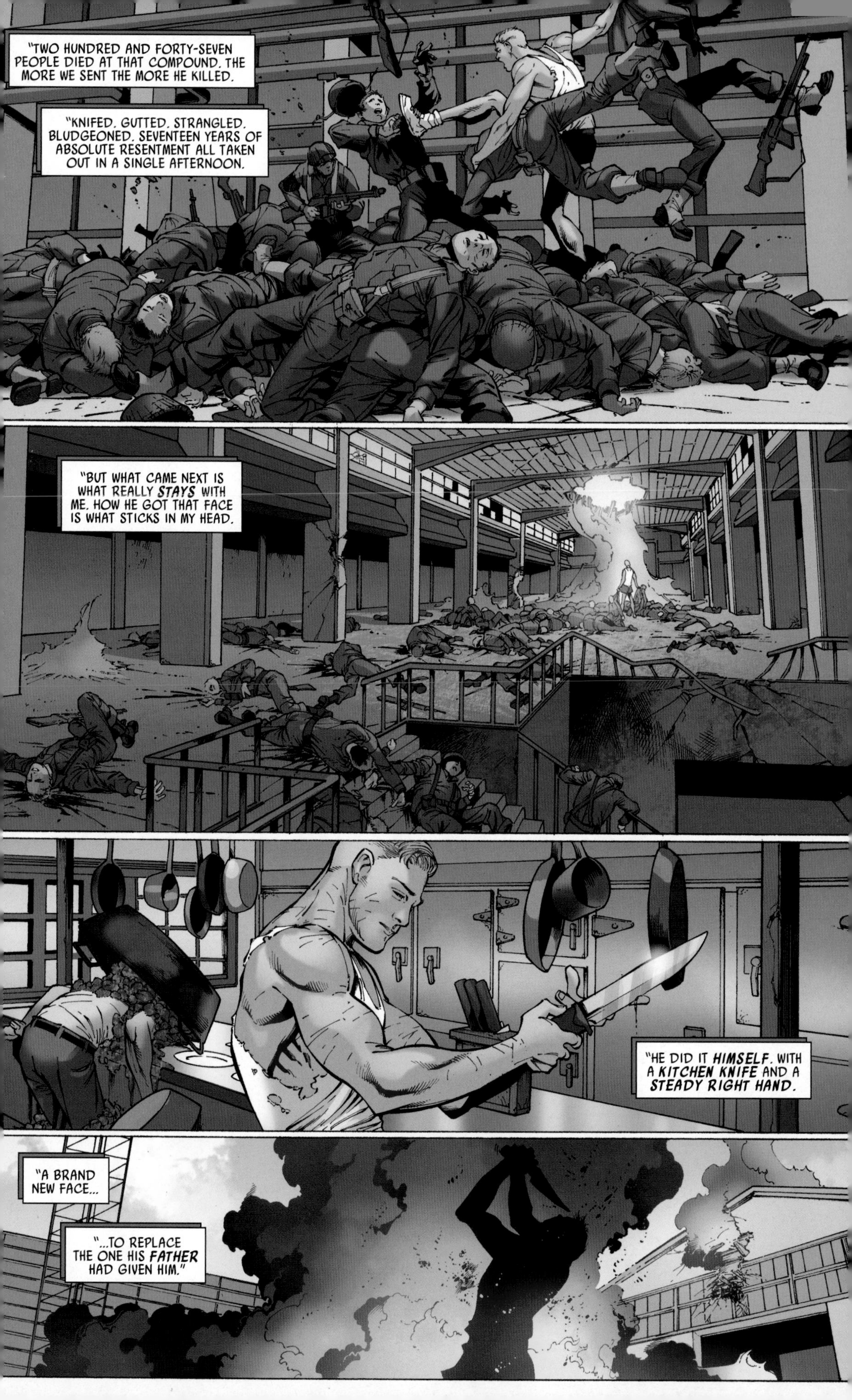
"TWO HUNDRED AND FORTY-SEVEN PEOPLE DIED AT THAT COMPOUND. THE MORE WE SENT THE MORE HE KILLED.
"KNIFED. GUTTED. STRANGLED. BLUDGEONED. SEVENTEEN YEARS OF ABSOLUTE RESENTMENT ALL TAKEN OUT IN A SINGLE AFTERNOON.
"BUT WHAT CAME NEXT IS WHAT REALLY STAYS WITH ME. HOW HE GOT THAT FACE IS WHAT STICKS IN MY HEAD.
"HE DID IT HIMSELF. WITH A KITCHEN KNIFE AND A STEADY RIGHT HAND.
"A BRAND NEW FACE...
"...TO REPLACE THE ONE HIS FATHER HAD GIVEN HIM."

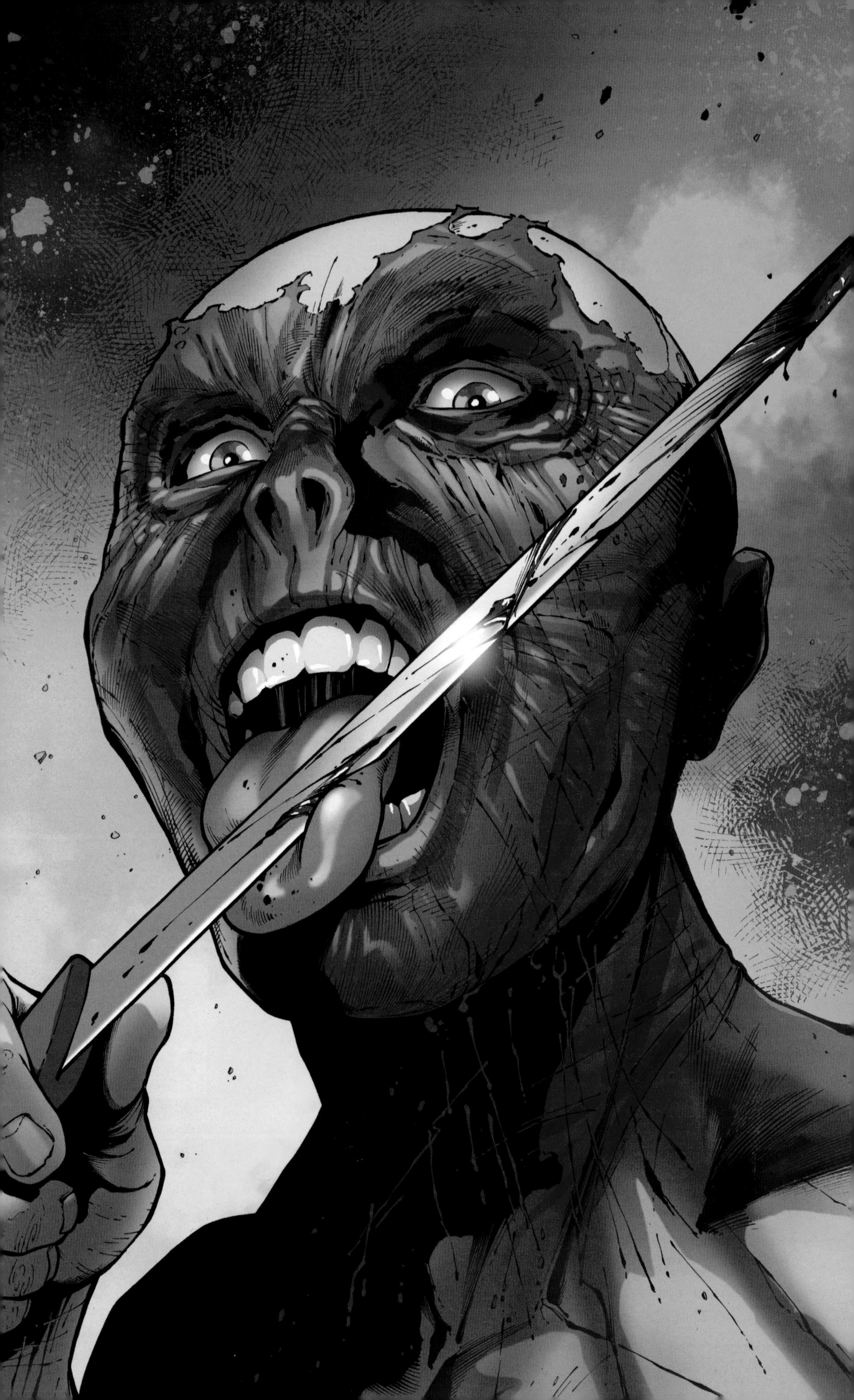

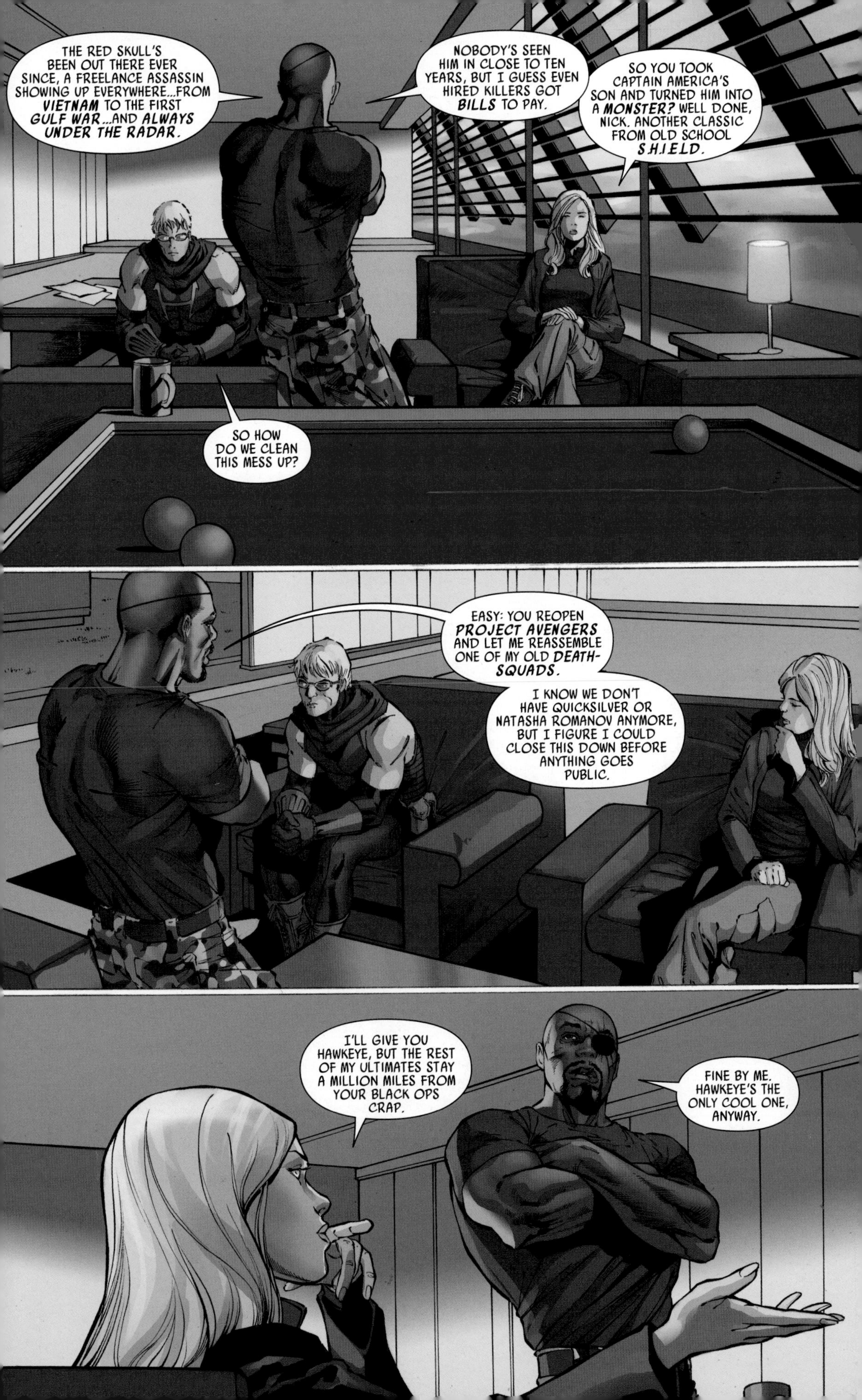
THE RED SKULL'S BEEN OUT THERE EVER SINCE, A FREELANCE ASSASSIN SHOWING UP EVERYWHERE...FROM VIETNAM TO THE FIRST GULF WAR...AND ALWAYS UNDER THE RADAR.
NOBODY'S SEEN HIM IN CLOSE TO TEN YEARS, BUT I GUESS EVEN HIRED KILLERS GOT BILLS TO PAY.
SO YOU TOOK CAPTAIN AMERICA'S SON AND TURNED HIM INTO A MONSTER? WELL DONE, NICK. ANOTHER CLASSIC FROM OLD SCHOOL S.H.I.E.L.D.
SO HOW DO WE CLEAN THIS MESS UP?
EASY: YOU REOPEN PROJECT AVENGERS AND LET ME REASSEMBLE ONE OF MY OLD DEATH-SQUADS.
I KNOW WE DON'T HAVE QUICKSILVER OR NATASHA ROMANOV ANYMORE, BUT I FIGURE I COULD CLOSE THIS DOWN BEFORE ANYTHING GOES PUBLIC.
I'LL GIVE YOU HAWKEYE, BUT THE REST OF MY ULTIMATES STAY A MILLION MILES FROM YOUR BLACK OPS CRAP.
FINE BY ME. HAWKEYE'S THE ONLY COOL ONE, ANYWAY.

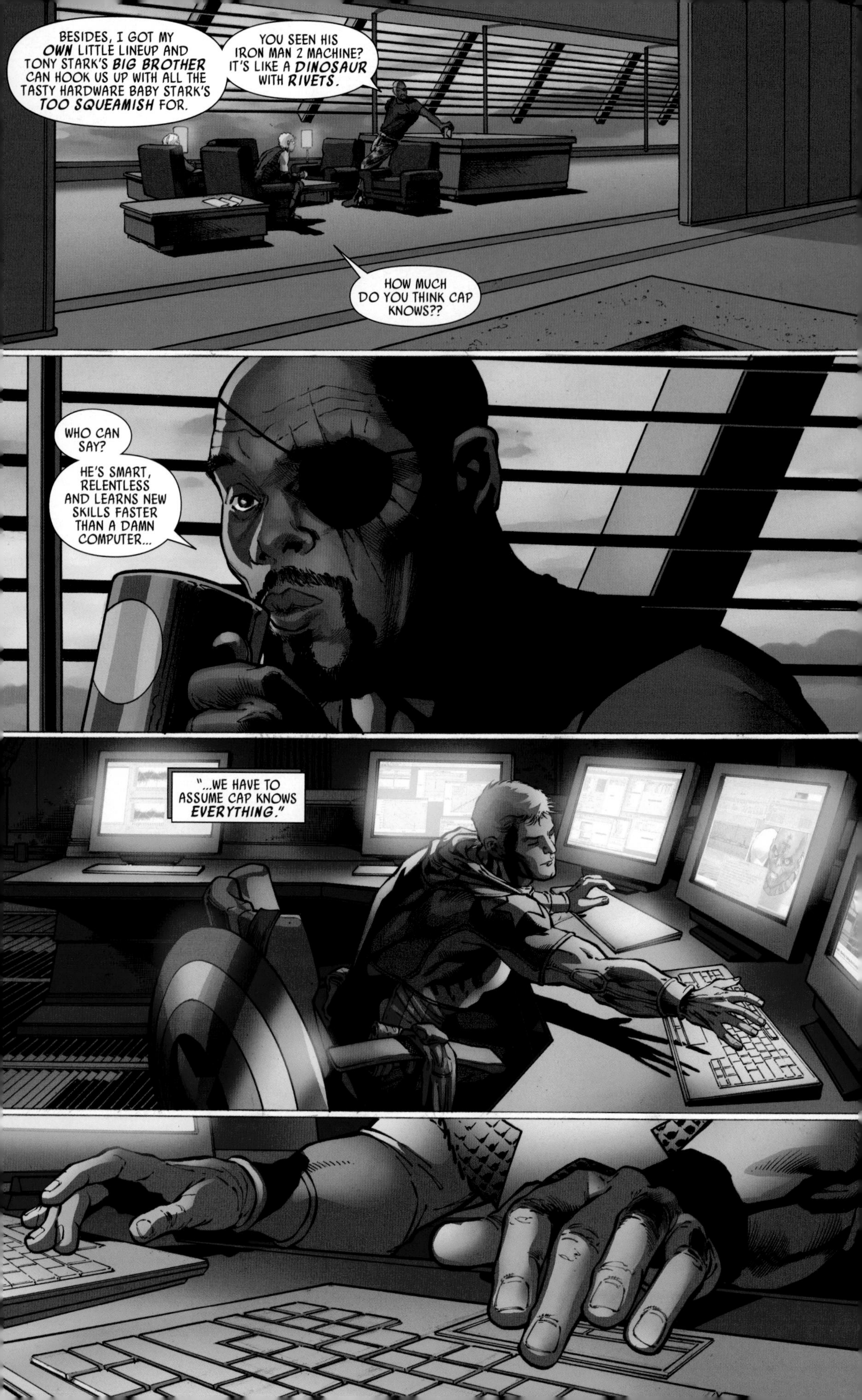
BESIDES, I GOT MY OWN LITTLE LINEUP AND TONY STARK'S BIG BROTHER CAN HOOK US UP WITH ALL THE TASTY HARDWARE BABY STARK'S TOO SQUEAMISH FOR.
YOU SEEN HIS IRON MAN 2 MACHINE? IT'S LIKE A DINOSAUR WITH RIVETS.
HOW MUCH DO YOU THINK CAP KNOWS??
WHO CAN SAY?
HE'S SMART, RELENTLESS AND LEARNS NEW SKILLS FASTER THAN A DAMN COMPUTER...
"...WE HAVE TO ASSUME CAP KNOWS EVERYTHING."

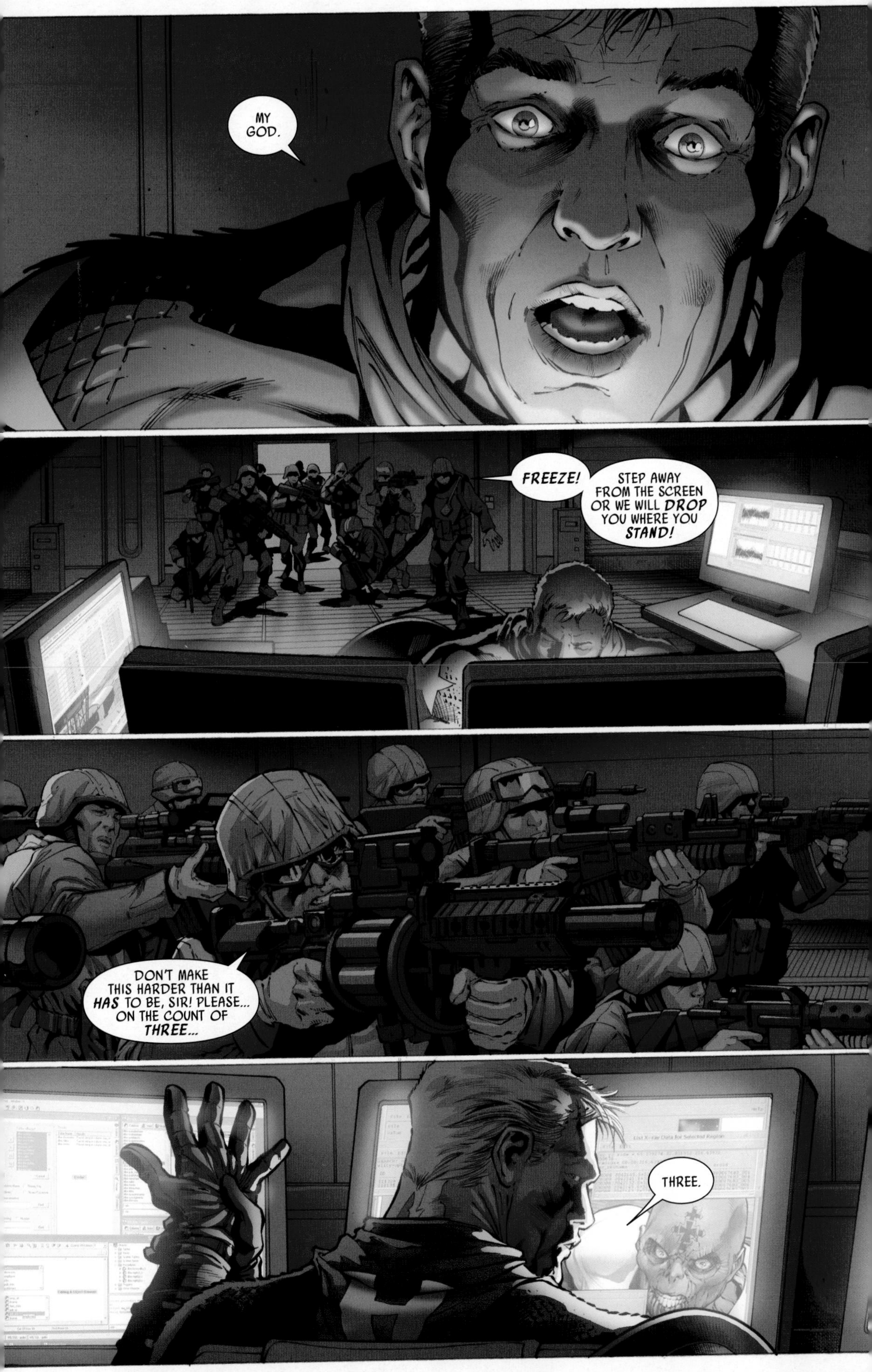
MY GOD.
FREEZE!
STEP AWAY FROM THE SCREEN OR WE WILL DROP YOU WHERE YOU STAND!
DON'T MAKE THIS HARDER THAN IT HAS TO BE, SIR! PLEASE... ON THE COUNT OF THREE...
THREE.

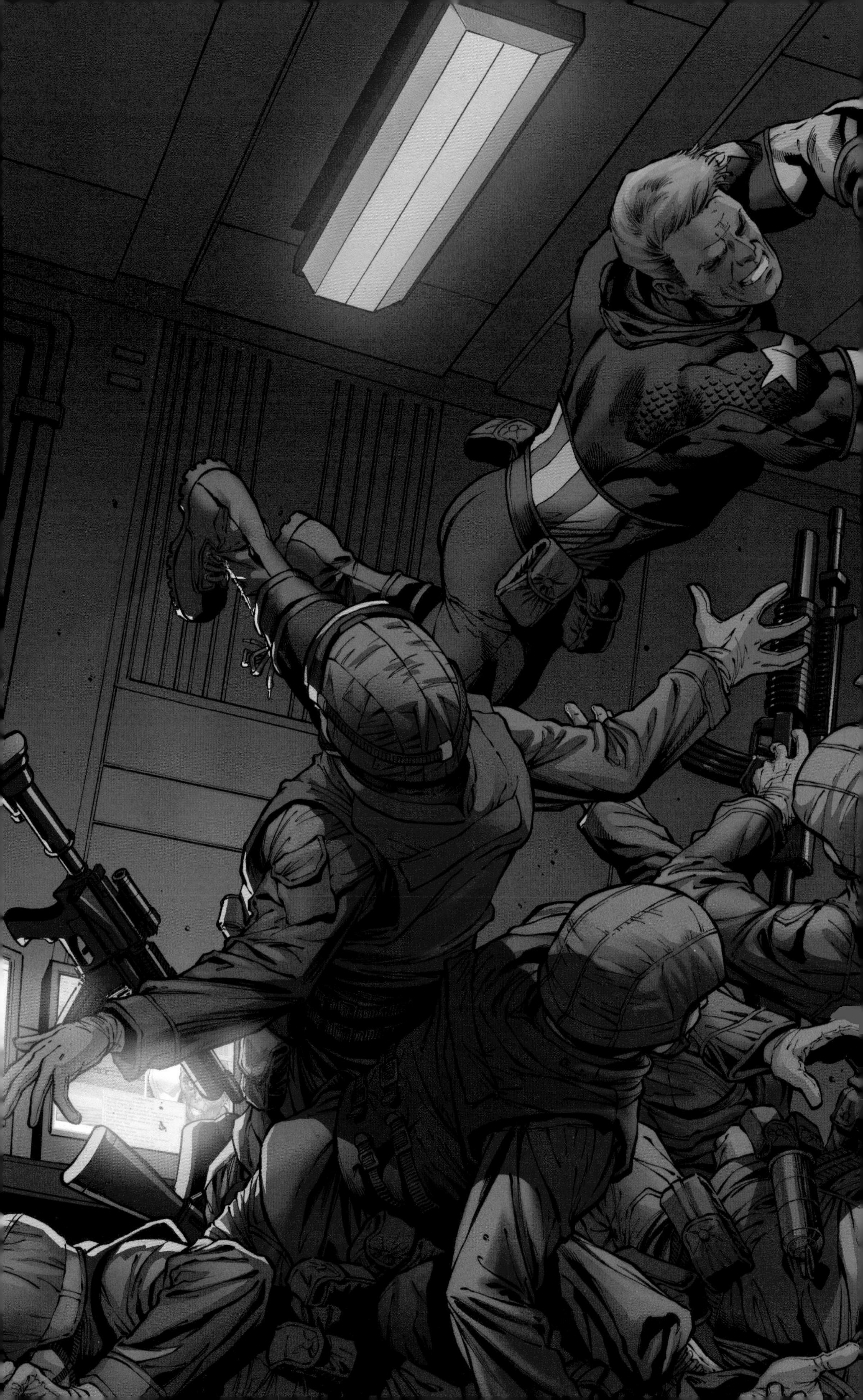

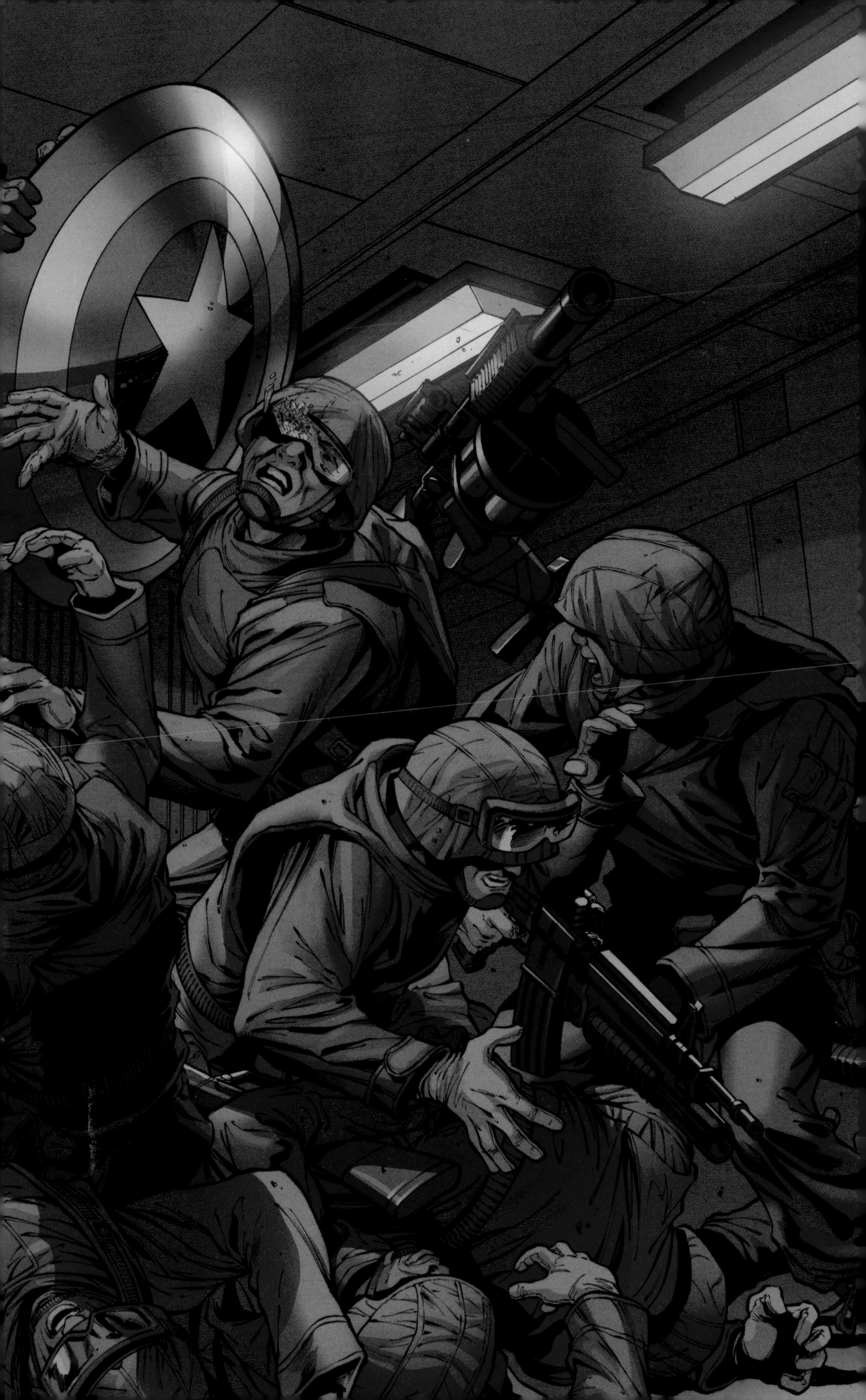

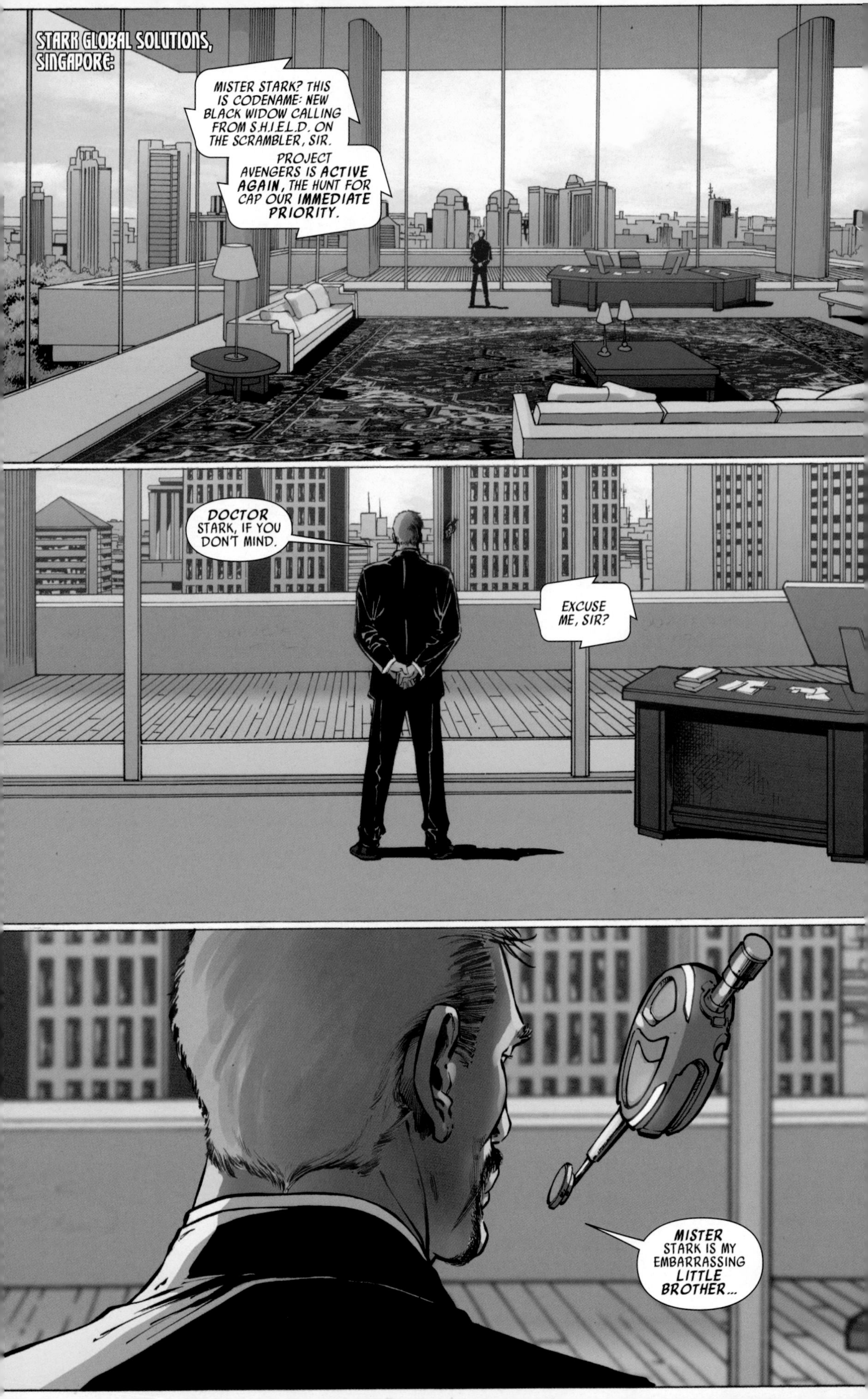
STARK GLOBAL SOLUTIONS, SINGAPORE:
MISTER STARK? THIS IS CODENAME: NEW BLACK WIDOW CALLING FROM S.H.I.E.L.D. ON THE SCRAMBLER, SIR.
PROJECT AVENGERS IS ACTIVE AGAIN, THE HUNT FOR CAP OUR IMMEDIATE PRIORITY.
DOCTOR STARK, IF YOU DON'T MIND.
EXCUSE ME, SIR?
MISTER STARK IS MY EMBARRASSING LITTLE BROTHER...

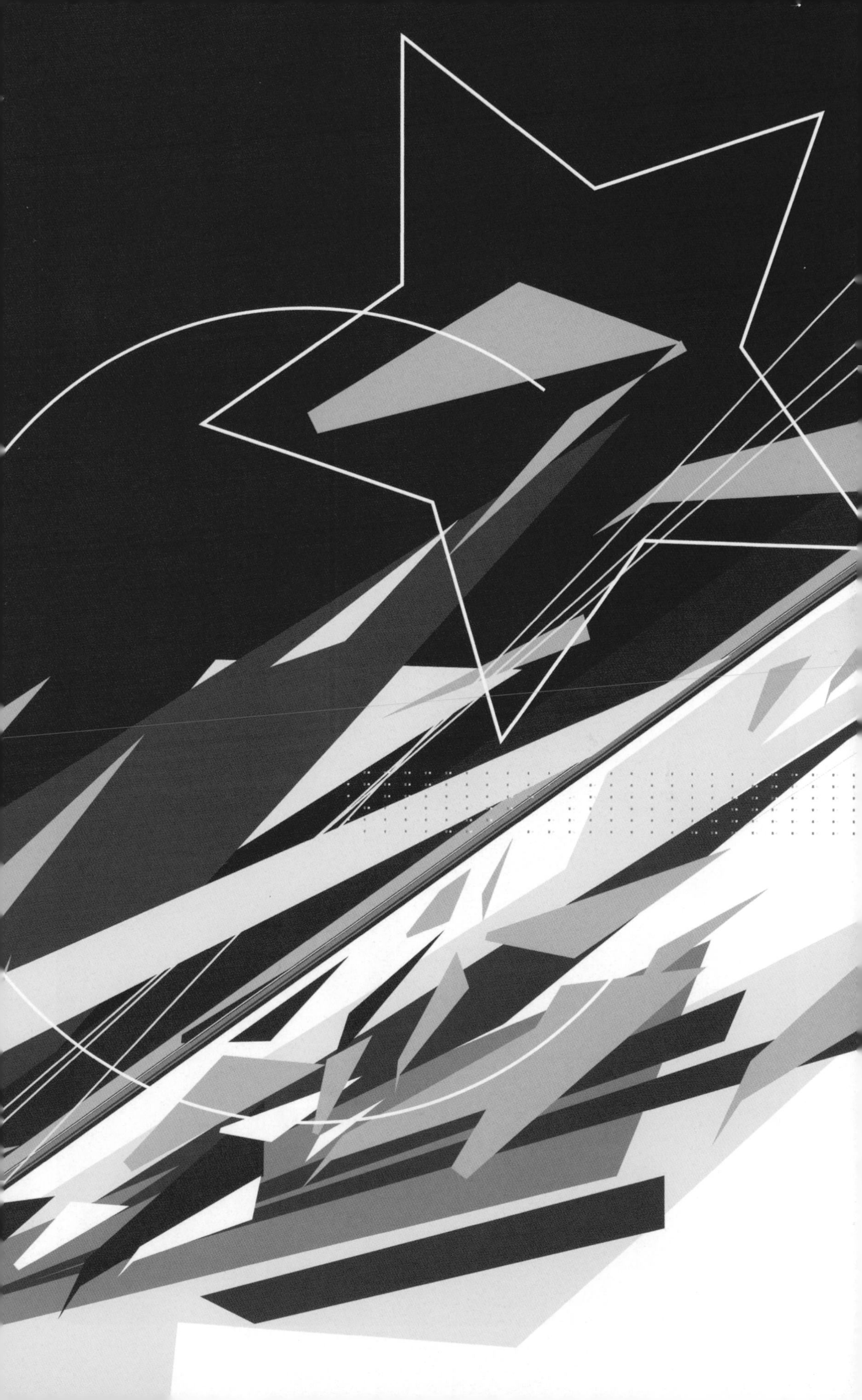

3

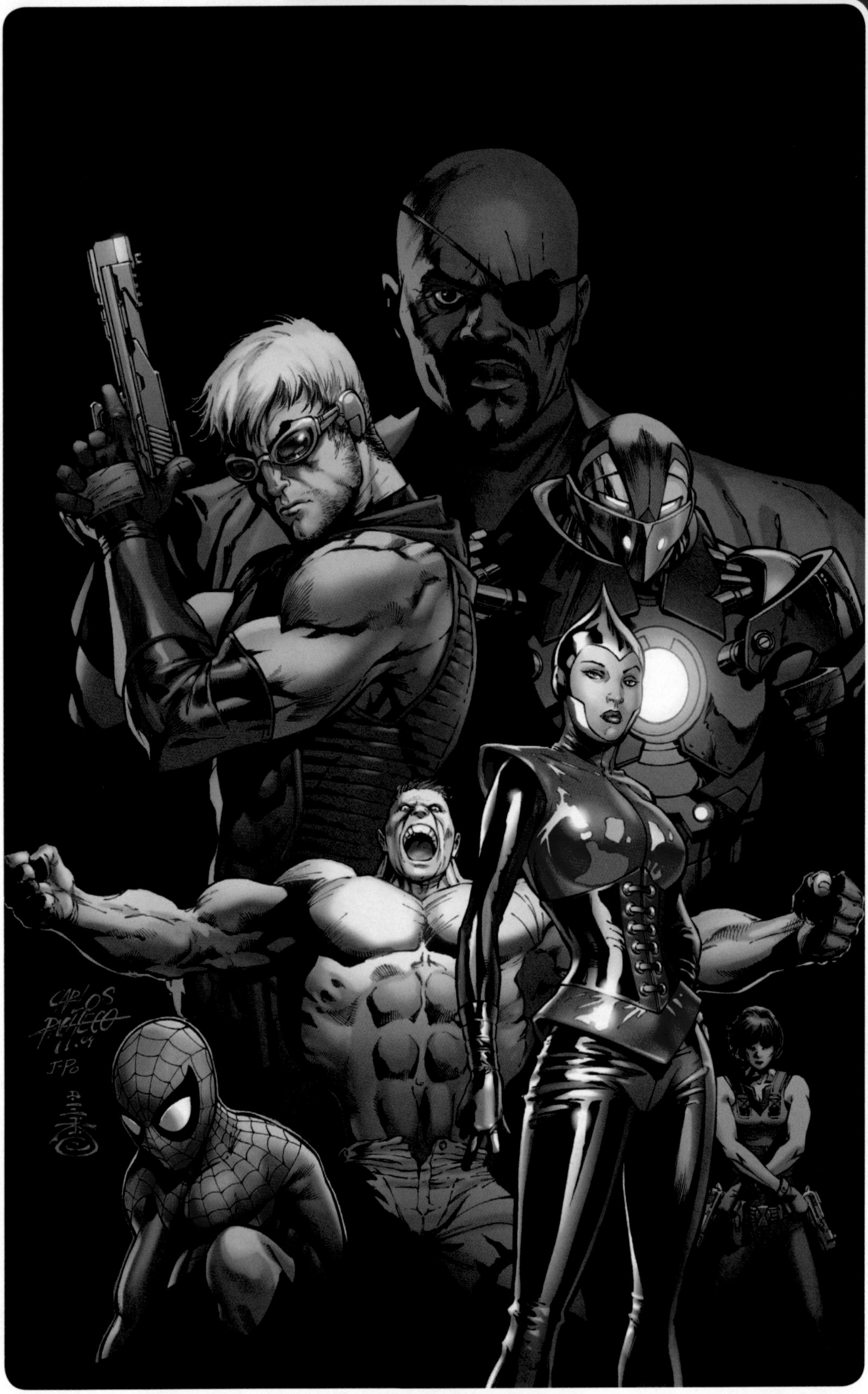

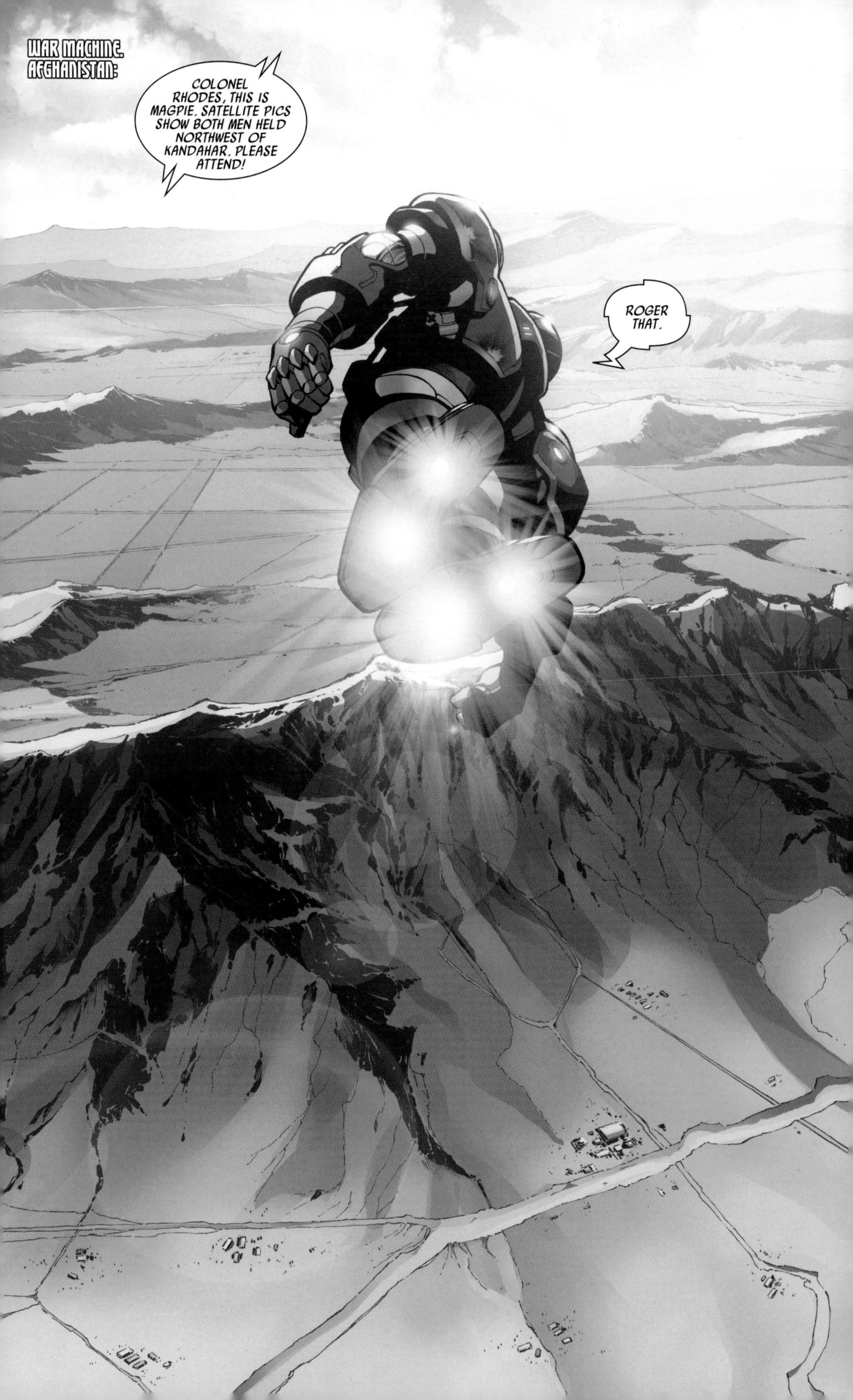
WAR MACHINE. AFGHANISTAN:
COLONEL RHODES, THIS IS MAGPIE. SATELLITE PICS SHOW BOTH MEN HELD NORTHWEST OF KANDAHAR. PLEASE ATTEND!
ROGER THAT.

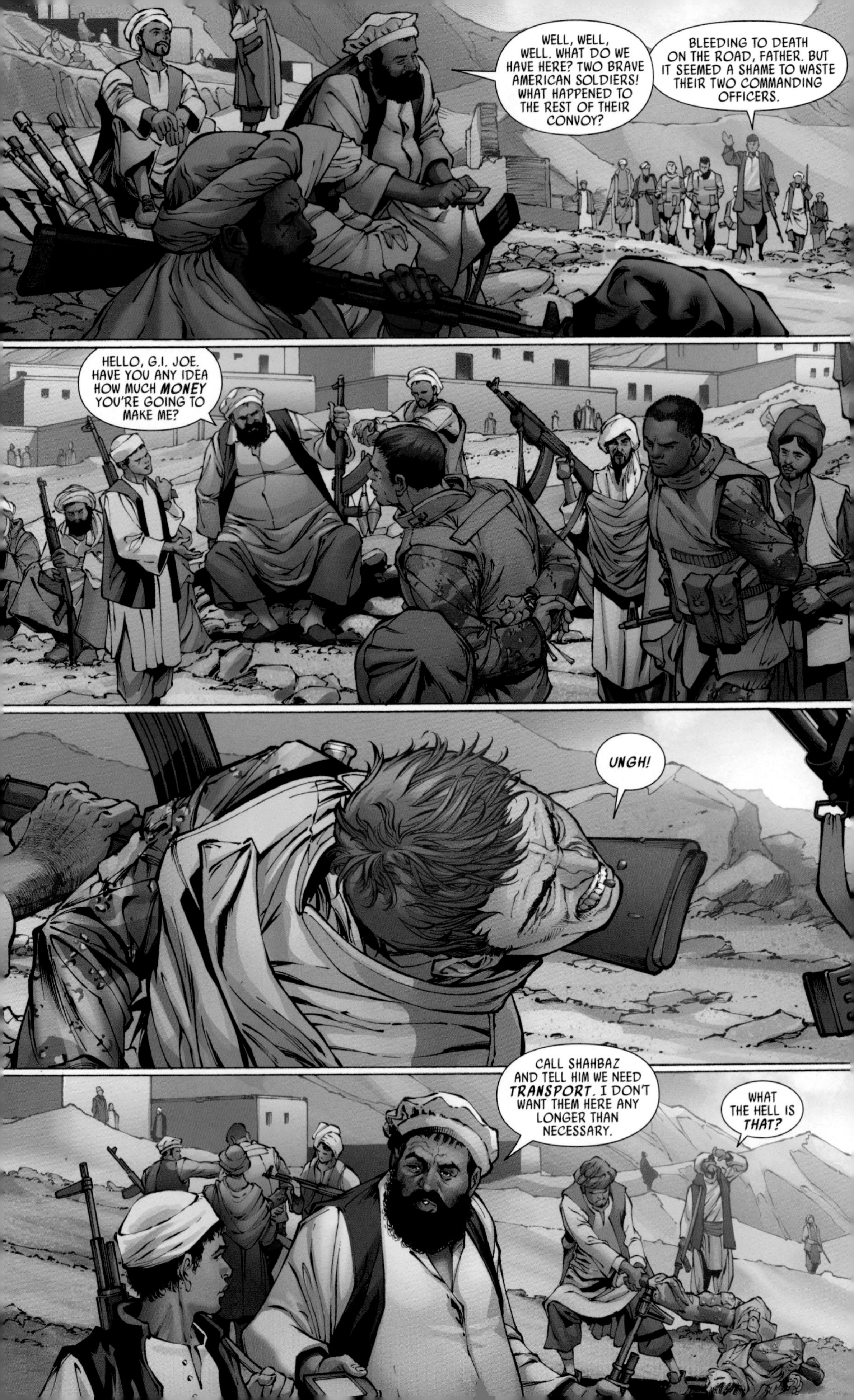
WELL, WELL, WELL. WHAT DO WE HAVE HERE? TWO BRAVE AMERICAN SOLDIERS! WHAT HAPPENED TO THE REST OF THEIR CONVOY?
BLEEDING TO DEATH ON THE ROAD, FATHER. BUT IT SEEMED A SHAME TO WASTE THEIR TWO COMMANDING OFFICERS.
HELLO, G.I. JOE. HAVE YOU ANY IDEA HOW MUCH MONEY YOU'RE GOING TO MAKE ME?
UNGH!
CALL SHAHBAZ AND TELL HIM WE NEED TRANSPORT. I DON'T WANT THEM HERE ANY LONGER THAN NECESSARY.
WHAT THE HELL IS THAT?

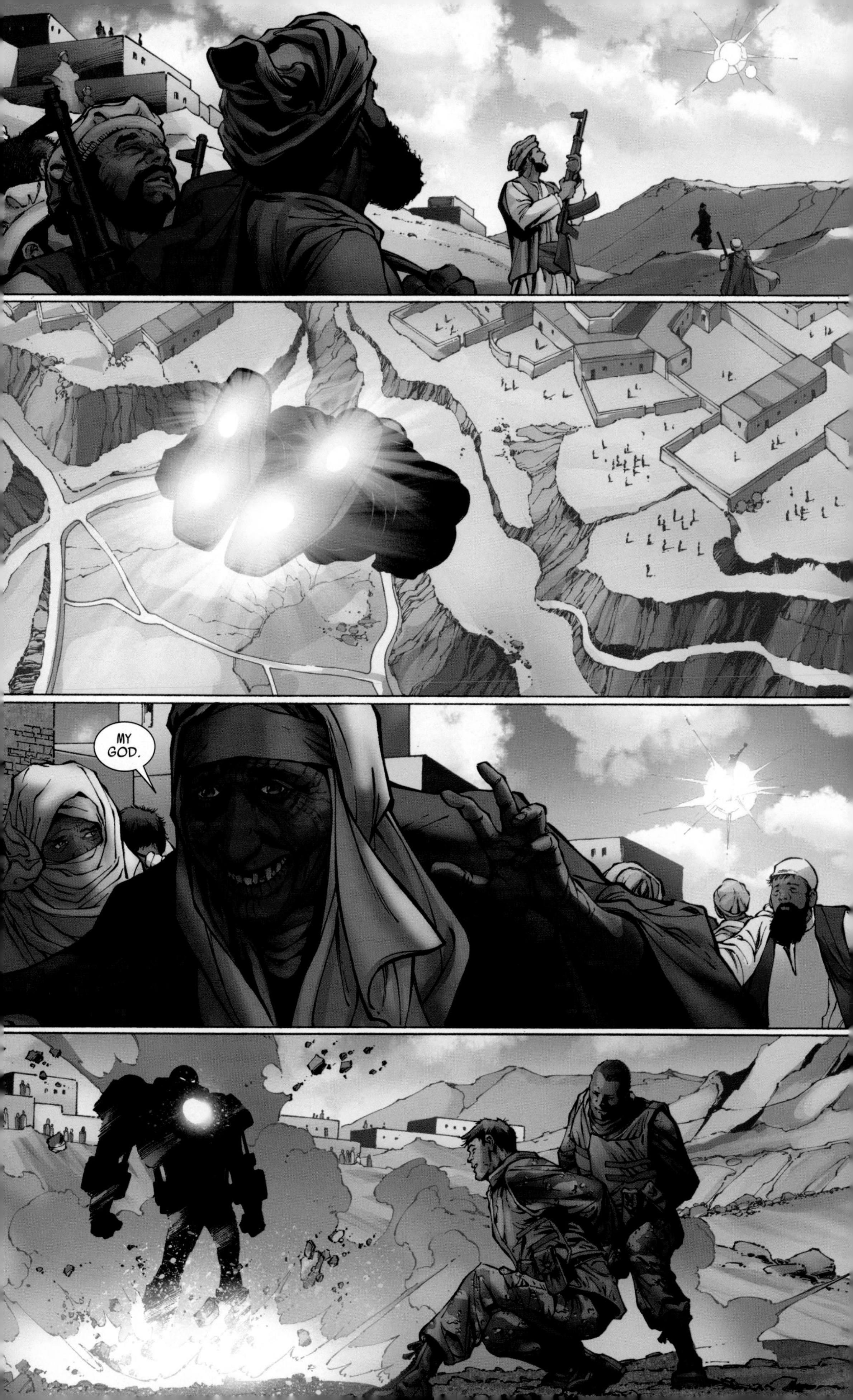
MY GOD.

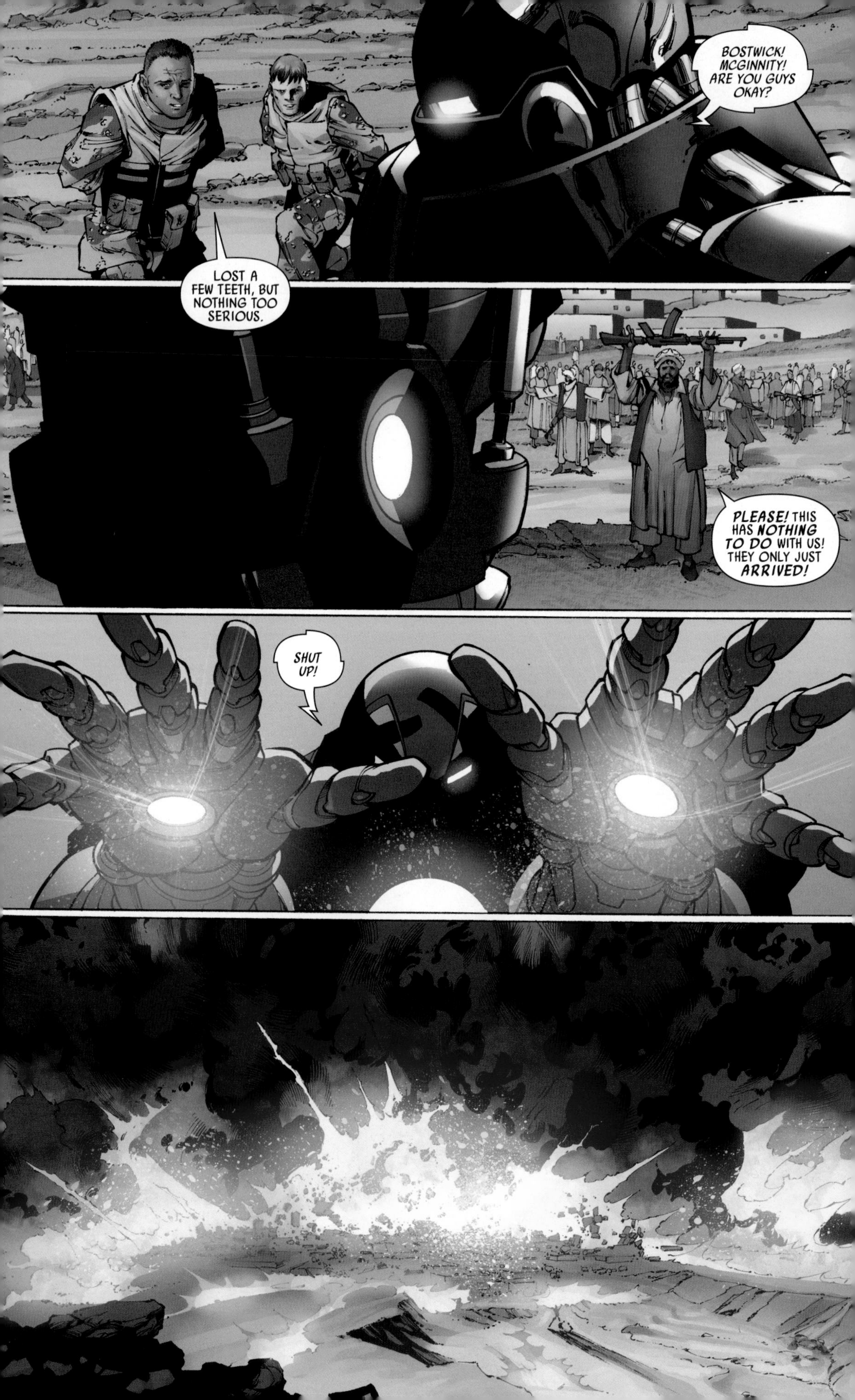
BOSTWICK! MCGINNITY! ARE YOU GUYS OKAY?
LOST A FEW TEETH, BUT NOTHING TOO SERIOUS.
PLEASE! THIS HAS NOTHING TO DO WITH US! THEY ONLY JUST ARRIVED!
SHUT UP!

RHODES! WHAT THE HELL ARE YOU DOING? THESE PEOPLE WERE *UNARMED* CIVILIANS!

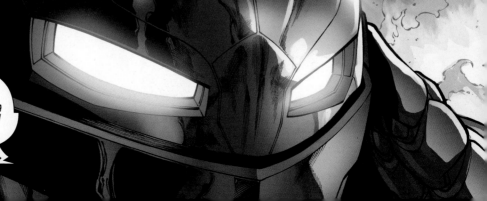

AW, GIMME A *BREAK!* FIVE MINUTES AGO THEY WERE PREPPING YOU FOR *YOUTUBE!*

NOW BUTTON IT, MICHAEL MOORE! I GOT A CALL COMING IN FROM *BASE-COMMAND...*

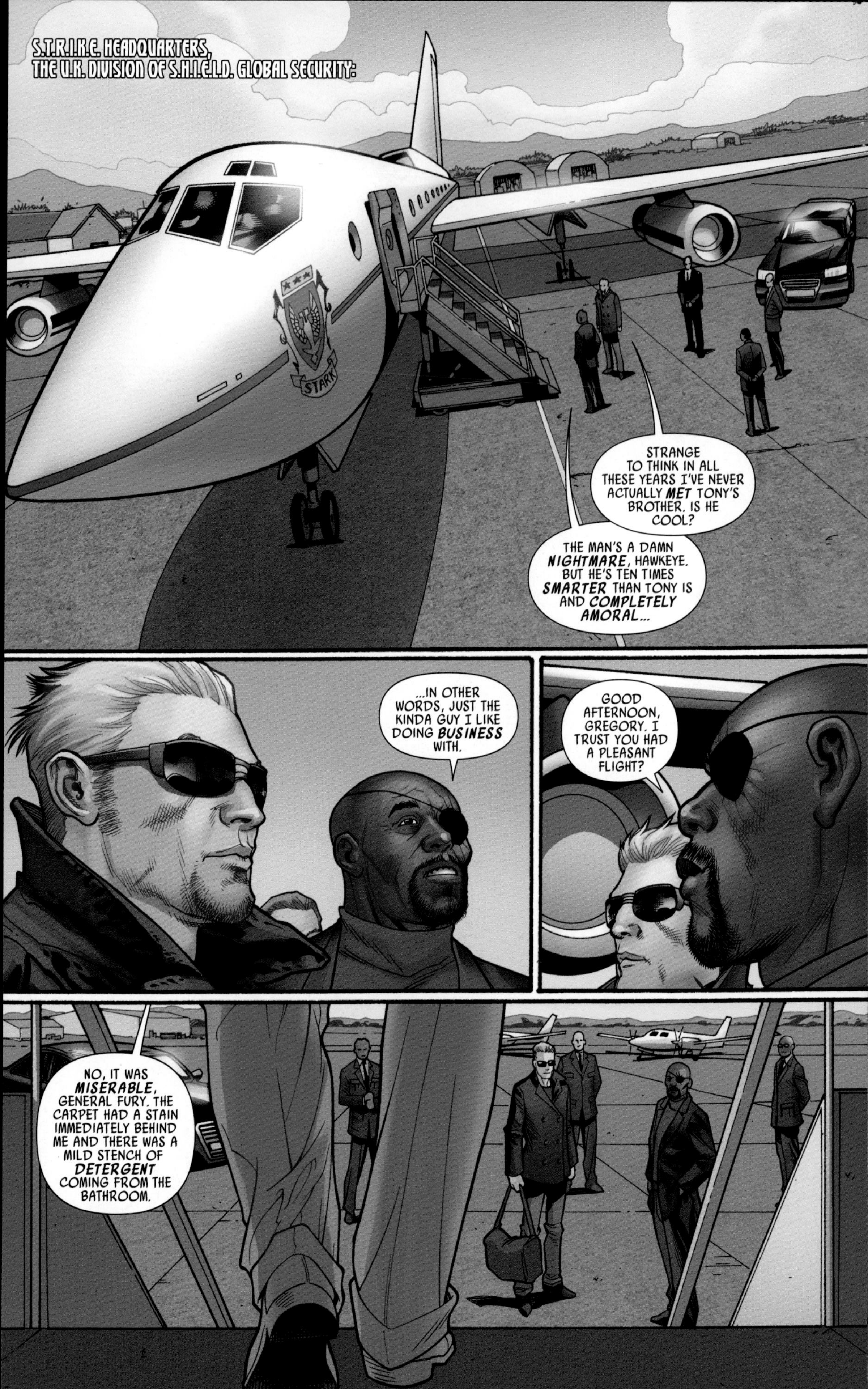
S.T.R.I.K.E. HEADQUARTERS, THE U.K. DIVISION OF S.H.I.E.L.D. GLOBAL SECURITY:
STARK
STRANGE TO THINK IN ALL THESE YEARS I'VE NEVER ACTUALLY MET TONY'S BROTHER. IS HE COOL?
THE MAN'S A DAMN NIGHTMARE, HAWKEYE. BUT HE'S TEN TIMES SMARTER THAN TONY IS AND COMPLETELY AMORAL...
...IN OTHER WORDS, JUST THE KINDA GUY I LIKE DOING BUSINESS WITH.
GOOD AFTERNOON, GREGORY. I TRUST YOU HAD A PLEASANT FLIGHT?
NO, IT WAS MISERABLE, GENERAL FURY. THE CARPET HAD A STAIN IMMEDIATELY BEHIND ME AND THERE WAS A MILD STENCH OF DETERGENT COMING FROM THE BATHROOM.

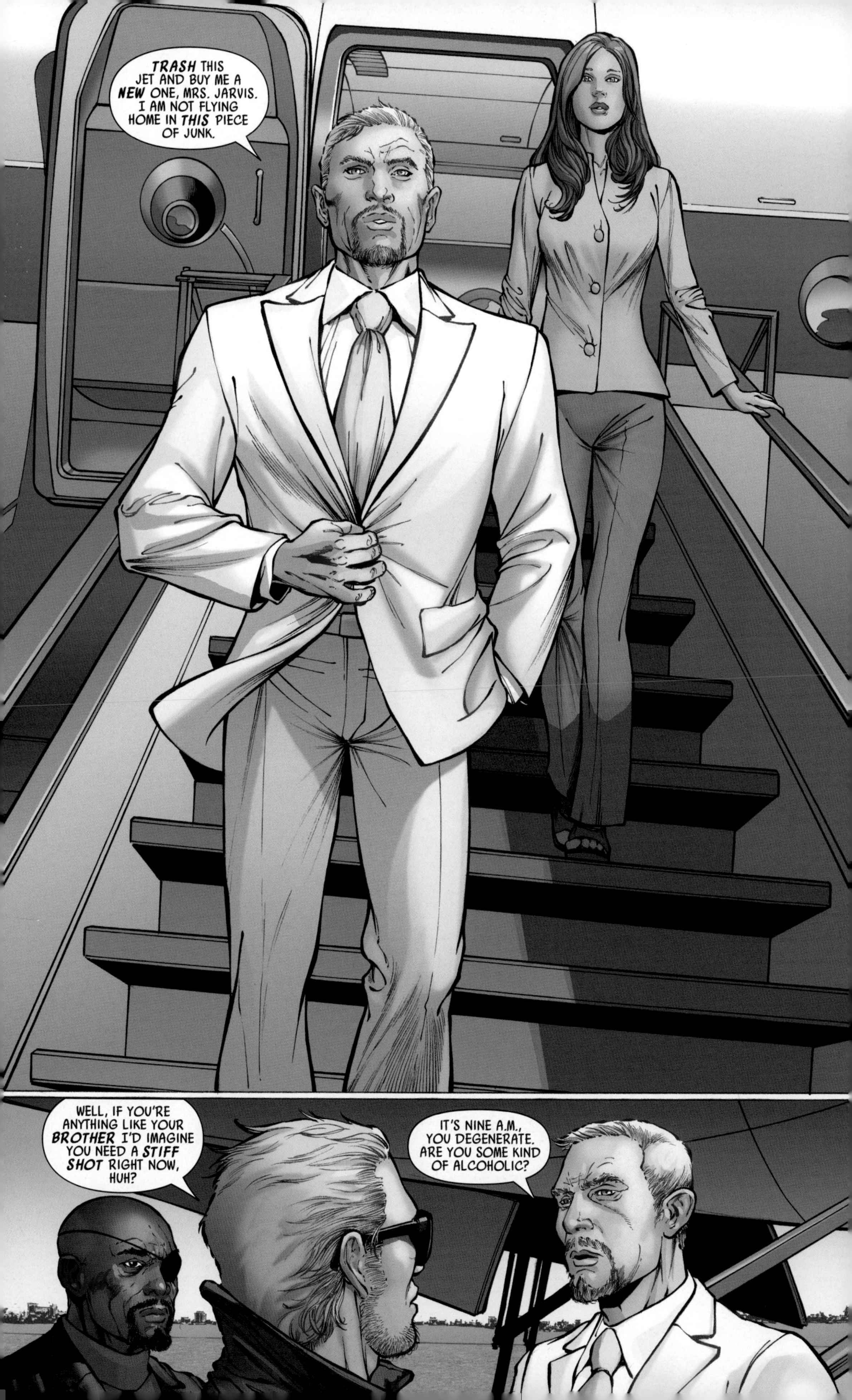
TRASH THIS JET AND BUY ME A NEW ONE, MRS. JARVIS. I AM NOT FLYING HOME IN THIS PIECE OF JUNK.
WELL, IF YOU'RE ANYTHING LIKE YOUR BROTHER I'D IMAGINE YOU NEED A STIFF SHOT RIGHT NOW, HUH?
IT'S NINE A.M., YOU DEGENERATE. ARE YOU SOME KIND OF ALCOHOLIC?

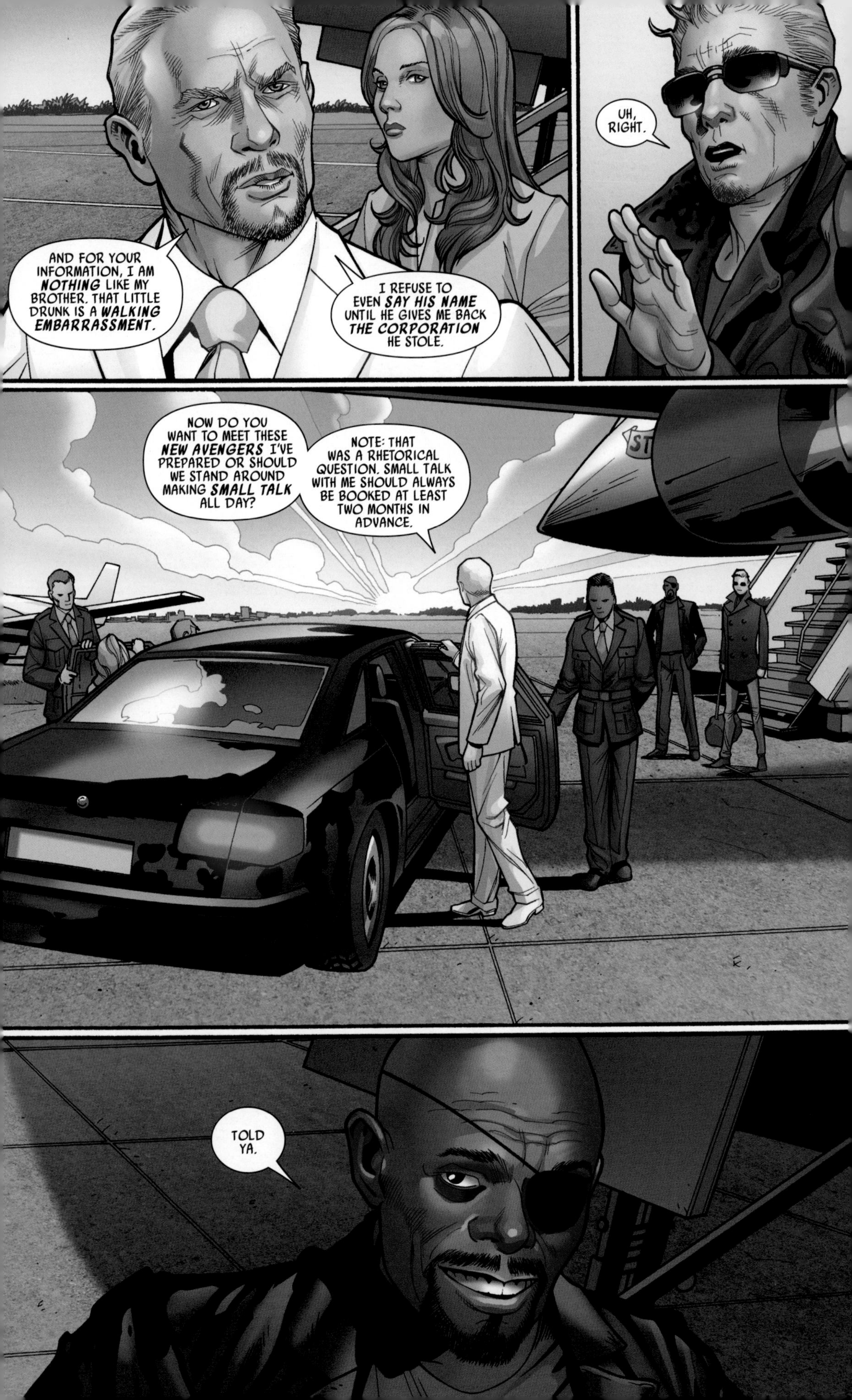
AND FOR YOUR INFORMATION, I AM NOTHING LIKE MY BROTHER. THAT LITTLE DRUNK IS A WALKING EMBARRASSMENT.
I REFUSE TO EVEN SAY HIS NAME UNTIL HE GIVES ME BACK THE CORPORATION HE STOLE.
UH, RIGHT.
NOW DO YOU WANT TO MEET THESE NEW AVENGERS I'VE PREPARED OR SHOULD WE STAND AROUND MAKING SMALL TALK ALL DAY?
NOTE: THAT WAS A RHETORICAL QUESTION. SMALL TALK WITH ME SHOULD ALWAYS BE BOOKED AT LEAST TWO MONTHS IN ADVANCE.
TOLD YA.

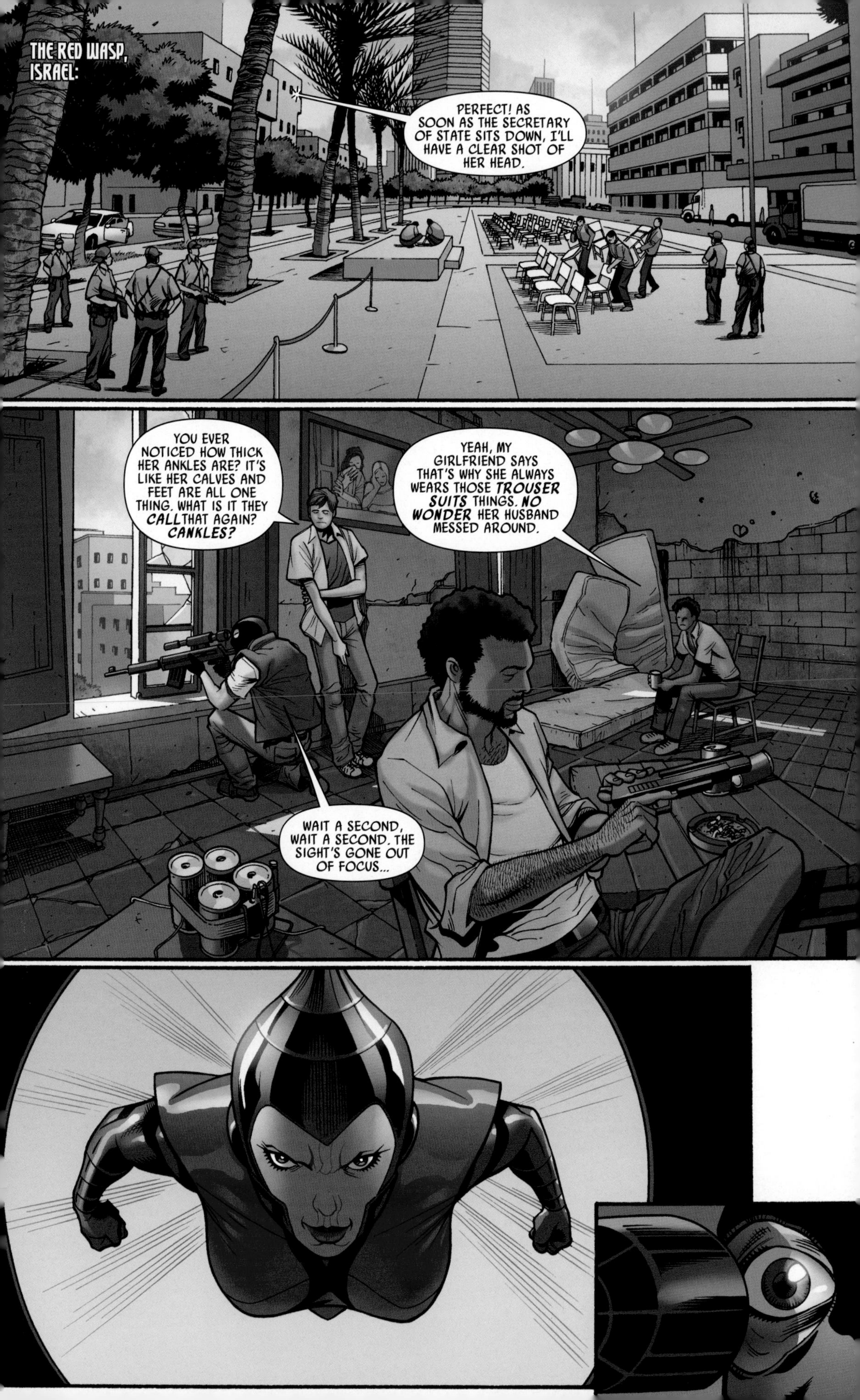
THE RED WASP, ISRAEL:
PERFECT! AS SOON AS THE SECRETARY OF STATE SITS DOWN, I'LL HAVE A CLEAR SHOT OF HER HEAD.
YOU EVER NOTICED HOW THICK HER ANKLES ARE? IT'S LIKE HER CALVES AND FEET ARE ALL ONE THING. WHAT IS IT THEY CALL THAT AGAIN? CANKLES?
YEAH, MY GIRLFRIEND SAYS THAT'S WHY SHE ALWAYS WEARS THOSE TROUSER SUITS THINGS. NO WONDER HER HUSBAND MESSED AROUND.
WAIT A SECOND, WAIT A SECOND. THE SIGHT'S GONE OUT OF FOCUS...

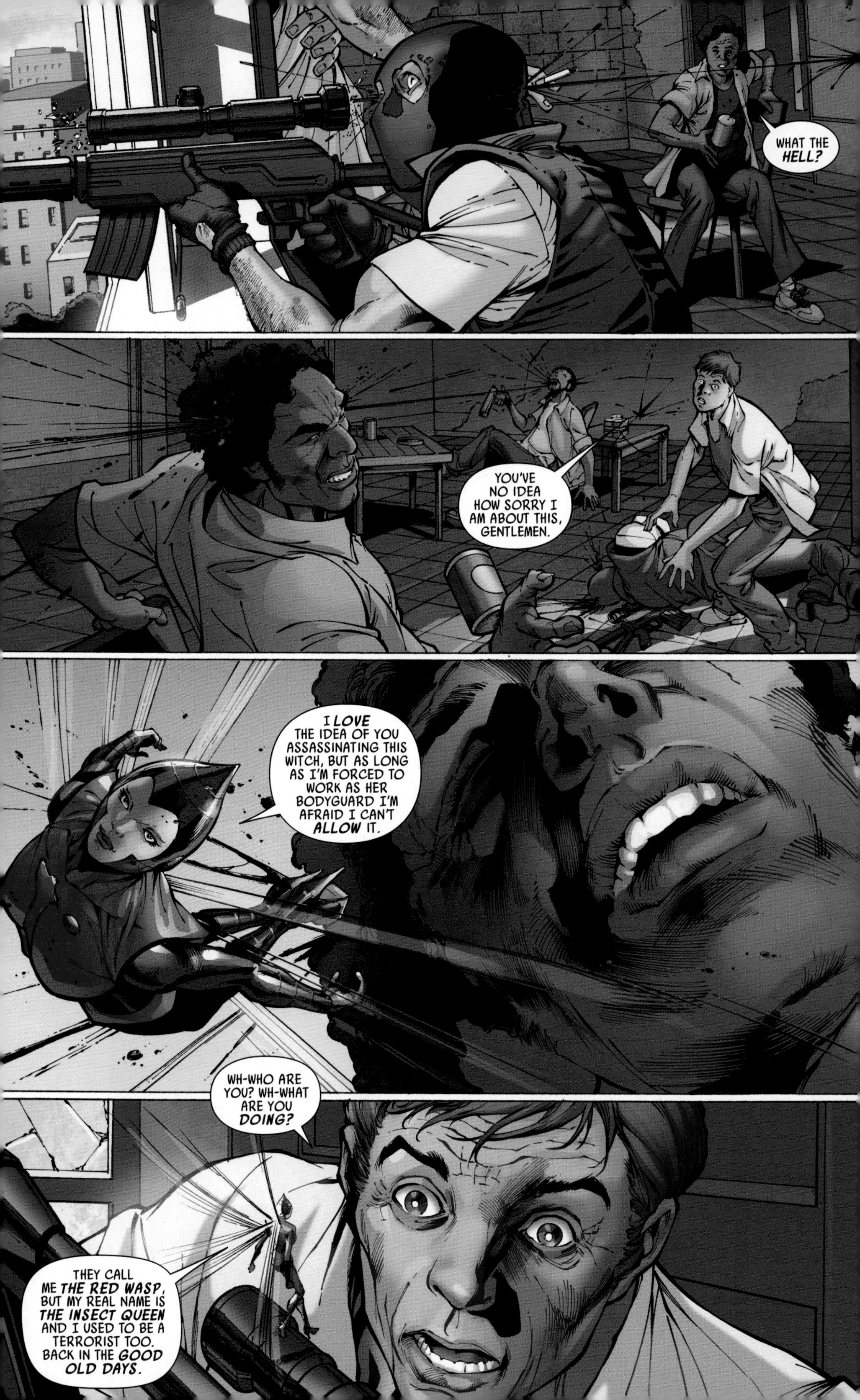
WHAT THE HELL?
YOU'VE NO IDEA HOW SORRY I AM ABOUT THIS, GENTLEMEN.
I LOVE THE IDEA OF YOU ASSASSINATING THIS WITCH, BUT AS LONG AS I'M FORCED TO WORK AS HER BODYGUARD I'M AFRAID I CAN'T ALLOW IT.
WH-WHO ARE YOU? WH-WHAT ARE YOU DOING?
THEY CALL ME THE RED WASP, BUT MY REAL NAME IS THE INSECT QUEEN AND I USED TO BE A TERRORIST TOO. BACK IN THE GOOD OLD DAYS.

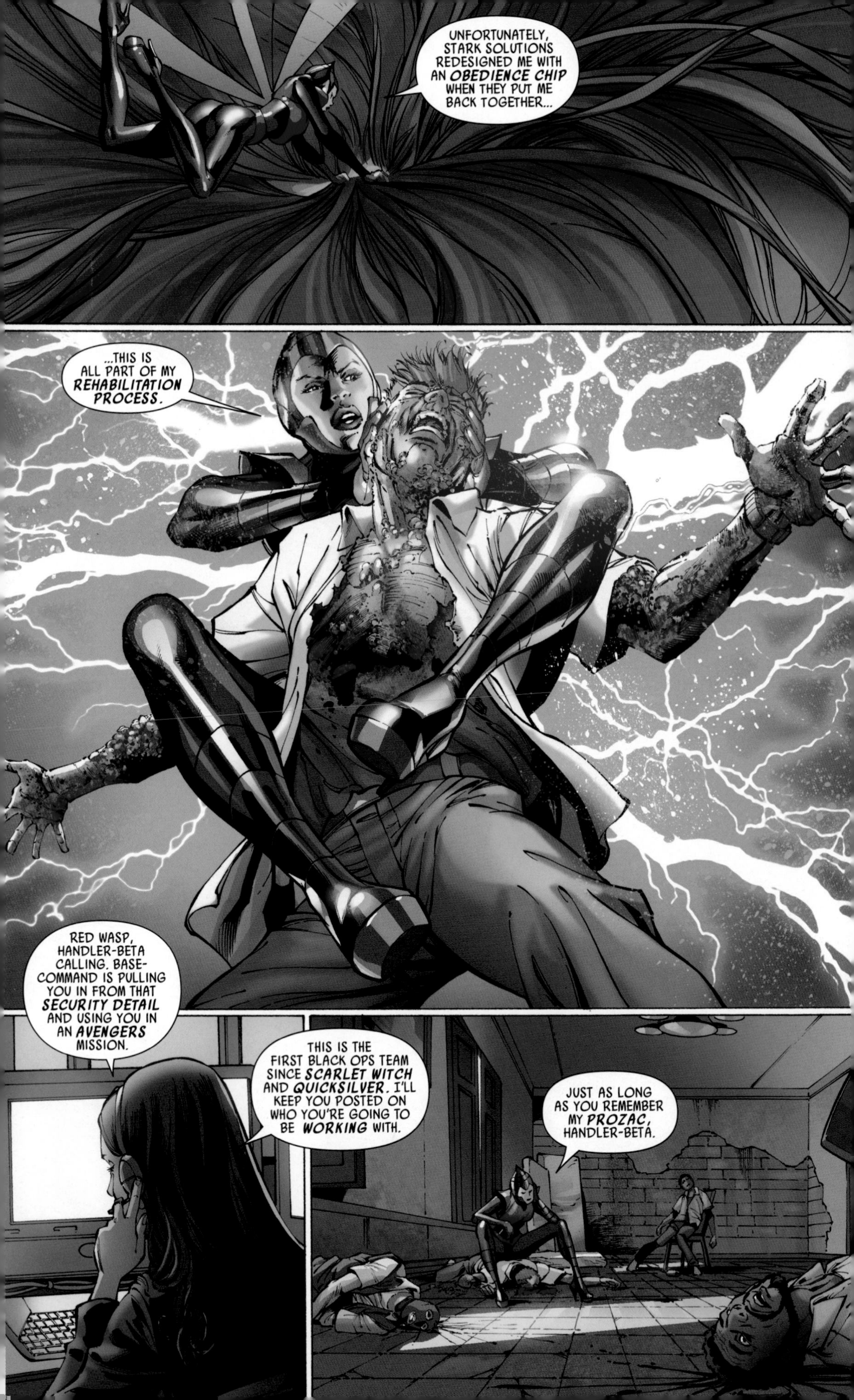
UNFORTUNATELY, STARK SOLUTIONS REDESIGNED ME WITH AN OBEDIENCE CHIP WHEN THEY PUT ME BACK TOGETHER...
...THIS IS ALL PART OF MY REHABILITATION PROCESS.
RED WASP, HANDLER-BETA CALLING. BASE-COMMAND IS PULLING YOU IN FROM THAT SECURITY DETAIL AND USING YOU IN AN AVENGERS MISSION.
THIS IS THE FIRST BLACK OPS TEAM SINCE SCARLET WITCH AND QUICKSILVER. I'LL KEEP YOU POSTED ON WHO YOU'RE GOING TO BE WORKING WITH.
JUST AS LONG AS YOU REMEMBER MY PROZAC, HANDLER-BETA.

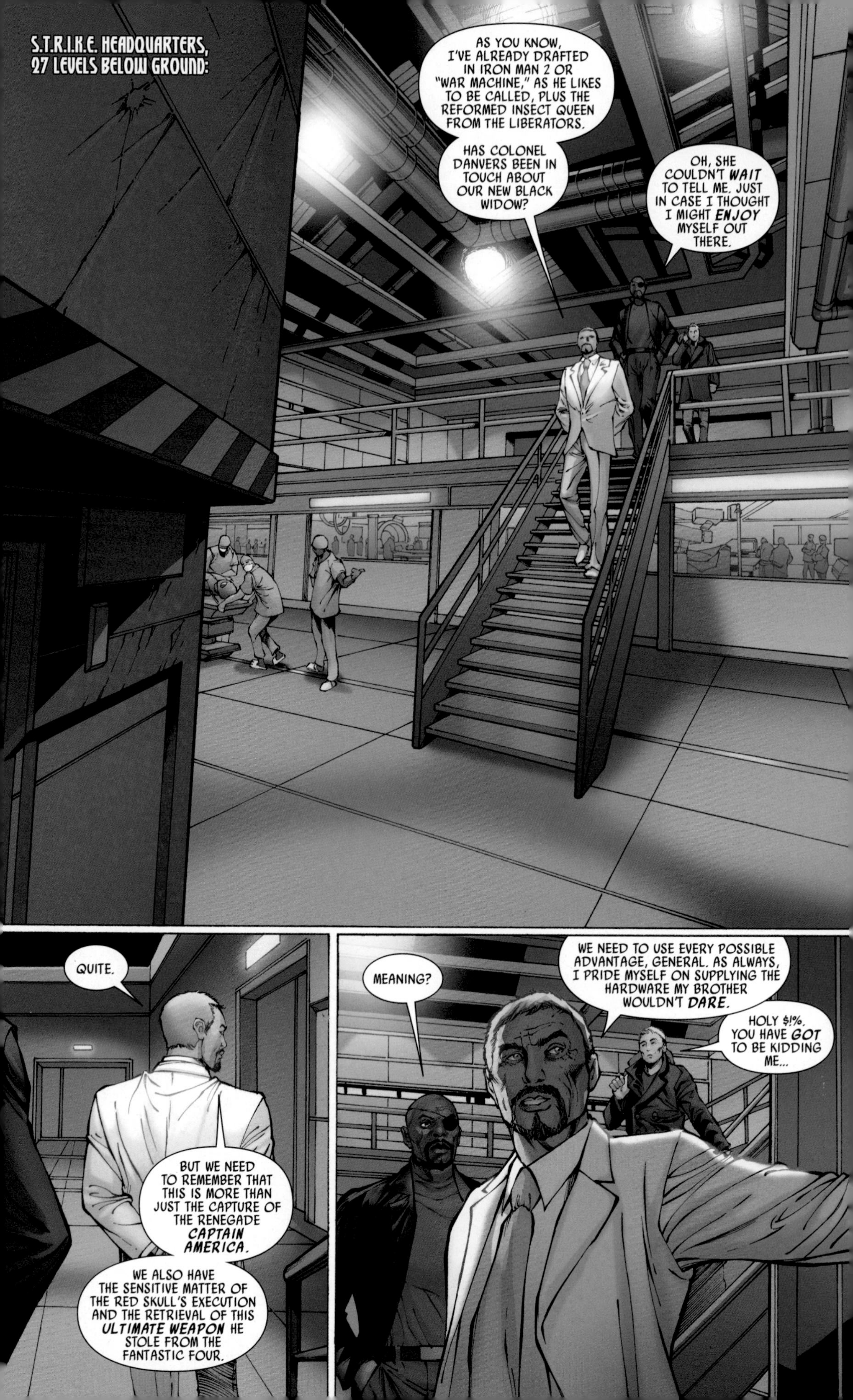
S.T.R.I.K.E. HEADQUARTERS, 27 LEVELS BELOW GROUND:
AS YOU KNOW, I'VE ALREADY DRAFTED IN IRON MAN 2 OR "WAR MACHINE," AS HE LIKES TO BE CALLED, PLUS THE REFORMED INSECT QUEEN FROM THE LIBERATORS.
HAS COLONEL DANVERS BEEN IN TOUCH ABOUT OUR NEW BLACK WIDOW?
OH, SHE COULDN'T WAIT TO TELL ME. JUST IN CASE I THOUGHT I MIGHT ENJOY MYSELF OUT THERE.
QUITE.
BUT WE NEED TO REMEMBER THAT THIS IS MORE THAN JUST THE CAPTURE OF THE RENEGADE CAPTAIN AMERICA.
WE ALSO HAVE THE SENSITIVE MATTER OF THE RED SKULL'S EXECUTION AND THE RETRIEVAL OF THIS ULTIMATE WEAPON HE STOLE FROM THE FANTASTIC FOUR.
MEANING?
WE NEED TO USE EVERY POSSIBLE ADVANTAGE, GENERAL. AS ALWAYS, I PRIDE MYSELF ON SUPPLYING THE HARDWARE MY BROTHER WOULDN'T DARE.
HOLY $!%. YOU HAVE GOT TO BE KIDDING ME...

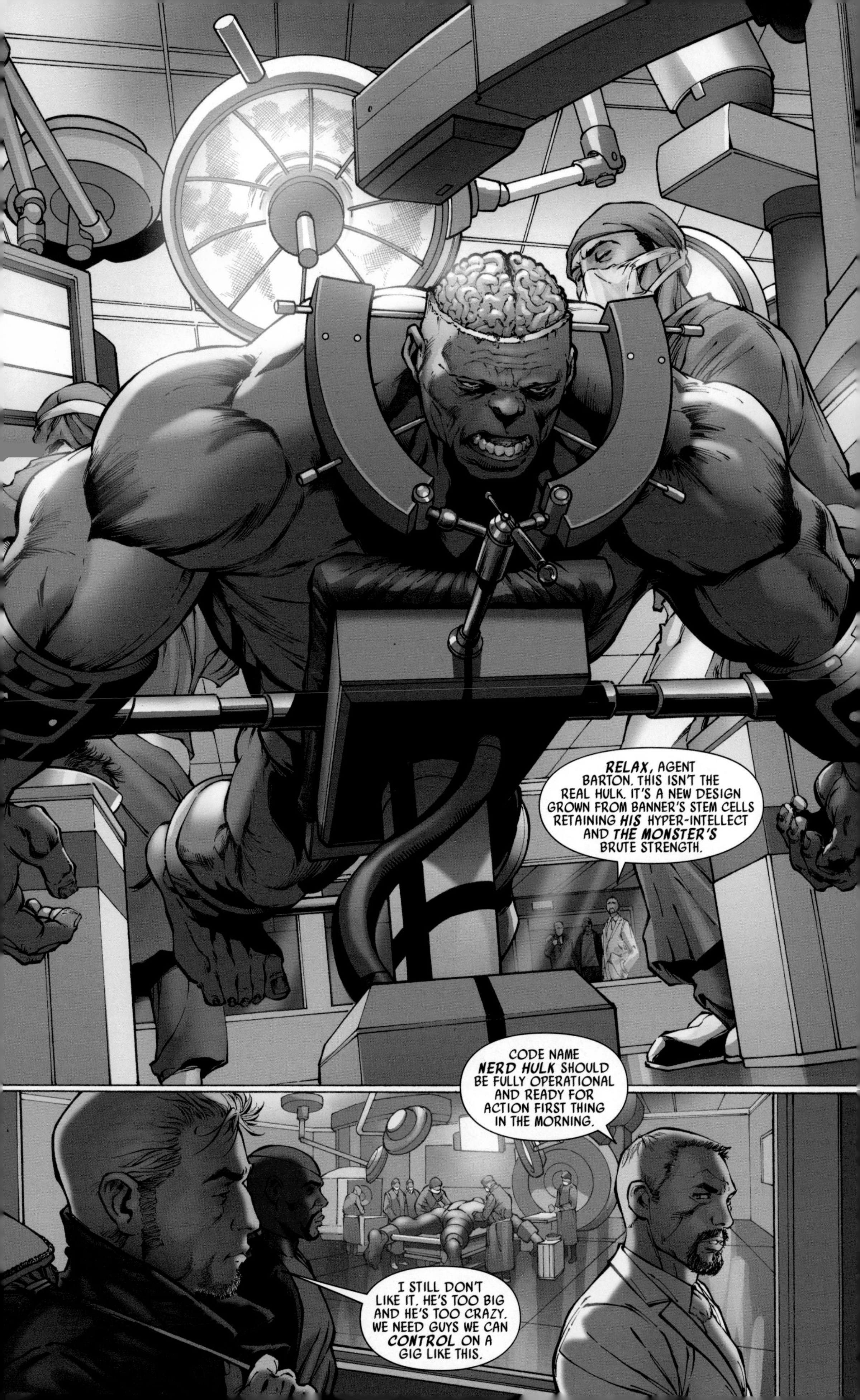
RELAX, AGENT BARTON. THIS ISN'T THE REAL HULK. IT'S A NEW DESIGN GROWN FROM BANNER'S STEM CELLS RETAINING HIS HYPER-INTELLECT AND THE MONSTER'S BRUTE STRENGTH.
CODE NAME NERD HULK SHOULD BE FULLY OPERATIONAL AND READY FOR ACTION FIRST THING IN THE MORNING.
I STILL DON'T LIKE IT. HE'S TOO BIG AND HE'S TOO CRAZY. WE NEED GUYS WE CAN CONTROL ON A GIG LIKE THIS.

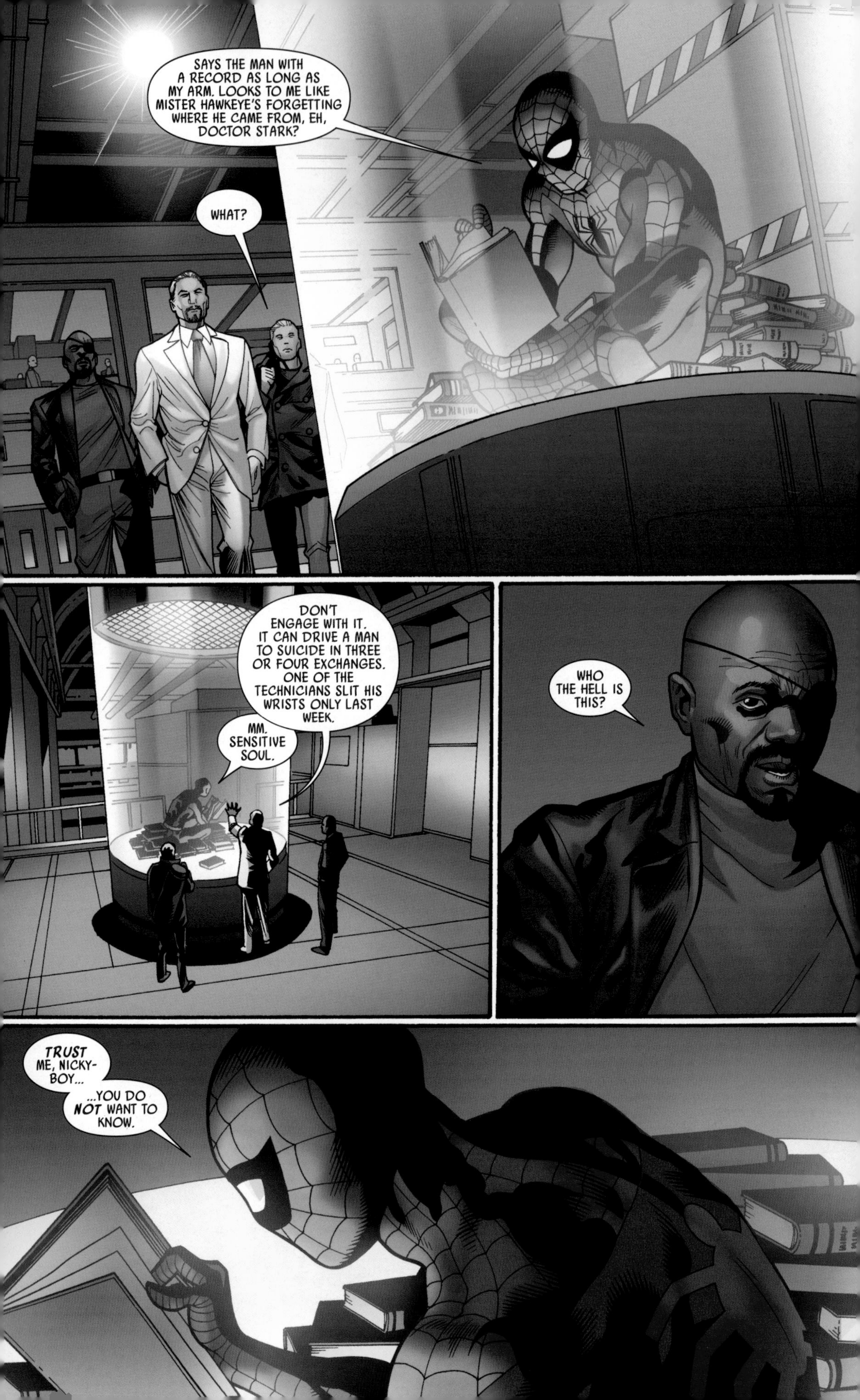

SAYS THE MAN WITH A RECORD AS LONG AS MY ARM. LOOKS TO ME LIKE MISTER HAWKEYE'S FORGETTING WHERE HE CAME FROM, EH, DOCTOR STARK?
WHAT?
DON'T ENGAGE WITH IT. IT CAN DRIVE A MAN TO SUICIDE IN THREE OR FOUR EXCHANGES. ONE OF THE TECHNICIANS SLIT HIS WRISTS ONLY LAST WEEK.
MM. SENSITIVE SOUL.
WHO THE HELL IS THIS?
TRUST ME, NICKY-BOY...
...YOU DO **NOT** WANT TO KNOW.

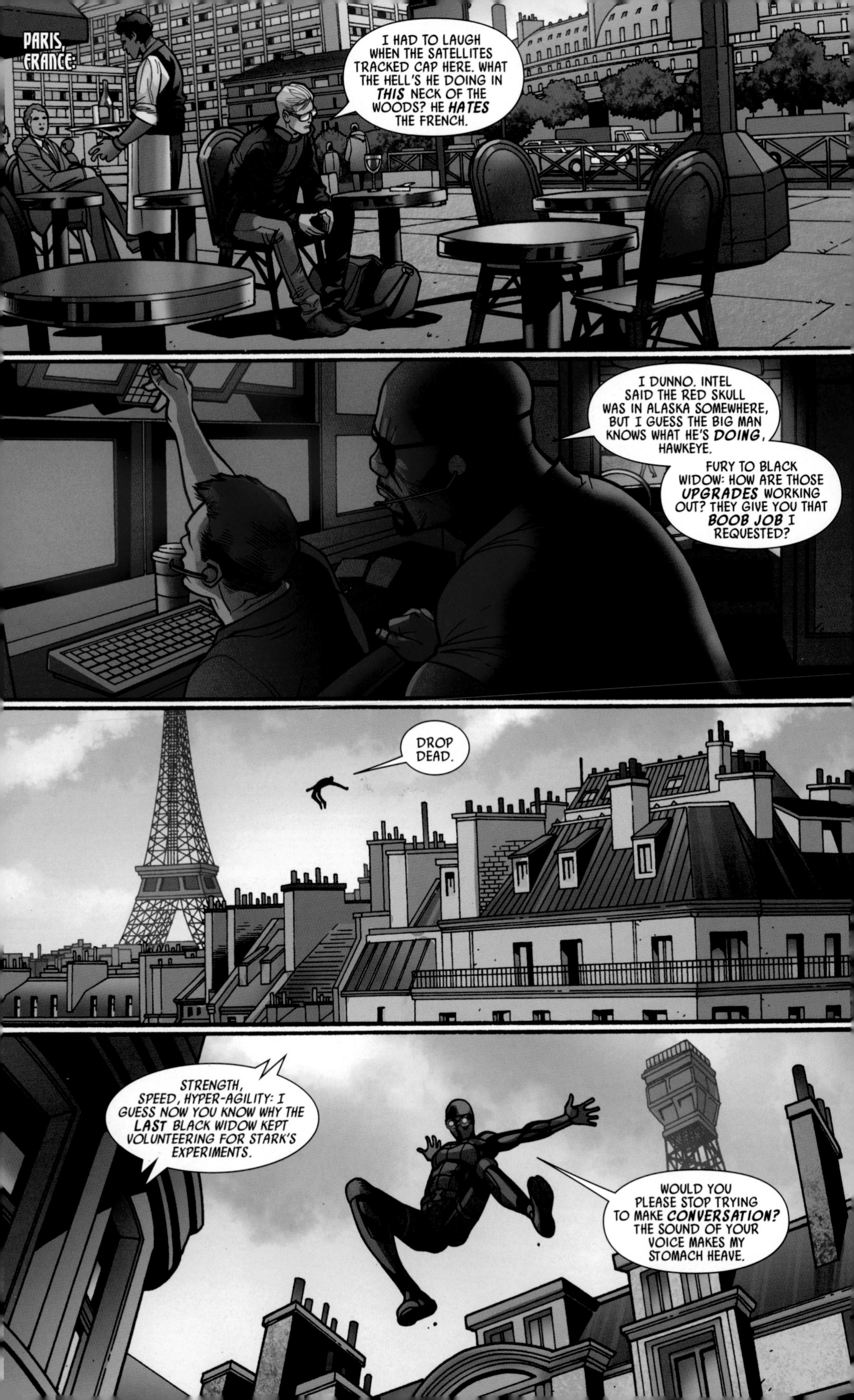
PARIS, FRANCE:
I HAD TO LAUGH WHEN THE SATELLITES TRACKED CAP HERE. WHAT THE HELL'S HE DOING IN THIS NECK OF THE WOODS? HE HATES THE FRENCH.
I DUNNO. INTEL SAID THE RED SKULL WAS IN ALASKA SOMEWHERE, BUT I GUESS THE BIG MAN KNOWS WHAT HE'S DOING, HAWKEYE.
FURY TO BLACK WIDOW: HOW ARE THOSE UPGRADES WORKING OUT? THEY GIVE YOU THAT BOOB JOB I REQUESTED?
DROP DEAD.
STRENGTH, SPEED, HYPER-AGILITY: I GUESS NOW YOU KNOW WHY THE LAST BLACK WIDOW KEPT VOLUNTEERING FOR STARK'S EXPERIMENTS.
WOULD YOU PLEASE STOP TRYING TO MAKE CONVERSATION? THE SOUND OF YOUR VOICE MAKES MY STOMACH HEAVE.

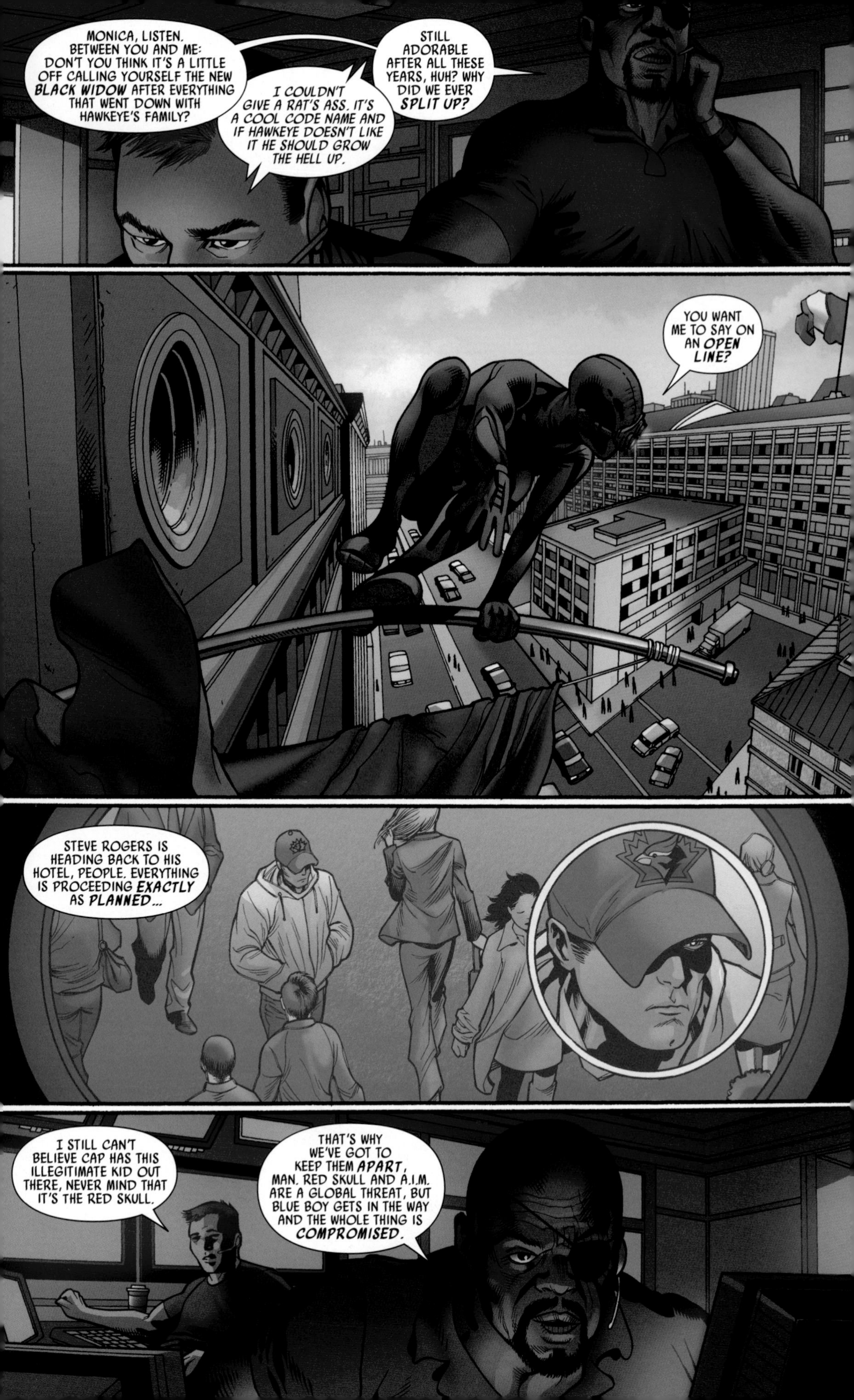
MONICA, LISTEN. BETWEEN YOU AND ME: DON'T YOU THINK IT'S A LITTLE OFF CALLING YOURSELF THE NEW BLACK WIDOW AFTER EVERYTHING THAT WENT DOWN WITH HAWKEYE'S FAMILY?
I COULDN'T GIVE A RAT'S ASS. IT'S A COOL CODE NAME AND IF HAWKEYE DOESN'T LIKE IT HE SHOULD GROW THE HELL UP.
STILL ADORABLE AFTER ALL THESE YEARS, HUH? WHY DID WE EVER SPLIT UP?
YOU WANT ME TO SAY ON AN OPEN LINE?
STEVE ROGERS IS HEADING BACK TO HIS HOTEL, PEOPLE. EVERYTHING IS PROCEEDING EXACTLY AS PLANNED...
I STILL CAN'T BELIEVE CAP HAS THIS ILLEGITIMATE KID OUT THERE, NEVER MIND THAT IT'S THE RED SKULL.
THAT'S WHY WE'VE GOT TO KEEP THEM APART, MAN. RED SKULL AND A.I.M. ARE A GLOBAL THREAT, BUT BLUE BOY GETS IN THE WAY AND THE WHOLE THING IS COMPROMISED.

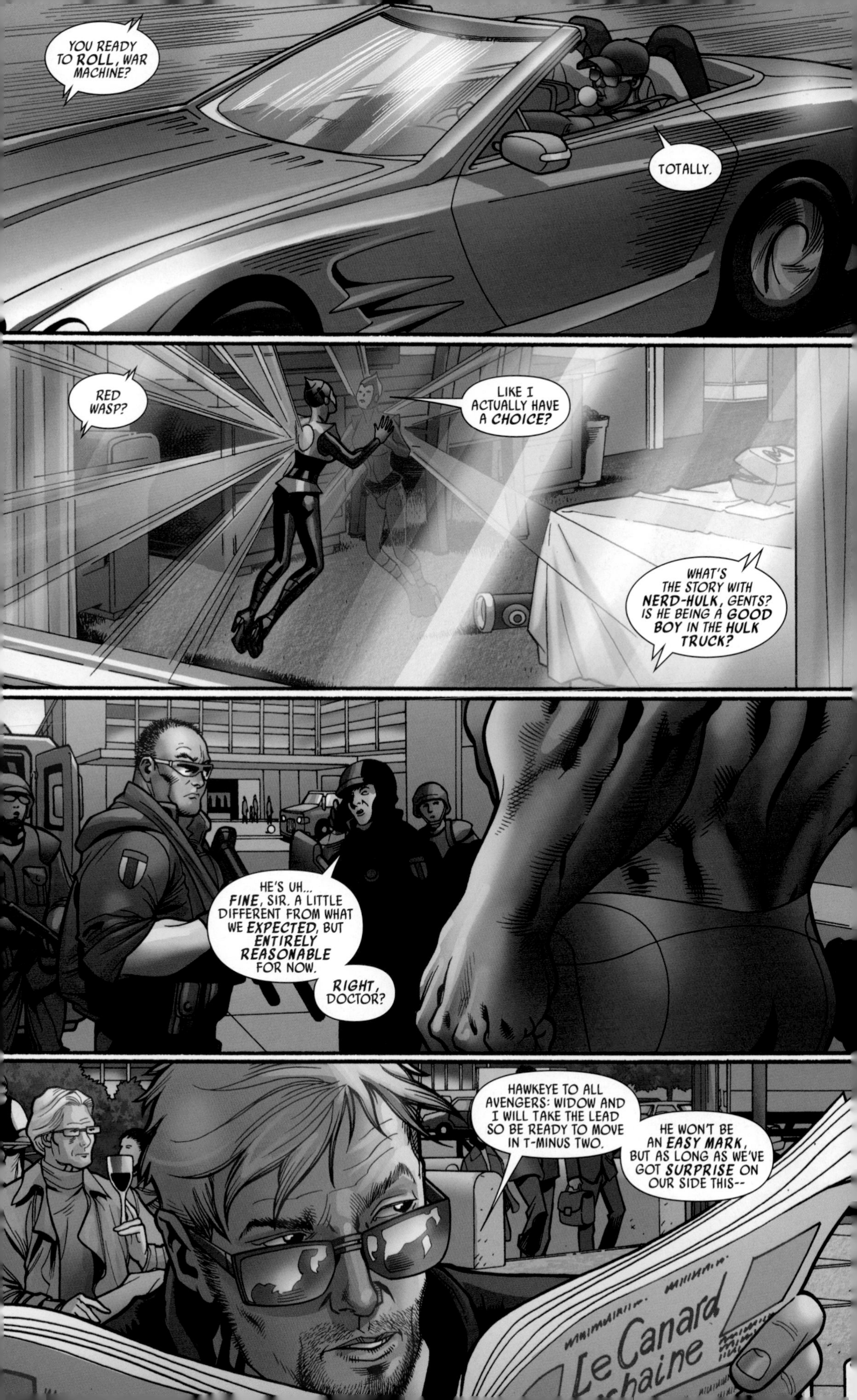
YOU READY TO ROLL, WAR MACHINE?
TOTALLY.
RED WASP?
LIKE I ACTUALLY HAVE A CHOICE?
WHAT'S THE STORY WITH NERD-HULK, GENTS? IS HE BEING A GOOD BOY IN THE HULK TRUCK?
HE'S UH... FINE, SIR. A LITTLE DIFFERENT FROM WHAT WE EXPECTED, BUT ENTIRELY REASONABLE FOR NOW.
RIGHT, DOCTOR?
HAWKEYE TO ALL AVENGERS: WIDOW AND I WILL TAKE THE LEAD SO BE READY TO MOVE IN T-MINUS TWO.
HE WON'T BE AN EASY MARK, BUT AS LONG AS WE'VE GOT SURPRISE ON OUR SIDE THIS--
Le Canard

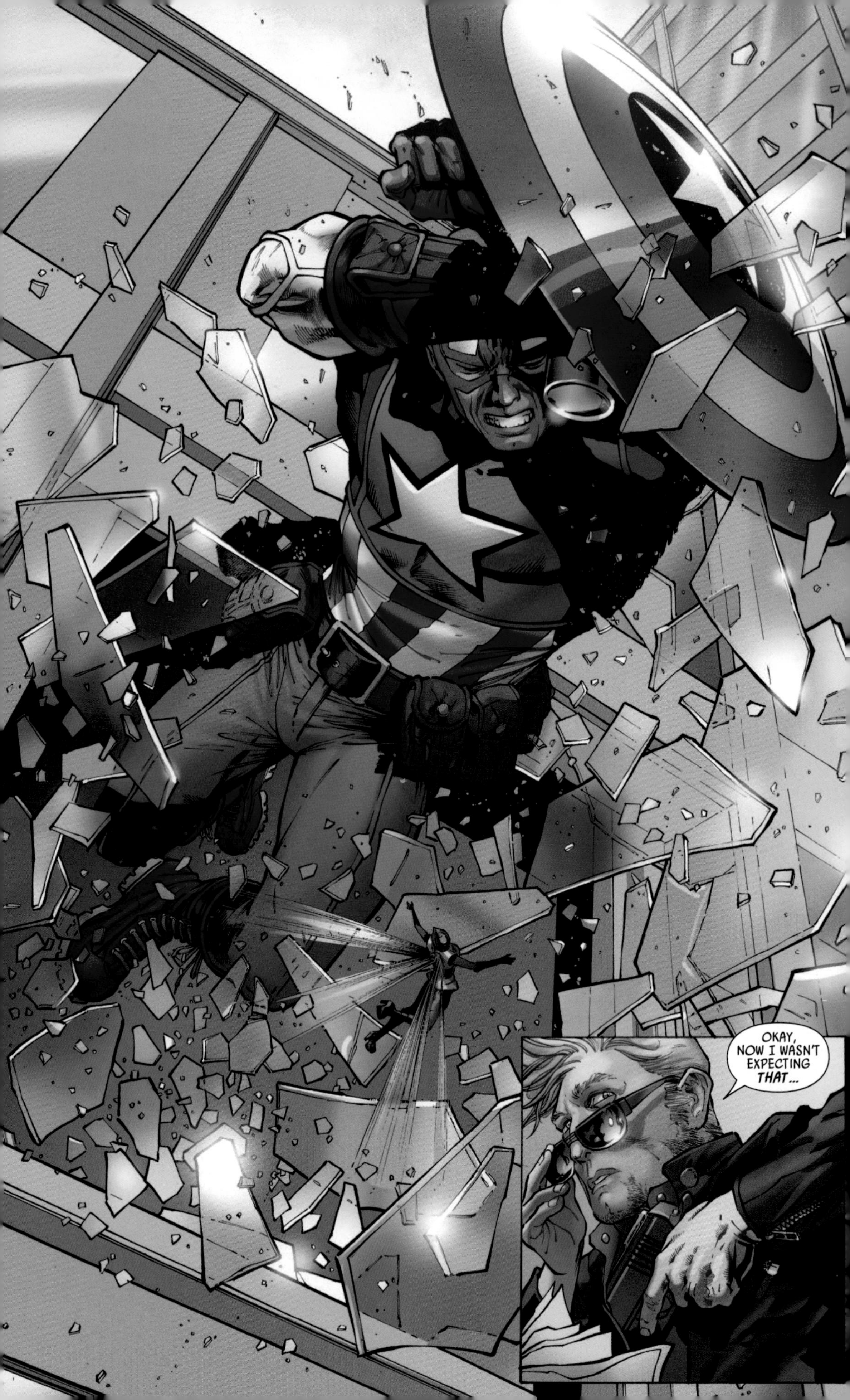
OKAY, NOW I WASN'T EXPECTING *THAT*...

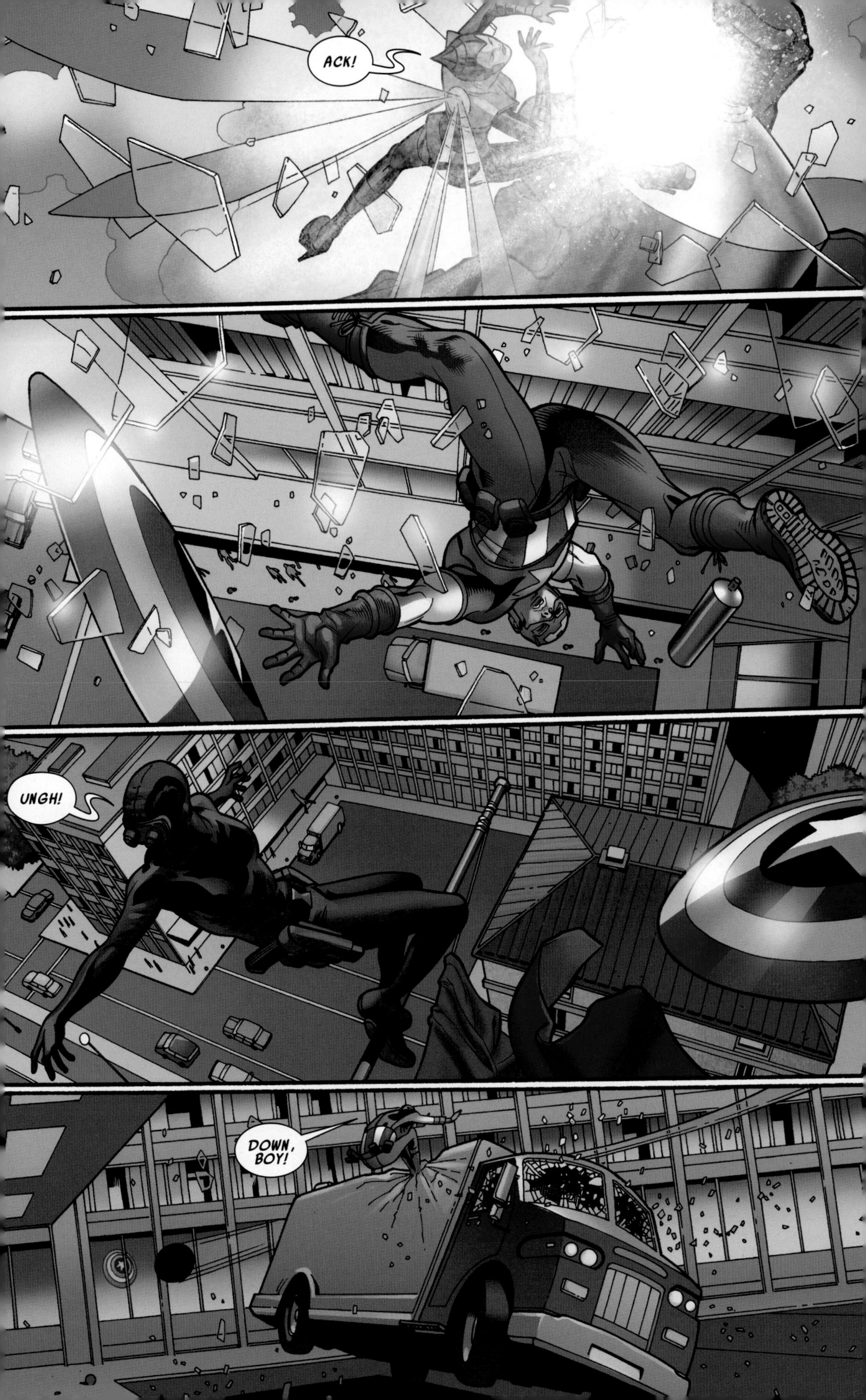
ACK!
UNGH!
DOWN, BOY!

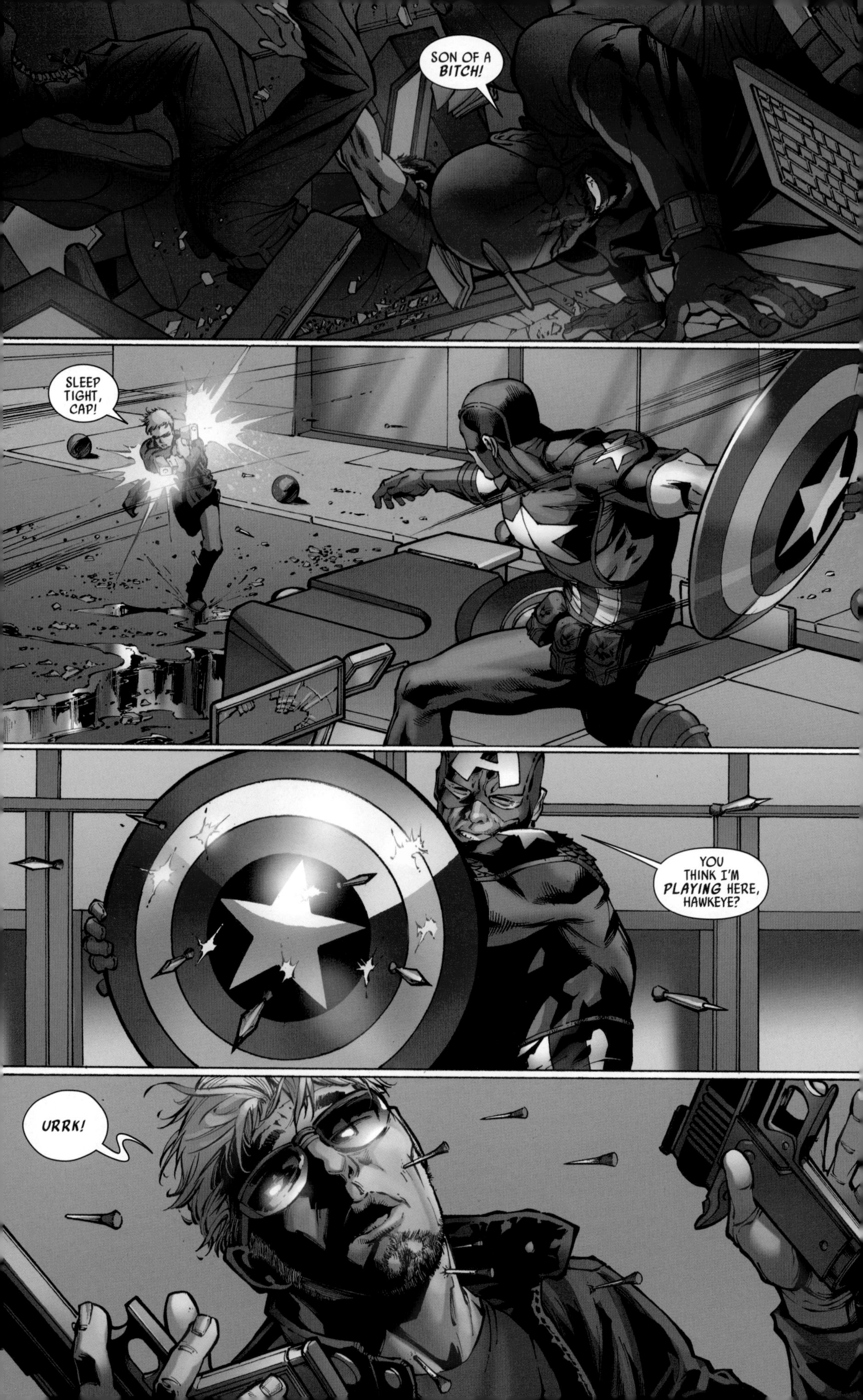
SON OF A BITCH!
SLEEP TIGHT, CAP!
YOU THINK I'M PLAYING HERE, HAWKEYE?
URRK!

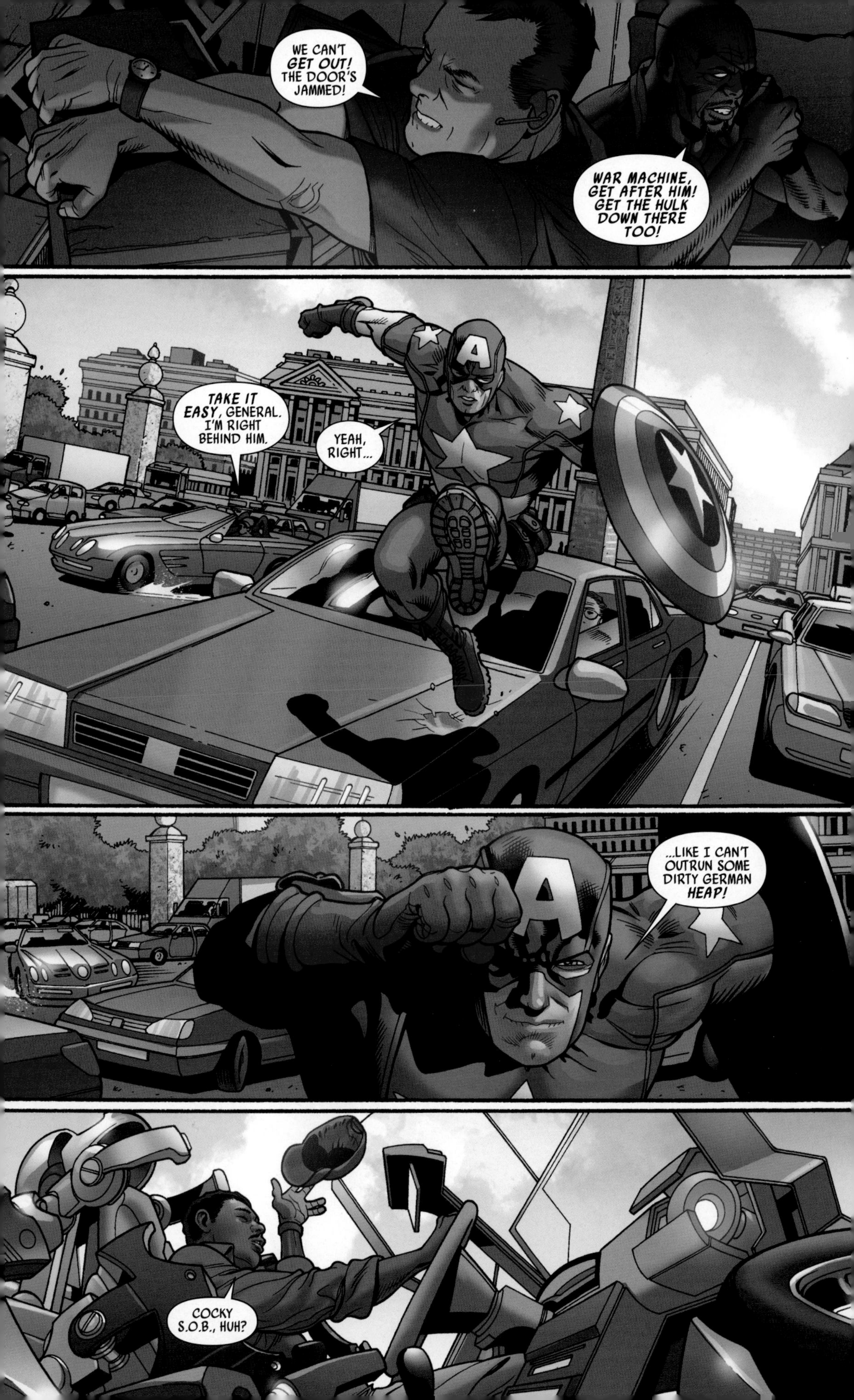
WE CAN'T GET OUT! THE DOOR'S JAMMED!
WAR MACHINE, GET AFTER HIM! GET THE HULK DOWN THERE TOO!
TAKE IT EASY, GENERAL. I'M RIGHT BEHIND HIM.
YEAH, RIGHT...
...LIKE I CAN'T OUTRUN SOME DIRTY GERMAN HEAP!
COCKY S.O.B., HUH?

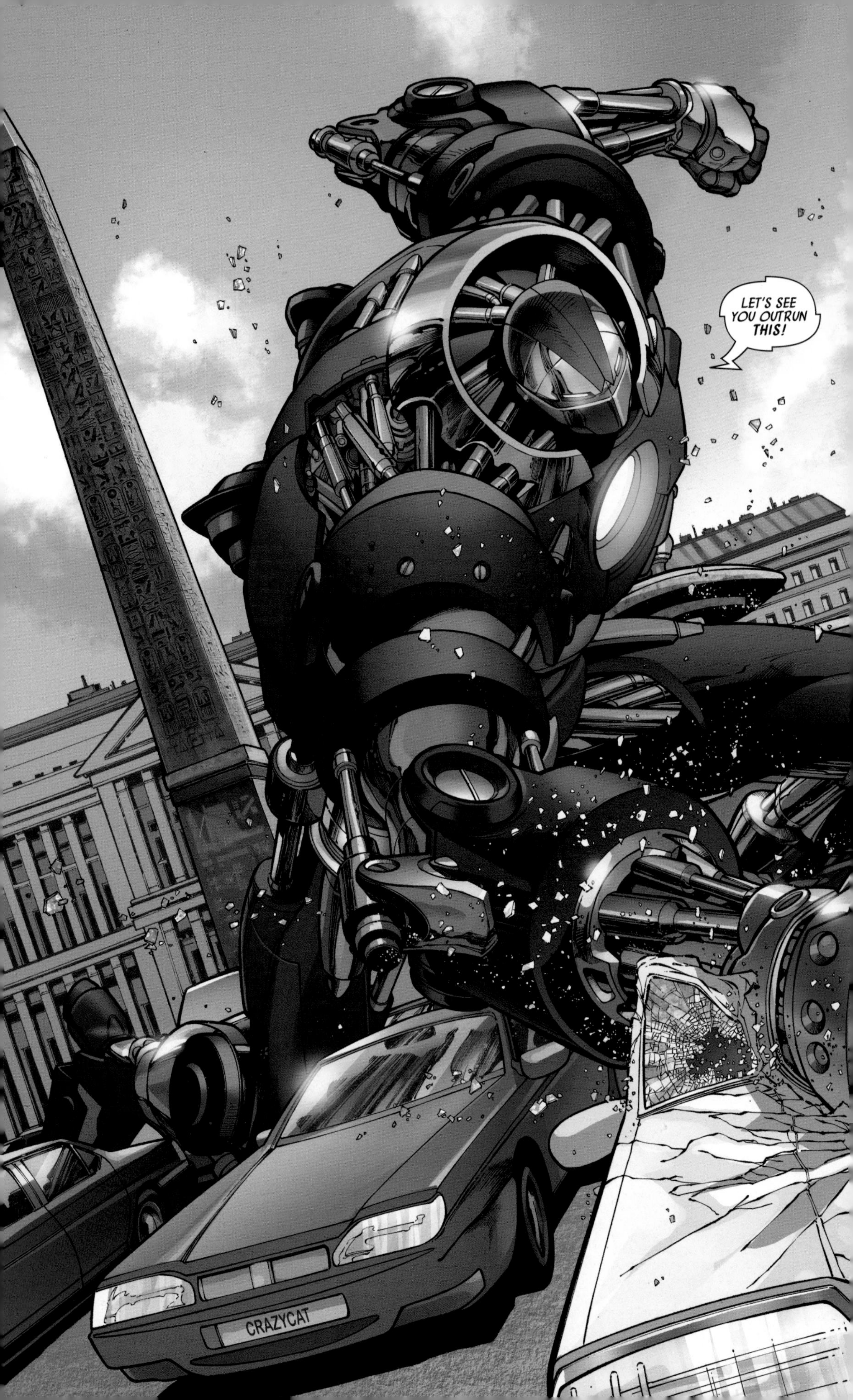
LET'S SEE YOU OUTRUN THIS!
CRAZYCAT

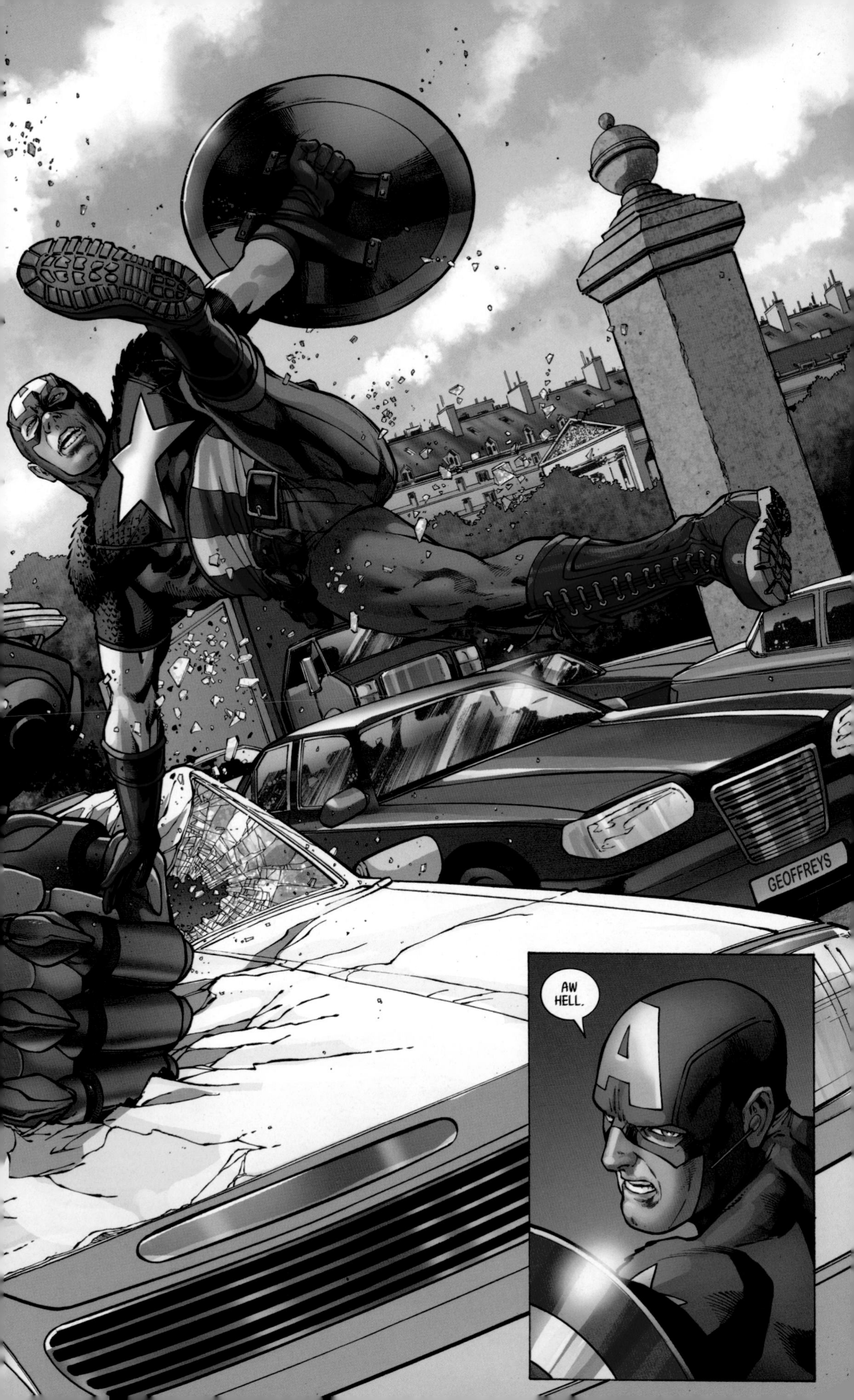
GEOFFREYS
AW HELL.

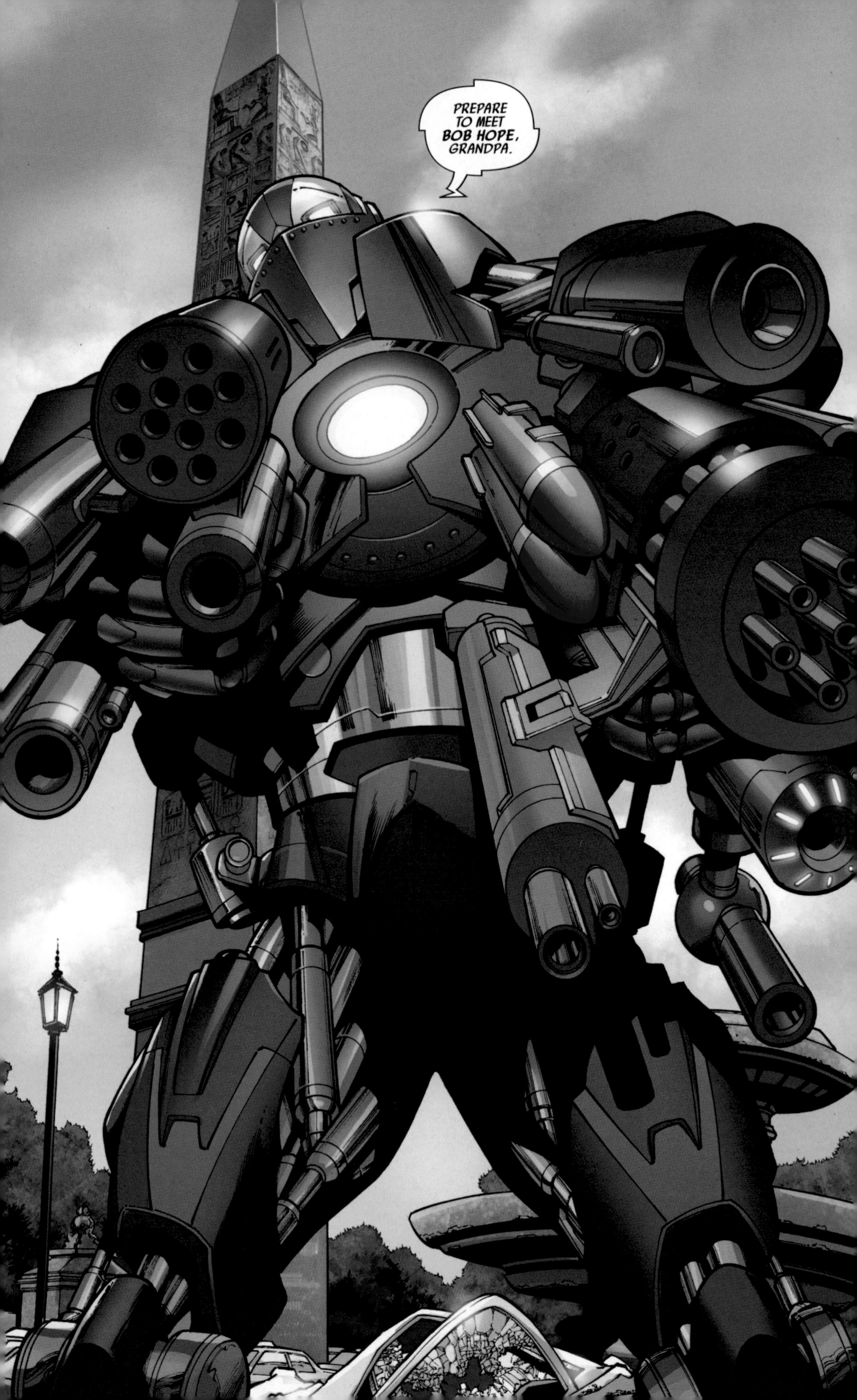
PREPARE TO MEET BOB HOPE, GRANDPA.

4

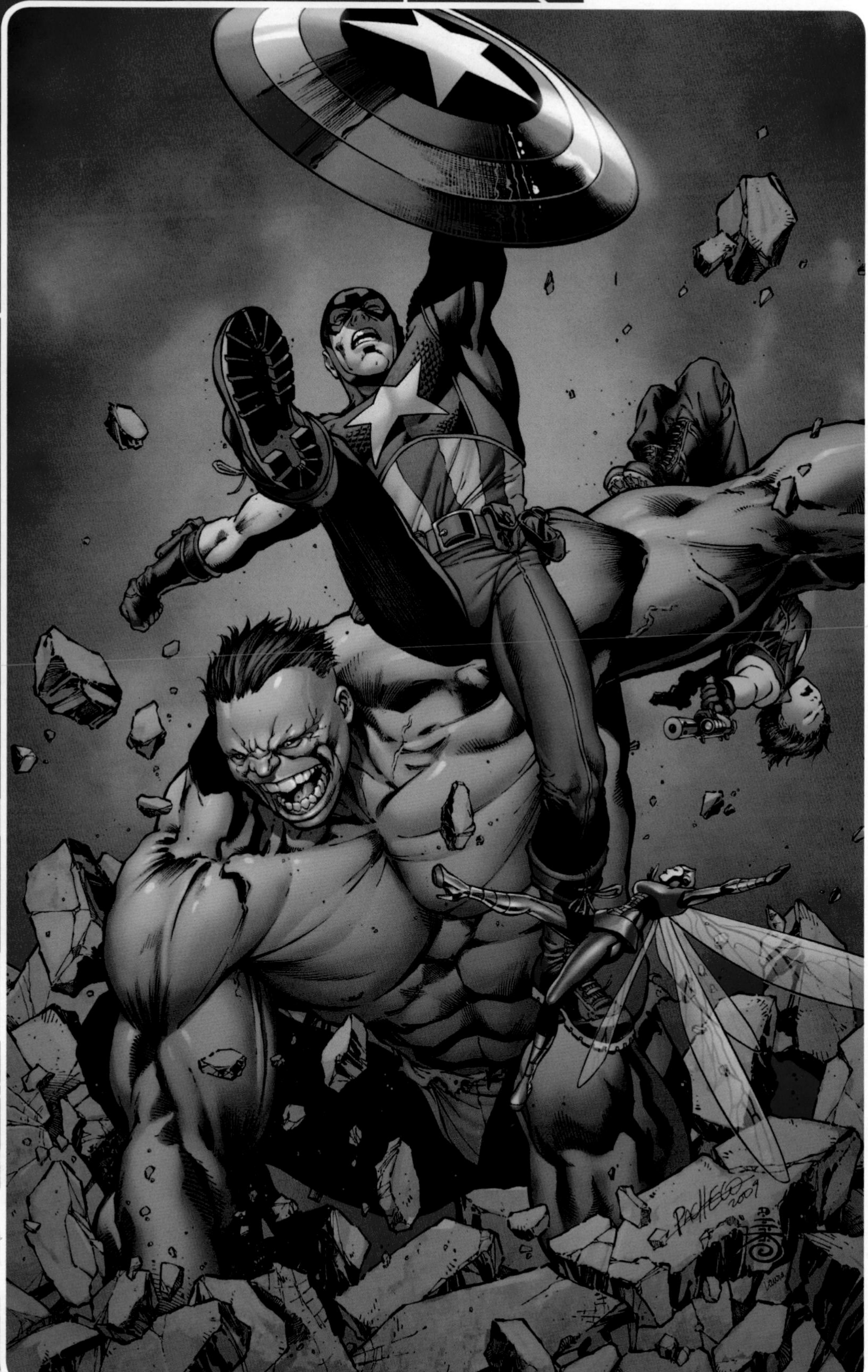
PACHECO 2009

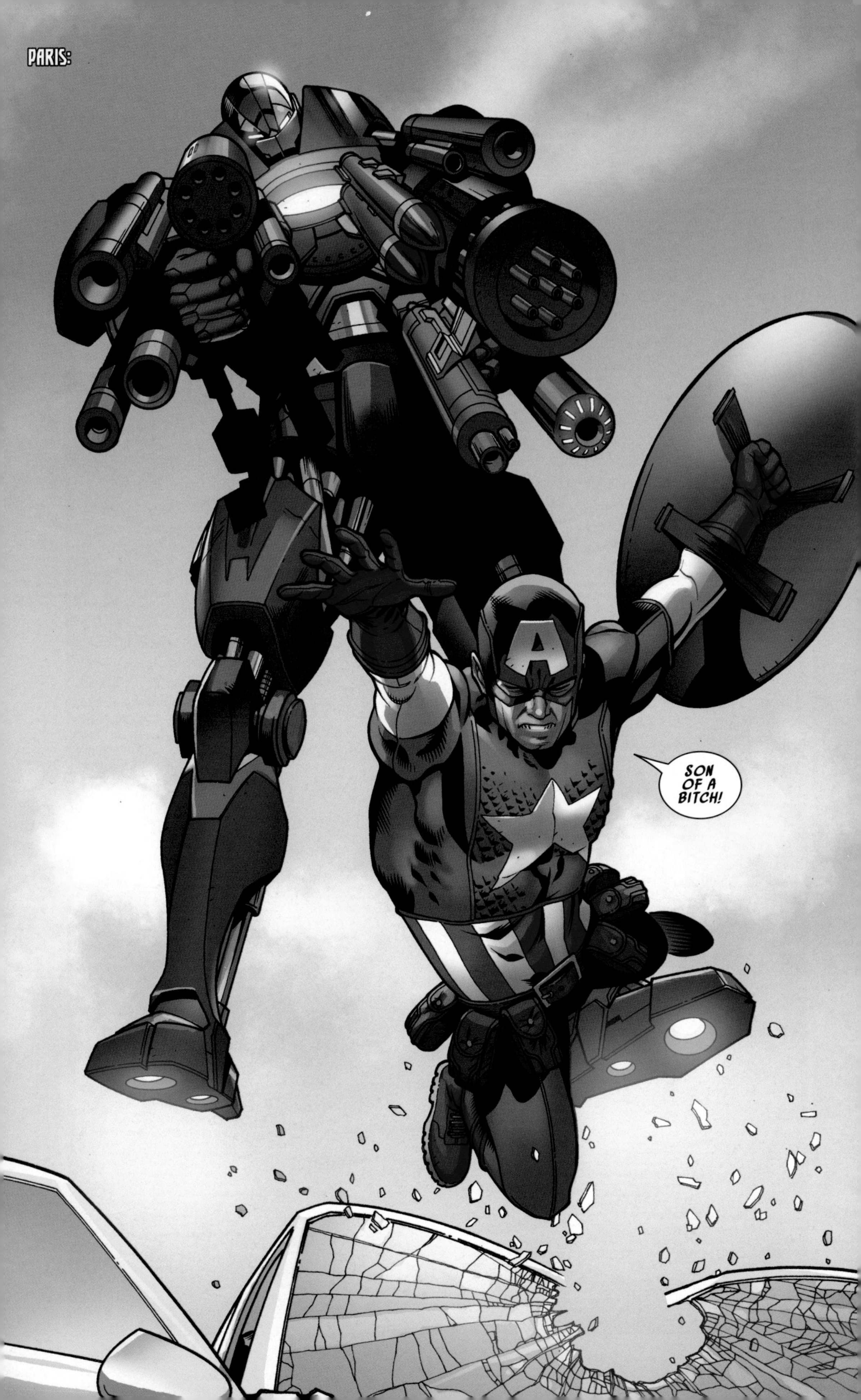
PARIS:
SON OF A BITCH!

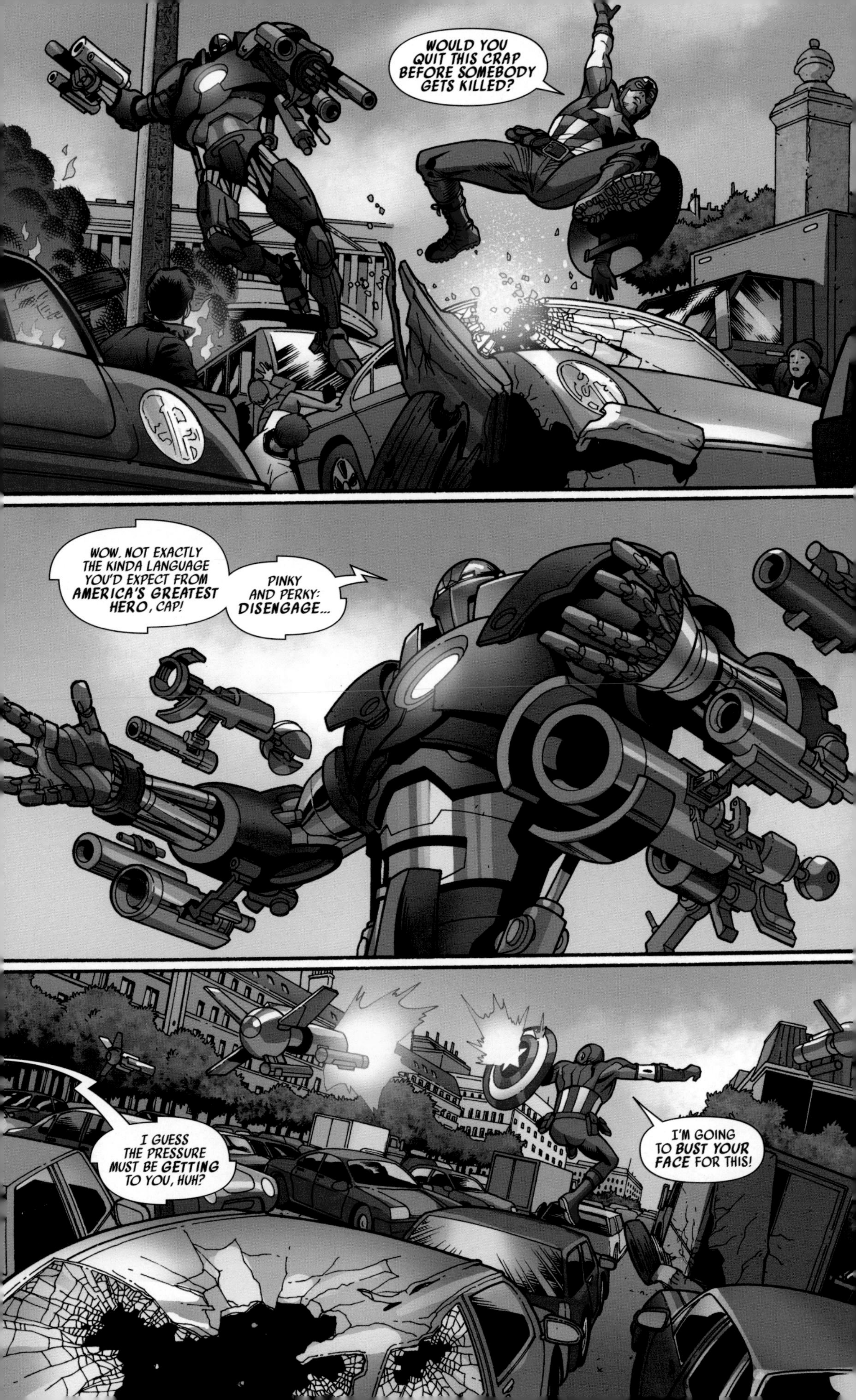
WOULD YOU QUIT THIS CRAP BEFORE SOMEBODY GETS KILLED?
WOW. NOT EXACTLY THE KINDA LANGUAGE YOU'D EXPECT FROM AMERICA'S GREATEST HERO, CAP!
PINKY AND PERKY: DISENGAGE...
I GUESS THE PRESSURE MUST BE GETTING TO YOU, HUH?
I'M GOING TO BUST YOUR FACE FOR THIS!

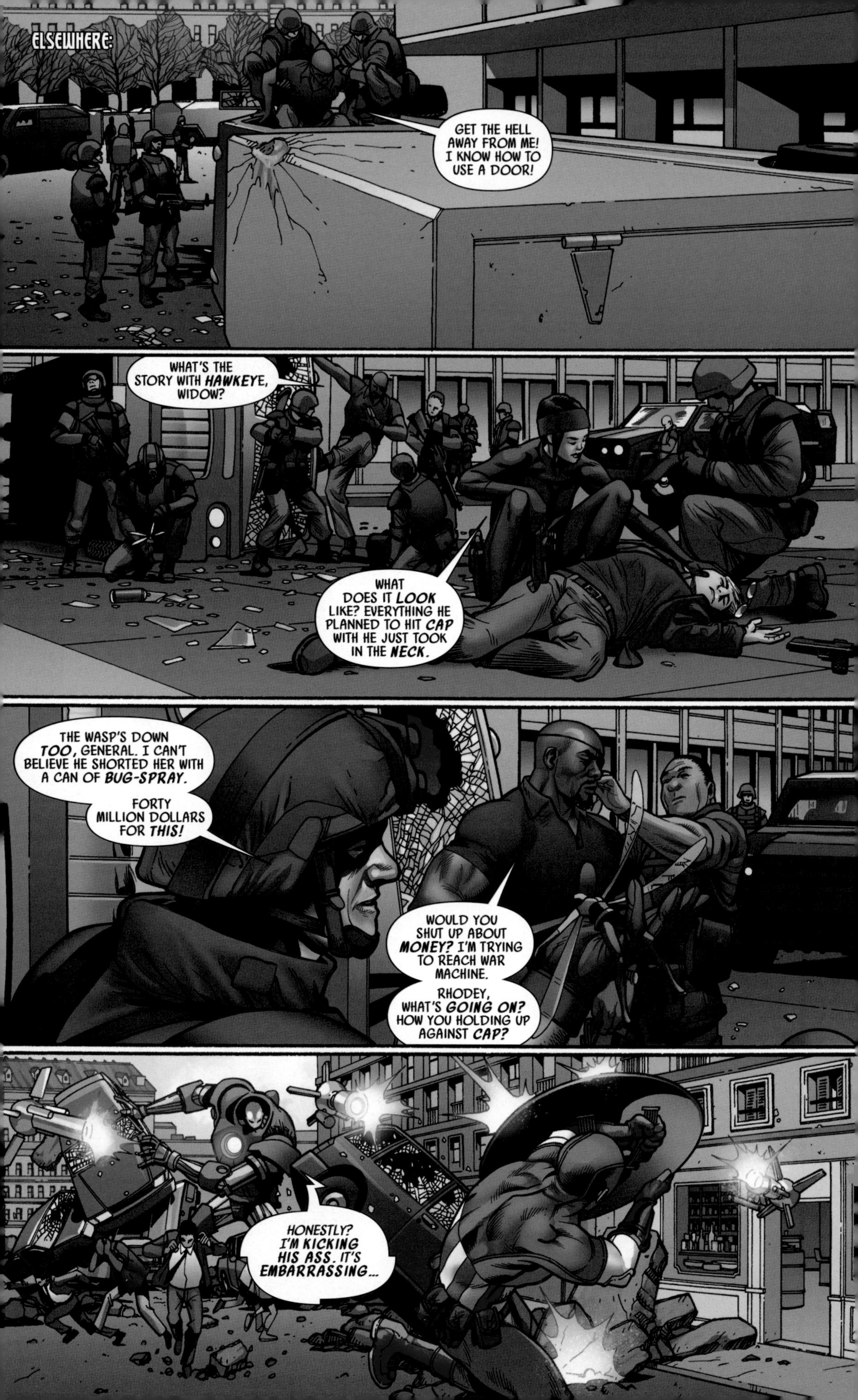
ELSEWHERE:
GET THE HELL AWAY FROM ME! I KNOW HOW TO USE A DOOR!
WHAT'S THE STORY WITH HAWKEYE, WIDOW?
WHAT DOES IT LOOK LIKE? EVERYTHING HE PLANNED TO HIT CAP WITH HE JUST TOOK IN THE NECK.
THE WASP'S DOWN TOO, GENERAL. I CAN'T BELIEVE HE SHORTED HER WITH A CAN OF BUG-SPRAY.
FORTY MILLION DOLLARS FOR THIS!
WOULD YOU SHUT UP ABOUT MONEY? I'M TRYING TO REACH WAR MACHINE.
RHODEY, WHAT'S GOING ON? HOW YOU HOLDING UP AGAINST CAP?
HONESTLY? I'M KICKING HIS ASS. IT'S EMBARRASSING...

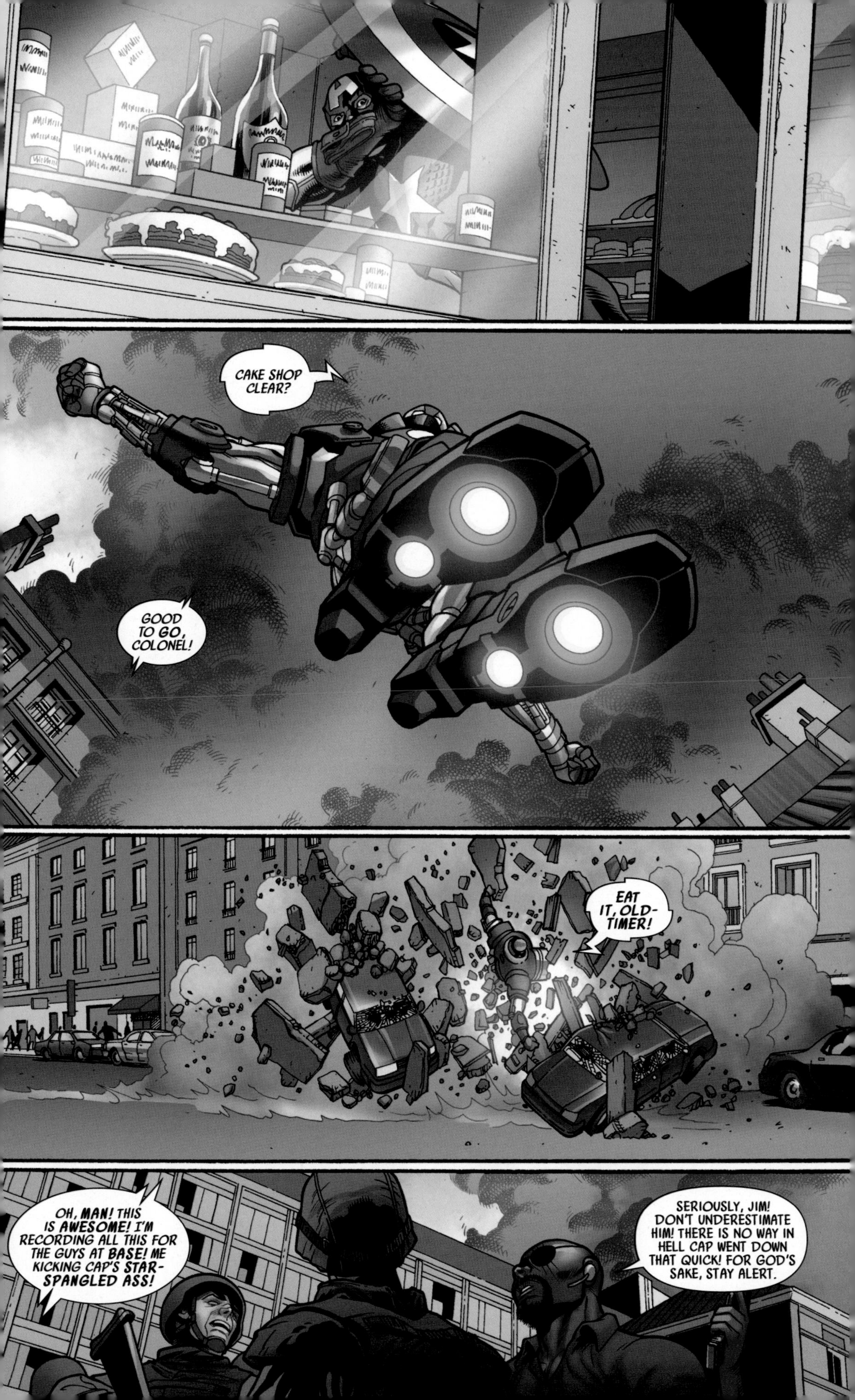
CAKE SHOP CLEAR?
GOOD TO GO, COLONEL!
EAT IT, OLD-TIMER!
OH, MAN! THIS IS AWESOME! I'M RECORDING ALL THIS FOR THE GUYS AT BASE! ME KICKING CAP'S STAR-SPANGLED ASS!
SERIOUSLY, JIM! DON'T UNDERESTIMATE HIM! THERE IS NO WAY IN HELL CAP WENT DOWN THAT QUICK! FOR GOD'S SAKE, STAY ALERT.

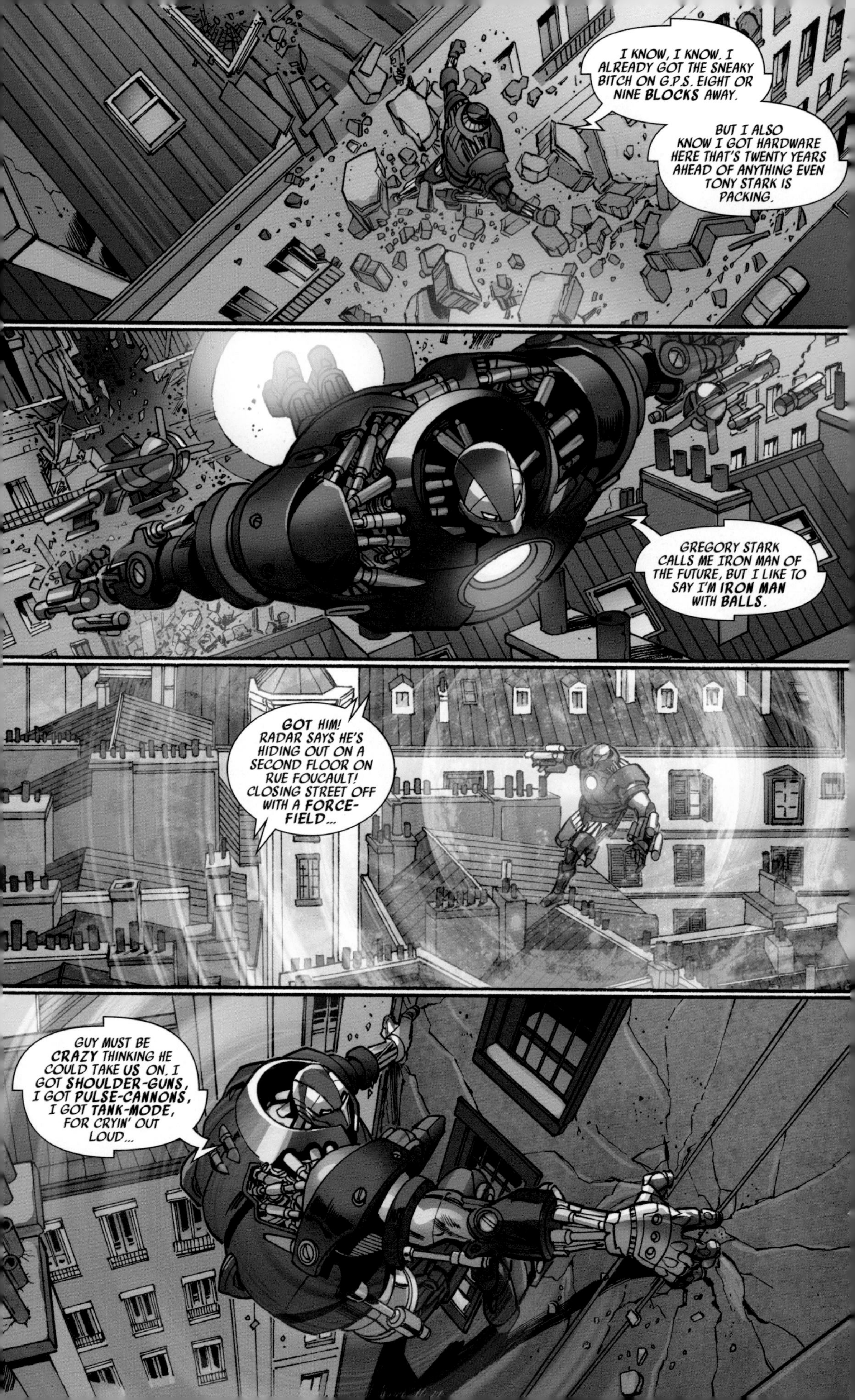
I KNOW, I KNOW. I ALREADY GOT THE SNEAKY BITCH ON G.P.S. EIGHT OR NINE BLOCKS AWAY.
BUT I ALSO KNOW I GOT HARDWARE HERE THAT'S TWENTY YEARS AHEAD OF ANYTHING EVEN TONY STARK IS PACKING.
GREGORY STARK CALLS ME IRON MAN OF THE FUTURE, BUT I LIKE TO SAY I'M IRON MAN WITH BALLS.
GOT HIM! RADAR SAYS HE'S HIDING OUT ON A SECOND FLOOR ON RUE FOUCAULT! CLOSING STREET OFF WITH A FORCE-FIELD...
GUY MUST BE CRAZY THINKING HE COULD TAKE US ON. I GOT SHOULDER-GUNS, I GOT PULSE-CANNONS, I GOT TANK-MODE, FOR CRYIN' OUT LOUD...

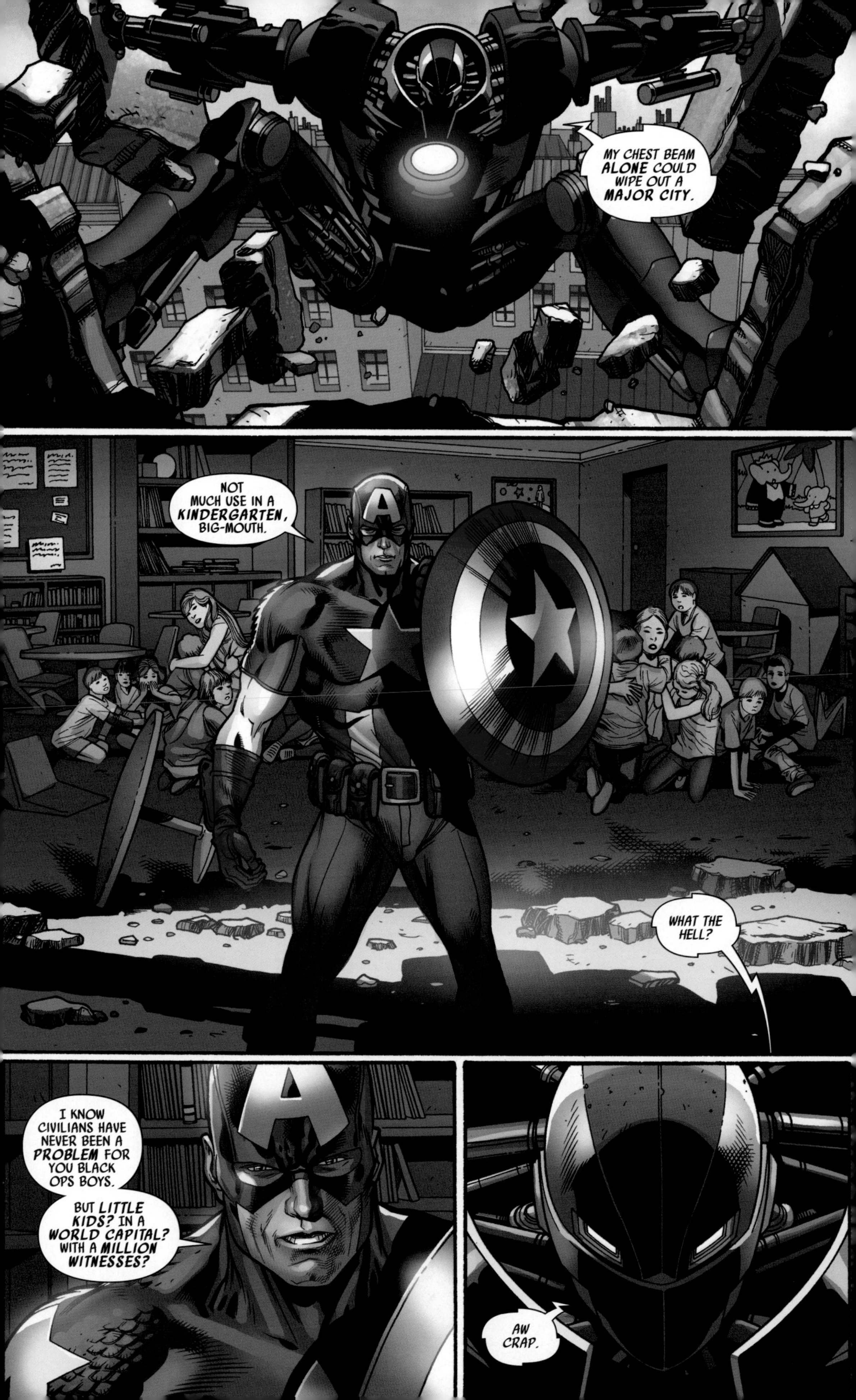
MY CHEST BEAM ALONE COULD WIPE OUT A MAJOR CITY.
NOT MUCH USE IN A KINDERGARTEN, BIG-MOUTH.
WHAT THE HELL?
I KNOW CIVILIANS HAVE NEVER BEEN A PROBLEM FOR YOU BLACK OPS BOYS.
BUT LITTLE KIDS? IN A WORLD CAPITAL? WITH A MILLION WITNESSES?
AW CRAP.

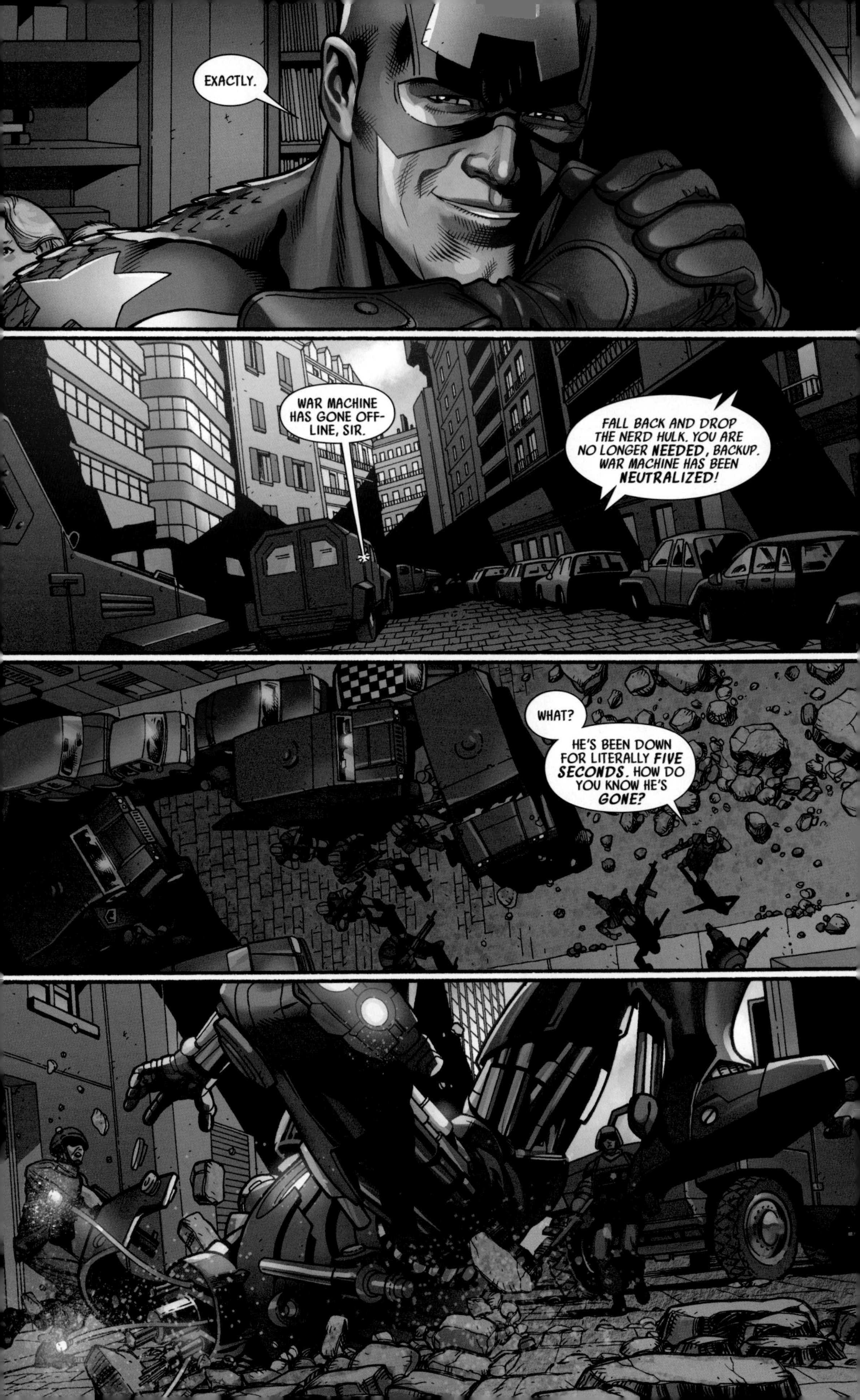
EXACTLY.
WAR MACHINE HAS GONE OFF-LINE, SIR.
FALL BACK AND DROP THE NERD HULK. YOU ARE NO LONGER NEEDED, BACKUP. WAR MACHINE HAS BEEN NEUTRALIZED!
WHAT?
HE'S BEEN DOWN FOR LITERALLY FIVE SECONDS. HOW DO YOU KNOW HE'S GONE?

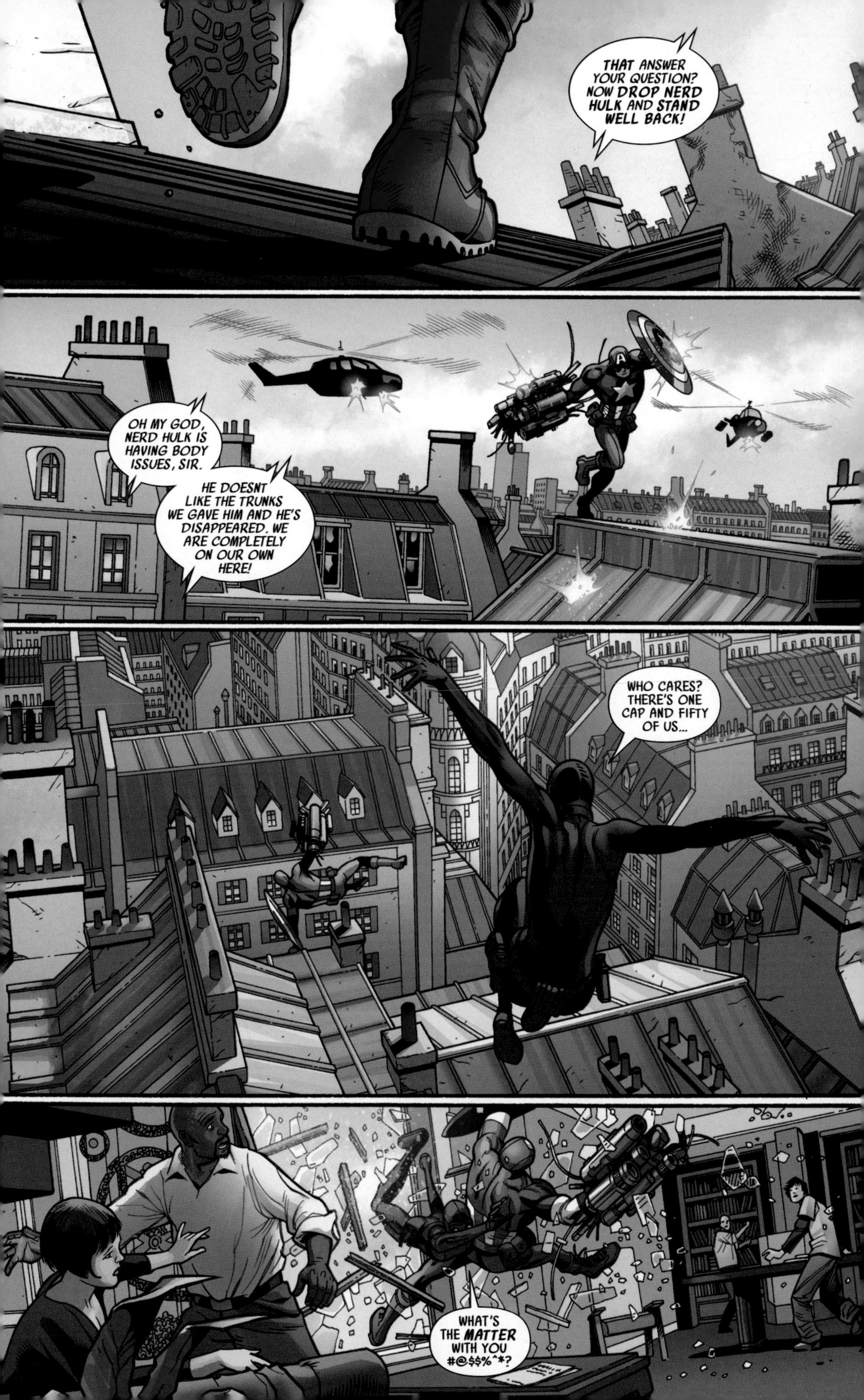
THAT ANSWER YOUR QUESTION? NOW DROP NERD HULK AND STAND WELL BACK!
OH MY GOD, NERD HULK IS HAVING BODY ISSUES, SIR.
HE DOESNT LIKE THE TRUNKS WE GAVE HIM AND HE'S DISAPPEARED. WE ARE COMPLETELY ON OUR OWN HERE!
WHO CARES? THERE'S ONE CAP AND FIFTY OF US...
WHAT'S THE MATTER WITH YOU #@$$%^*?

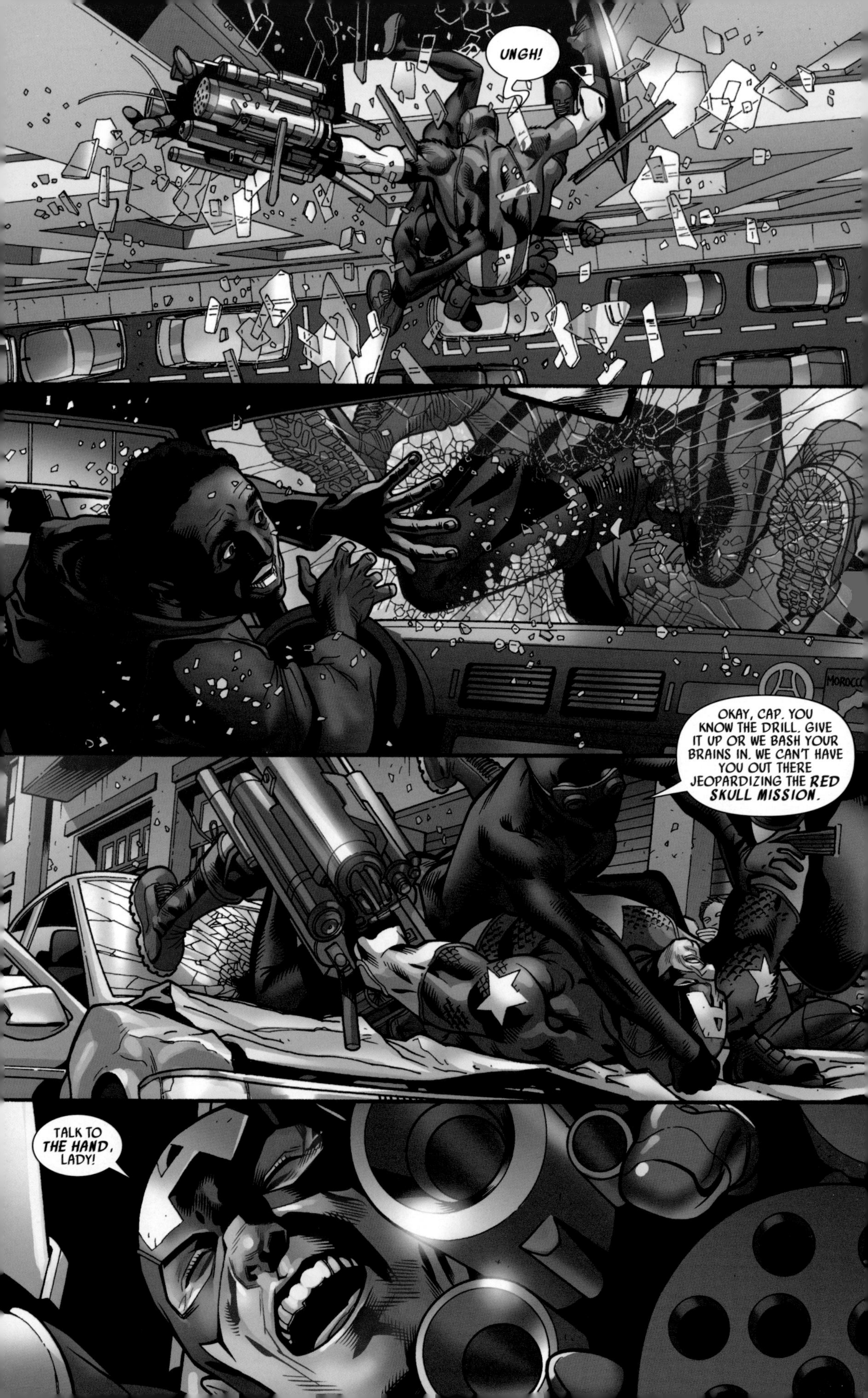
UNGH!
MOROCCO
OKAY, CAP. YOU KNOW THE DRILL. GIVE IT UP OR WE BASH YOUR BRAINS IN. WE CAN'T HAVE YOU OUT THERE JEOPARDIZING THE RED SKULL MISSION.
TALK TO THE HAND, LADY!

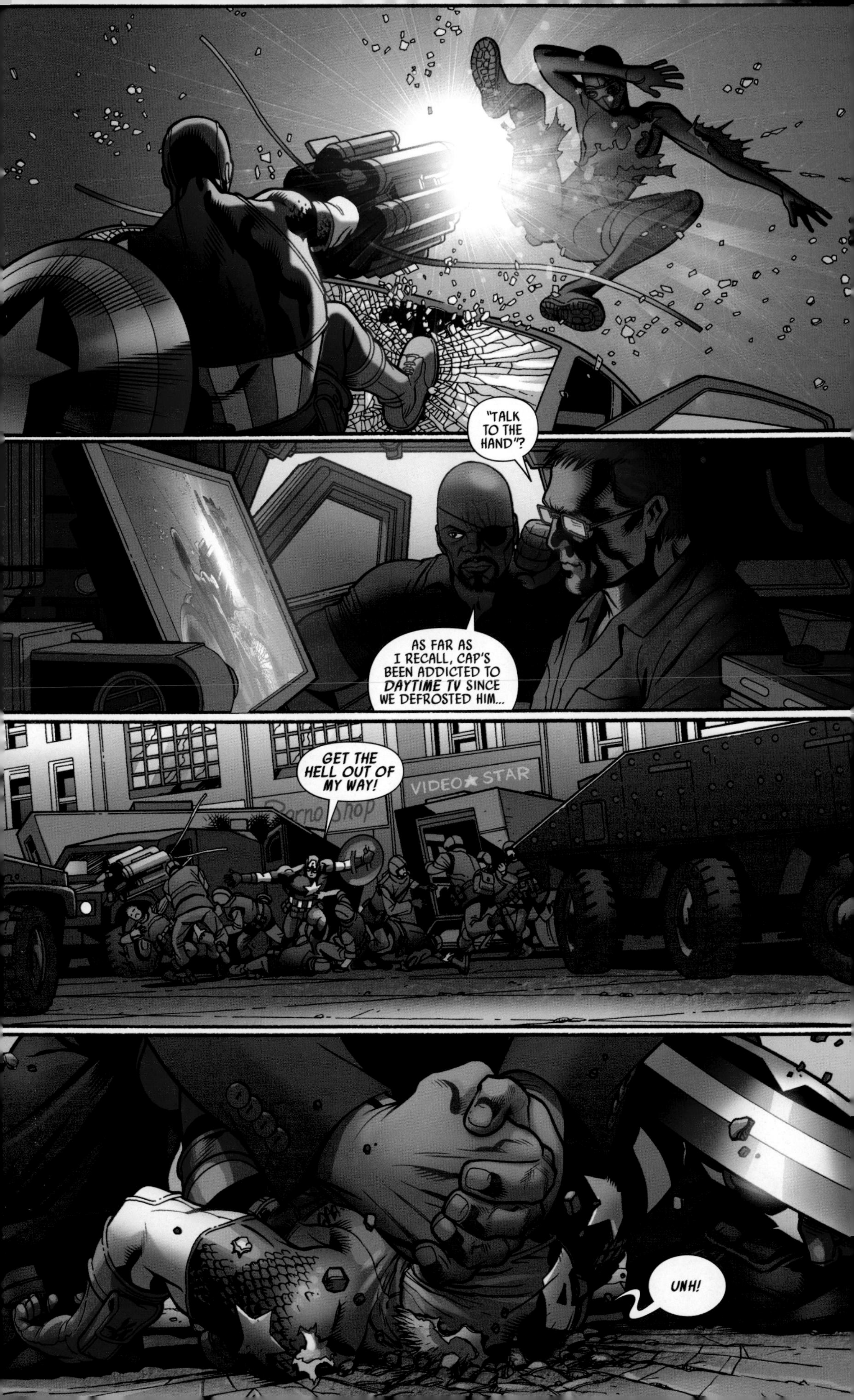
"TALK TO THE HAND"?
AS FAR AS I RECALL, CAP'S BEEN ADDICTED TO DAYTIME TV SINCE WE DEFROSTED HIM...
GET THE HELL OUT OF MY WAY!
VIDEO STAR
Porno Shop
UNH!

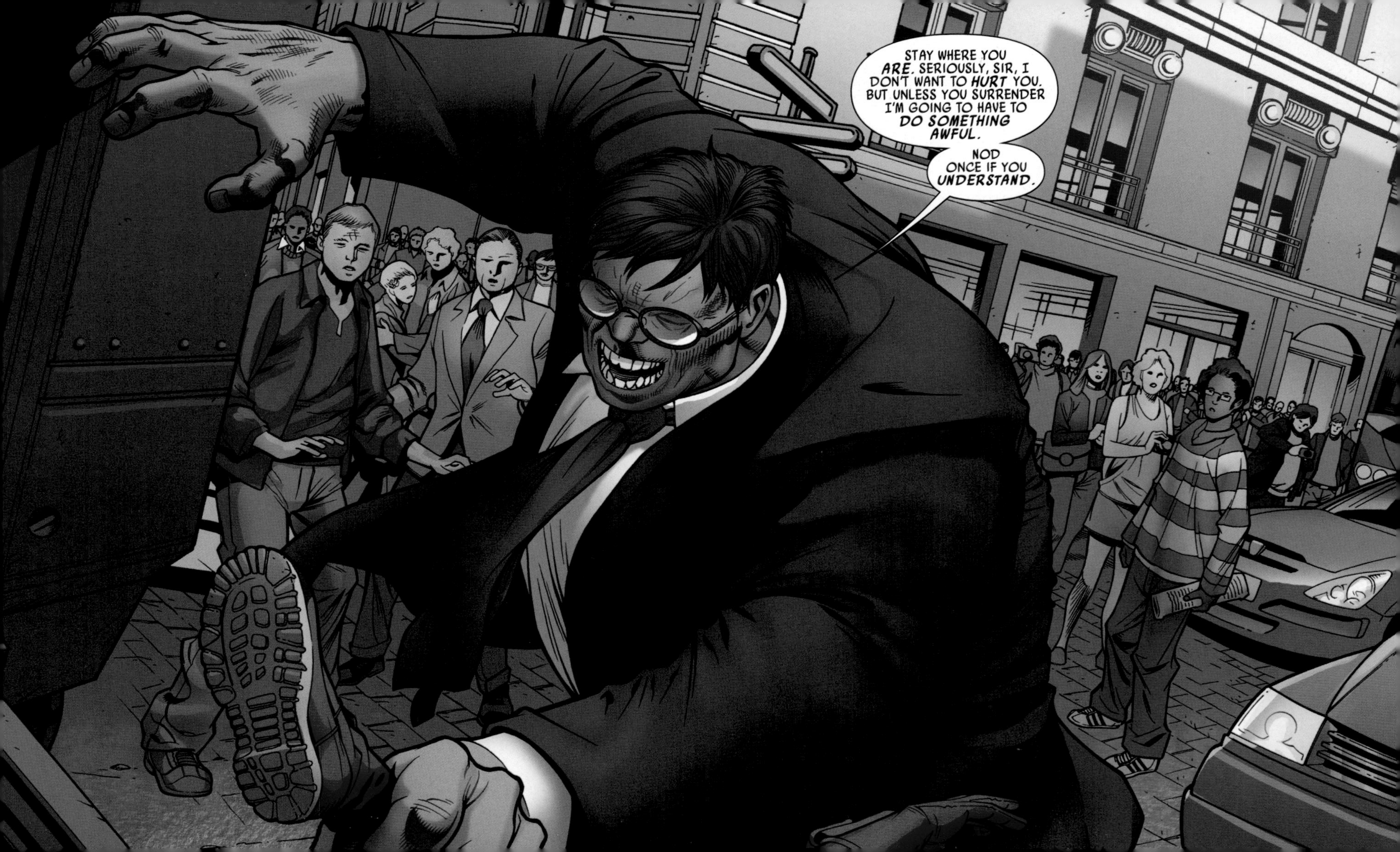
STAY WHERE YOU ARE. SERIOUSLY, SIR, I DON'T WANT TO HURT YOU. BUT UNLESS YOU SURRENDER I'M GOING TO HAVE TO DO SOMETHING AWFUL.
NOD ONCE IF YOU UNDERSTAND.

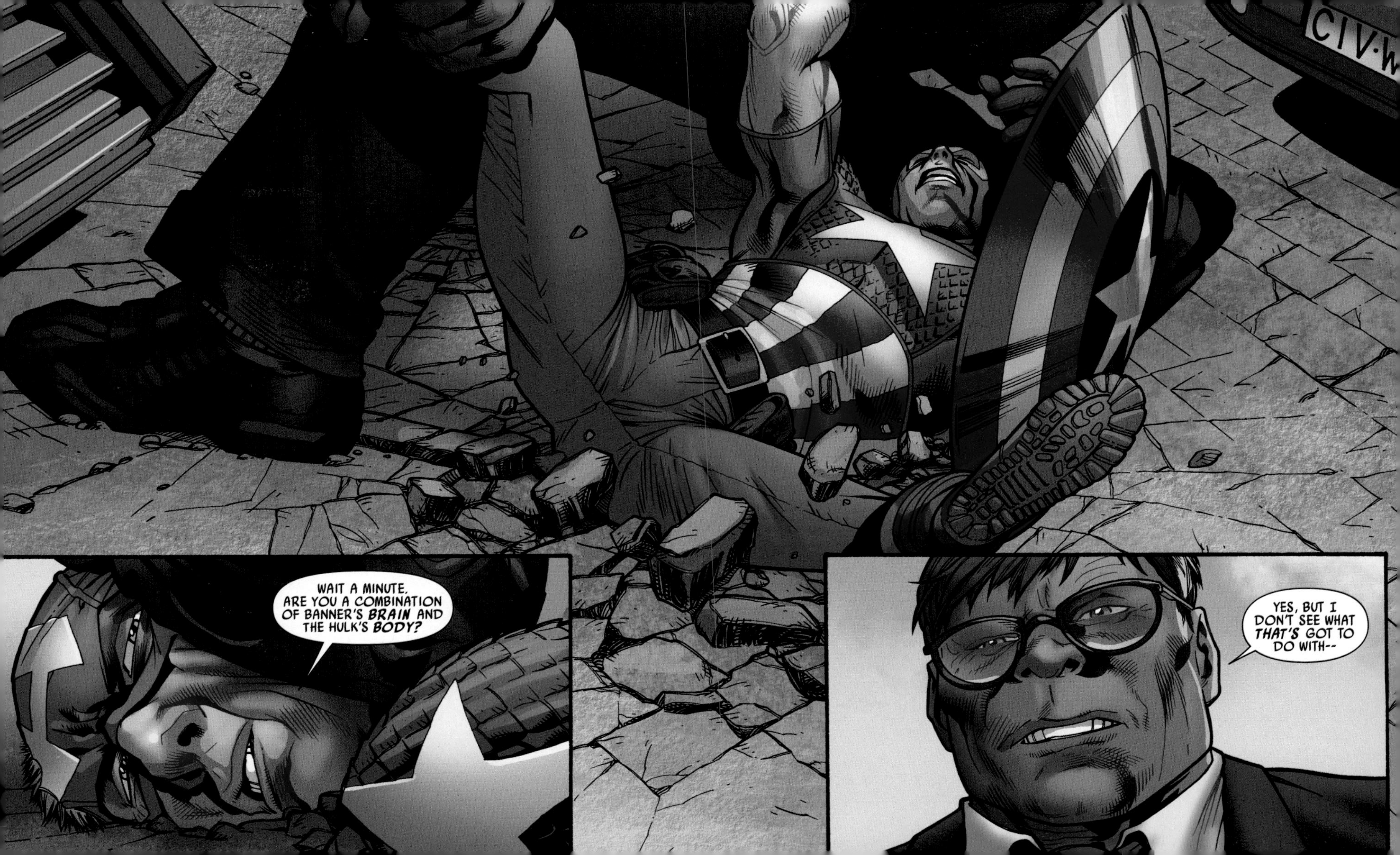
CIV·W
WAIT A MINUTE. ARE YOU A COMBINATION OF BANNER'S ***BRAIN*** AND THE HULK'S ***BODY?***
YES, BUT I DON'T SEE WHAT ***THAT'S*** GOT TO DO WITH--

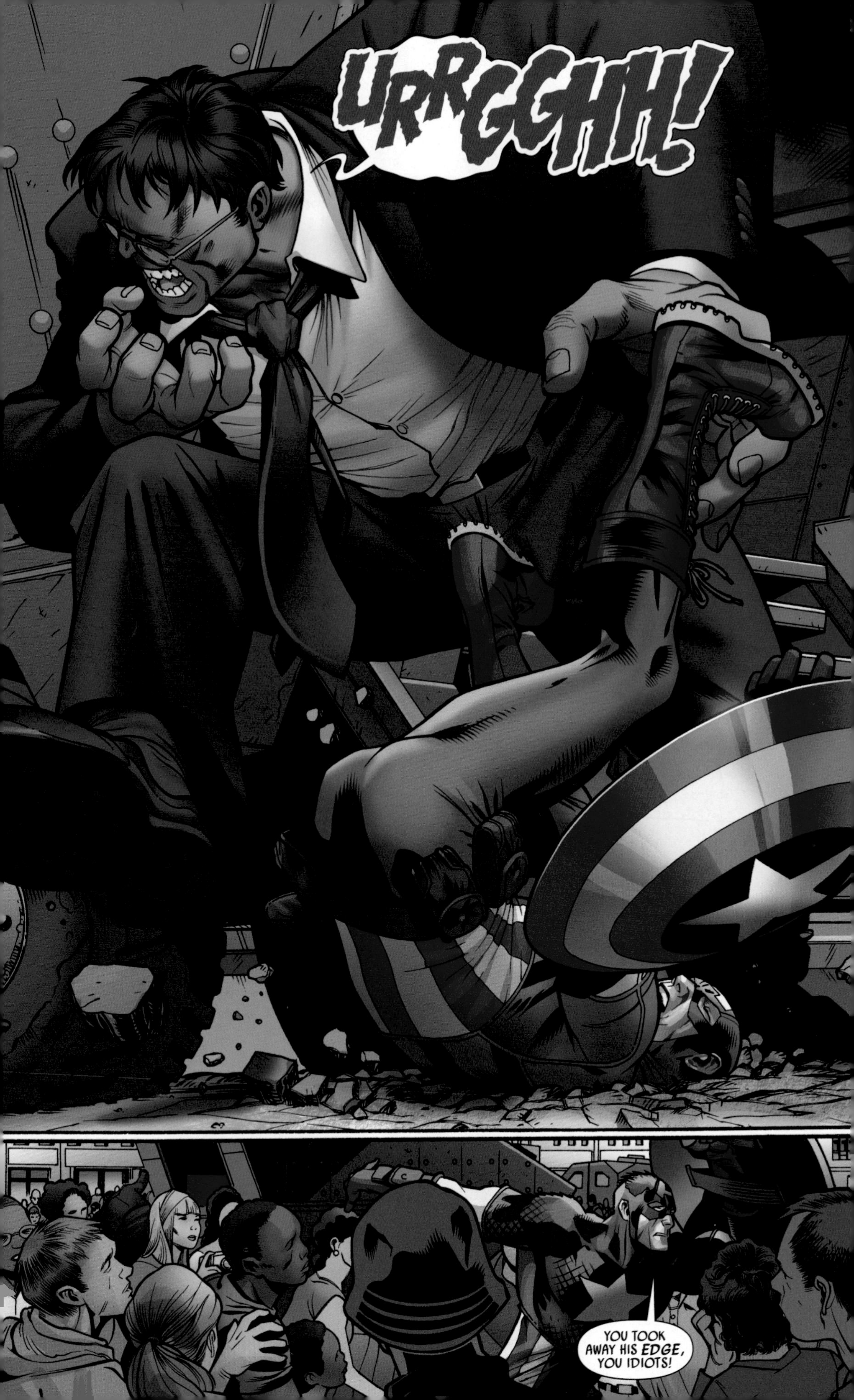
URRGGHH!
YOU TOOK AWAY HIS EDGE, YOU IDIOTS!

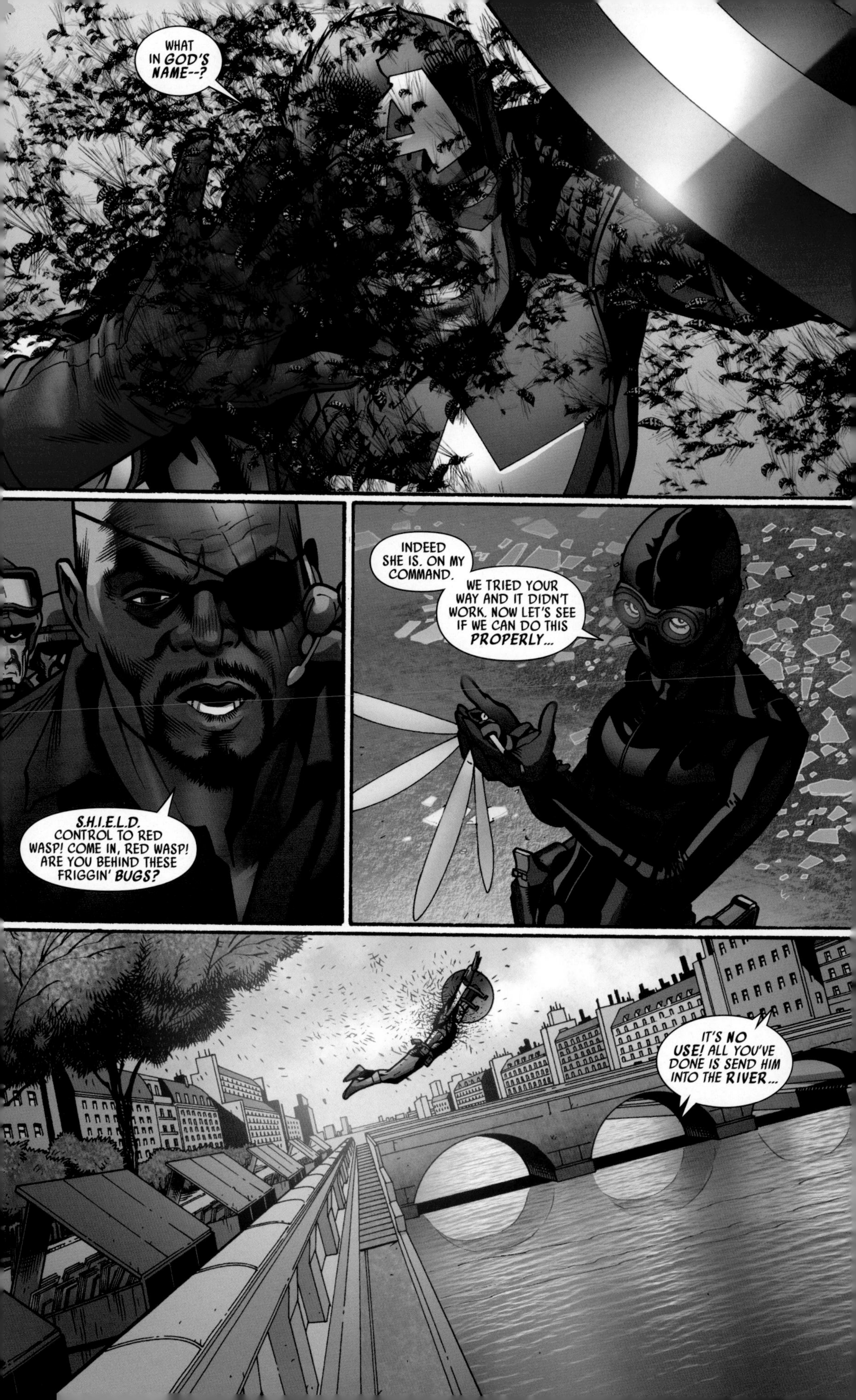
WHAT IN GOD'S NAME--?
S.H.I.E.L.D. CONTROL TO RED WASP! COME IN, RED WASP! ARE YOU BEHIND THESE FRIGGIN' BUGS?
INDEED SHE IS. ON MY COMMAND.
WE TRIED YOUR WAY AND IT DIDN'T WORK. NOW LET'S SEE IF WE CAN DO THIS PROPERLY...
IT'S NO USE! ALL YOU'VE DONE IS SEND HIM INTO THE RIVER...

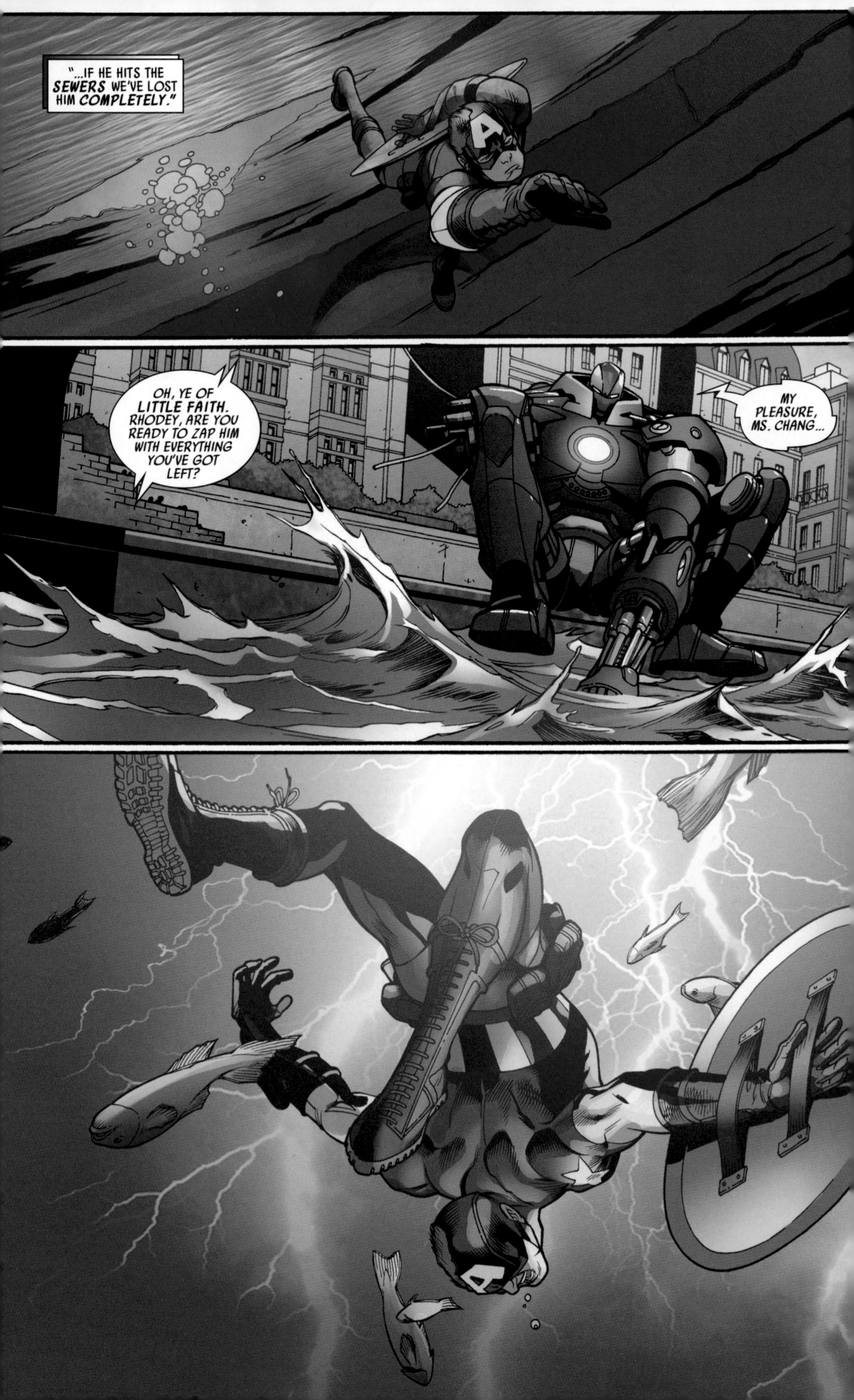
"...IF HE HITS THE SEWERS WE'VE LOST HIM COMPLETELY."
OH, YE OF LITTLE FAITH. RHODEY, ARE YOU READY TO ZAP HIM WITH EVERYTHING YOU'VE GOT LEFT?
MY PLEASURE, MS. CHANG...

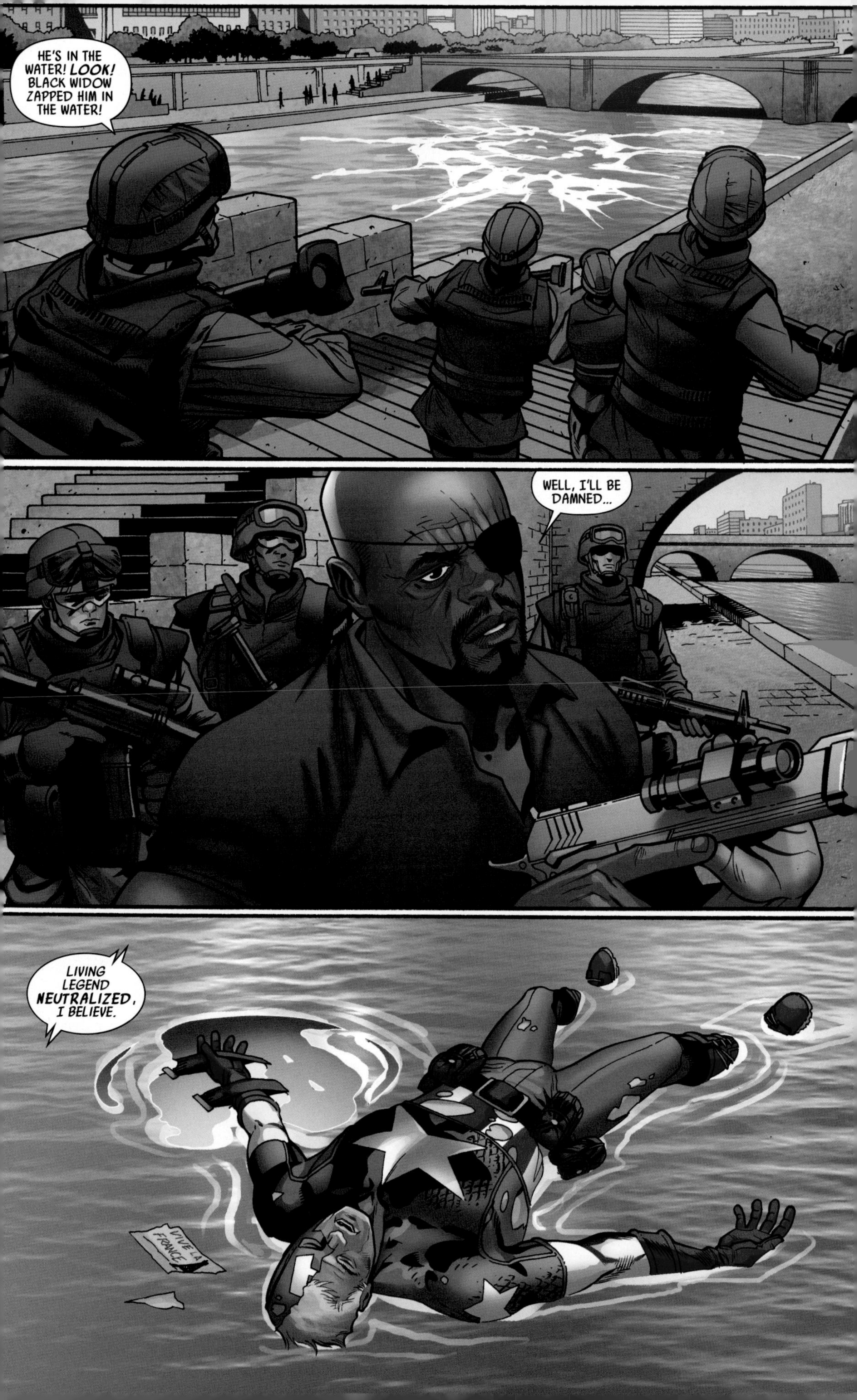
HE'S IN THE WATER! LOOK! BLACK WIDOW ZAPPED HIM IN THE WATER!
WELL, I'LL BE DAMNED...
LIVING LEGEND NEUTRALIZED, I BELIEVE.
VIVE LA FRANCE

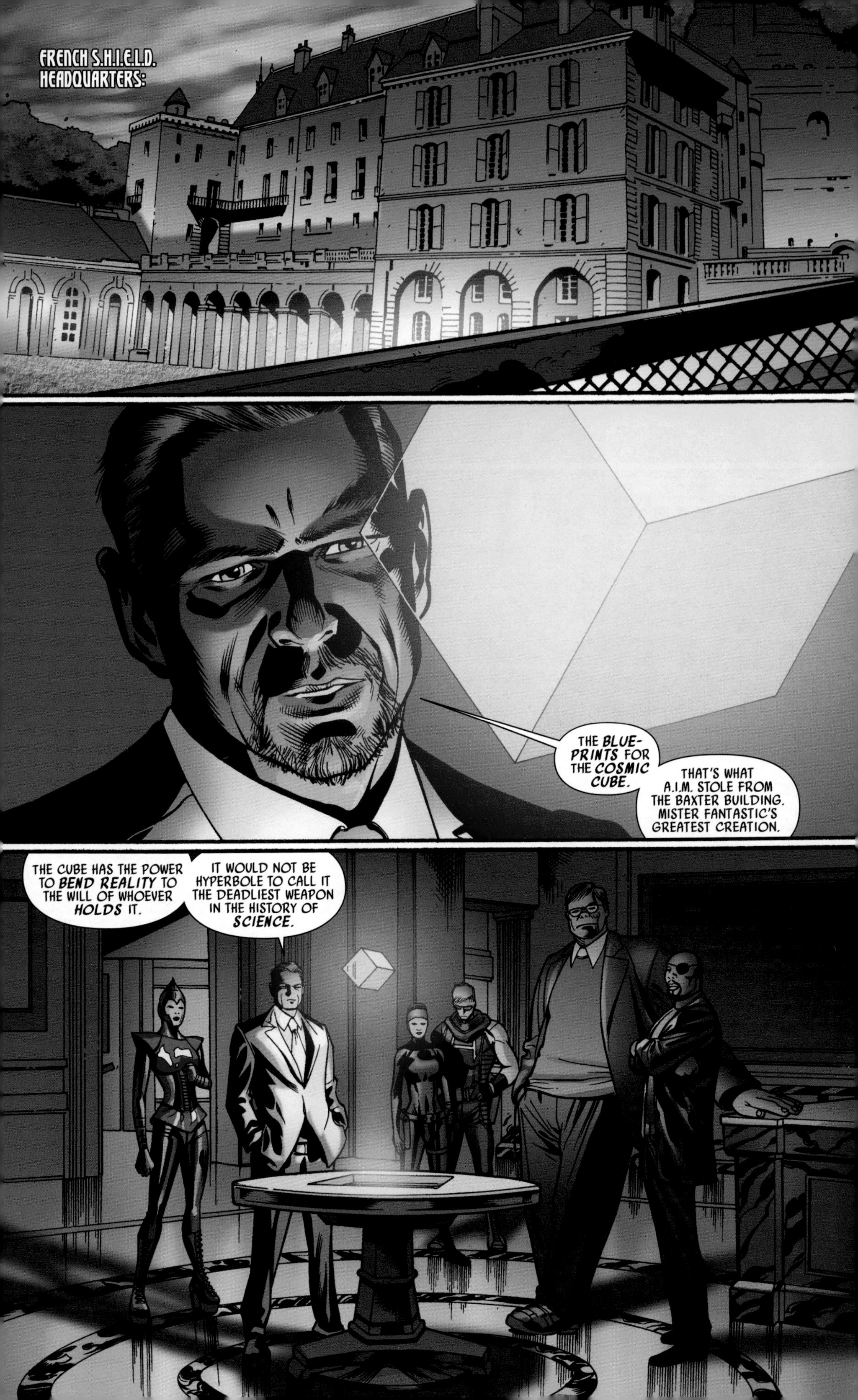
FRENCH S.H.I.E.L.D. HEADQUARTERS:
THE BLUE-PRINTS FOR THE COSMIC CUBE.
THAT'S WHAT A.I.M. STOLE FROM THE BAXTER BUILDING. MISTER FANTASTIC'S GREATEST CREATION.
THE CUBE HAS THE POWER TO BEND REALITY TO THE WILL OF WHOEVER HOLDS IT.
IT WOULD NOT BE HYPERBOLE TO CALL IT THE DEADLIEST WEAPON IN THE HISTORY OF SCIENCE.

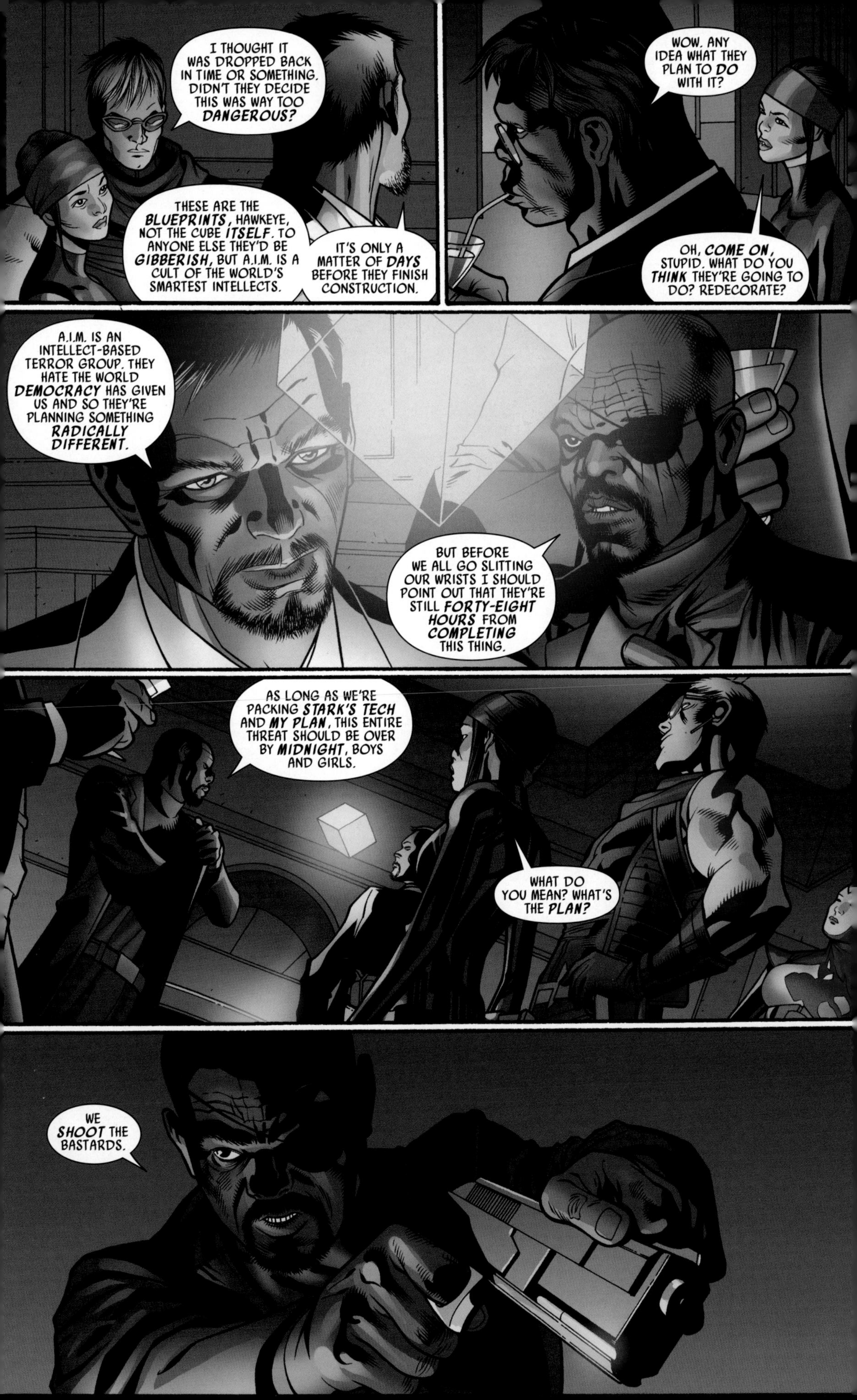
I THOUGHT IT WAS DROPPED BACK IN TIME OR SOMETHING. DIDN'T THEY DECIDE THIS WAS WAY TOO DANGEROUS?
THESE ARE THE BLUEPRINTS, HAWKEYE, NOT THE CUBE ITSELF. TO ANYONE ELSE THEY'D BE GIBBERISH, BUT A.I.M. IS A CULT OF THE WORLD'S SMARTEST INTELLECTS.
IT'S ONLY A MATTER OF DAYS BEFORE THEY FINISH CONSTRUCTION.
WOW. ANY IDEA WHAT THEY PLAN TO DO WITH IT?
OH, COME ON, STUPID. WHAT DO YOU THINK THEY'RE GOING TO DO? REDECORATE?
A.I.M. IS AN INTELLECT-BASED TERROR GROUP. THEY HATE THE WORLD DEMOCRACY HAS GIVEN US AND SO THEY'RE PLANNING SOMETHING RADICALLY DIFFERENT.
BUT BEFORE WE ALL GO SLITTING OUR WRISTS I SHOULD POINT OUT THAT THEY'RE STILL FORTY-EIGHT HOURS FROM COMPLETING THIS THING.
AS LONG AS WE'RE PACKING STARK'S TECH AND MY PLAN, THIS ENTIRE THREAT SHOULD BE OVER BY MIDNIGHT, BOYS AND GIRLS.
WHAT DO YOU MEAN? WHAT'S THE PLAN?
WE SHOOT THE BASTARDS.

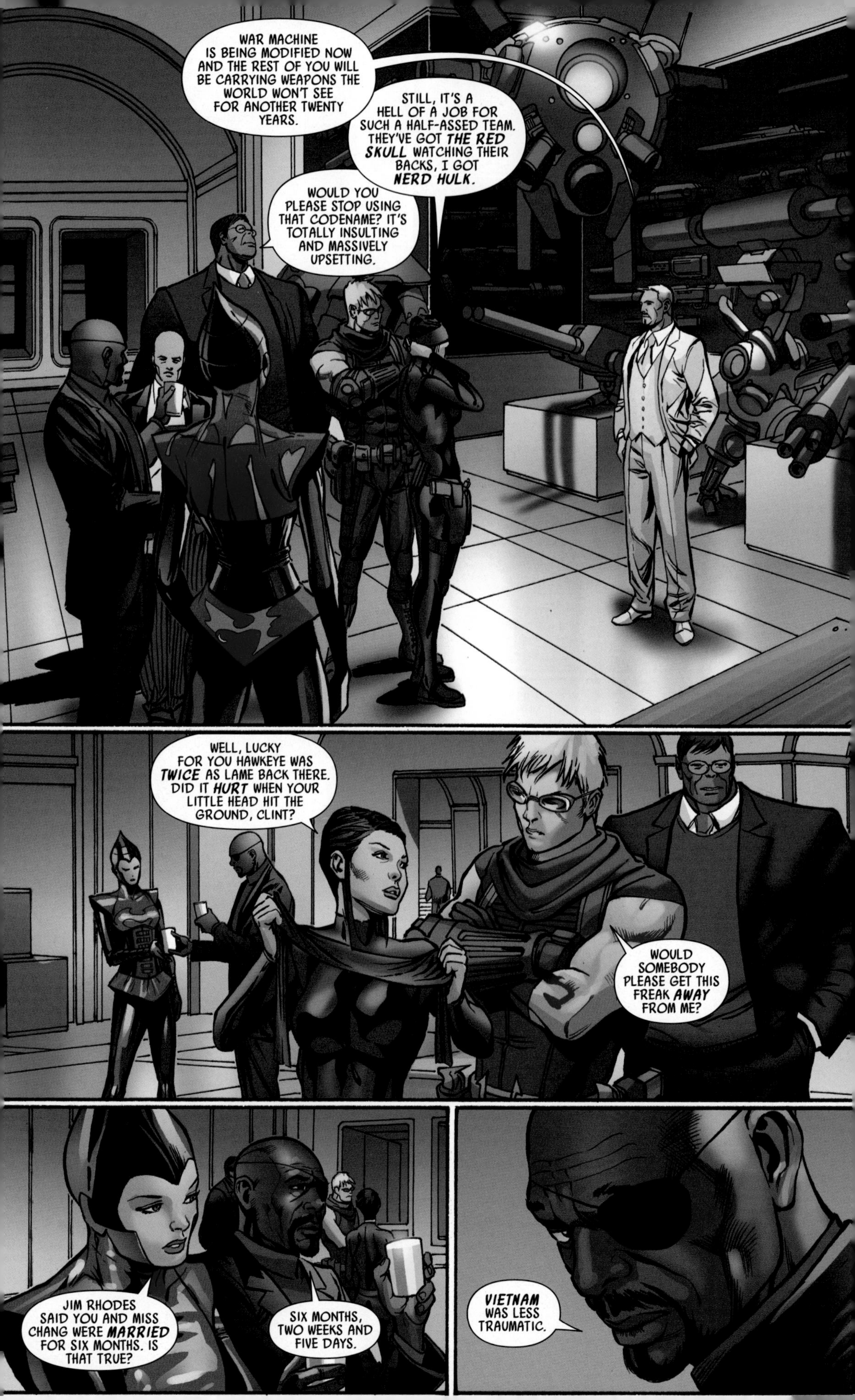
WAR MACHINE IS BEING MODIFIED NOW AND THE REST OF YOU WILL BE CARRYING WEAPONS THE WORLD WON'T SEE FOR ANOTHER TWENTY YEARS.
STILL, IT'S A HELL OF A JOB FOR SUCH A HALF-ASSED TEAM. THEY'VE GOT THE RED SKULL WATCHING THEIR BACKS, I GOT NERD HULK.
WOULD YOU PLEASE STOP USING THAT CODENAME? IT'S TOTALLY INSULTING AND MASSIVELY UPSETTING.
WELL, LUCKY FOR YOU HAWKEYE WAS TWICE AS LAME BACK THERE. DID IT HURT WHEN YOUR LITTLE HEAD HIT THE GROUND, CLINT?
WOULD SOMEBODY PLEASE GET THIS FREAK AWAY FROM ME?
JIM RHODES SAID YOU AND MISS CHANG WERE MARRIED FOR SIX MONTHS. IS THAT TRUE?
SIX MONTHS, TWO WEEKS AND FIVE DAYS.
VIETNAM WAS LESS TRAUMATIC.

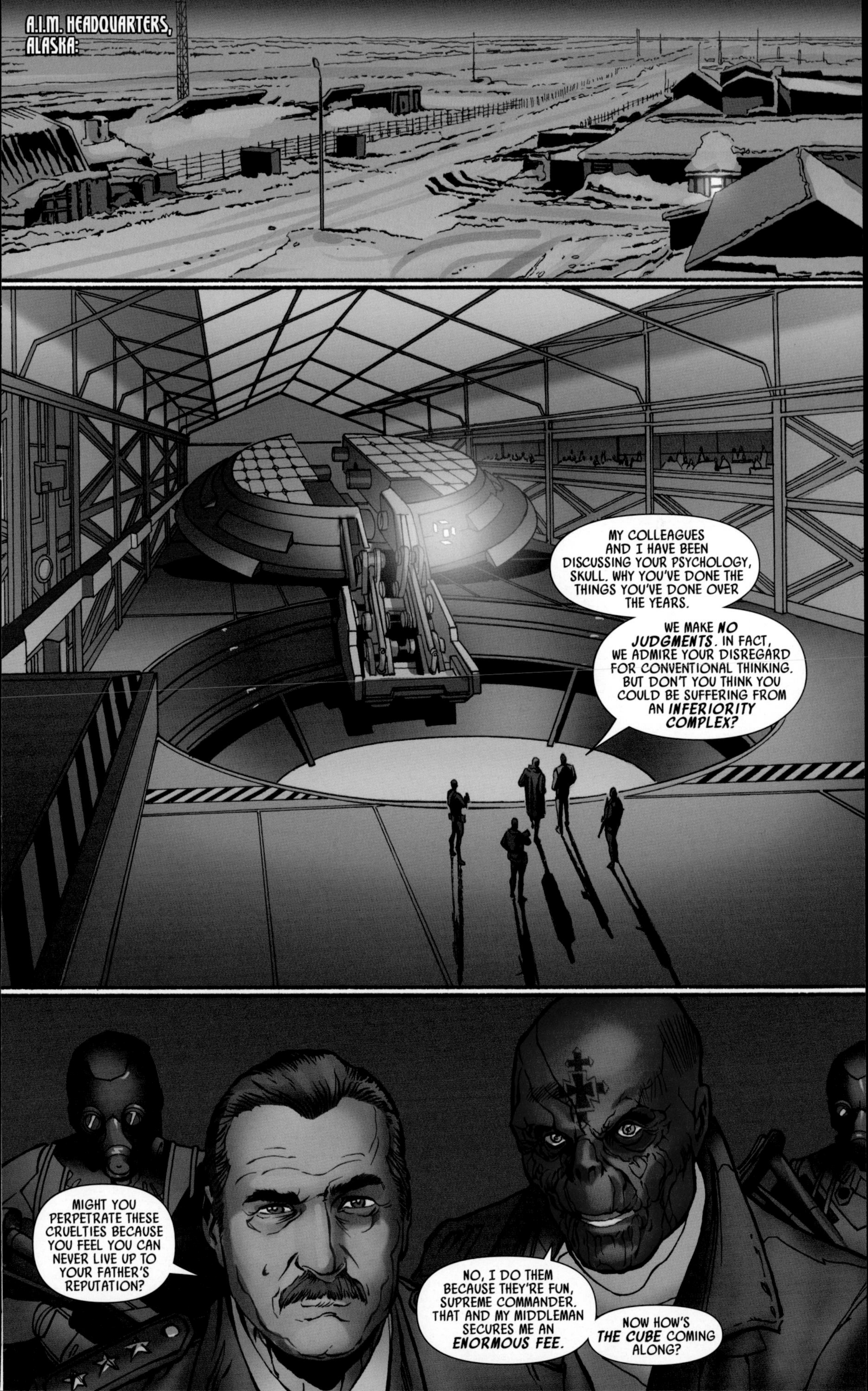
A.I.M. HEADQUARTERS, ALASKA:
MY COLLEAGUES AND I HAVE BEEN DISCUSSING YOUR PSYCHOLOGY, SKULL. WHY YOU'VE DONE THE THINGS YOU'VE DONE OVER THE YEARS.
WE MAKE NO JUDGMENTS. IN FACT, WE ADMIRE YOUR DISREGARD FOR CONVENTIONAL THINKING. BUT DON'T YOU THINK YOU COULD BE SUFFERING FROM AN INFERIORITY COMPLEX?
MIGHT YOU PERPETRATE THESE CRUELTIES BECAUSE YOU FEEL YOU CAN NEVER LIVE UP TO YOUR FATHER'S REPUTATION?
NO, I DO THEM BECAUSE THEY'RE FUN, SUPREME COMMANDER. THAT AND MY MIDDLEMAN SECURES ME AN ENORMOUS FEE.
NOW HOW'S THE CUBE COMING ALONG?

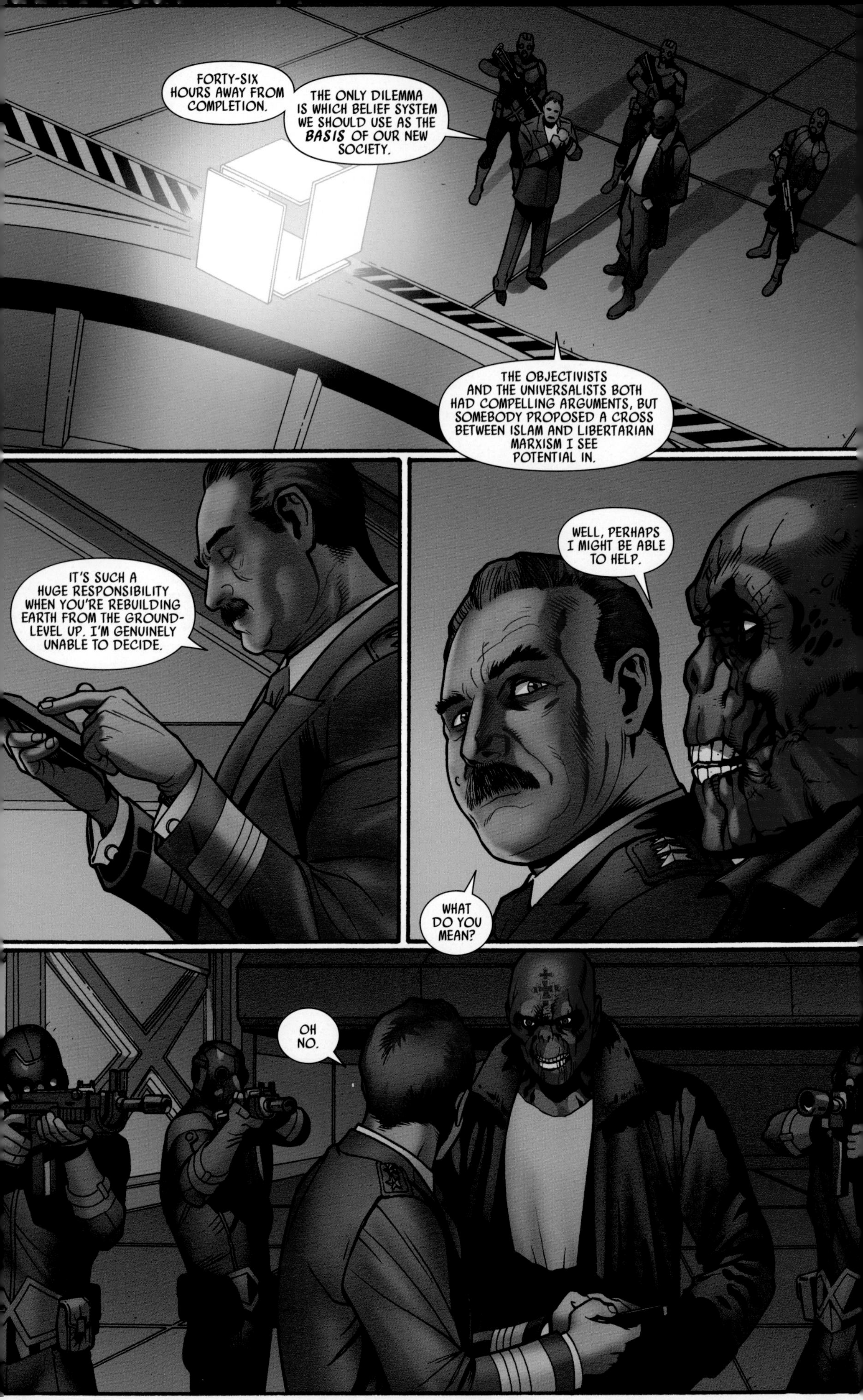

FORTY-SIX HOURS AWAY FROM COMPLETION.
THE ONLY DILEMMA IS WHICH BELIEF SYSTEM WE SHOULD USE AS THE *BASIS* OF OUR NEW SOCIETY.
THE OBJECTIVISTS AND THE UNIVERSALISTS BOTH HAD COMPELLING ARGUMENTS, BUT SOMEBODY PROPOSED A CROSS BETWEEN ISLAM AND LIBERTARIAN MARXISM I SEE POTENTIAL IN.
IT'S SUCH A HUGE RESPONSIBILITY WHEN YOU'RE REBUILDING EARTH FROM THE GROUND-LEVEL UP. I'M GENUINELY UNABLE TO DECIDE.
WELL, PERHAPS I MIGHT BE ABLE TO HELP.
WHAT DO YOU MEAN?
OH NO.

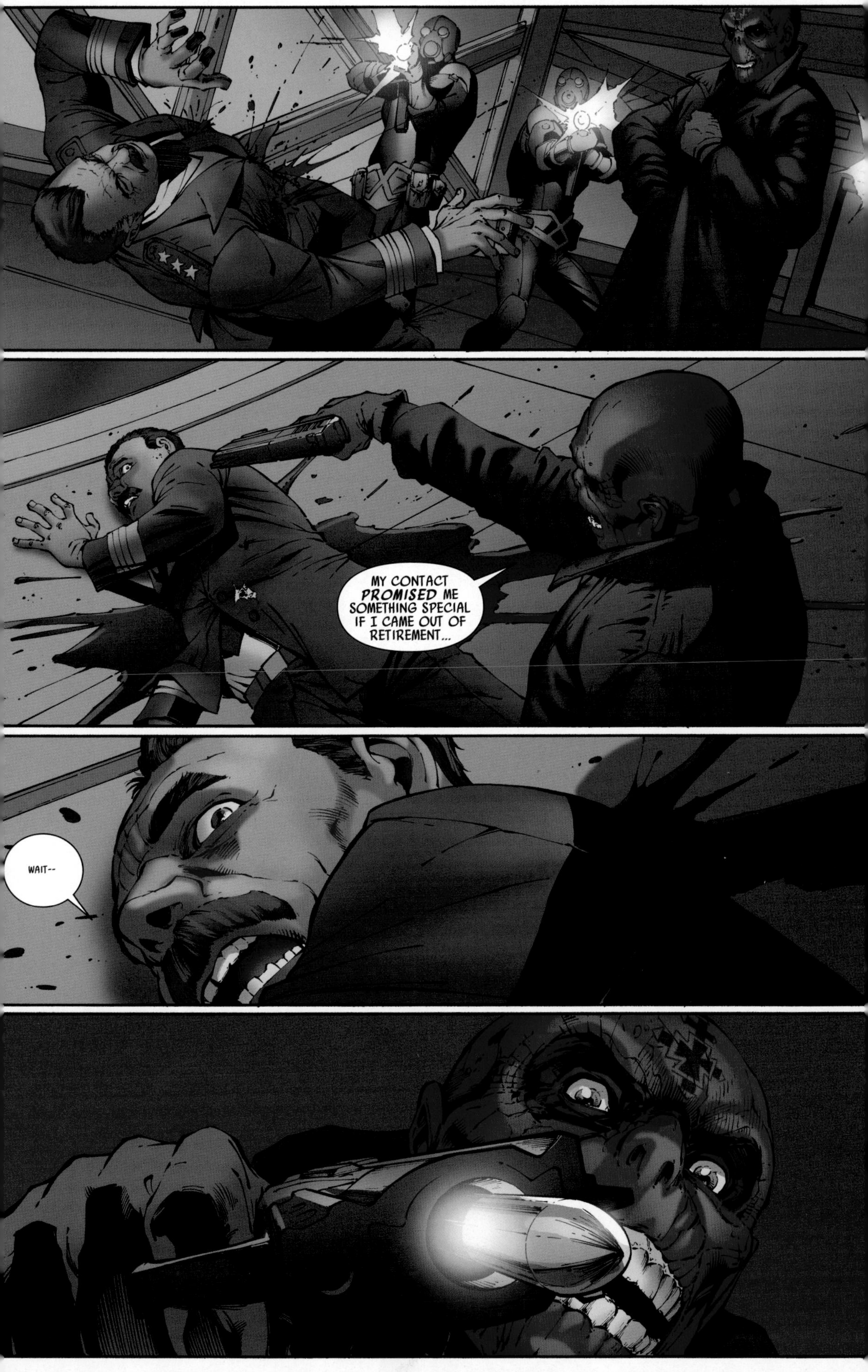
MY CONTACT PROMISED ME SOMETHING SPECIAL IF I CAME OUT OF RETIREMENT...
WAIT--

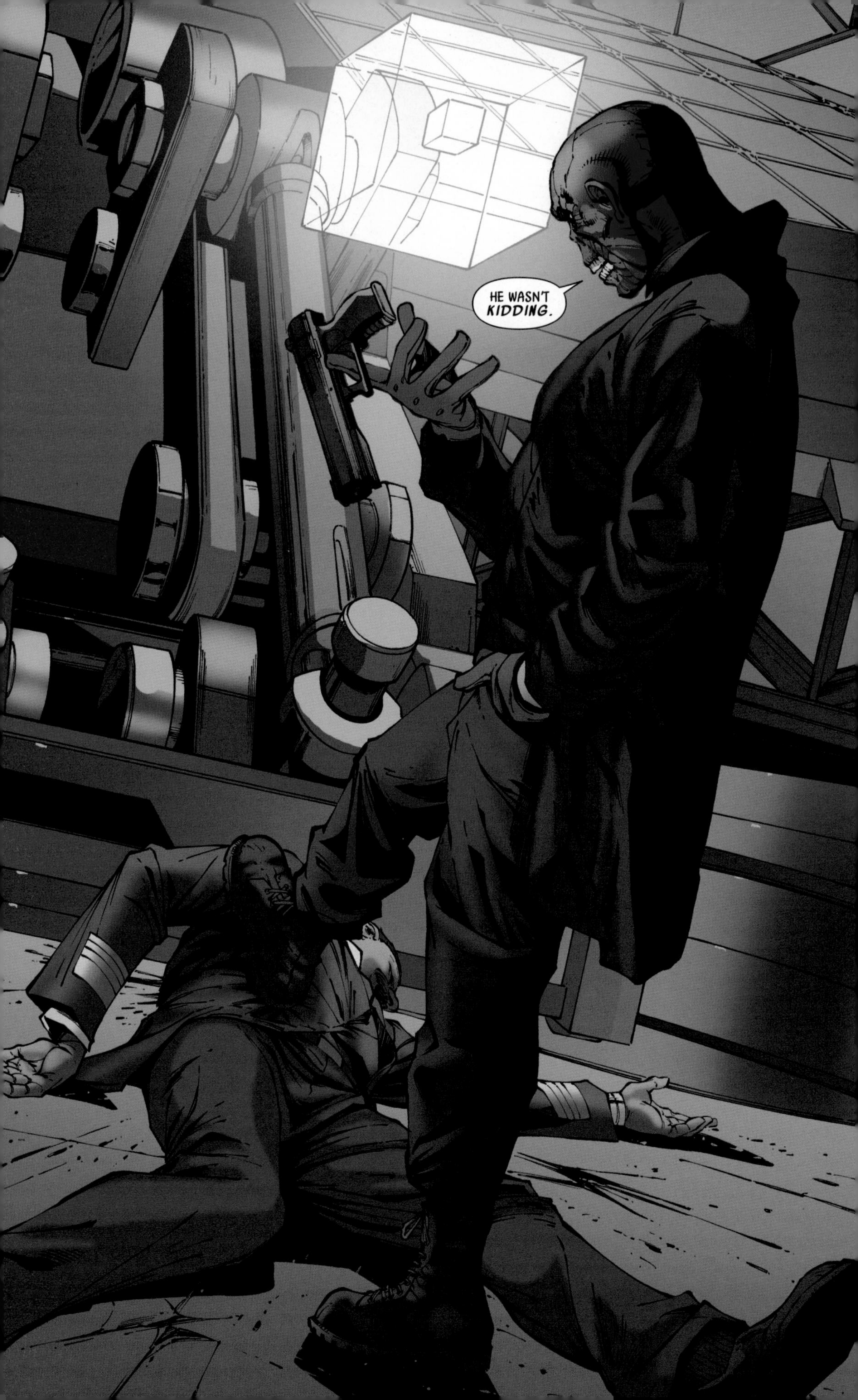
HE WASN'T KIDDING.

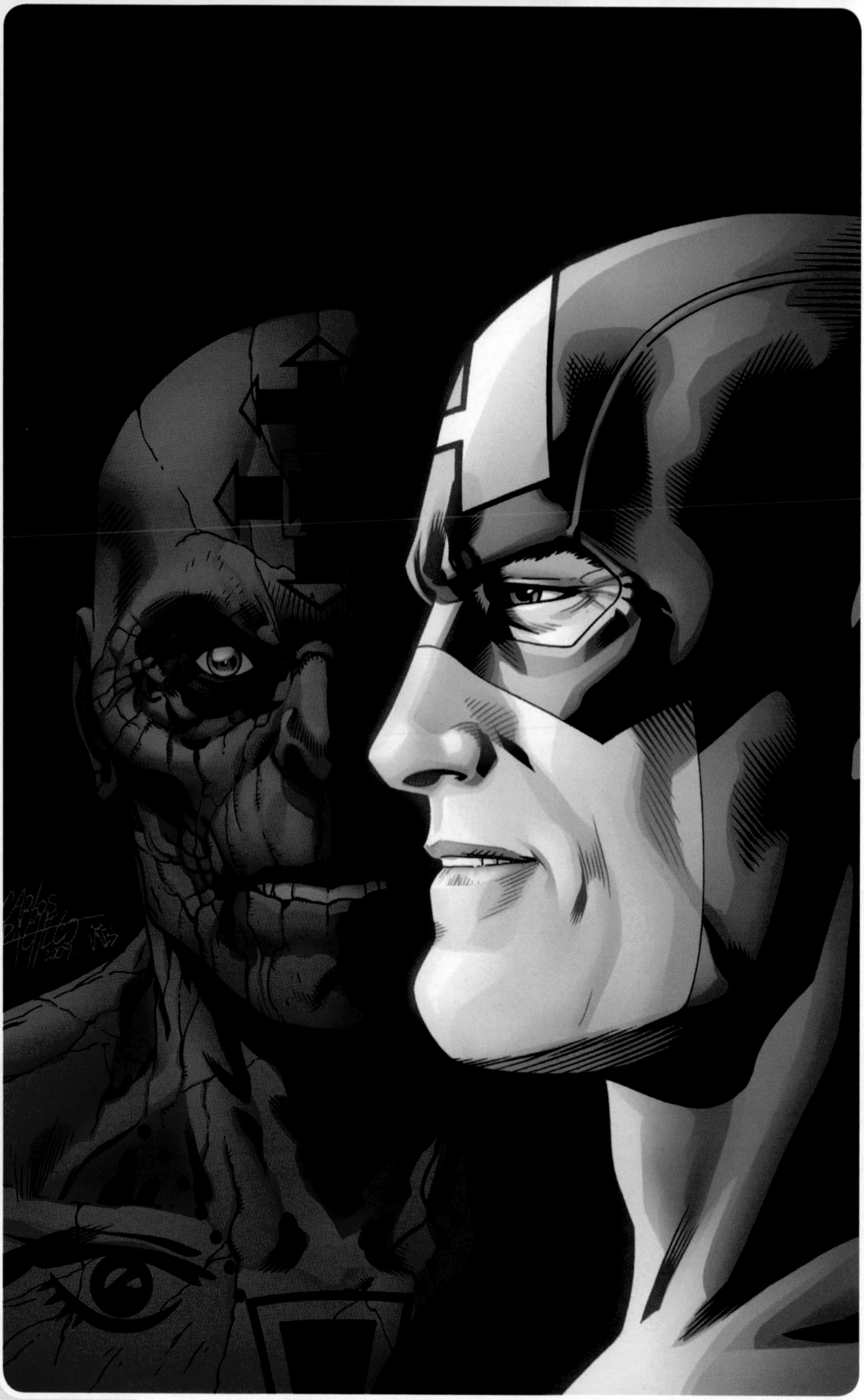

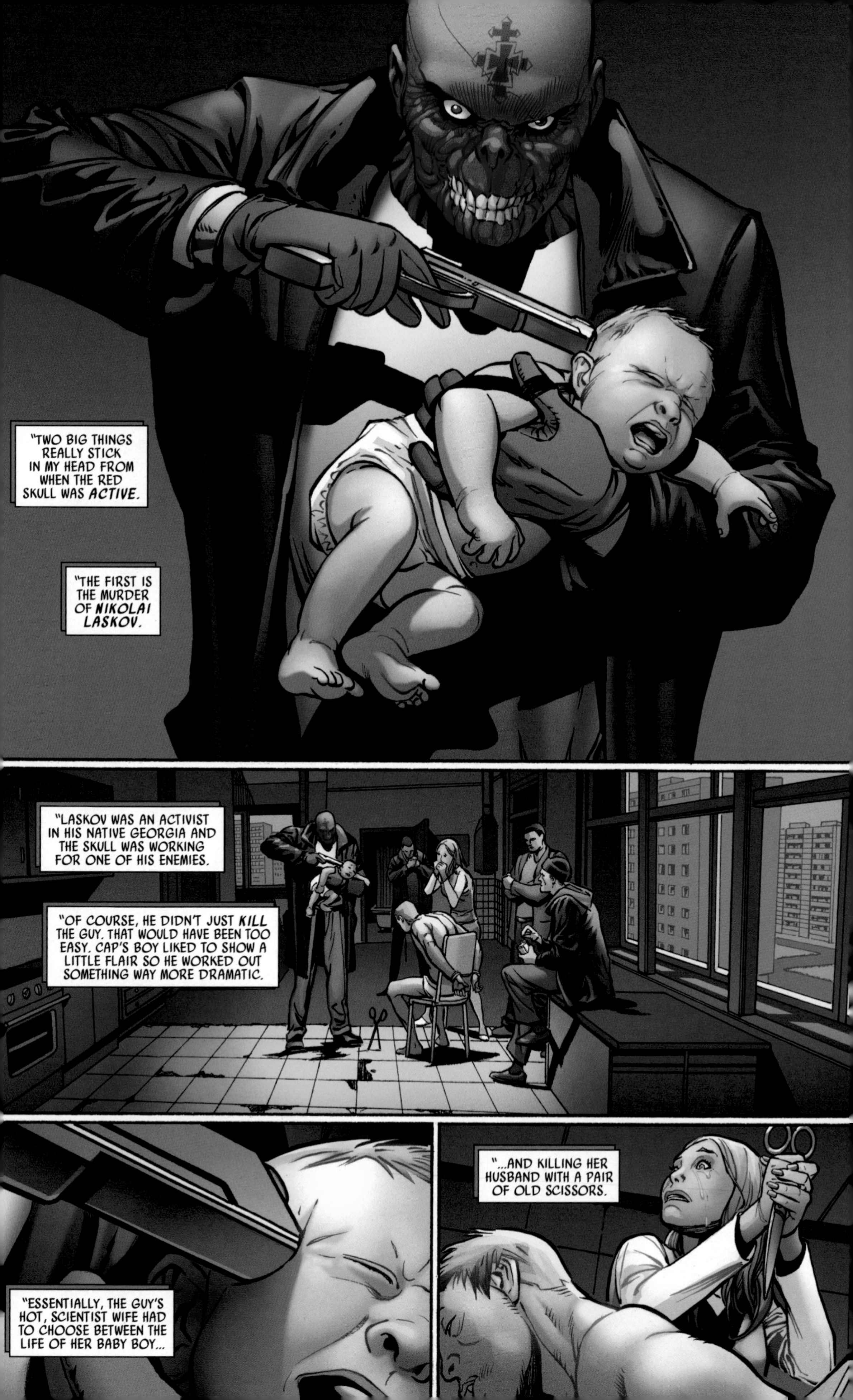
"TWO BIG THINGS REALLY STICK IN MY HEAD FROM WHEN THE RED SKULL WAS ACTIVE.
"THE FIRST IS THE MURDER OF NIKOLAI LASKOV.
"LASKOV WAS AN ACTIVIST IN HIS NATIVE GEORGIA AND THE SKULL WAS WORKING FOR ONE OF HIS ENEMIES.
"OF COURSE, HE DIDN'T JUST KILL THE GUY. THAT WOULD HAVE BEEN TOO EASY. CAP'S BOY LIKED TO SHOW A LITTLE FLAIR SO HE WORKED OUT SOMETHING WAY MORE DRAMATIC.
"ESSENTIALLY, THE GUY'S HOT, SCIENTIST WIFE HAD TO CHOOSE BETWEEN THE LIFE OF HER BABY BOY...
"...AND KILLING HER HUSBAND WITH A PAIR OF OLD SCISSORS.

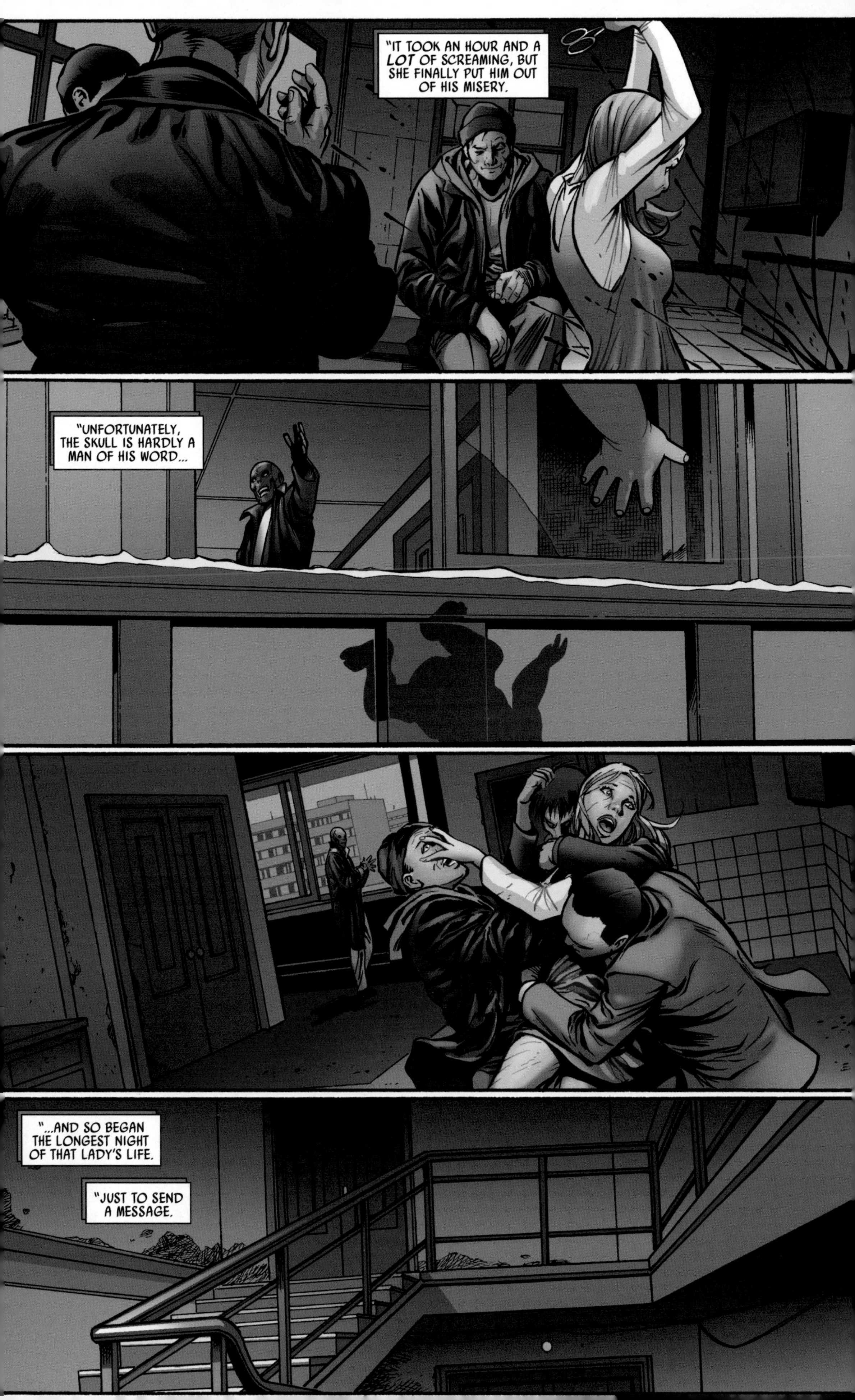
"IT TOOK AN HOUR AND A *LOT* OF SCREAMING, BUT SHE FINALLY PUT HIM OUT OF HIS MISERY.
"UNFORTUNATELY, THE SKULL IS HARDLY A MAN OF HIS WORD...
"...AND SO BEGAN THE LONGEST NIGHT OF THAT LADY'S LIFE.
"JUST TO SEND A MESSAGE.

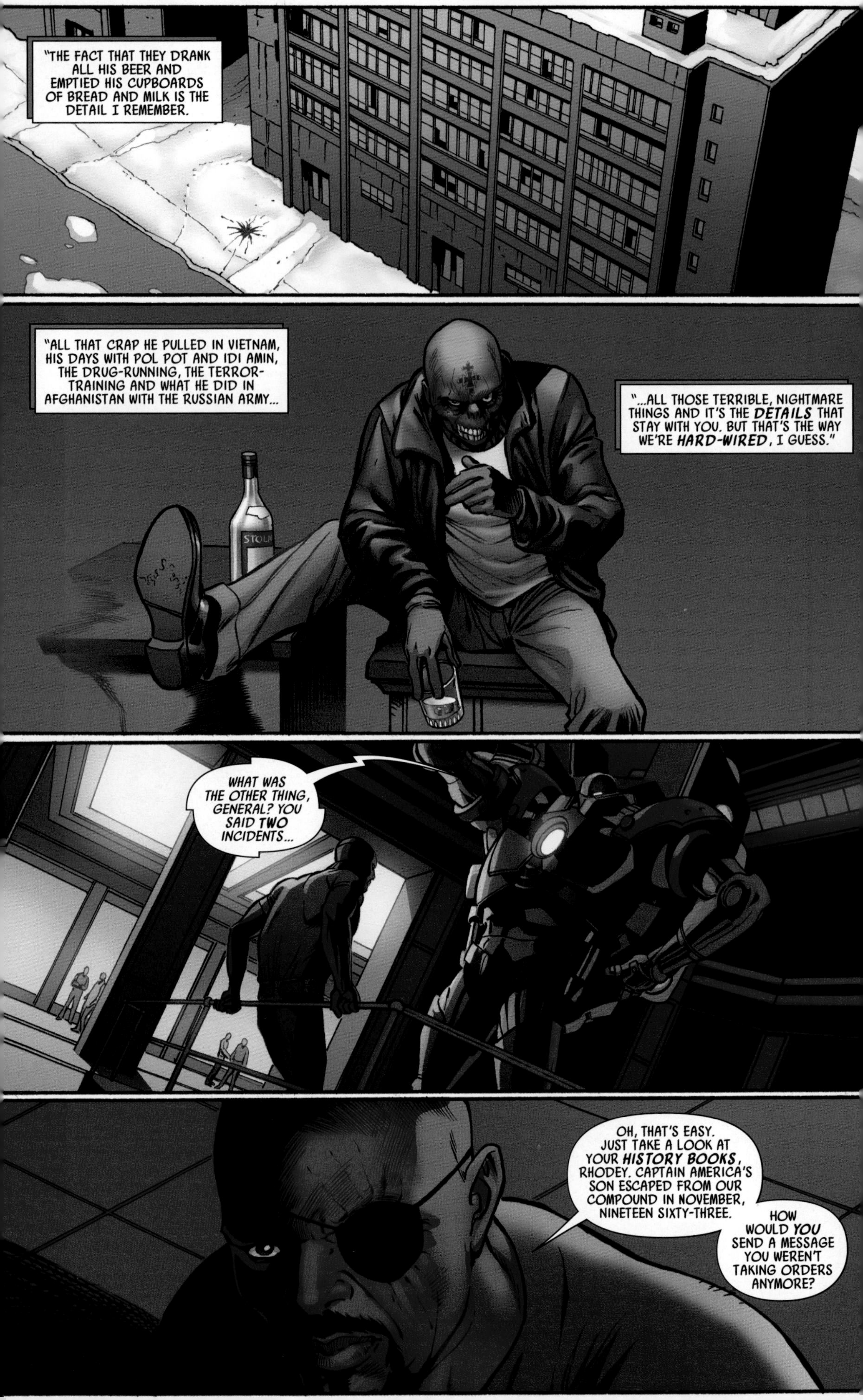
"THE FACT THAT THEY DRANK ALL HIS BEER AND EMPTIED HIS CUPBOARDS OF BREAD AND MILK IS THE DETAIL I REMEMBER.
"ALL THAT CRAP HE PULLED IN VIETNAM, HIS DAYS WITH POL POT AND IDI AMIN, THE DRUG-RUNNING, THE TERROR-TRAINING AND WHAT HE DID IN AFGHANISTAN WITH THE RUSSIAN ARMY...
"...ALL THOSE TERRIBLE, NIGHTMARE THINGS AND IT'S THE DETAILS THAT STAY WITH YOU. BUT THAT'S THE WAY WE'RE HARD-WIRED, I GUESS."
WHAT WAS THE OTHER THING, GENERAL? YOU SAID TWO INCIDENTS...
OH, THAT'S EASY. JUST TAKE A LOOK AT YOUR HISTORY BOOKS, RHODEY. CAPTAIN AMERICA'S SON ESCAPED FROM OUR COMPOUND IN NOVEMBER, NINETEEN SIXTY-THREE.
HOW WOULD YOU SEND A MESSAGE YOU WEREN'T TAKING ORDERS ANYMORE?

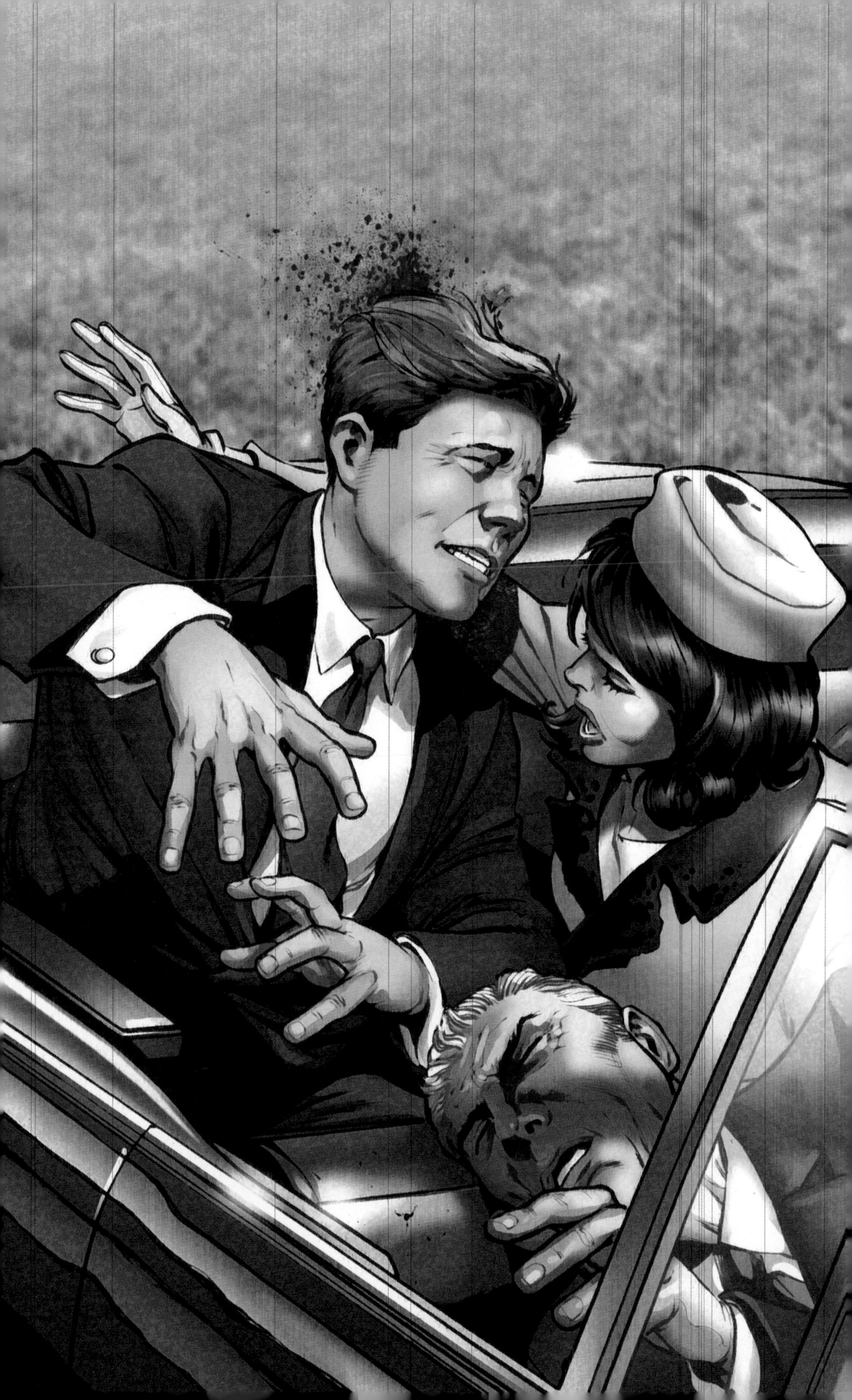

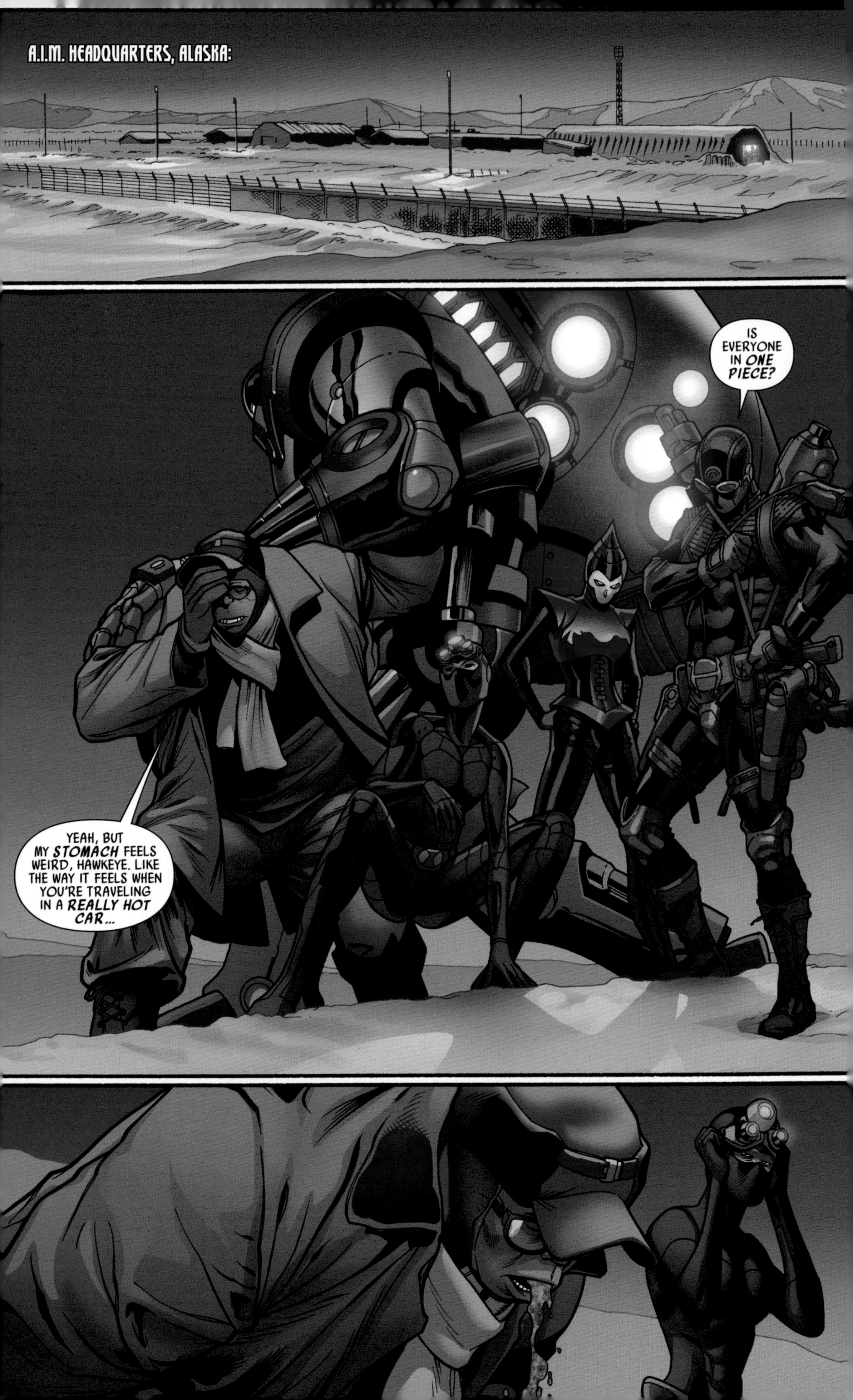
A.I.M. HEADQUARTERS, ALASKA:
IS EVERYONE IN ONE PIECE?
YEAH, BUT MY STOMACH FEELS WEIRD, HAWKEYE. LIKE THE WAY IT FEELS WHEN YOU'RE TRAVELING IN A REALLY HOT CAR...

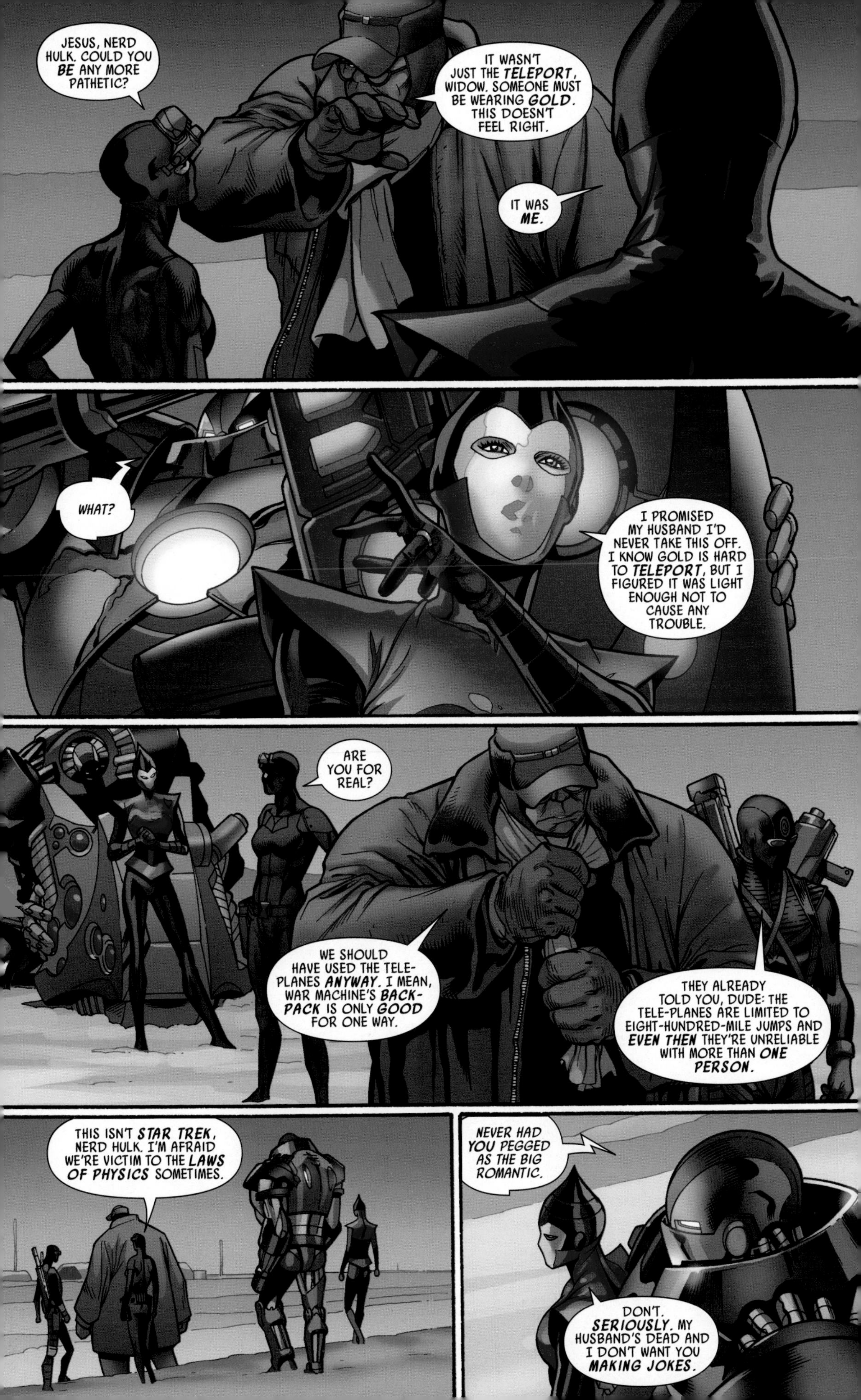

JESUS, NERD HULK. COULD YOU BE ANY MORE PATHETIC?
IT WASN'T JUST THE TELEPORT, WIDOW. SOMEONE MUST BE WEARING GOLD. THIS DOESN'T FEEL RIGHT.
IT WAS ME.
WHAT?
I PROMISED MY HUSBAND I'D NEVER TAKE THIS OFF. I KNOW GOLD IS HARD TO TELEPORT, BUT I FIGURED IT WAS LIGHT ENOUGH NOT TO CAUSE ANY TROUBLE.
ARE YOU FOR REAL?
WE SHOULD HAVE USED THE TELE-PLANES ANYWAY. I MEAN, WAR MACHINE'S BACK-PACK IS ONLY GOOD FOR ONE WAY.
THEY ALREADY TOLD YOU, DUDE: THE TELE-PLANES ARE LIMITED TO EIGHT-HUNDRED-MILE JUMPS AND EVEN THEN THEY'RE UNRELIABLE WITH MORE THAN ONE PERSON.
THIS ISN'T STAR TREK, NERD HULK. I'M AFRAID WE'RE VICTIM TO THE LAWS OF PHYSICS SOMETIMES.
NEVER HAD YOU PEGGED AS THE BIG ROMANTIC.
DON'T. SERIOUSLY. MY HUSBAND'S DEAD AND I DON'T WANT YOU MAKING JOKES.

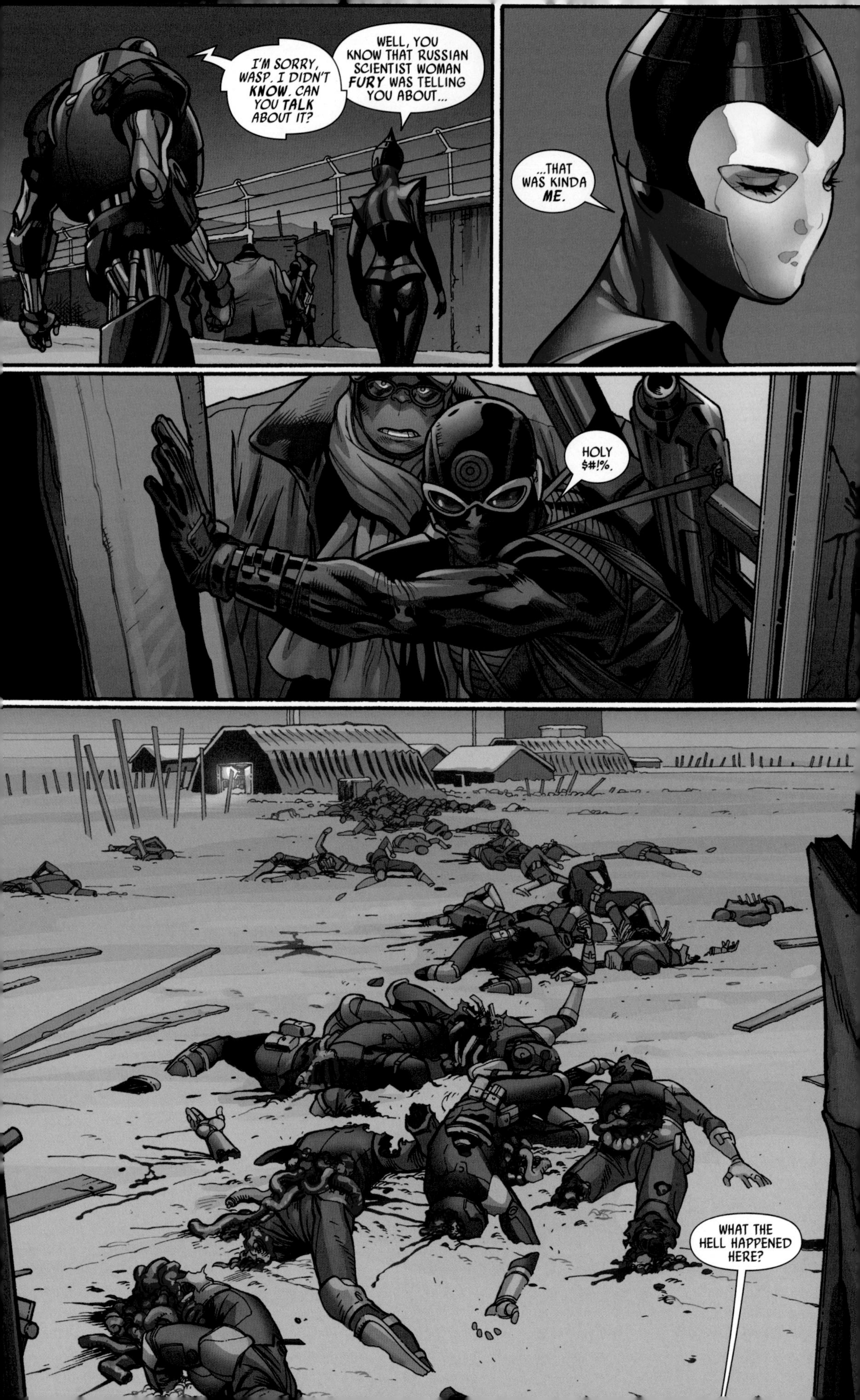
I'M SORRY, WASP. I DIDN'T KNOW. CAN YOU TALK ABOUT IT?
WELL, YOU KNOW THAT RUSSIAN SCIENTIST WOMAN FURY WAS TELLING YOU ABOUT...
...THAT WAS KINDA ME.
HOLY $#!%.
WHAT THE HELL HAPPENED HERE?

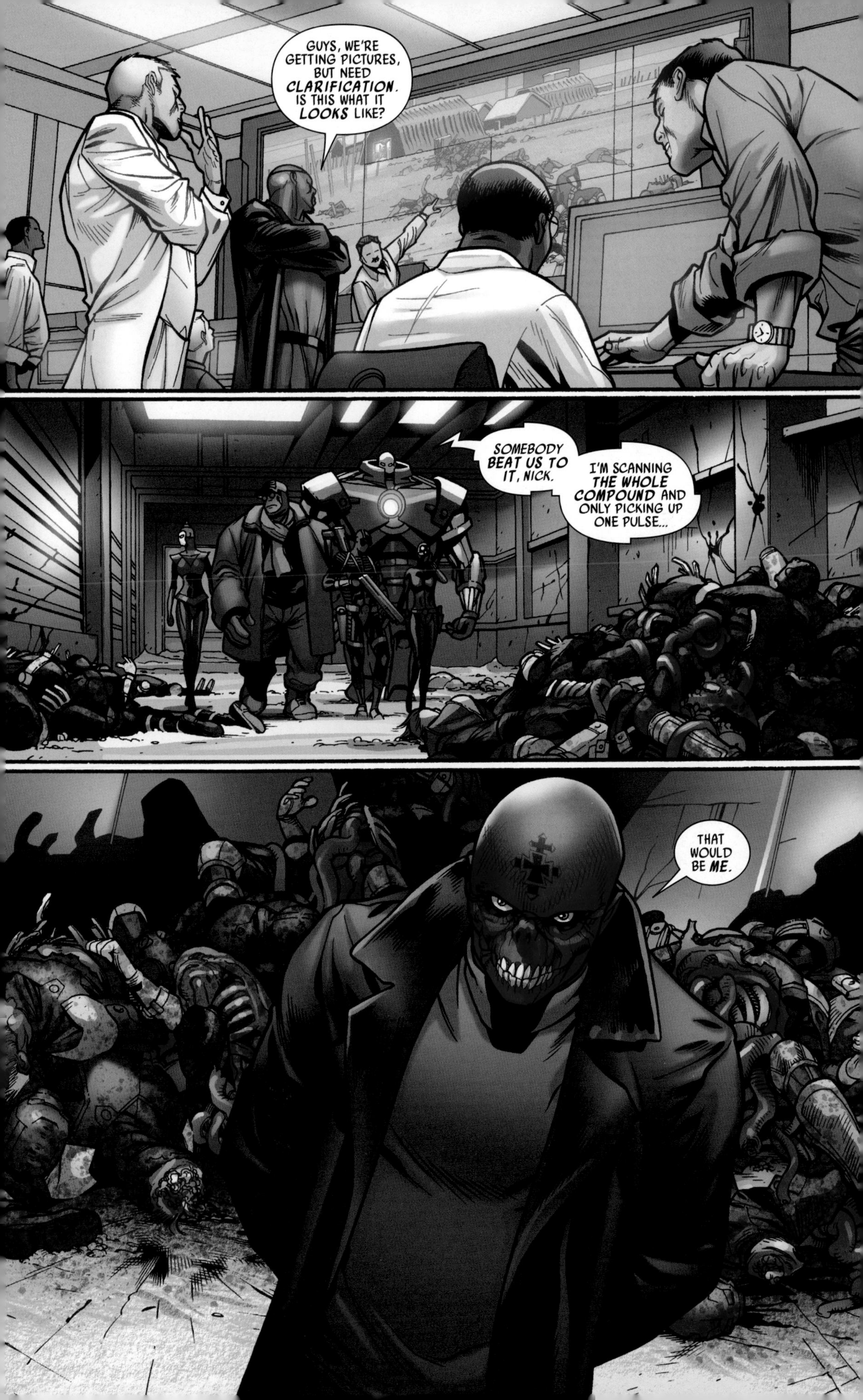
GUYS, WE'RE GETTING PICTURES, BUT NEED CLARIFICATION. IS THIS WHAT IT LOOKS LIKE?
SOMEBODY BEAT US TO IT, NICK.
I'M SCANNING THE WHOLE COMPOUND AND ONLY PICKING UP ONE PULSE...
THAT WOULD BE ME.

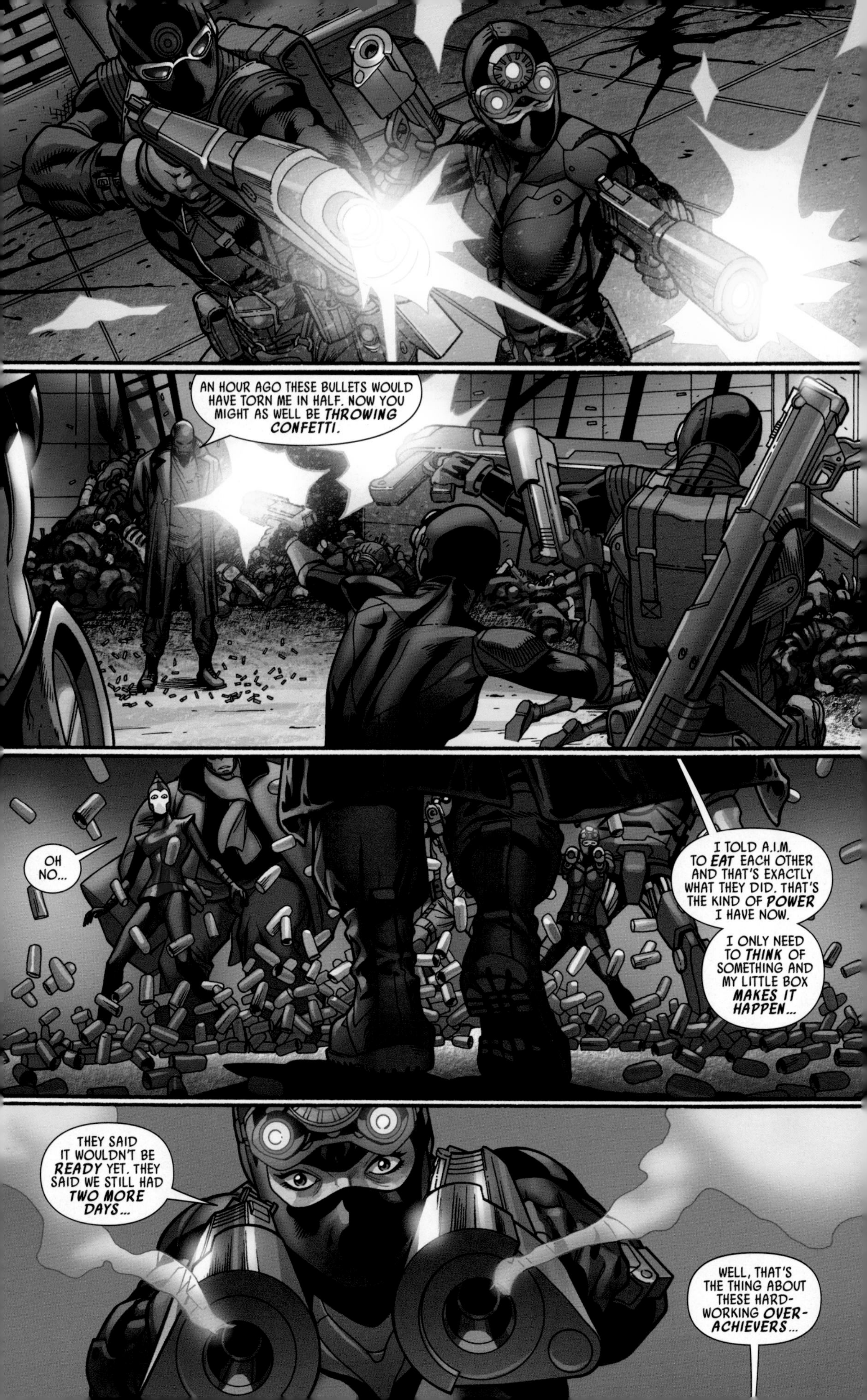
AN HOUR AGO THESE BULLETS WOULD HAVE TORN ME IN HALF. NOW YOU MIGHT AS WELL BE THROWING CONFETTI.
OH NO...
I TOLD A.I.M. TO EAT EACH OTHER AND THAT'S EXACTLY WHAT THEY DID. THAT'S THE KIND OF POWER I HAVE NOW.
I ONLY NEED TO THINK OF SOMETHING AND MY LITTLE BOX MAKES IT HAPPEN...
THEY SAID IT WOULDN'T BE READY YET. THEY SAID WE STILL HAD TWO MORE DAYS...
WELL, THAT'S THE THING ABOUT THESE HARD-WORKING OVER-ACHIEVERS...

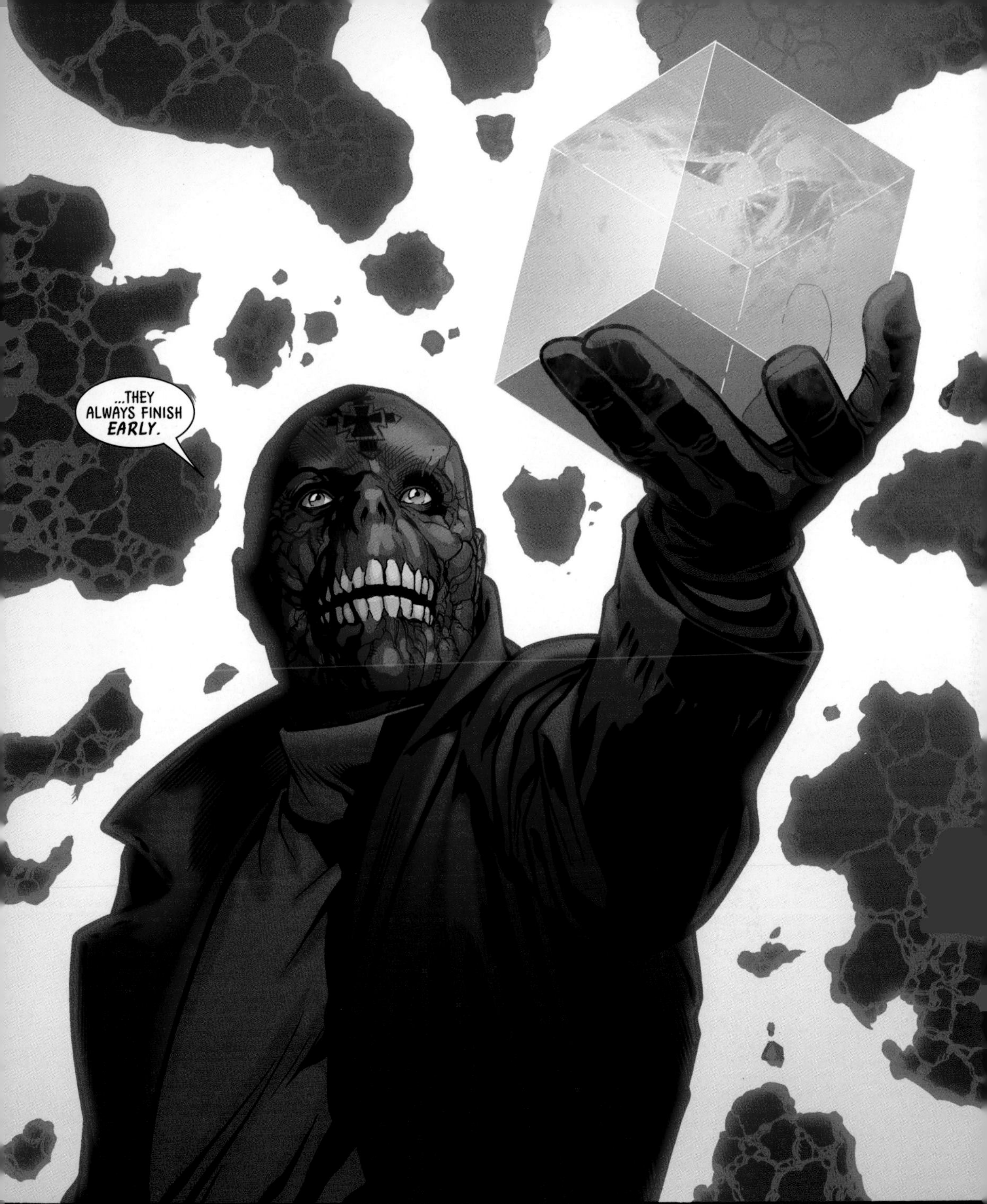
...THEY ALWAYS FINISH EARLY.
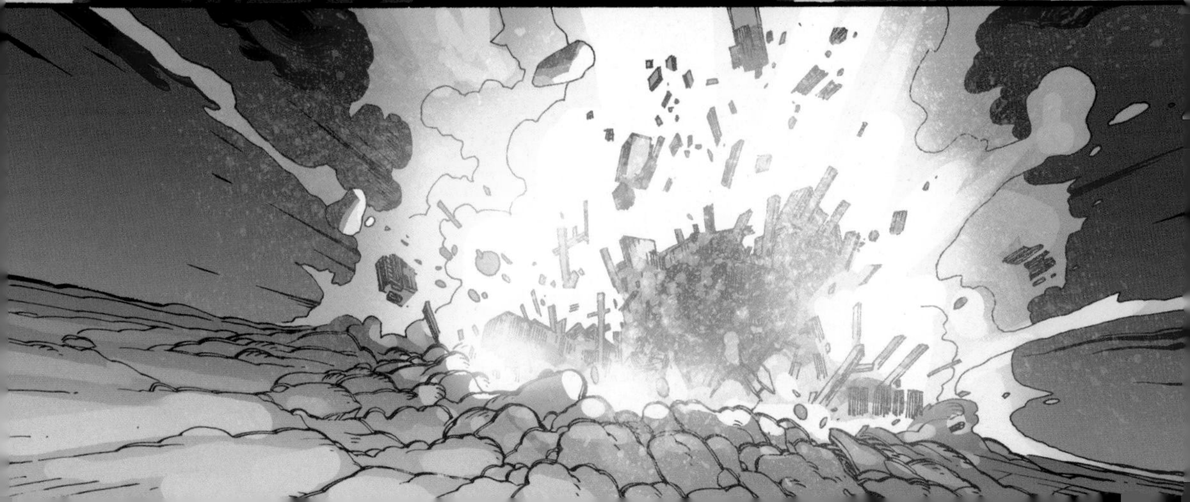

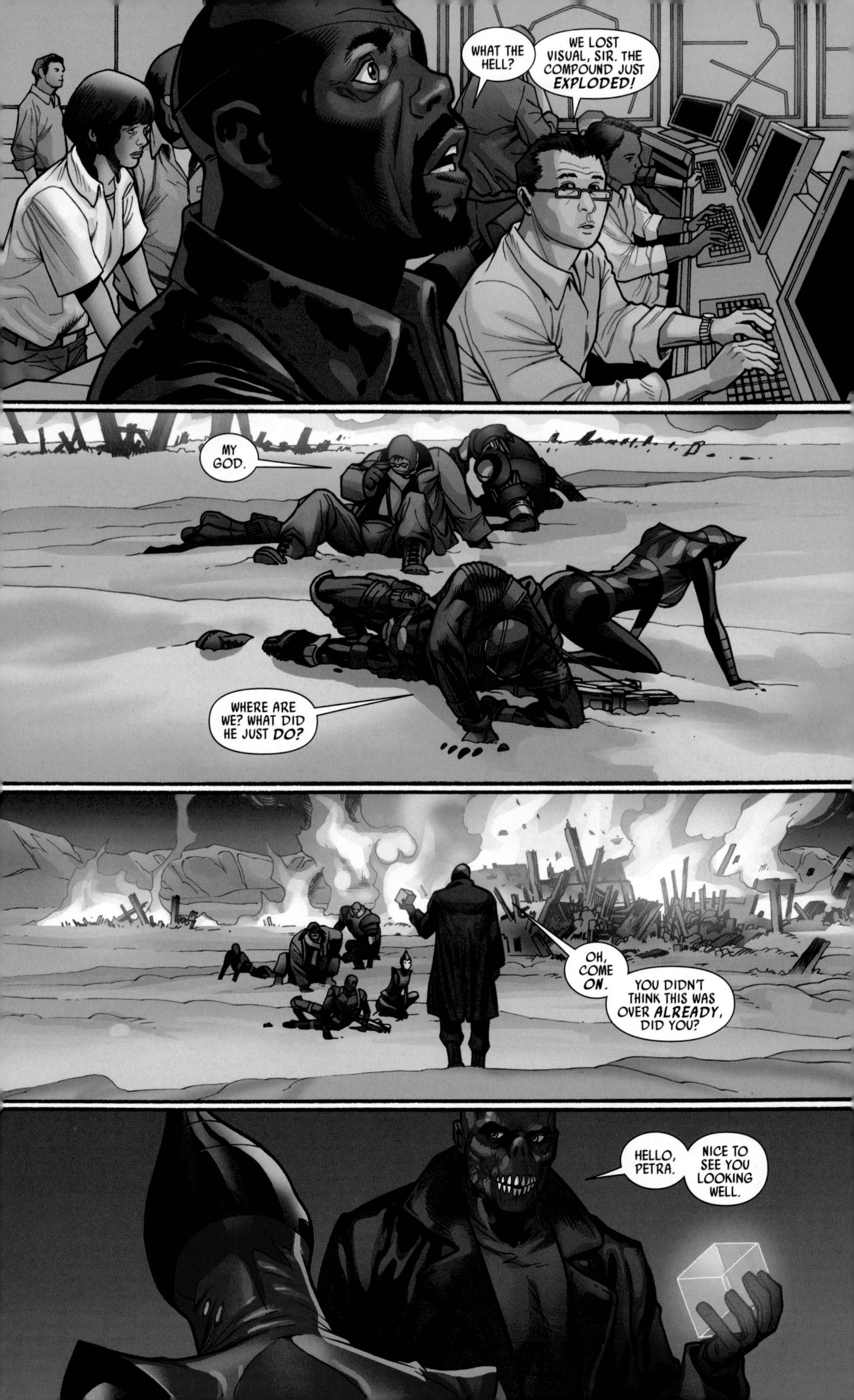
WHAT THE HELL?
WE LOST VISUAL, SIR. THE COMPOUND JUST EXPLODED!
MY GOD.
WHERE ARE WE? WHAT DID HE JUST DO?
OH, COME ON.
YOU DIDN'T THINK THIS WAS OVER ALREADY, DID YOU?
HELLO, PETRA.
NICE TO SEE YOU LOOKING WELL.

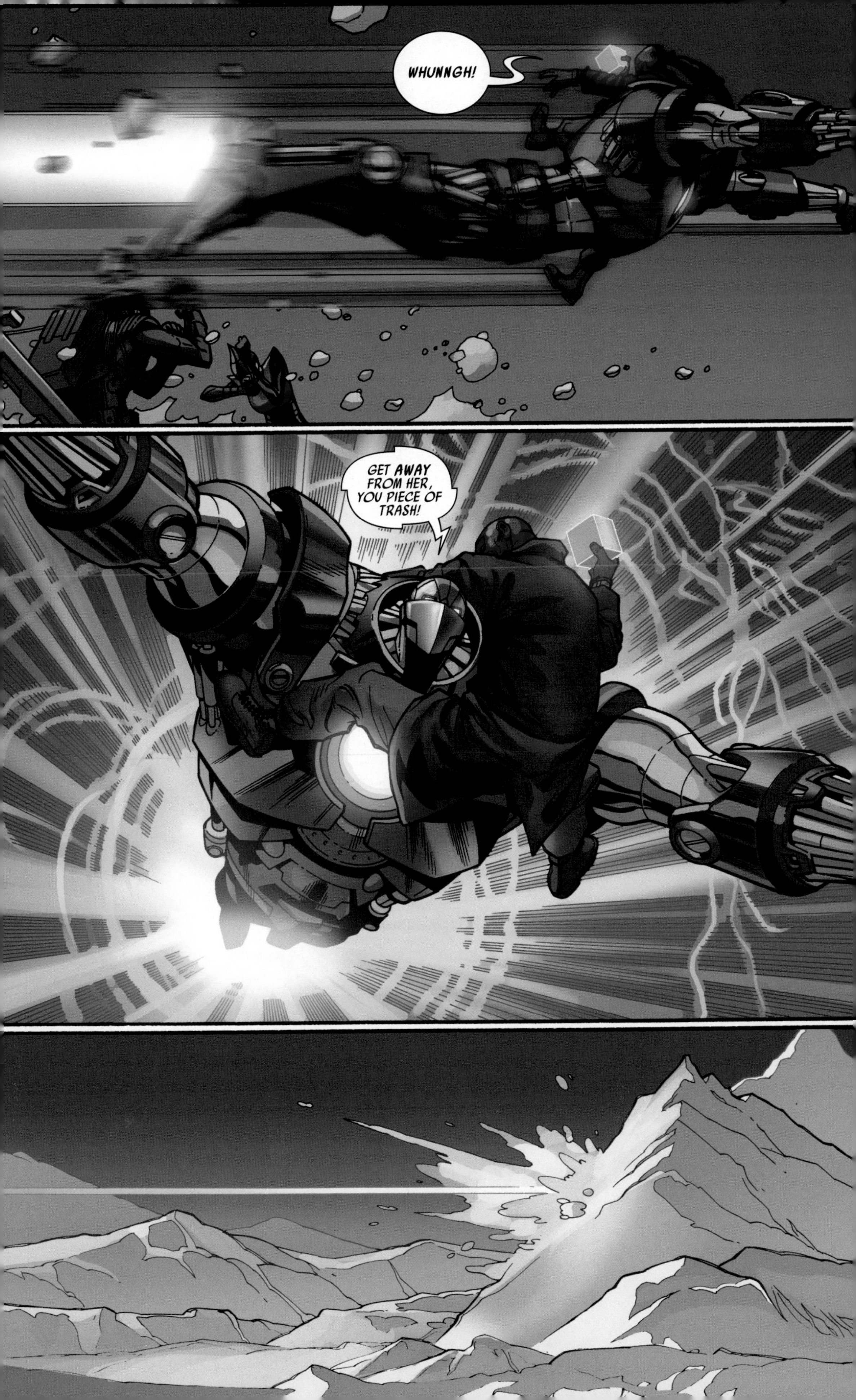
WHUNNGH!
GET AWAY FROM HER, YOU PIECE OF TRASH!

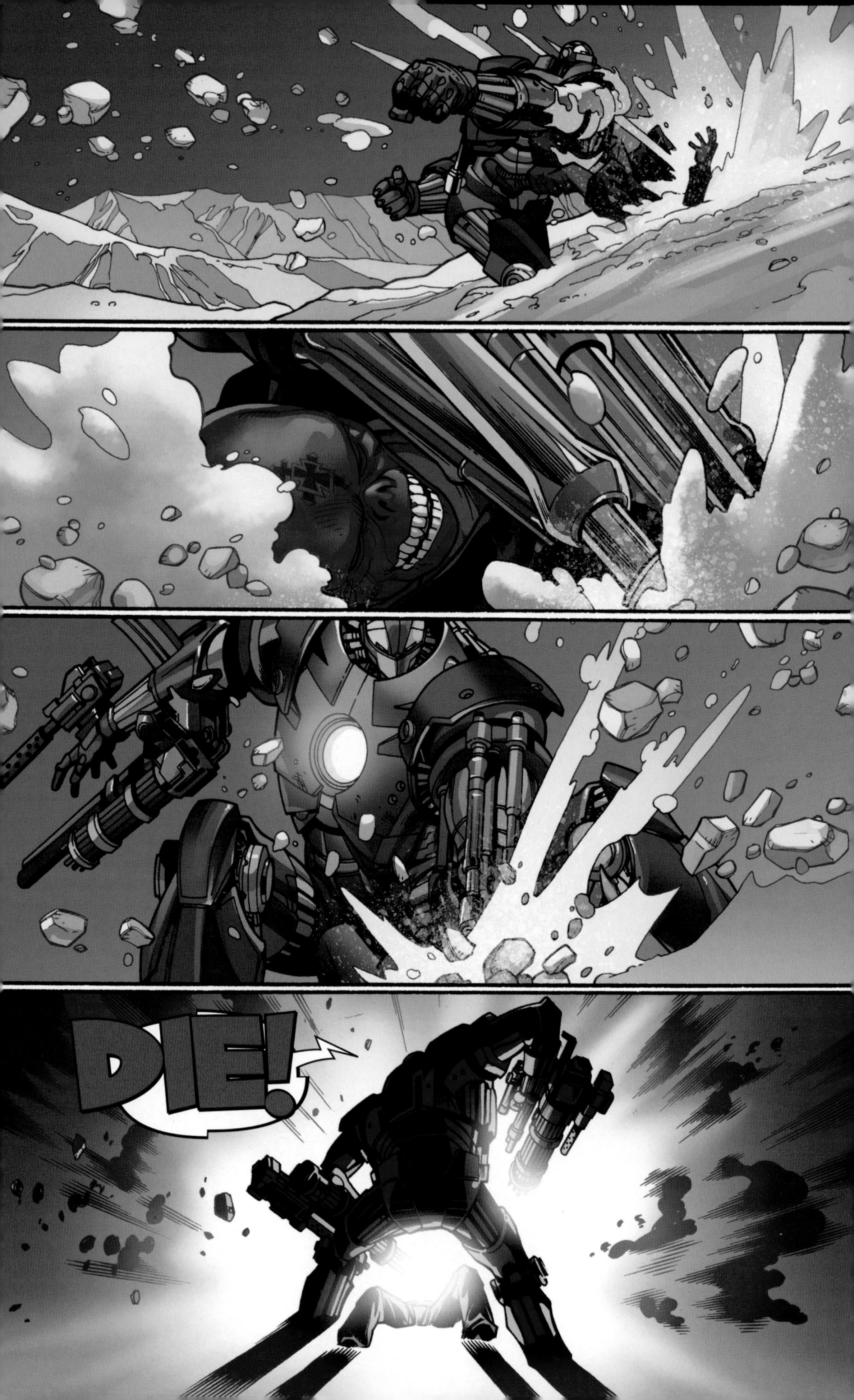
DIE!

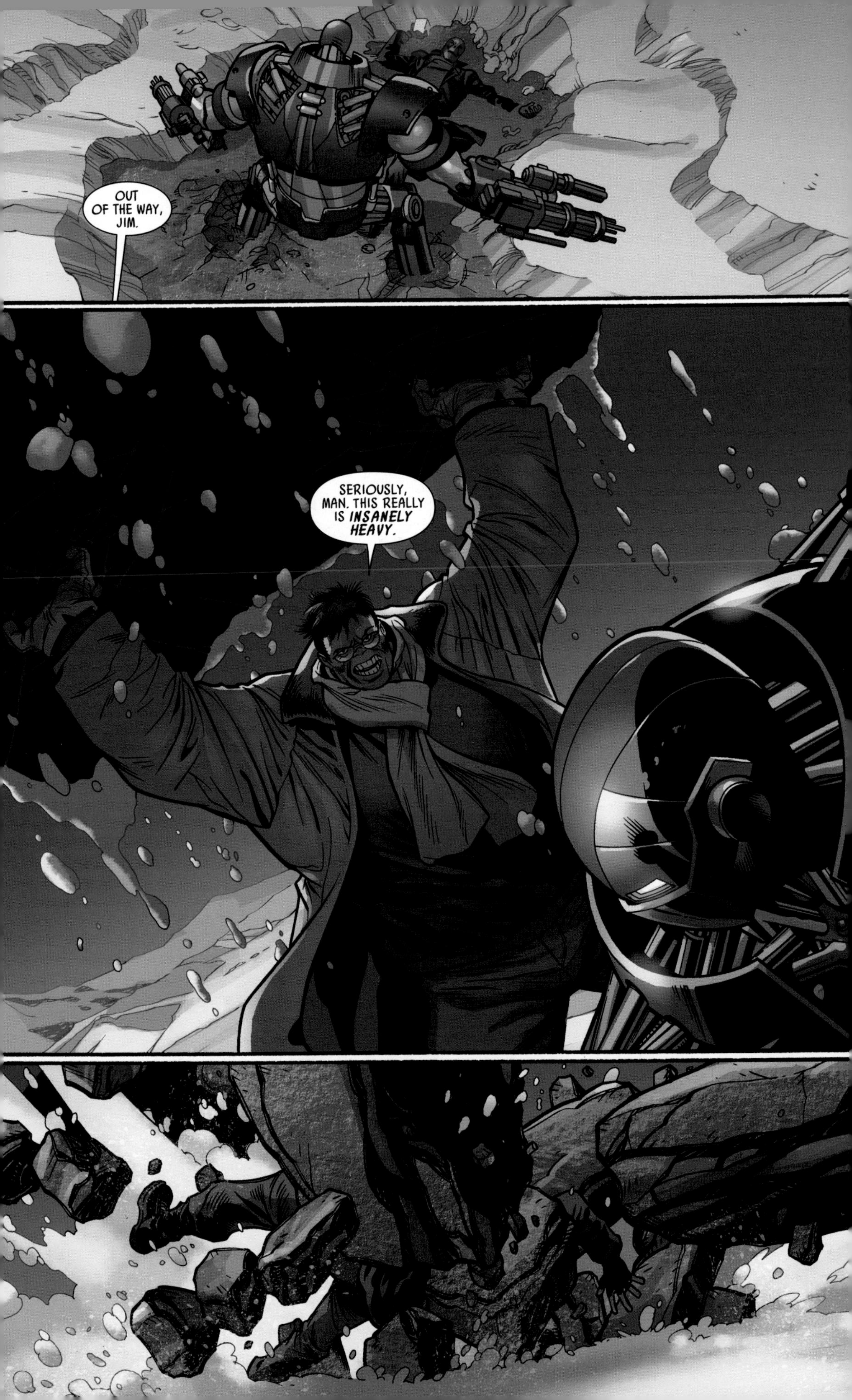
OUT OF THE WAY, JIM.
SERIOUSLY, MAN. THIS REALLY IS INSANELY HEAVY.

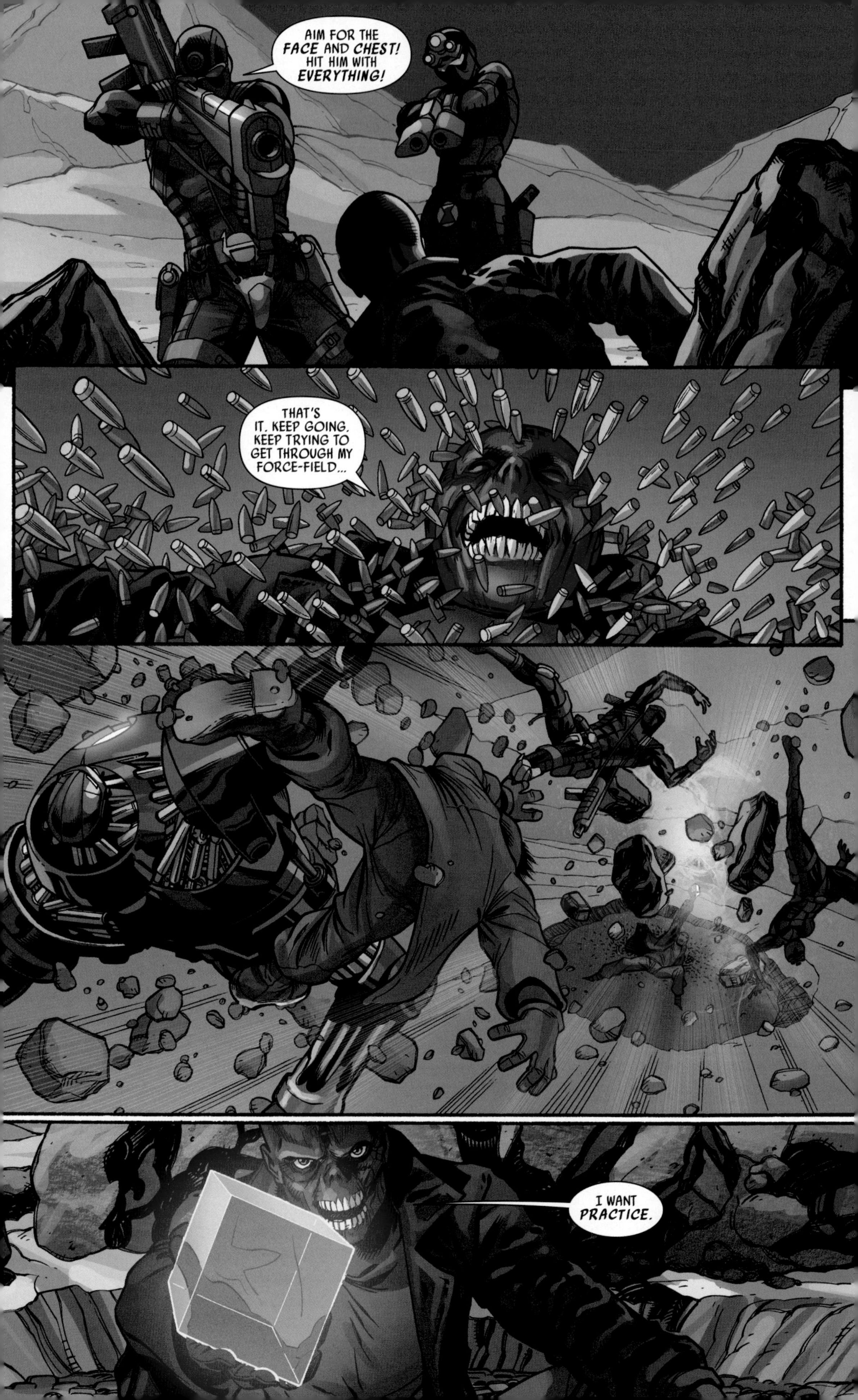
AIM FOR THE FACE AND CHEST! HIT HIM WITH EVERYTHING!
THAT'S IT. KEEP GOING. KEEP TRYING TO GET THROUGH MY FORCE-FIELD...
I WANT PRACTICE.

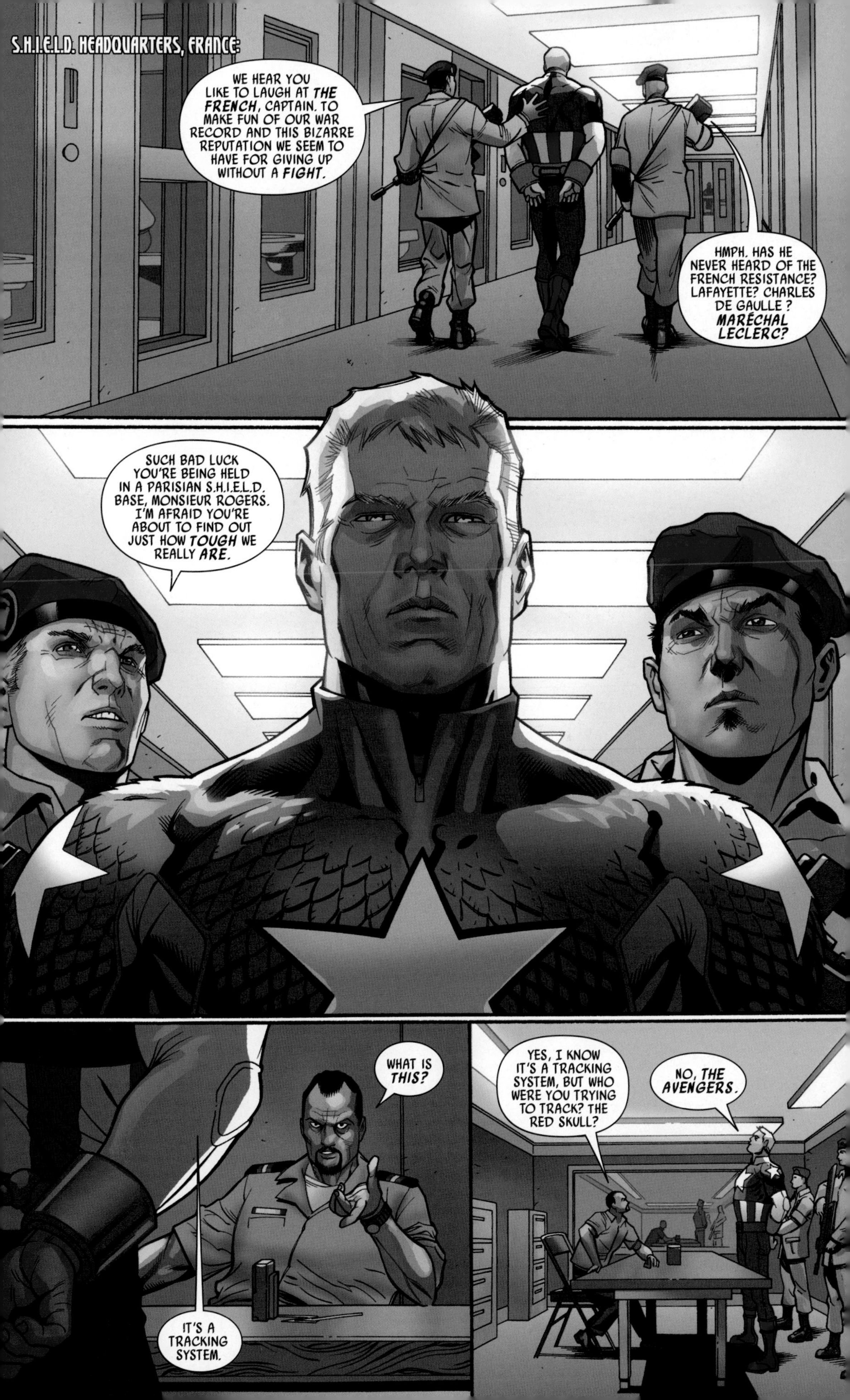
S.H.I.E.L.D. HEADQUARTERS, FRANCE:
WE HEAR YOU LIKE TO LAUGH AT THE FRENCH, CAPTAIN. TO MAKE FUN OF OUR WAR RECORD AND THIS BIZARRE REPUTATION WE SEEM TO HAVE FOR GIVING UP WITHOUT A FIGHT.
HMPH. HAS HE NEVER HEARD OF THE FRENCH RESISTANCE? LAFAYETTE? CHARLES DE GAULLE ? MARÉCHAL LECLERC?
SUCH BAD LUCK YOU'RE BEING HELD IN A PARISIAN S.H.I.E.L.D. BASE, MONSIEUR ROGERS. I'M AFRAID YOU'RE ABOUT TO FIND OUT JUST HOW TOUGH WE REALLY ARE.
WHAT IS THIS?
IT'S A TRACKING SYSTEM.
YES, I KNOW IT'S A TRACKING SYSTEM, BUT WHO WERE YOU TRYING TO TRACK? THE RED SKULL?
NO, THE AVENGERS.

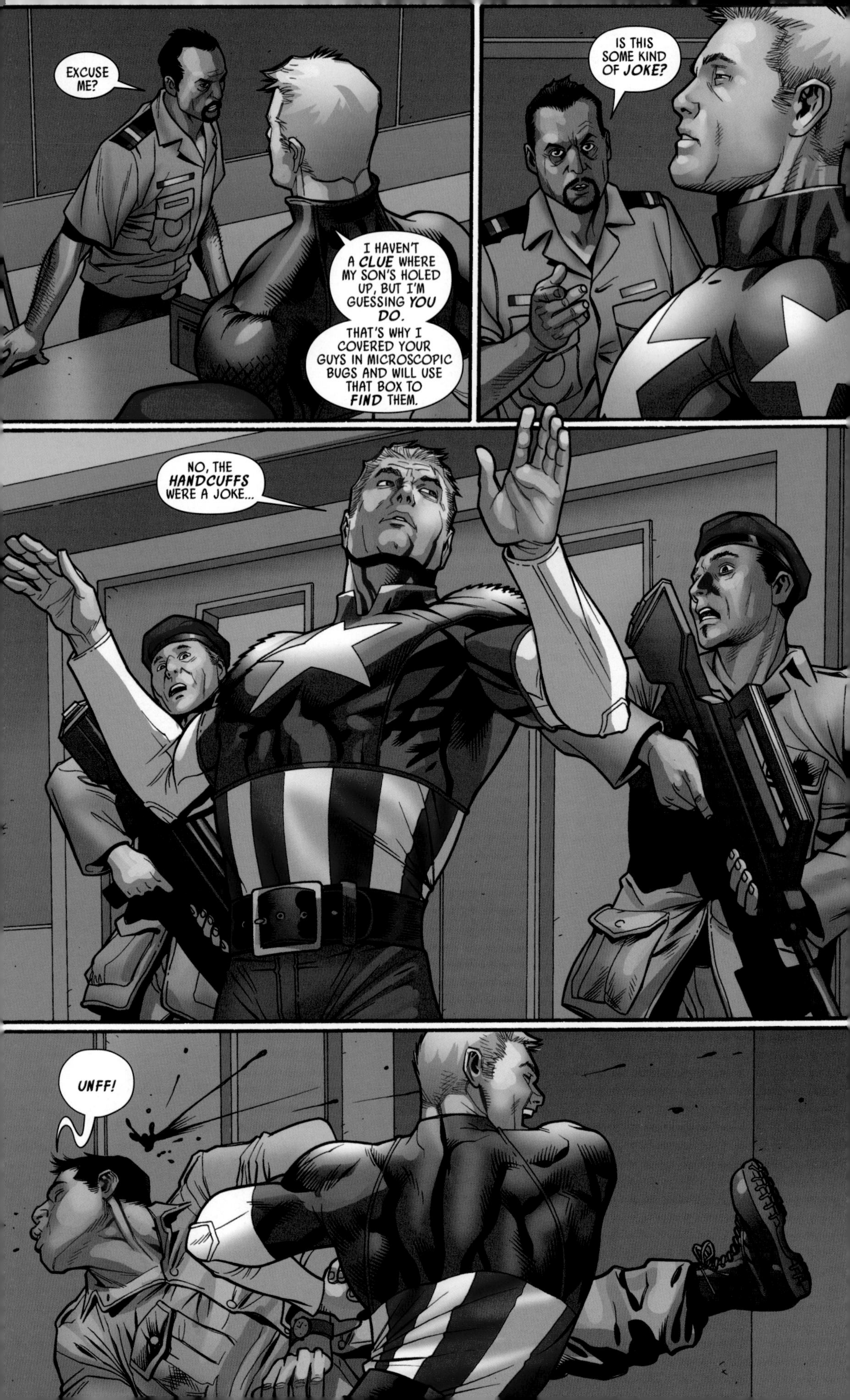
EXCUSE ME?
I HAVEN'T A CLUE WHERE MY SON'S HOLED UP, BUT I'M GUESSING YOU DO.
THAT'S WHY I COVERED YOUR GUYS IN MICROSCOPIC BUGS AND WILL USE THAT BOX TO FIND THEM.
IS THIS SOME KIND OF JOKE?
NO, THE HANDCUFFS WERE A JOKE...
UNFF!

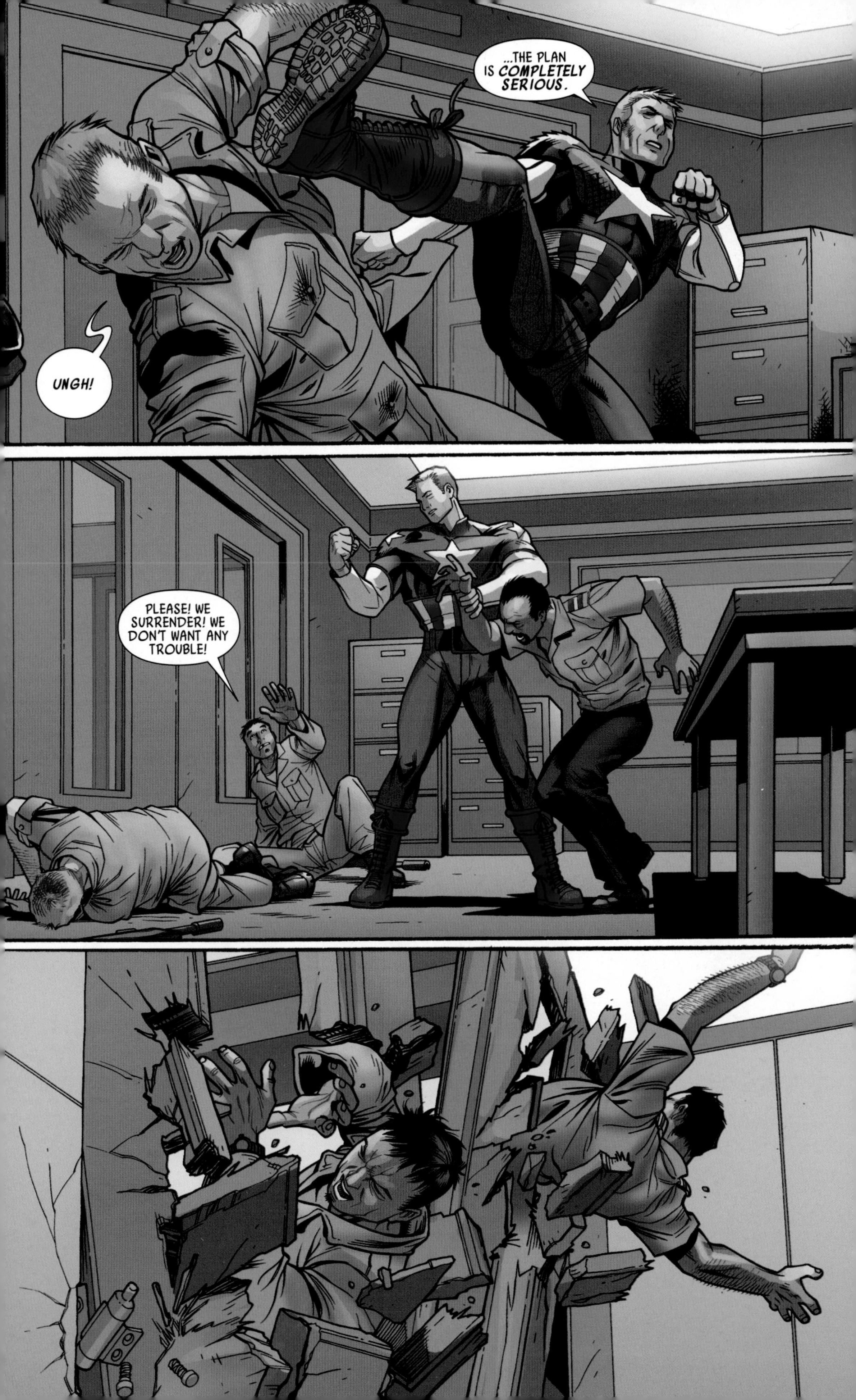
...THE PLAN IS COMPLETELY SERIOUS.
UNGH!
PLEASE! WE SURRENDER! WE DON'T WANT ANY TROUBLE!

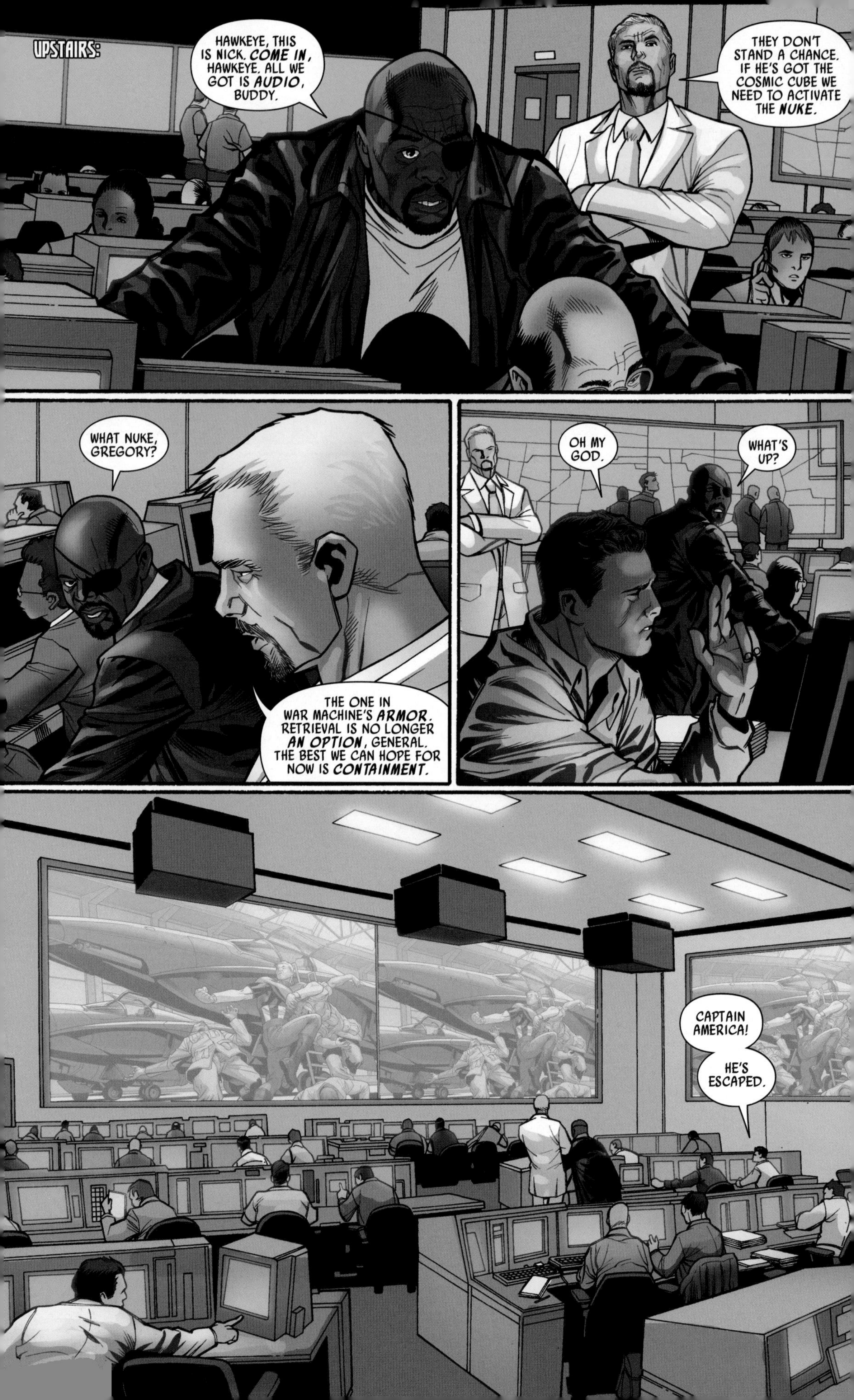
UPSTAIRS:
HAWKEYE, THIS IS NICK. COME IN, HAWKEYE. ALL WE GOT IS AUDIO, BUDDY.
THEY DON'T STAND A CHANCE. IF HE'S GOT THE COSMIC CUBE WE NEED TO ACTIVATE THE NUKE.
WHAT NUKE, GREGORY?
THE ONE IN WAR MACHINE'S ARMOR. RETRIEVAL IS NO LONGER AN OPTION, GENERAL. THE BEST WE CAN HOPE FOR NOW IS CONTAINMENT.
OH MY GOD.
WHAT'S UP?
CAPTAIN AMERICA!
HE'S ESCAPED.

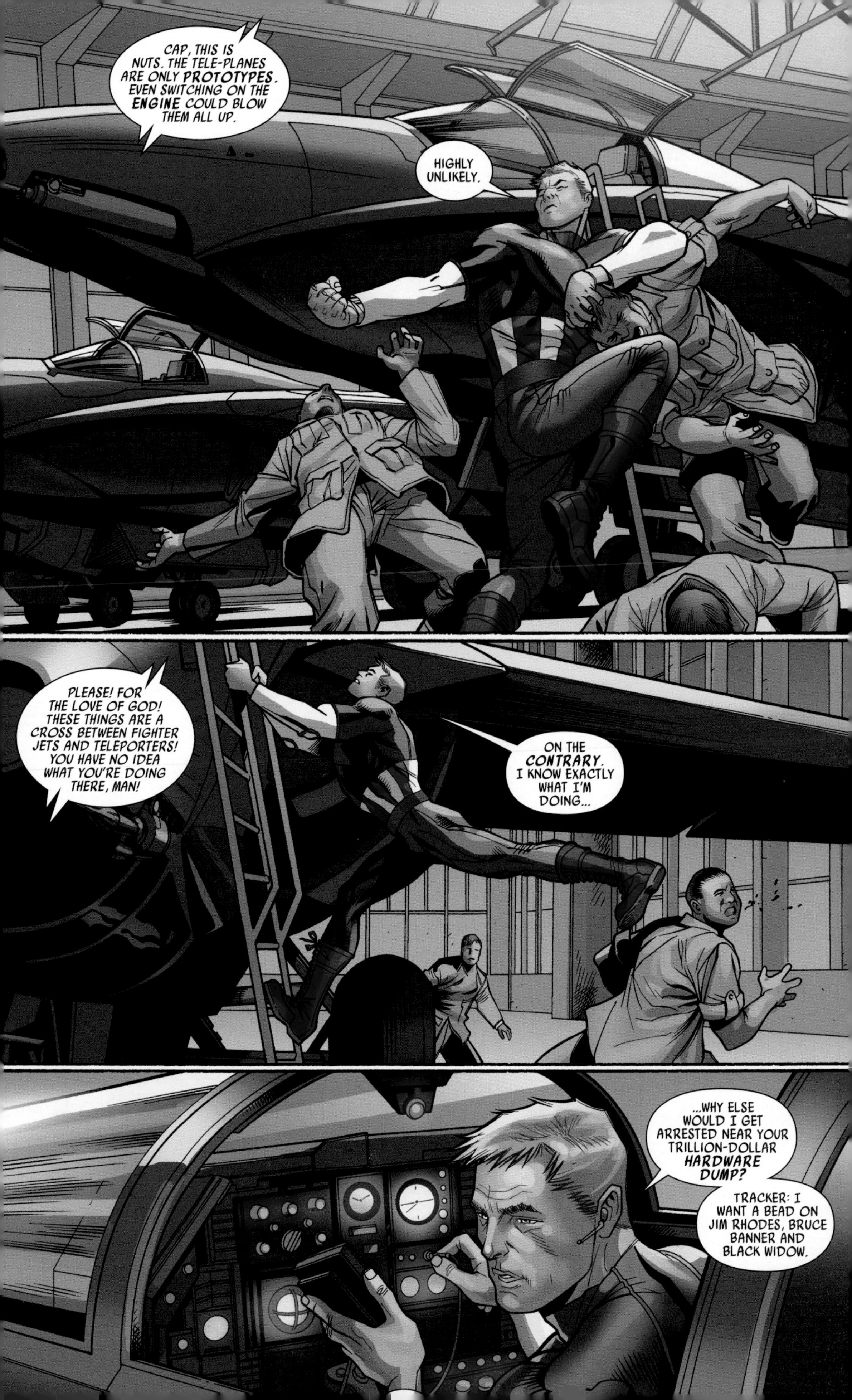
CAP, THIS IS NUTS. THE TELE-PLANES ARE ONLY PROTOTYPES. EVEN SWITCHING ON THE ENGINE COULD BLOW THEM ALL UP.
HIGHLY UNLIKELY.
PLEASE! FOR THE LOVE OF GOD! THESE THINGS ARE A CROSS BETWEEN FIGHTER JETS AND TELEPORTERS! YOU HAVE NO IDEA WHAT YOU'RE DOING THERE, MAN!
ON THE CONTRARY. I KNOW EXACTLY WHAT I'M DOING...
...WHY ELSE WOULD I GET ARRESTED NEAR YOUR TRILLION-DOLLAR HARDWARE DUMP?
TRACKER: I WANT A BEAD ON JIM RHODES, BRUCE BANNER AND BLACK WIDOW.

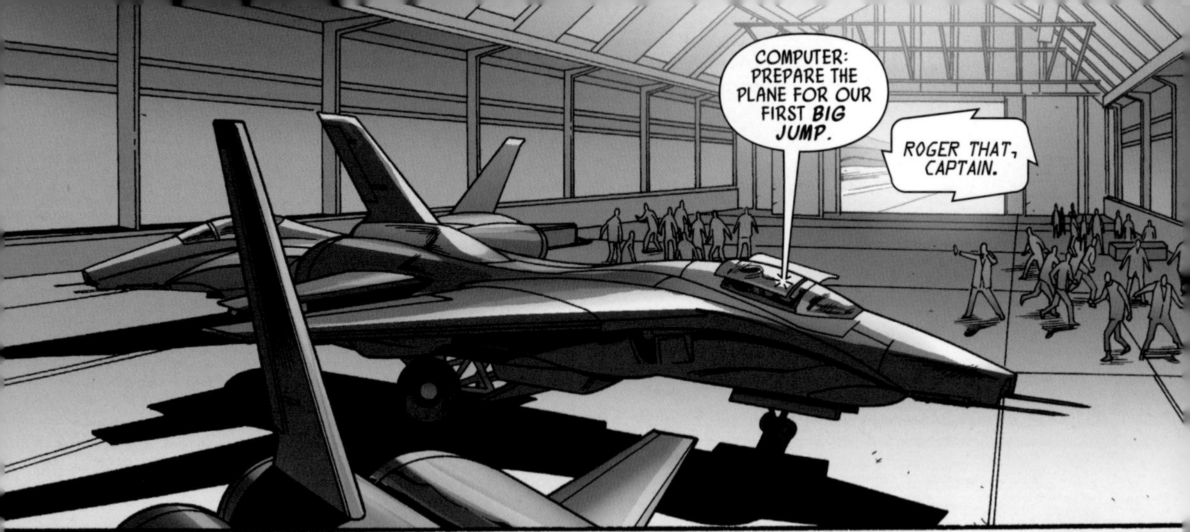
COMPUTER: PREPARE THE PLANE FOR OUR FIRST BIG JUMP.
ROGER THAT, CAPTAIN.

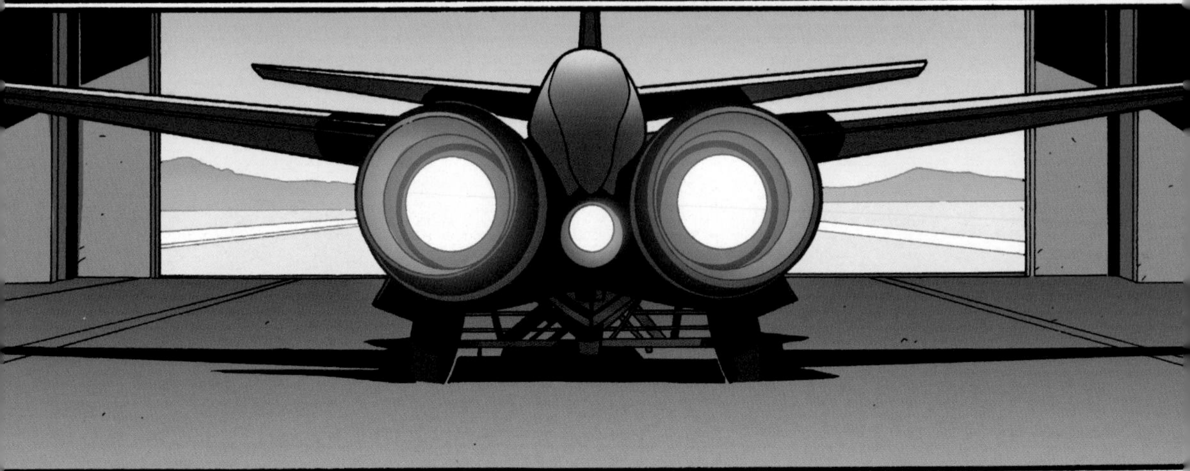

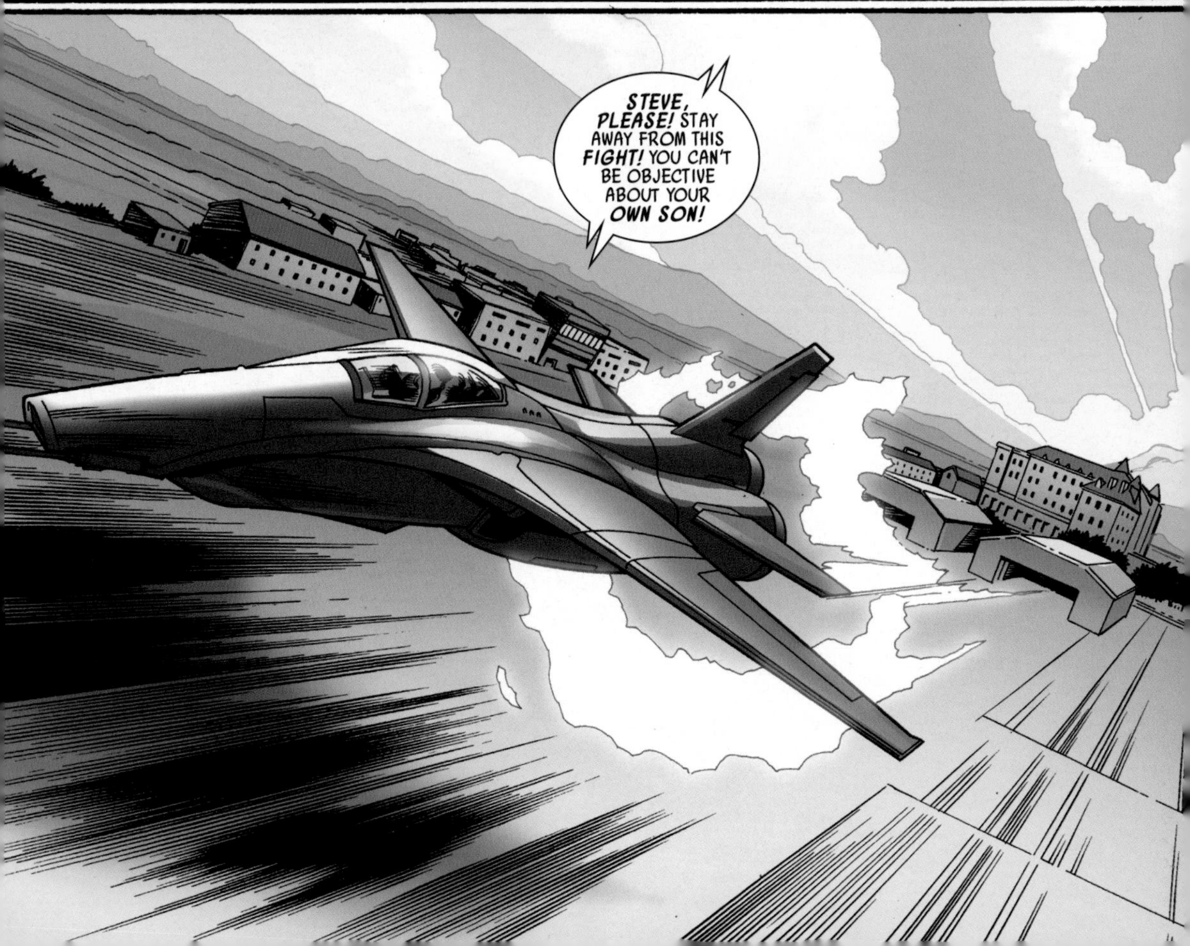
STEVE, PLEASE! STAY AWAY FROM THIS FIGHT! YOU CAN'T BE OBJECTIVE ABOUT YOUR OWN SON!

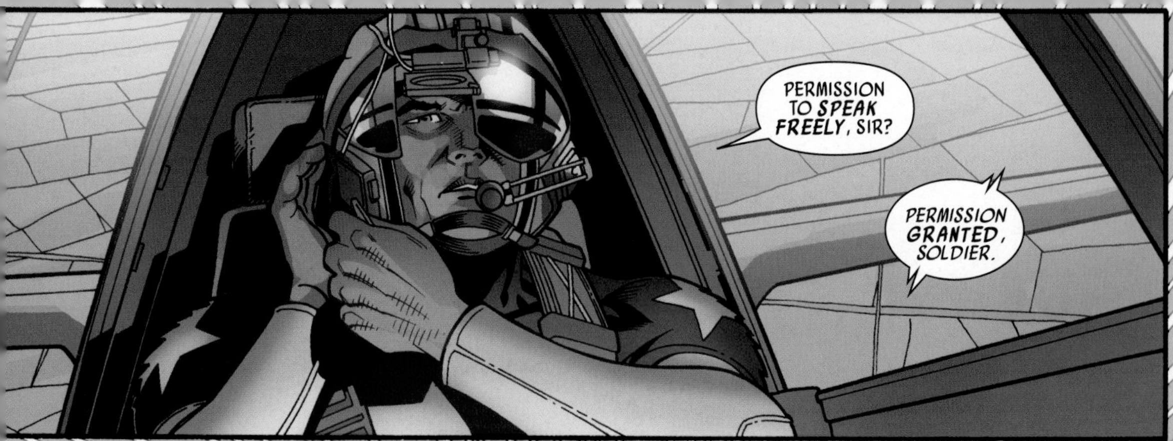
PERMISSION TO SPEAK FREELY, SIR?
PERMISSION GRANTED, SOLDIER.

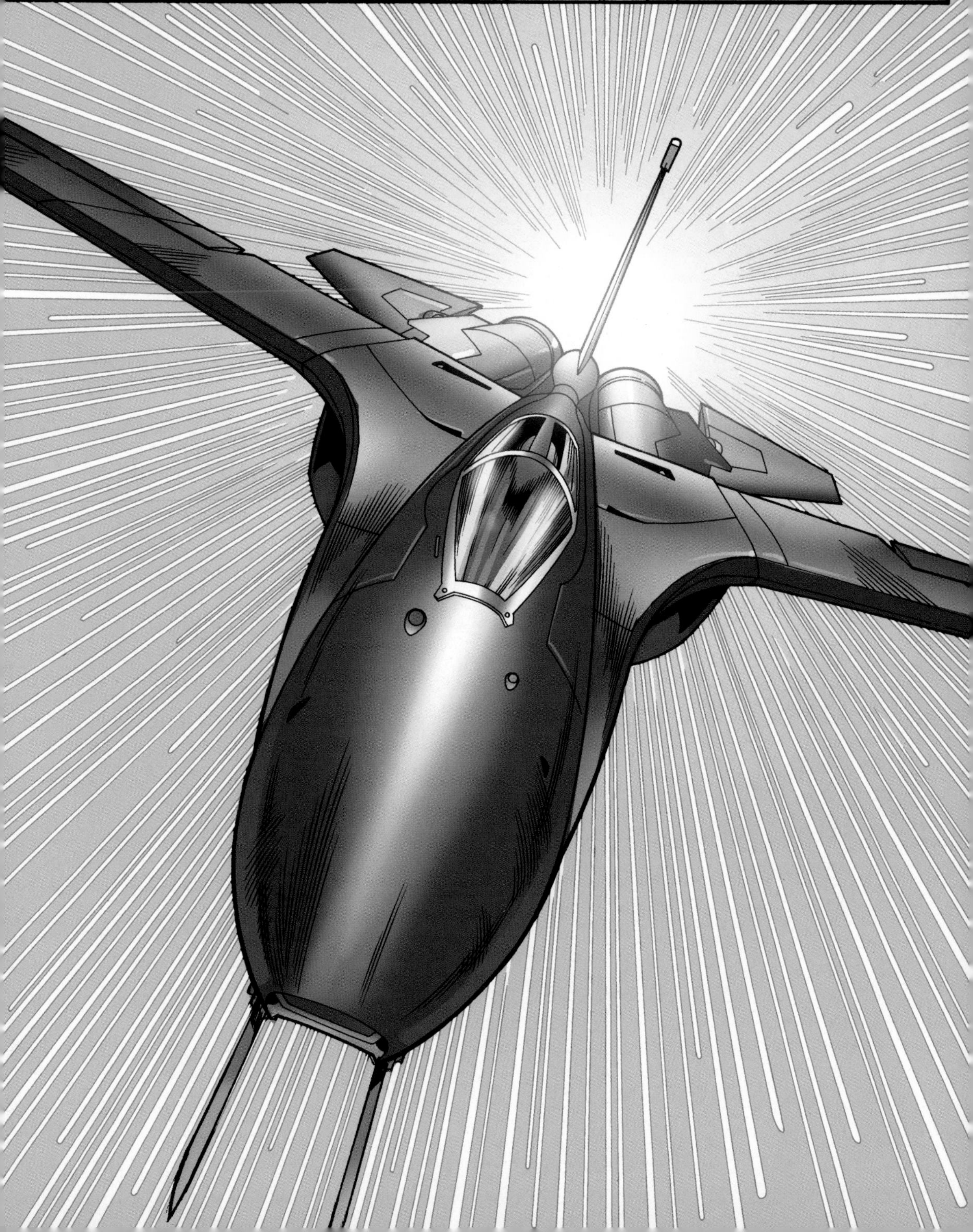

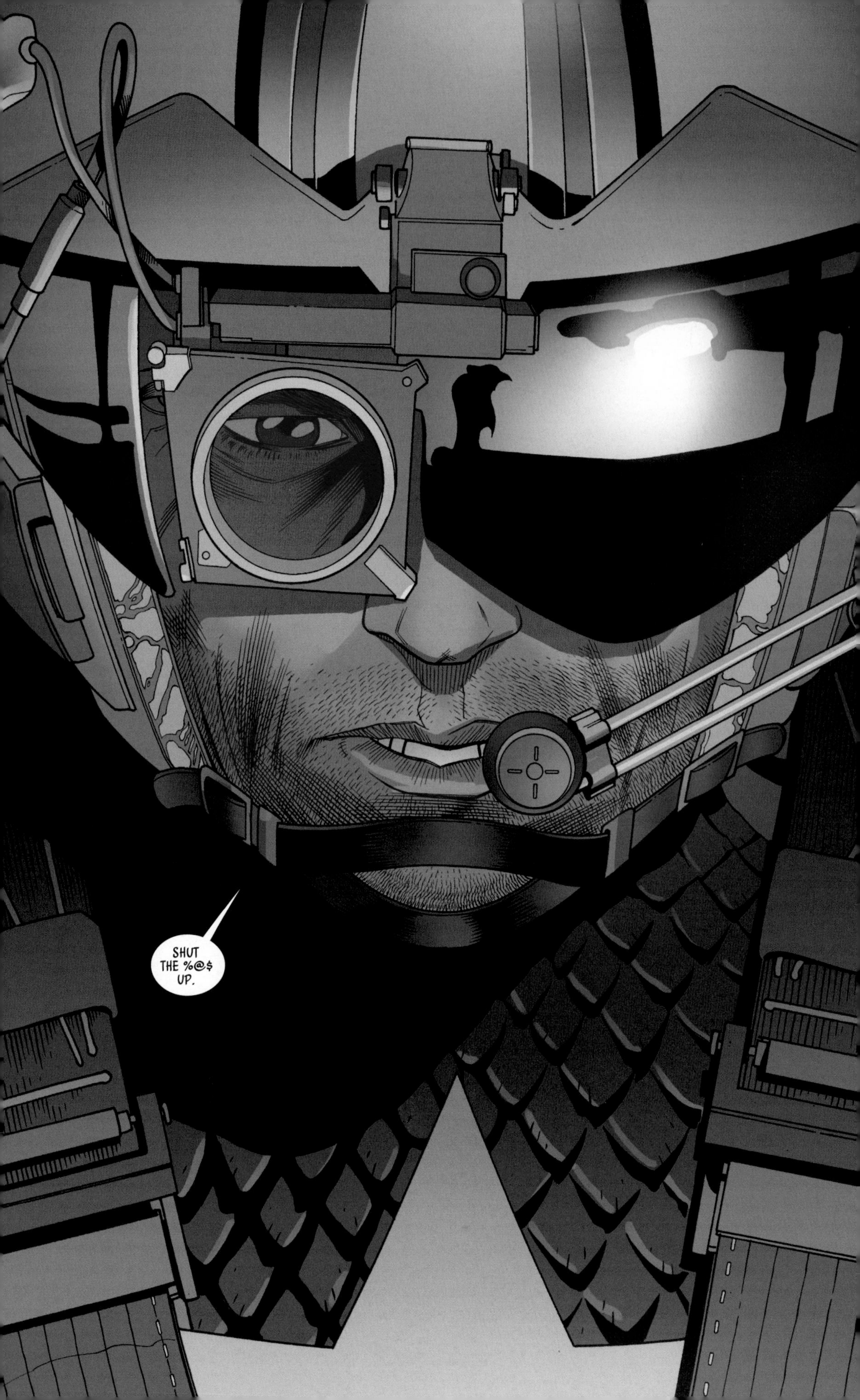
SHUT THE %@$ UP.

6

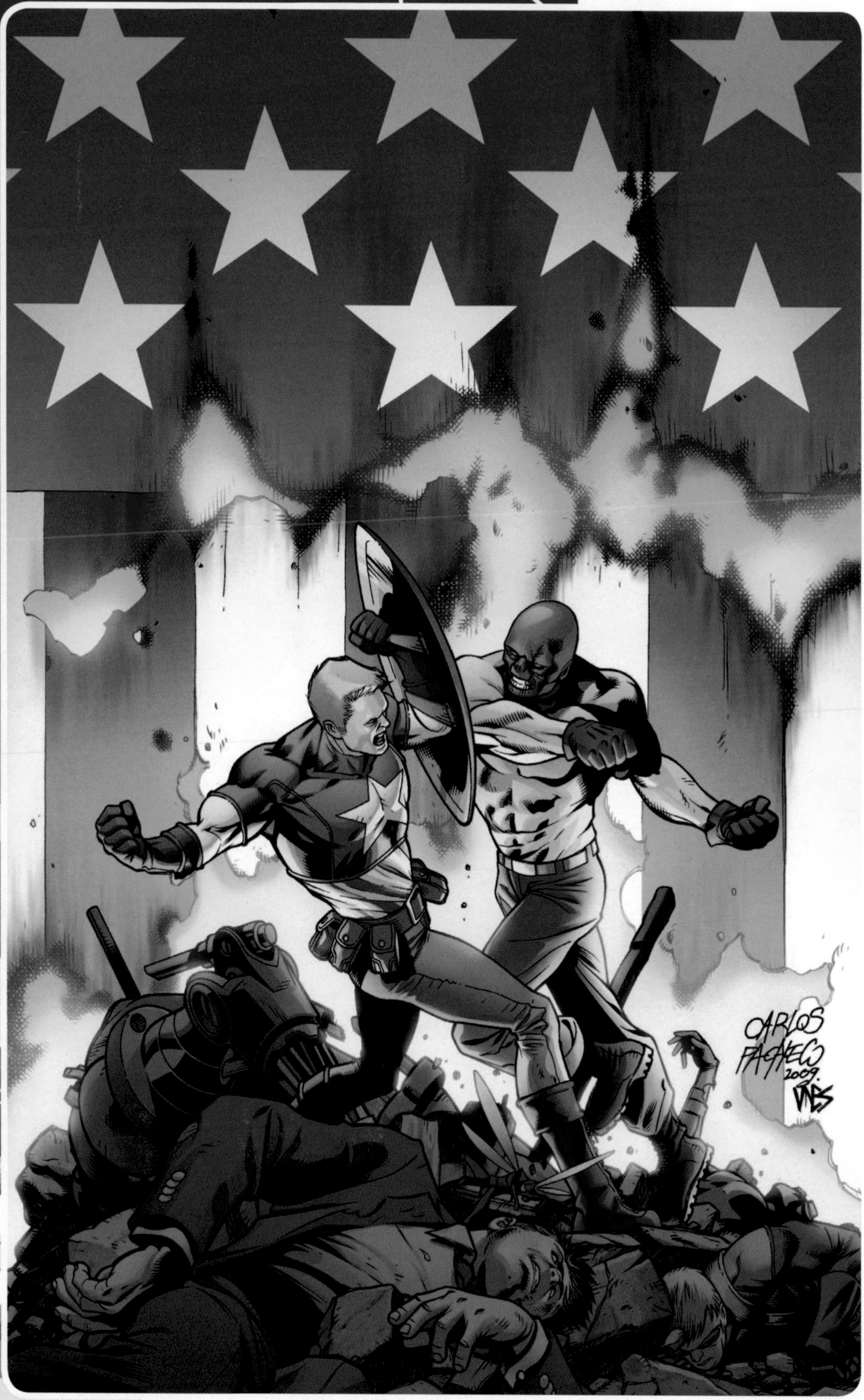
CARLOS PACHECO 2009.

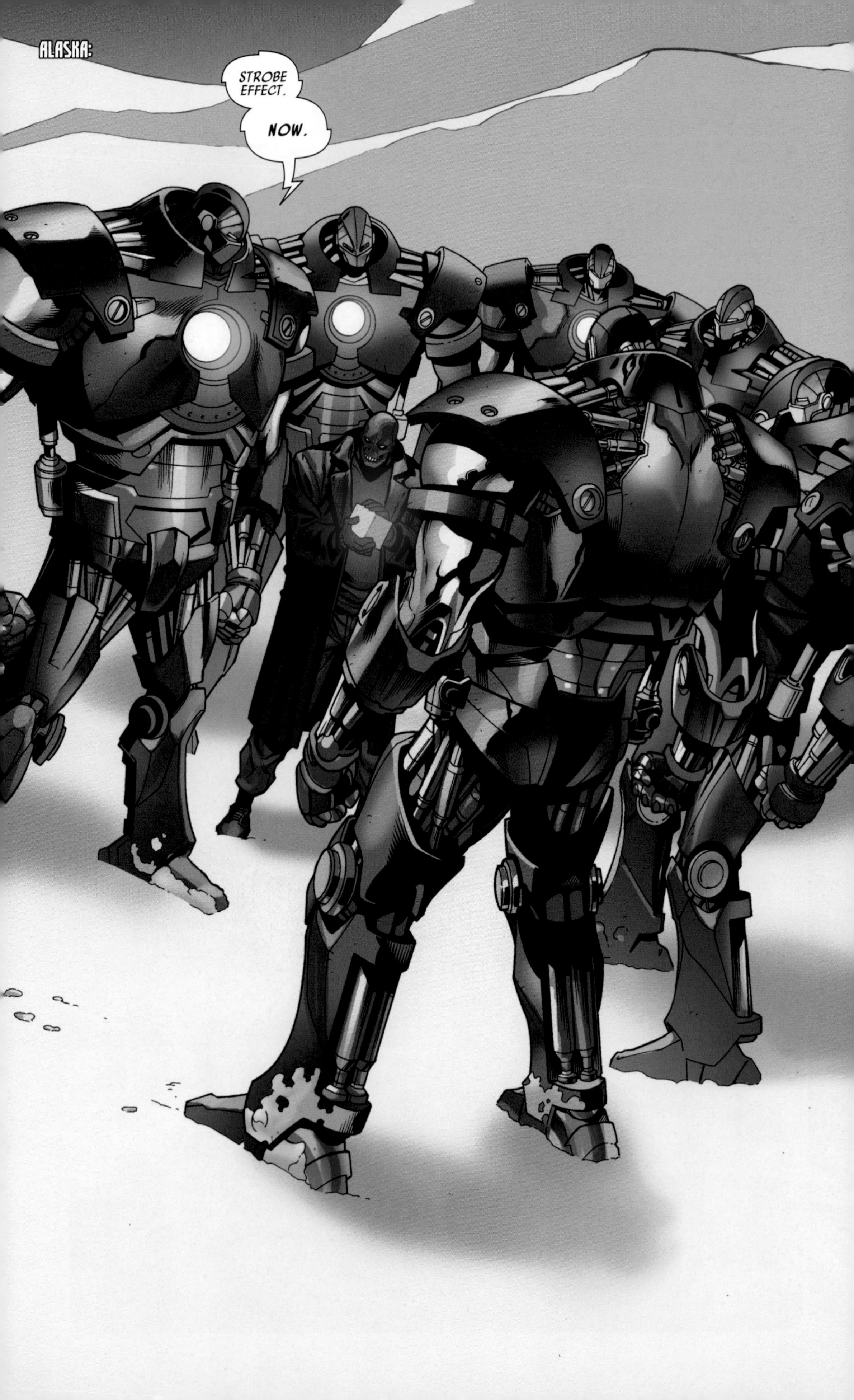
ALASKA:
STROBE EFFECT.
NOW.

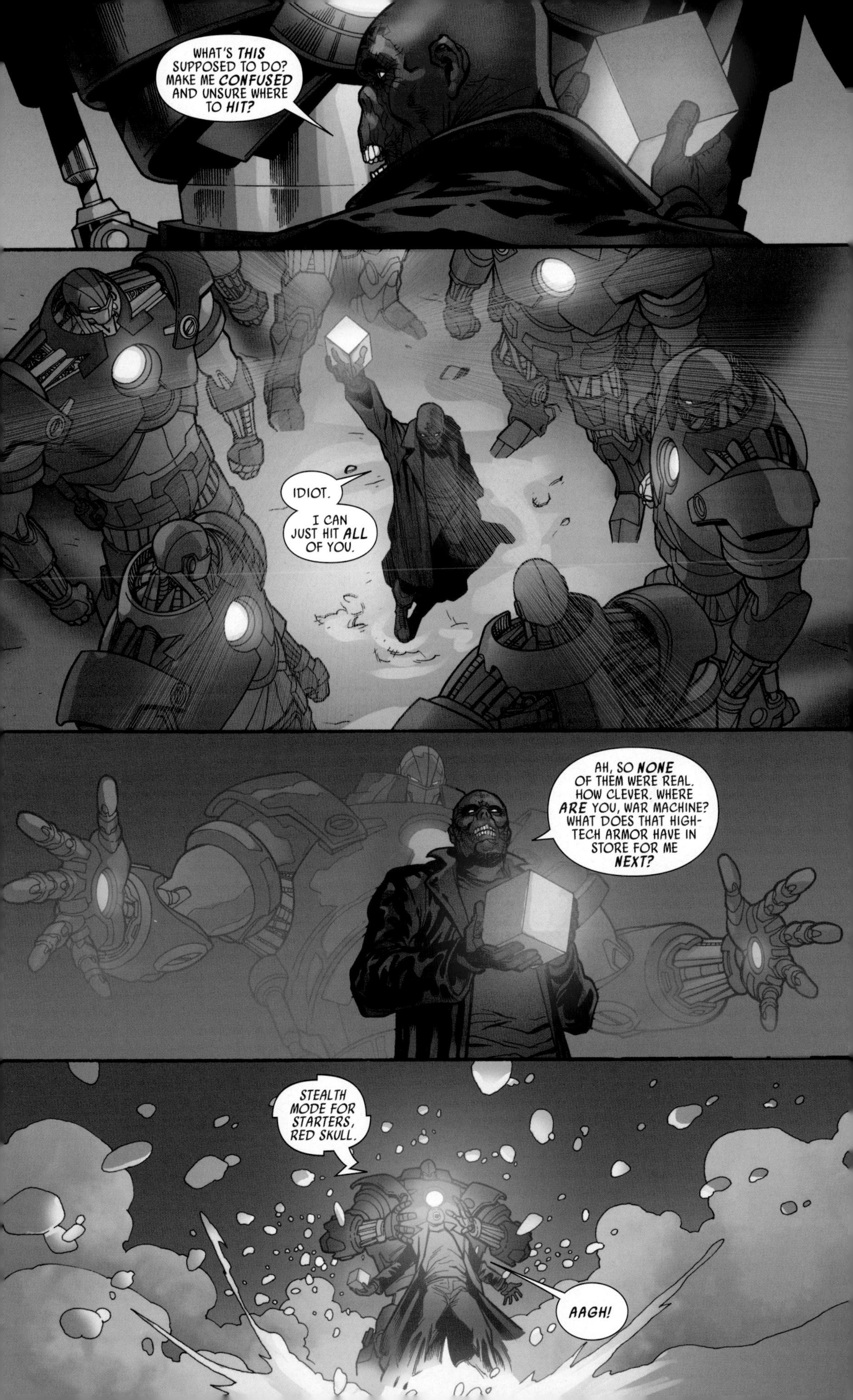
WHAT'S THIS SUPPOSED TO DO? MAKE ME CONFUSED AND UNSURE WHERE TO HIT?
IDIOT.
I CAN JUST HIT ALL OF YOU.
AH, SO NONE OF THEM WERE REAL. HOW CLEVER. WHERE ARE YOU, WAR MACHINE? WHAT DOES THAT HIGH-TECH ARMOR HAVE IN STORE FOR ME NEXT?
STEALTH MODE FOR STARTERS, RED SKULL.
AAGH!

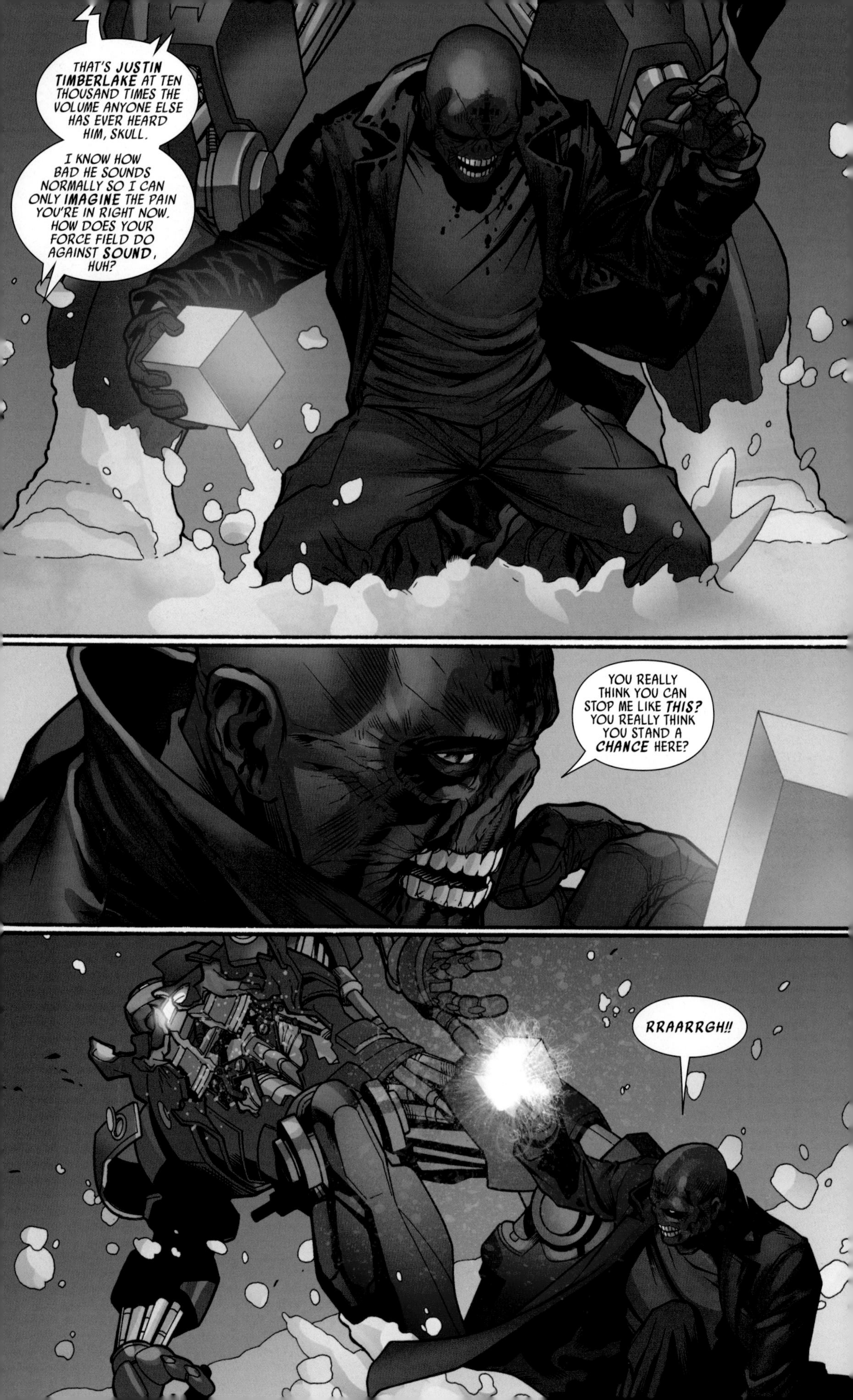
THAT'S JUSTIN TIMBERLAKE AT TEN THOUSAND TIMES THE VOLUME ANYONE ELSE HAS EVER HEARD HIM, SKULL.
I KNOW HOW BAD HE SOUNDS NORMALLY SO I CAN ONLY IMAGINE THE PAIN YOU'RE IN RIGHT NOW. HOW DOES YOUR FORCE FIELD DO AGAINST SOUND, HUH?
YOU REALLY THINK YOU CAN STOP ME LIKE THIS? YOU REALLY THINK YOU STAND A CHANCE HERE?
RRAARRGH!!

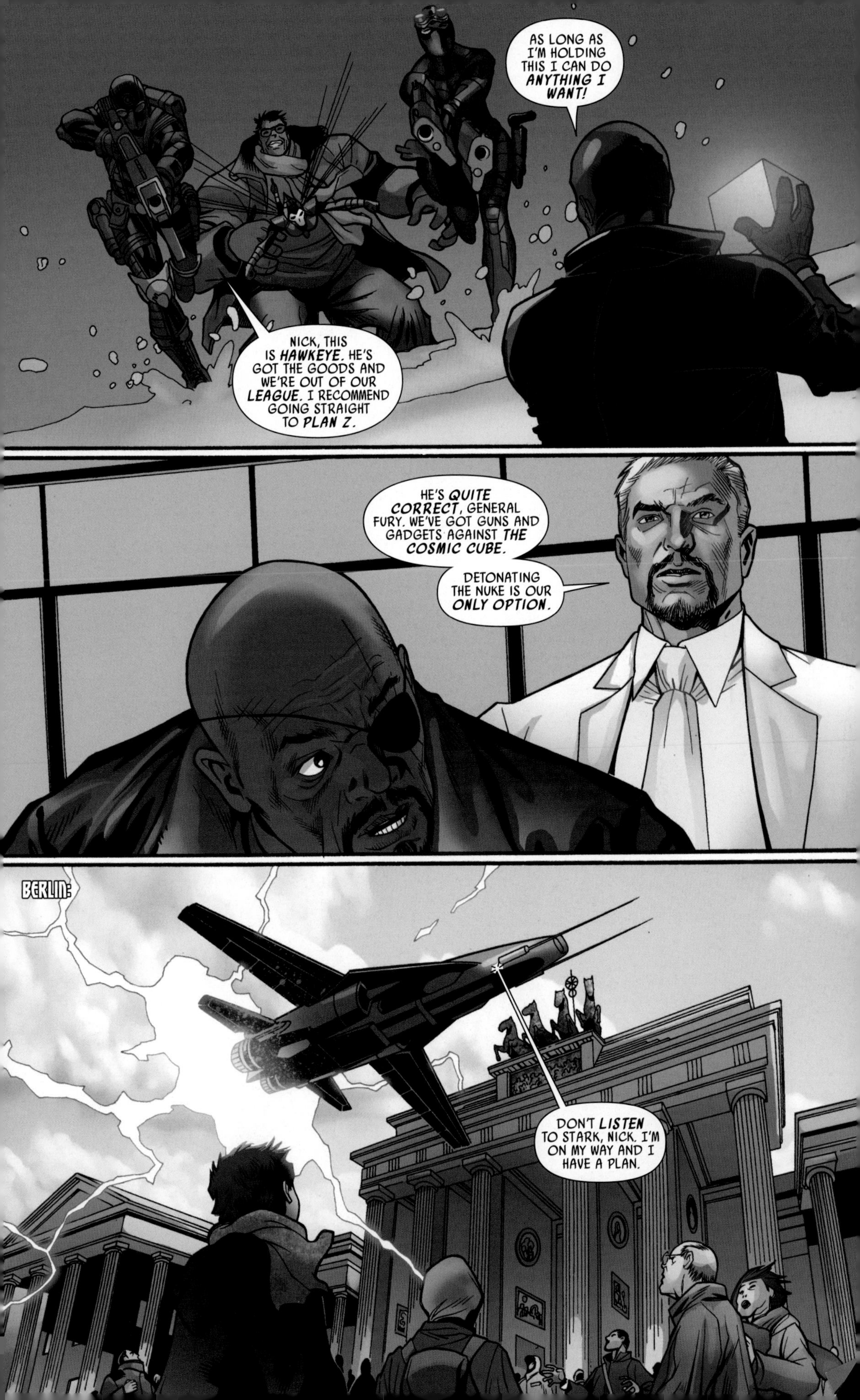
AS LONG AS I'M HOLDING THIS I CAN DO ANYTHING I WANT!
NICK, THIS IS HAWKEYE. HE'S GOT THE GOODS AND WE'RE OUT OF OUR LEAGUE. I RECOMMEND GOING STRAIGHT TO PLAN Z.
HE'S QUITE CORRECT, GENERAL FURY. WE'VE GOT GUNS AND GADGETS AGAINST THE COSMIC CUBE.
DETONATING THE NUKE IS OUR ONLY OPTION.
BERLIN:
DON'T LISTEN TO STARK, NICK. I'M ON MY WAY AND I HAVE A PLAN.

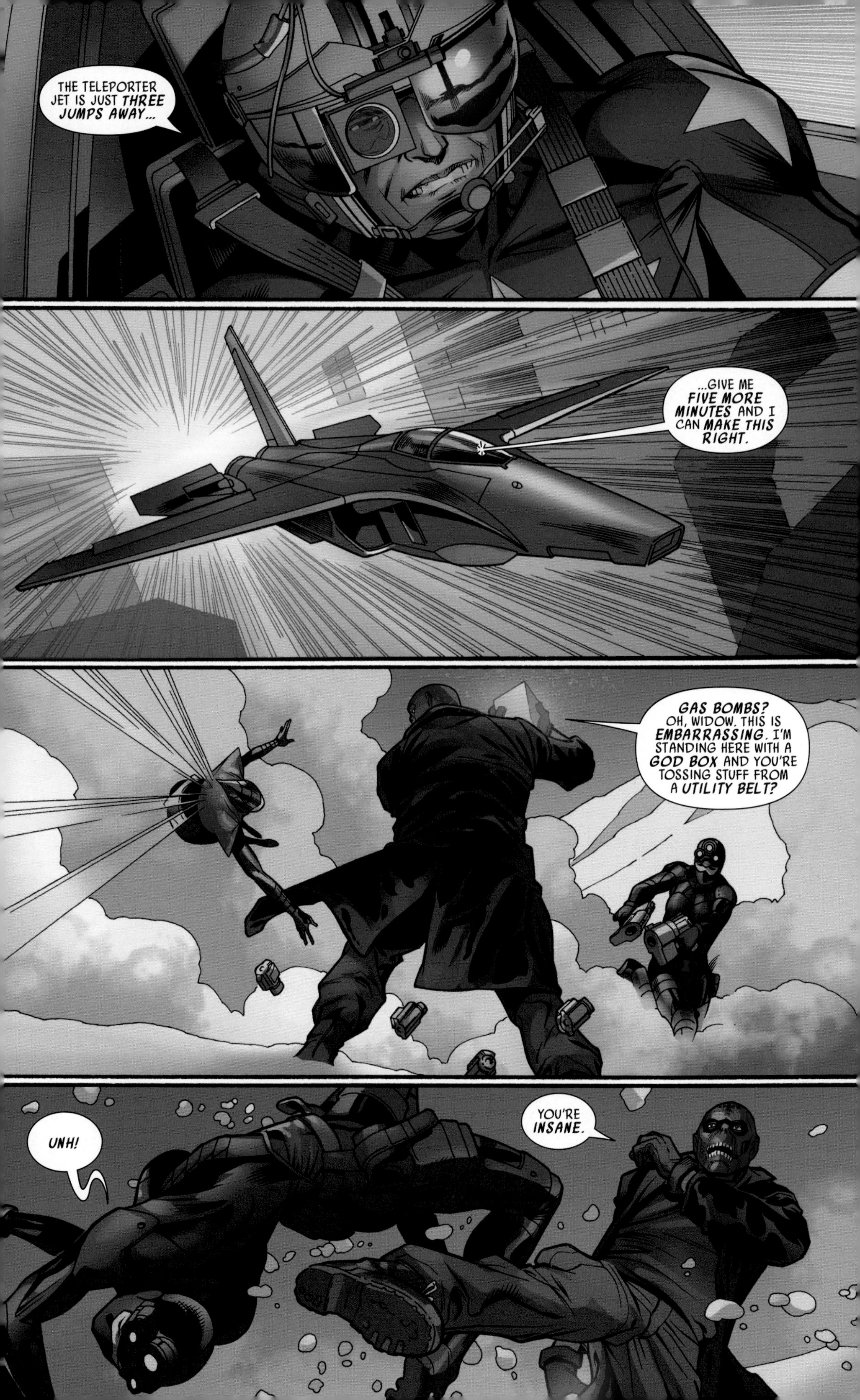
THE TELEPORTER JET IS JUST THREE JUMPS AWAY...
...GIVE ME FIVE MORE MINUTES AND I CAN MAKE THIS RIGHT.
GAS BOMBS? OH, WIDOW. THIS IS EMBARRASSING. I'M STANDING HERE WITH A GOD BOX AND YOU'RE TOSSING STUFF FROM A UTILITY BELT?
UNH!
YOU'RE INSANE.

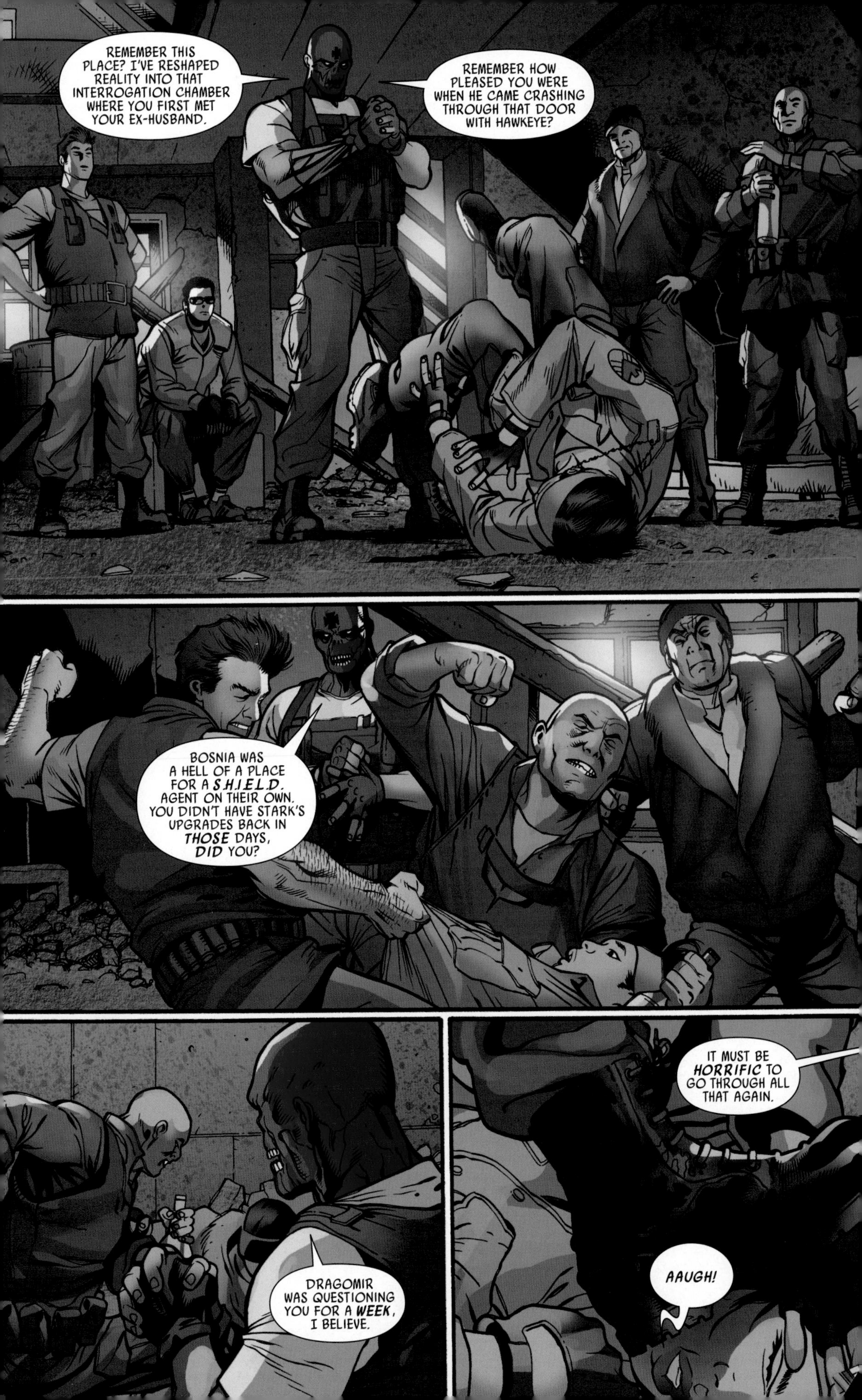
REMEMBER THIS PLACE? I'VE RESHAPED REALITY INTO THAT INTERROGATION CHAMBER WHERE YOU FIRST MET YOUR EX-HUSBAND.
REMEMBER HOW PLEASED YOU WERE WHEN HE CAME CRASHING THROUGH THAT DOOR WITH HAWKEYE?
BOSNIA WAS A HELL OF A PLACE FOR A S.H.I.E.L.D. AGENT ON THEIR OWN. YOU DIDN'T HAVE STARK'S UPGRADES BACK IN THOSE DAYS, DID YOU?
DRAGOMIR WAS QUESTIONING YOU FOR A WEEK, I BELIEVE.
IT MUST BE HORRIFIC TO GO THROUGH ALL THAT AGAIN.
AAUGH!

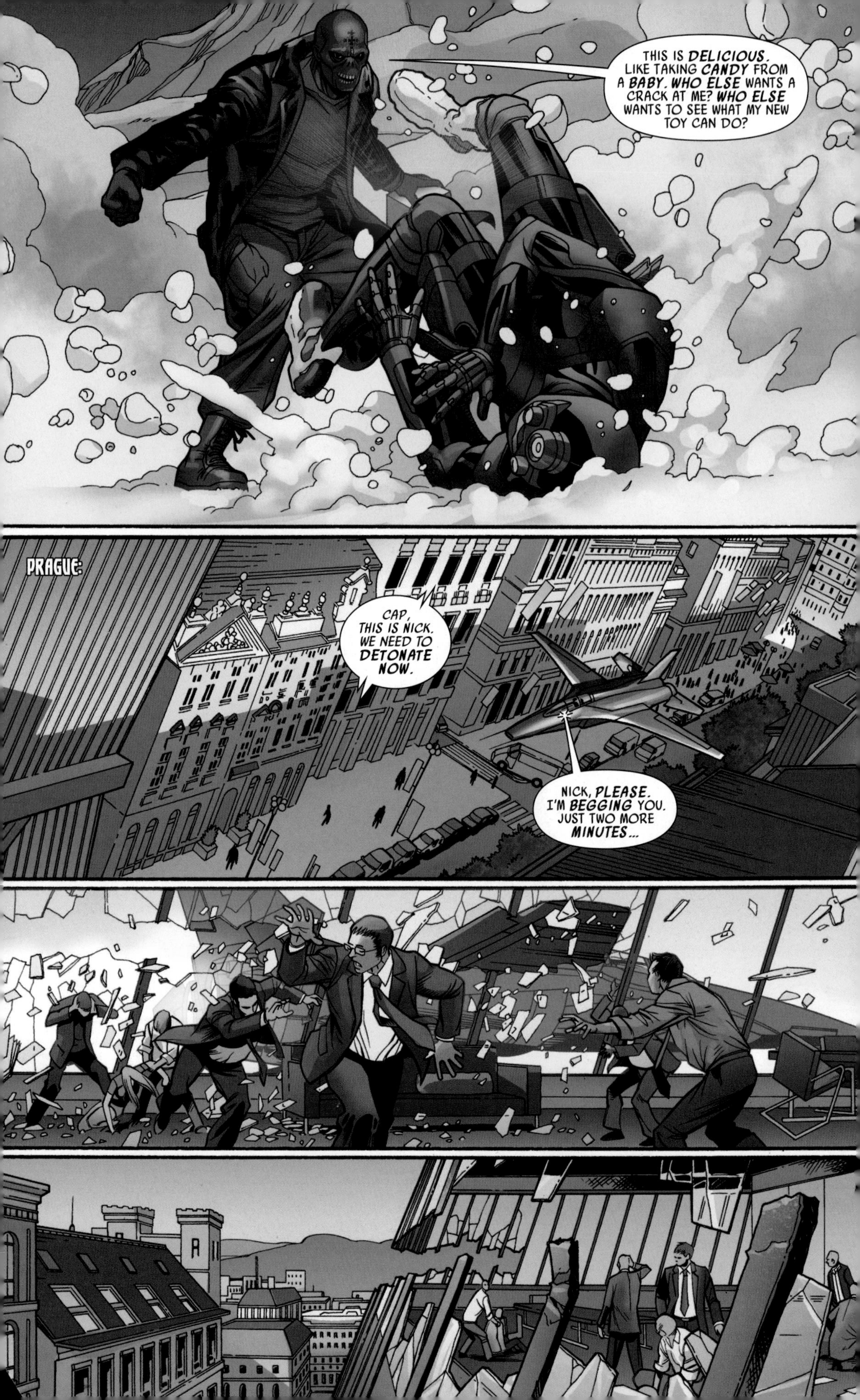
THIS IS DELICIOUS. LIKE TAKING CANDY FROM A BABY. WHO ELSE WANTS A CRACK AT ME? WHO ELSE WANTS TO SEE WHAT MY NEW TOY CAN DO?
PRAGUE:
CAP, THIS IS NICK. WE NEED TO DETONATE NOW.
NICK, PLEASE. I'M BEGGING YOU. JUST TWO MORE MINUTES...

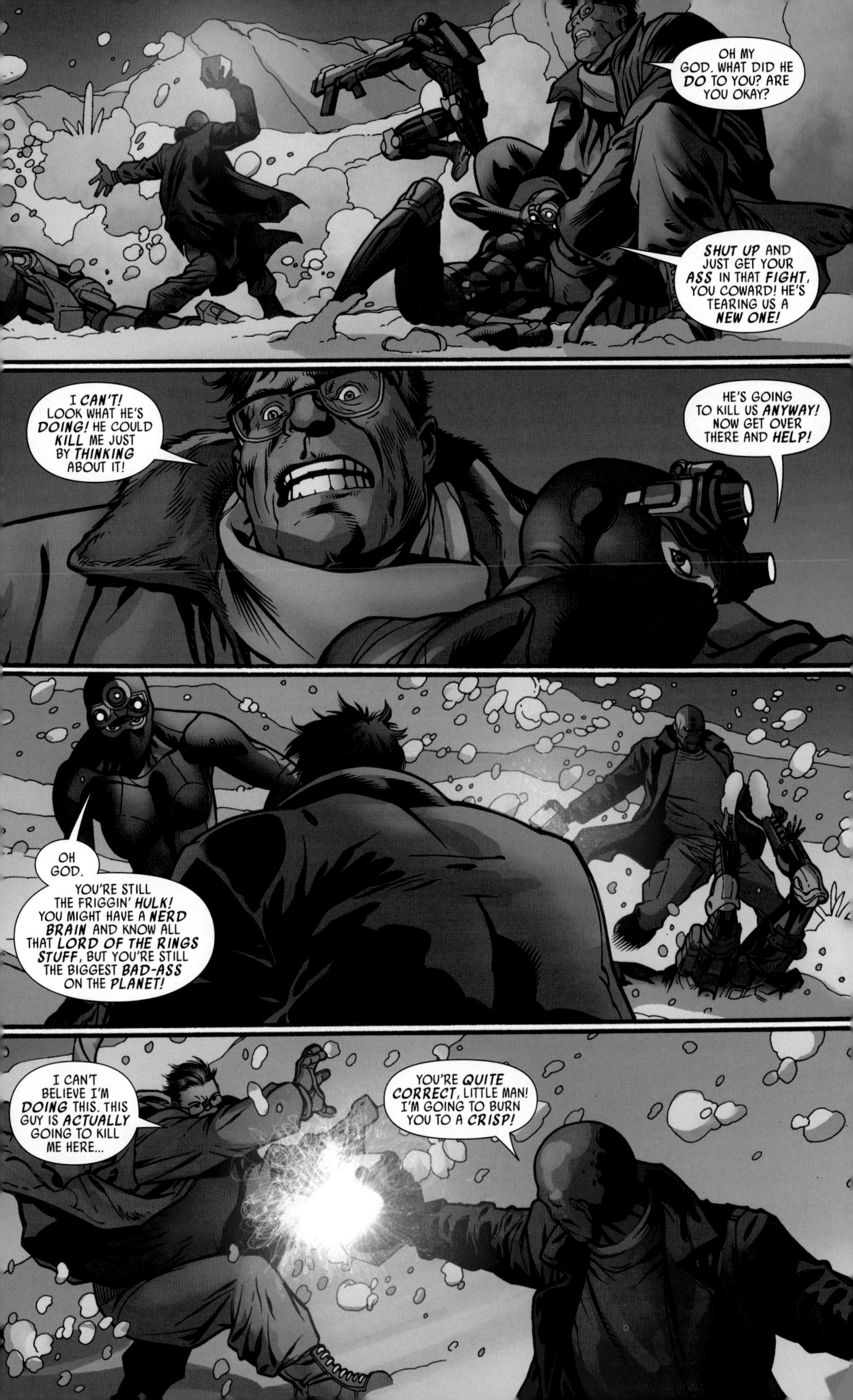
OH MY GOD. WHAT DID HE DO TO YOU? ARE YOU OKAY?
SHUT UP AND JUST GET YOUR ASS IN THAT FIGHT, YOU COWARD! HE'S TEARING US A NEW ONE!
I CAN'T! LOOK WHAT HE'S DOING! HE COULD KILL ME JUST BY THINKING ABOUT IT!
HE'S GOING TO KILL US ANYWAY! NOW GET OVER THERE AND HELP!
OH GOD.
YOU'RE STILL THE FRIGGIN' HULK! YOU MIGHT HAVE A NERD BRAIN AND KNOW ALL THAT LORD OF THE RINGS STUFF, BUT YOU'RE STILL THE BIGGEST BAD-ASS ON THE PLANET!
I CAN'T BELIEVE I'M DOING THIS. THIS GUY IS ACTUALLY GOING TO KILL ME HERE...
YOU'RE QUITE CORRECT, LITTLE MAN! I'M GOING TO BURN YOU TO A CRISP!

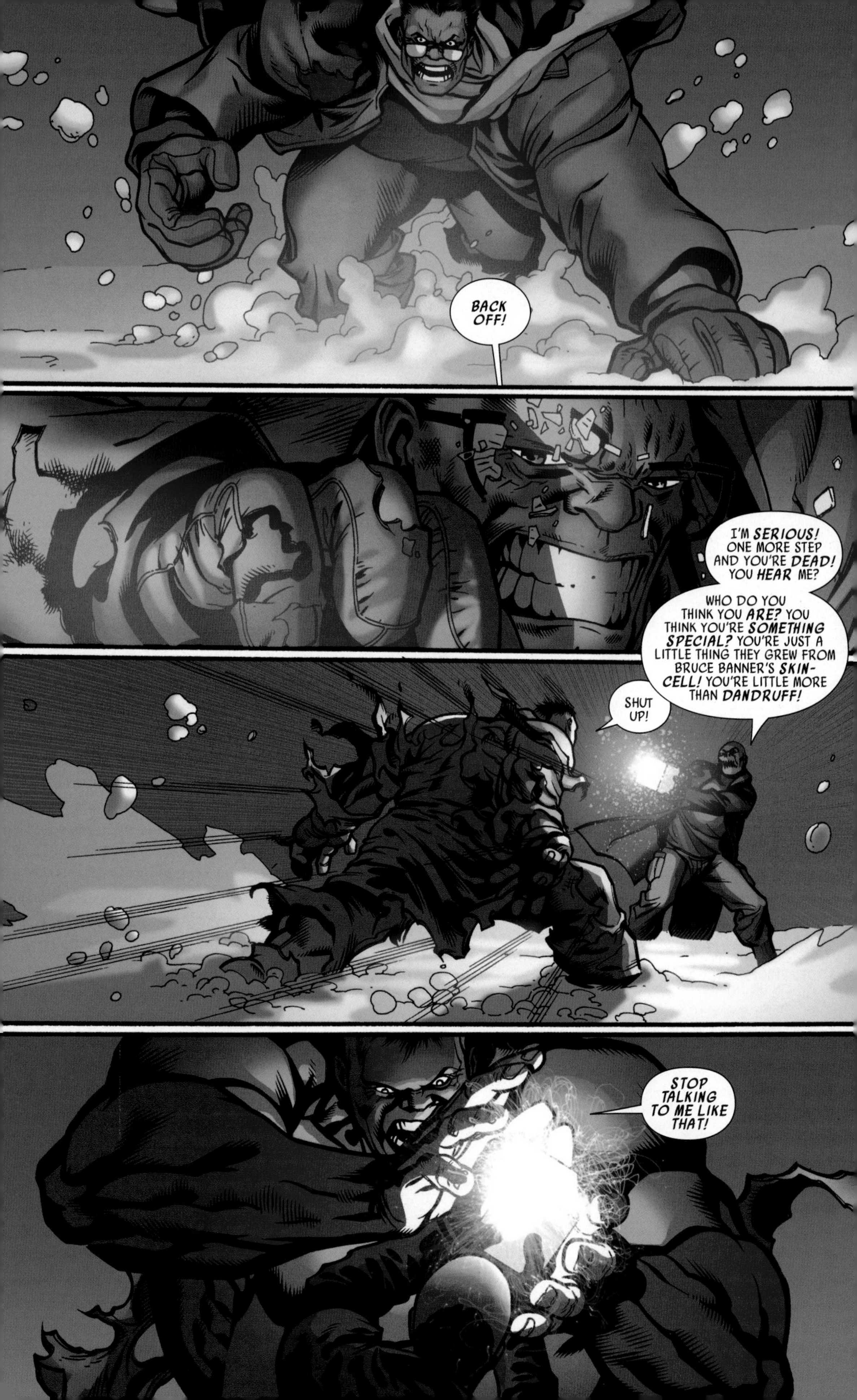
BACK OFF!
I'M SERIOUS! ONE MORE STEP AND YOU'RE DEAD! YOU HEAR ME?
WHO DO YOU THINK YOU ARE? YOU THINK YOU'RE SOMETHING SPECIAL? YOU'RE JUST A LITTLE THING THEY GREW FROM BRUCE BANNER'S SKIN-CELL! YOU'RE LITTLE MORE THAN DANDRUFF!
SHUT UP!
STOP TALKING TO ME LIKE THAT!

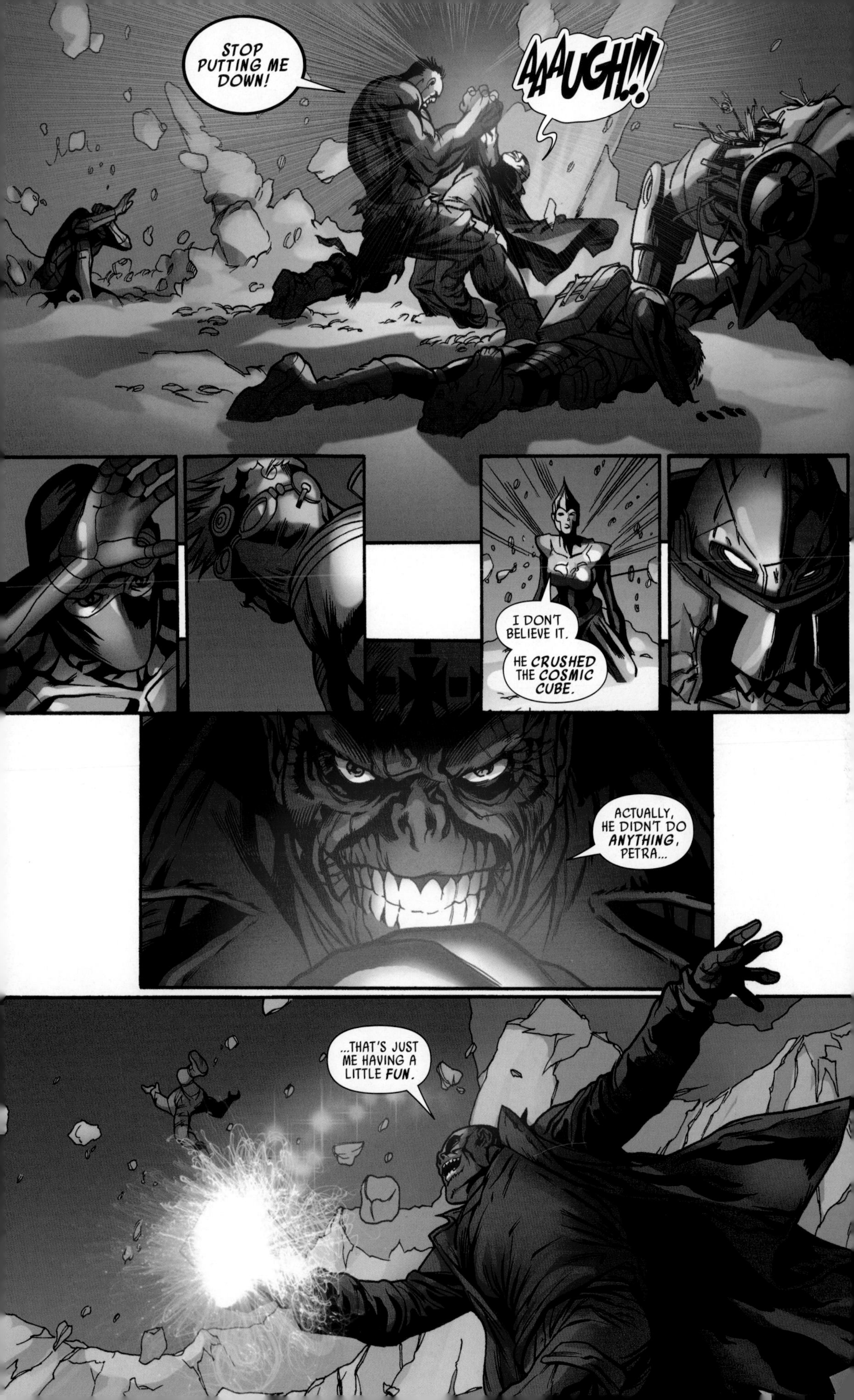
STOP PUTTING ME DOWN!
AAAUGH!!!
I DON'T BELIEVE IT.
HE CRUSHED THE COSMIC CUBE.
ACTUALLY, HE DIDN'T DO ANYTHING, PETRA...
...THAT'S JUST ME HAVING A LITTLE FUN.

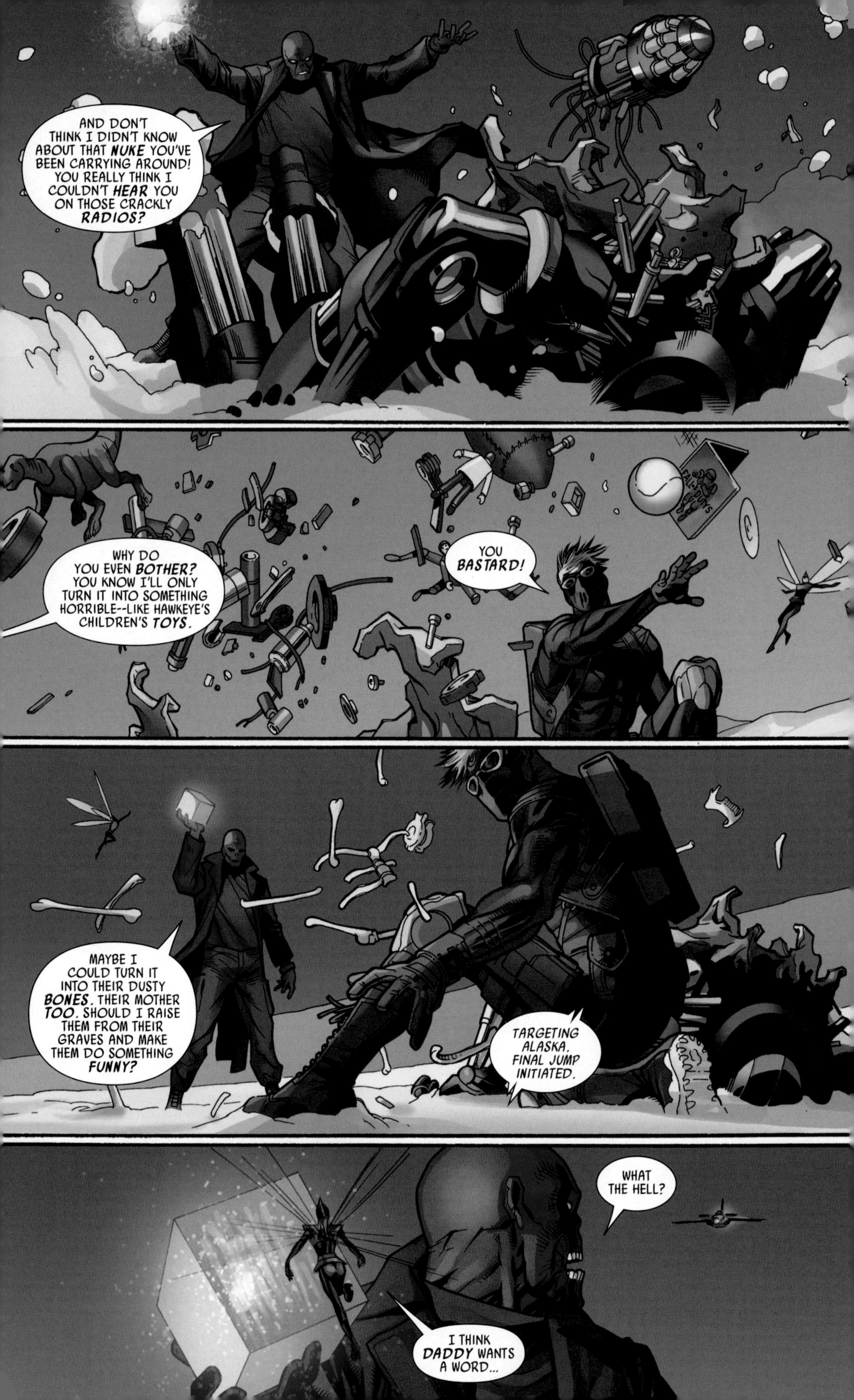
AND DON'T THINK I DIDN'T KNOW ABOUT THAT NUKE YOU'VE BEEN CARRYING AROUND! YOU REALLY THINK I COULDN'T HEAR YOU ON THOSE CRACKLY RADIOS?
WHY DO YOU EVEN BOTHER? YOU KNOW I'LL ONLY TURN IT INTO SOMETHING HORRIBLE--LIKE HAWKEYE'S CHILDREN'S TOYS.
YOU BASTARD!
MAYBE I COULD TURN IT INTO THEIR DUSTY BONES. THEIR MOTHER TOO. SHOULD I RAISE THEM FROM THEIR GRAVES AND MAKE THEM DO SOMETHING FUNNY?
TARGETING ALASKA. FINAL JUMP INITIATED.
WHAT THE HELL?
I THINK DADDY WANTS A WORD...

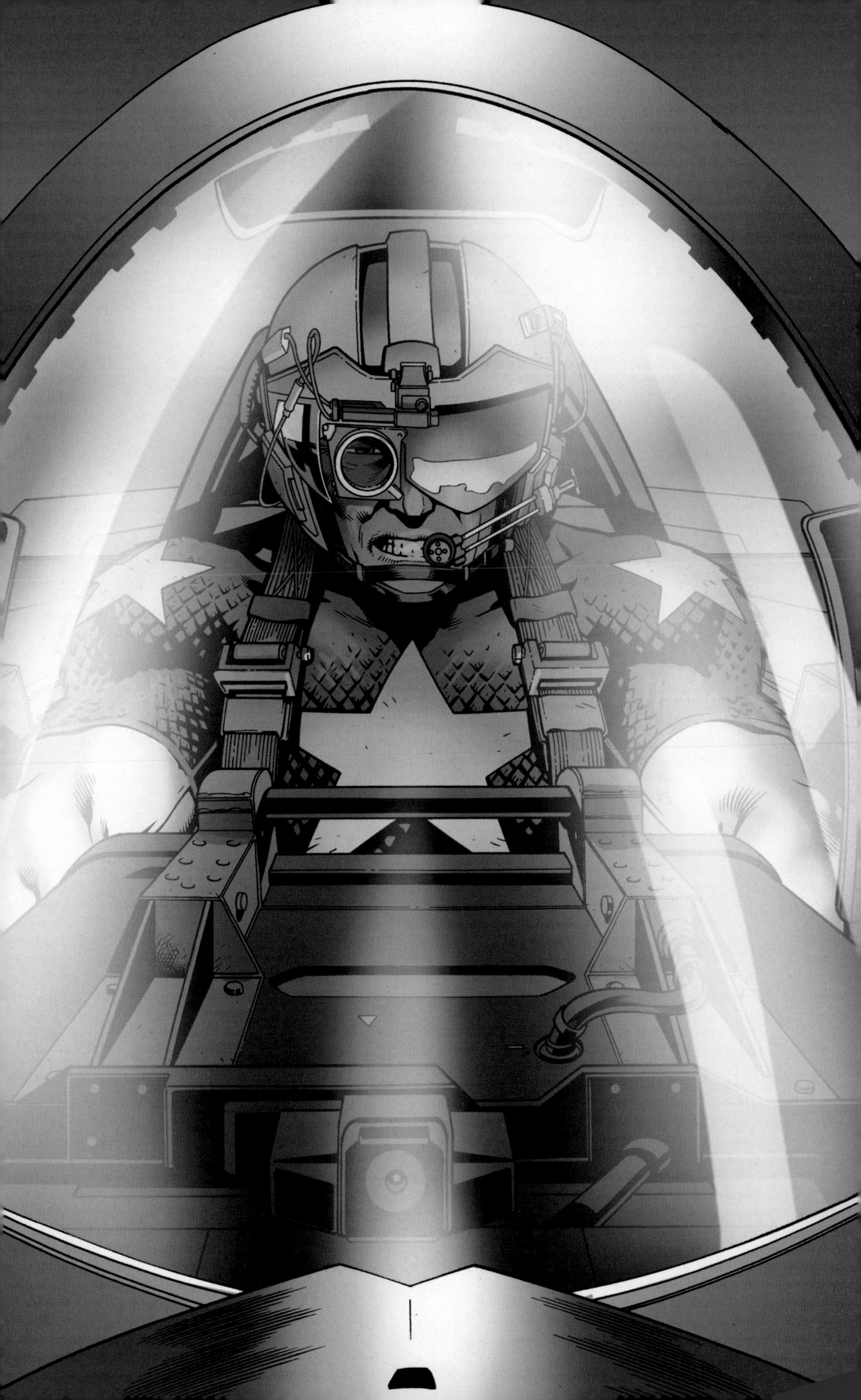

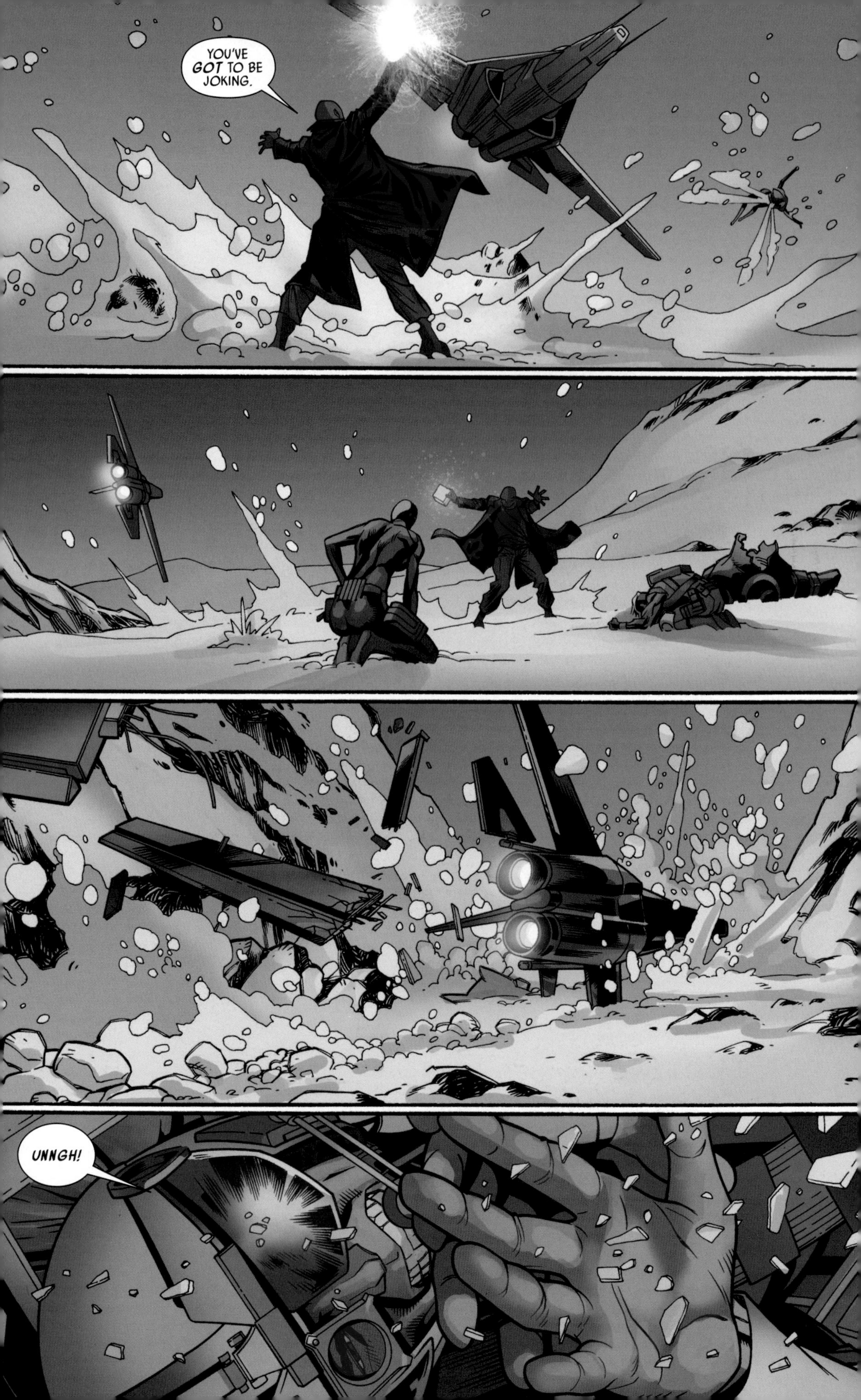
YOU'VE GOT TO BE JOKING.
UNNGH!

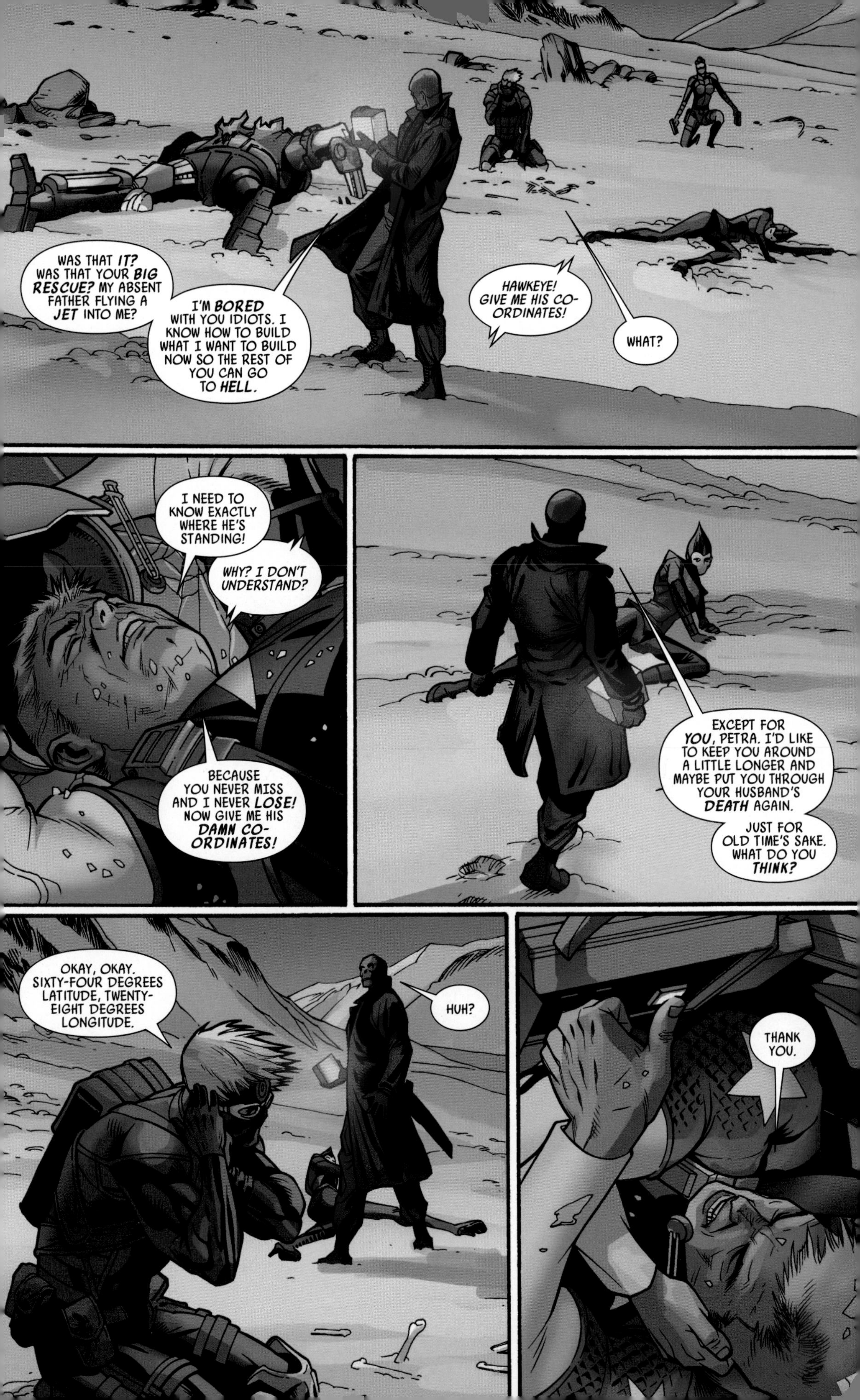
WAS THAT IT? WAS THAT YOUR BIG RESCUE? MY ABSENT FATHER FLYING A JET INTO ME?
I'M BORED WITH YOU IDIOTS. I KNOW HOW TO BUILD WHAT I WANT TO BUILD NOW SO THE REST OF YOU CAN GO TO HELL.
HAWKEYE! GIVE ME HIS CO-ORDINATES!
WHAT?
I NEED TO KNOW EXACTLY WHERE HE'S STANDING!
WHY? I DON'T UNDERSTAND?
BECAUSE YOU NEVER MISS AND I NEVER LOSE! NOW GIVE ME HIS DAMN CO-ORDINATES!
EXCEPT FOR YOU, PETRA. I'D LIKE TO KEEP YOU AROUND A LITTLE LONGER AND MAYBE PUT YOU THROUGH YOUR HUSBAND'S DEATH AGAIN.
JUST FOR OLD TIME'S SAKE. WHAT DO YOU THINK?
OKAY, OKAY. SIXTY-FOUR DEGREES LATITUDE, TWENTY-EIGHT DEGREES LONGITUDE.
HUH?
THANK YOU.

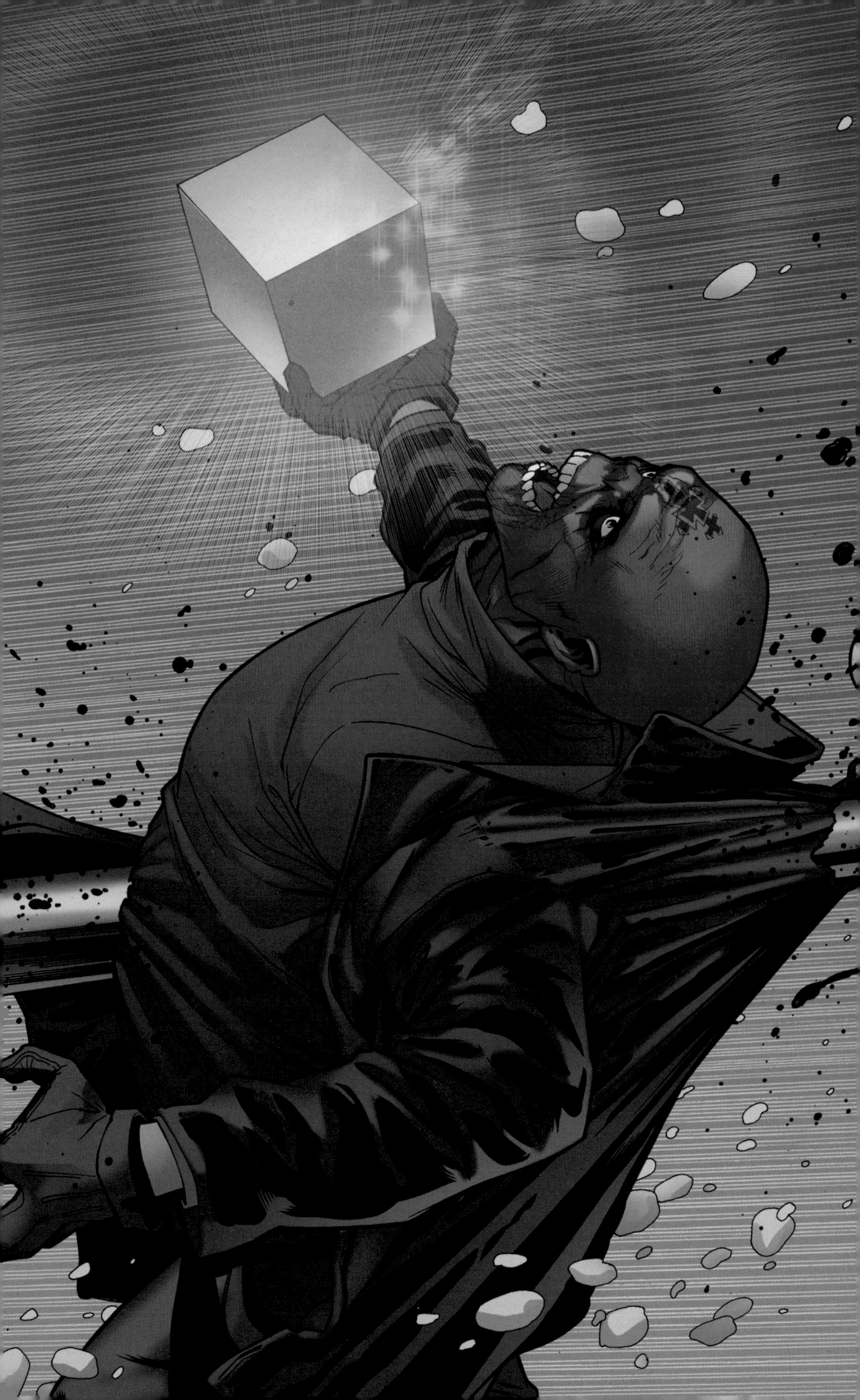

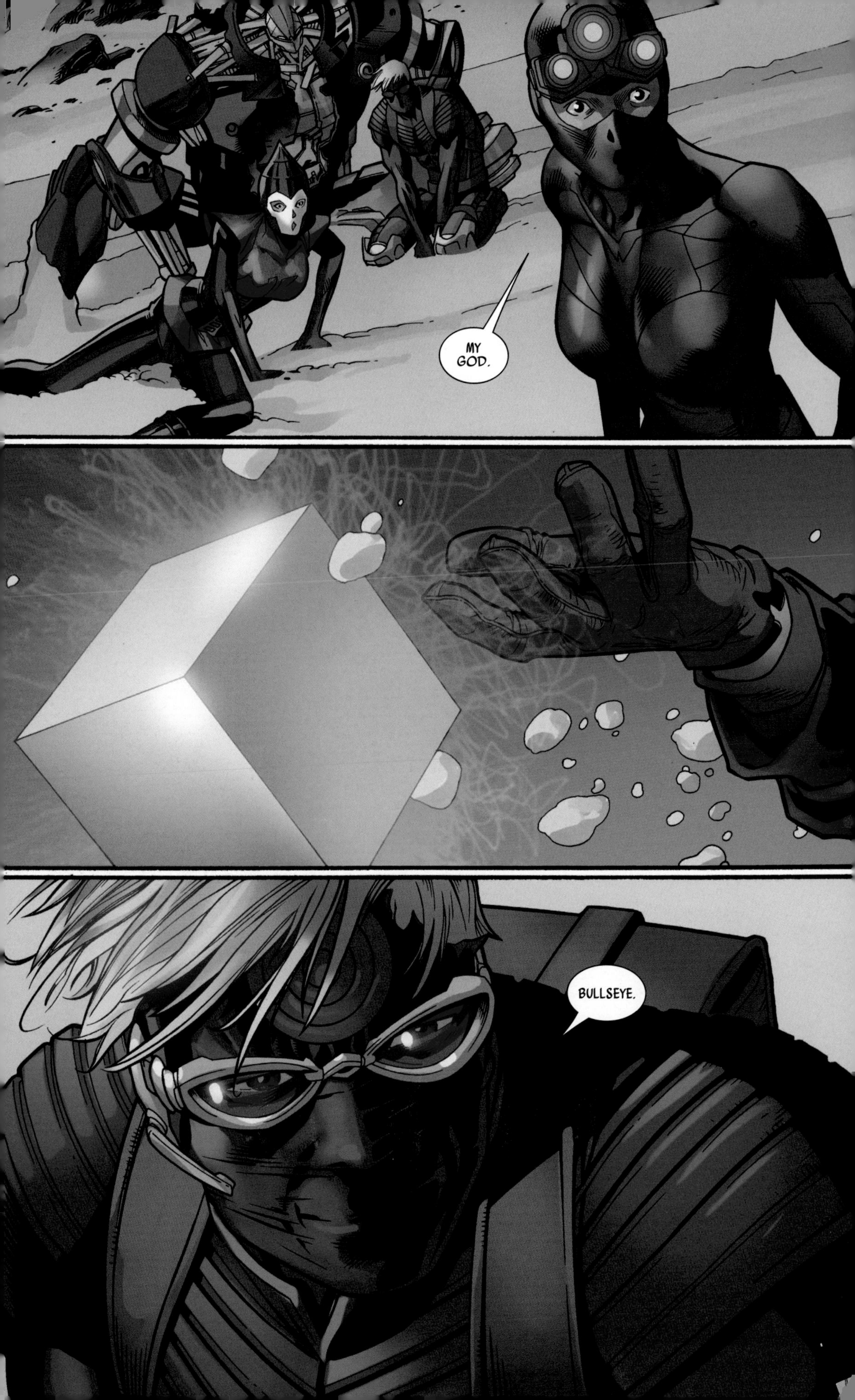
MY GOD.
BULLSEYE.

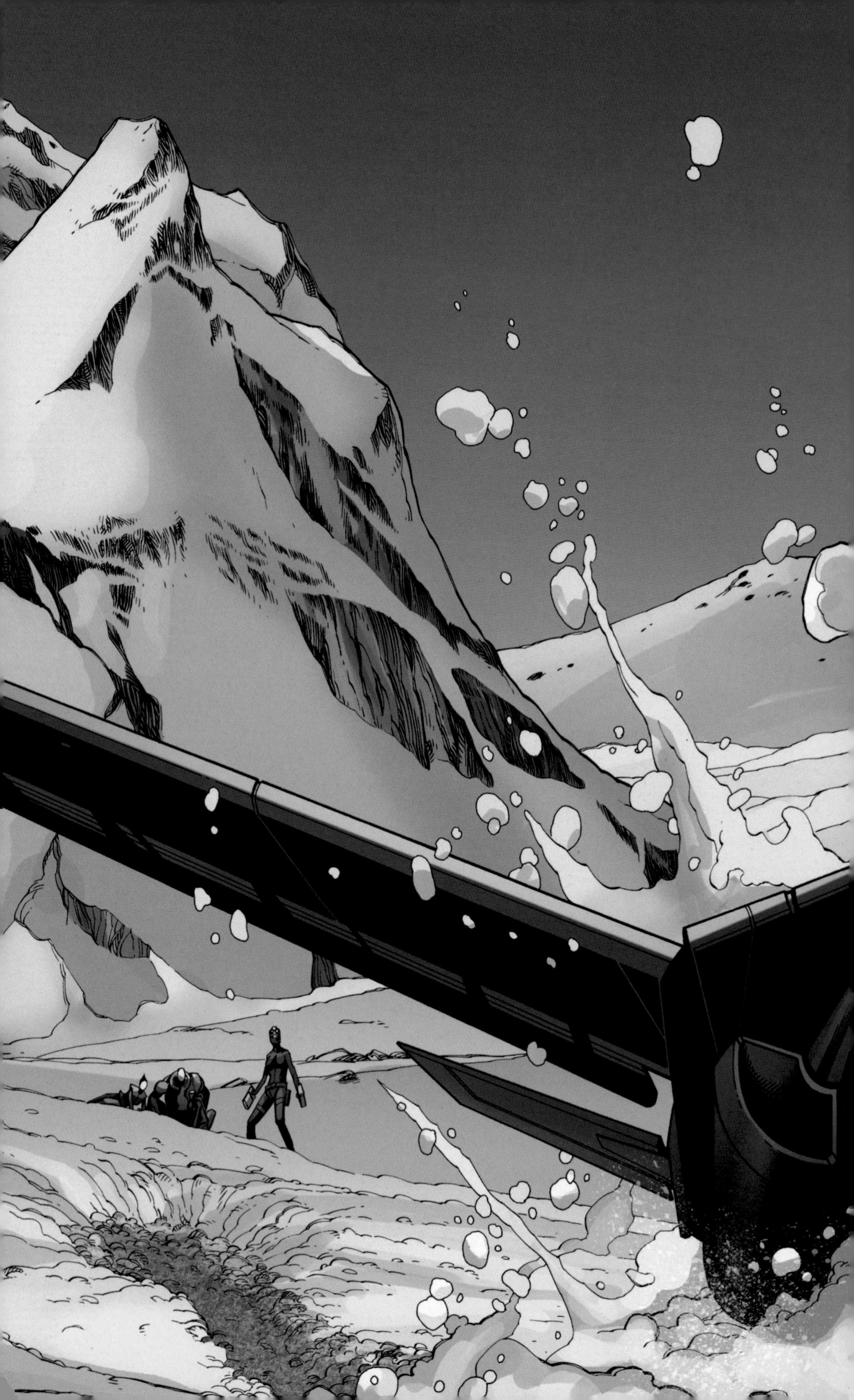

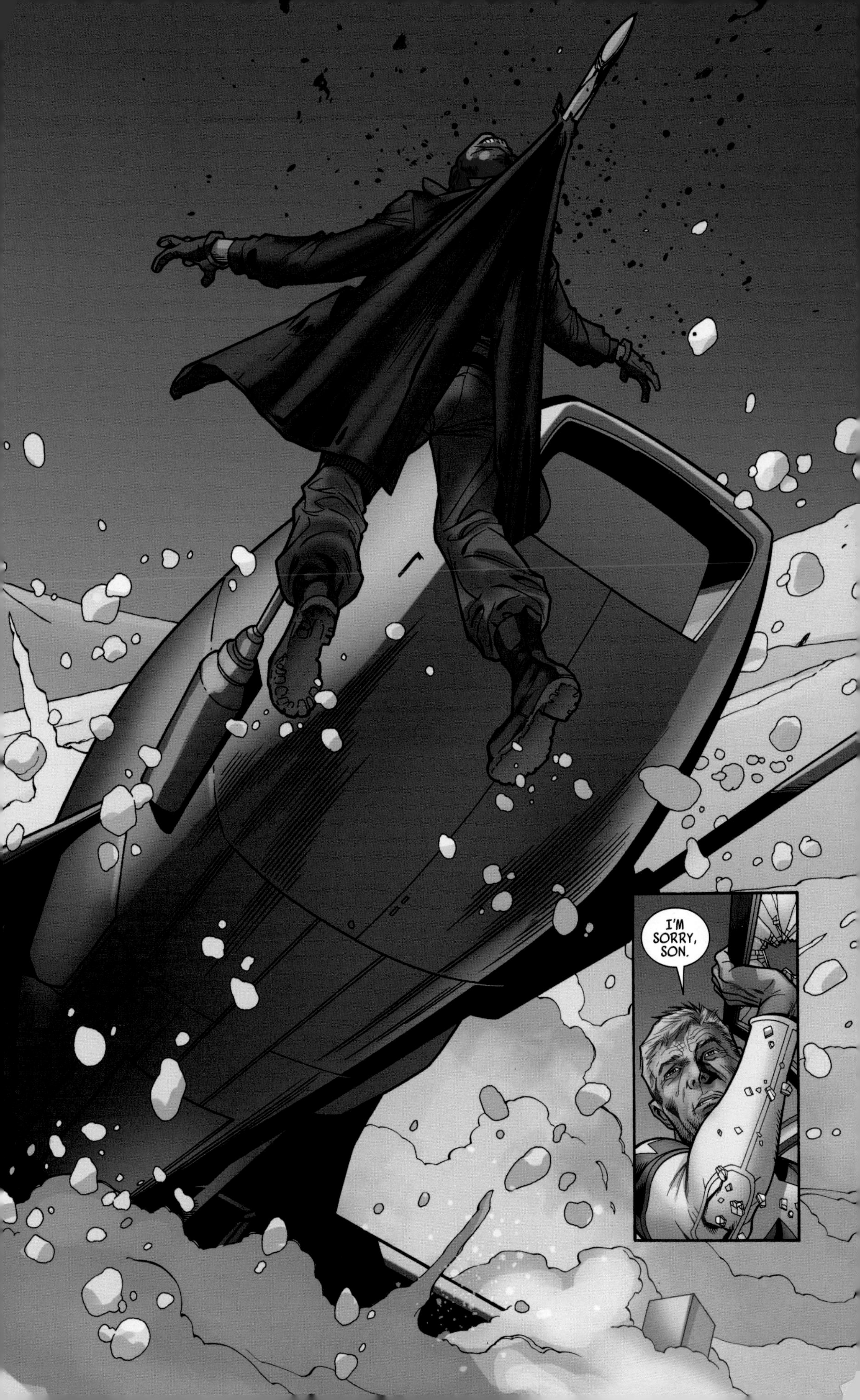
I'M SORRY, SON.

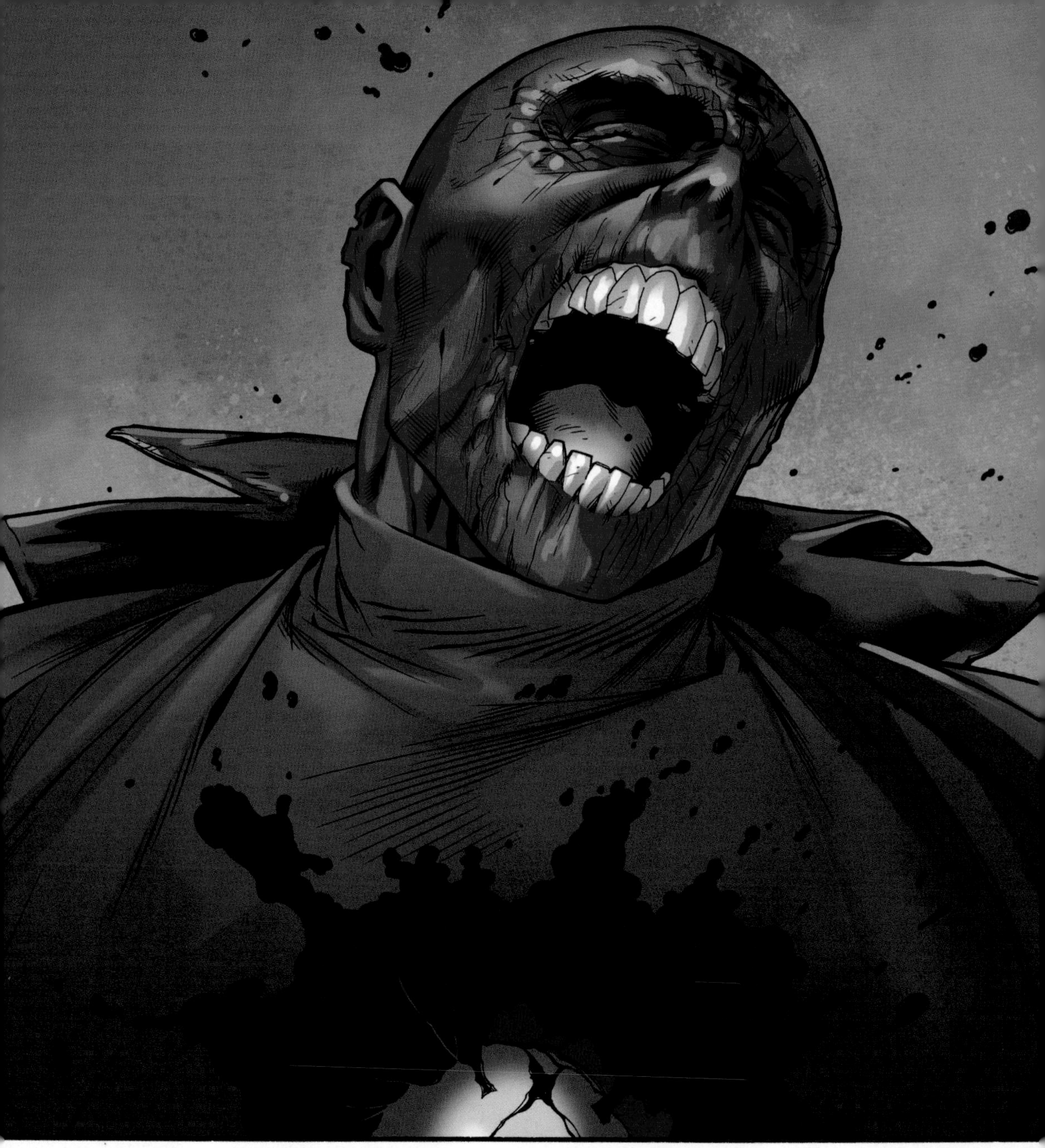

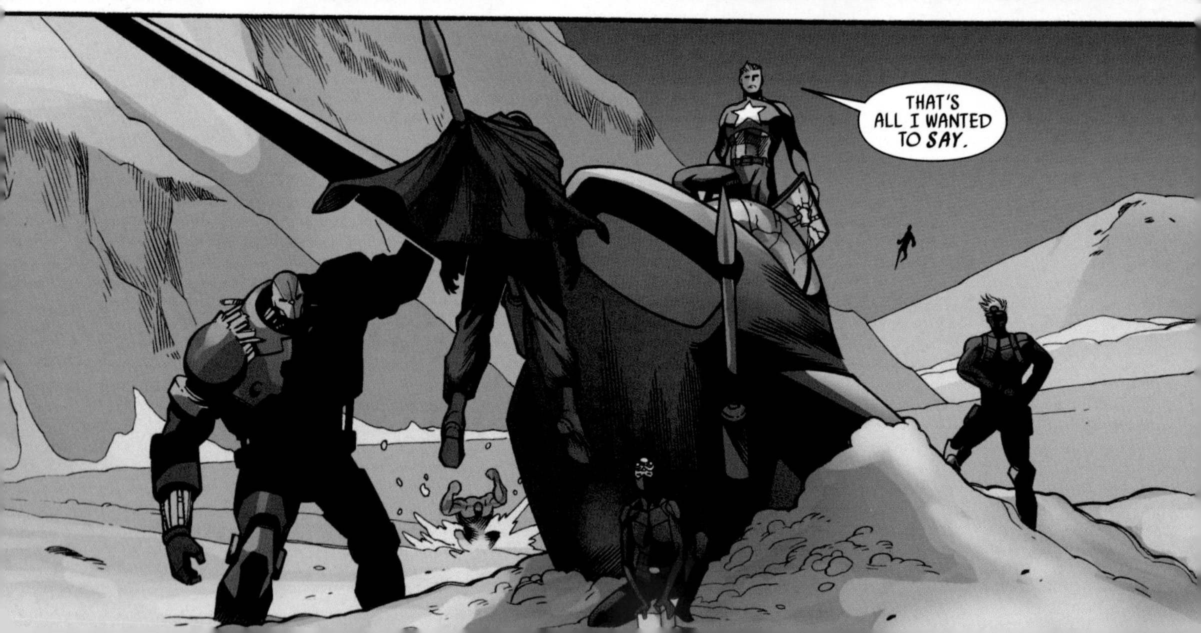
THAT'S ALL I WANTED TO SAY.

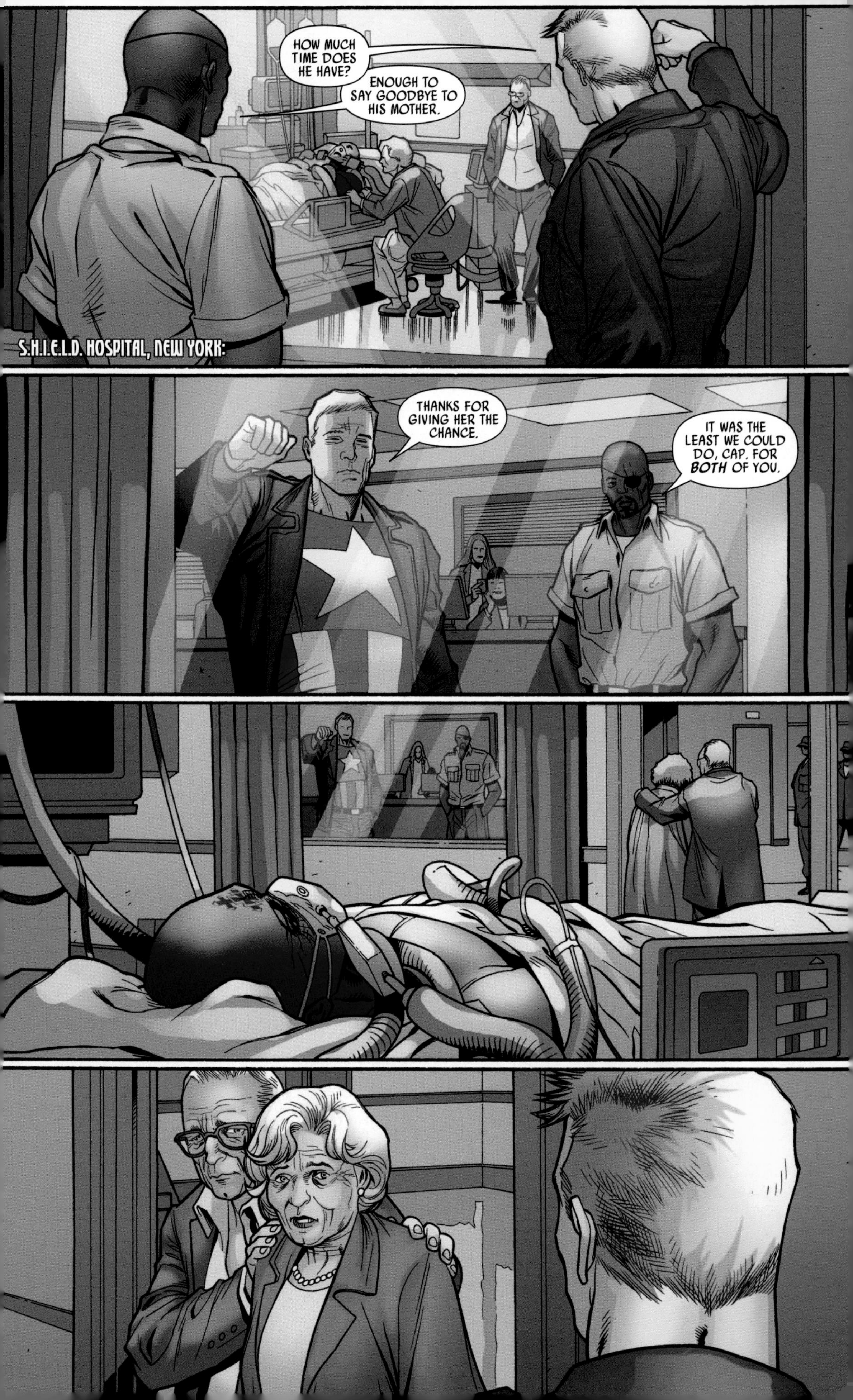
HOW MUCH TIME DOES HE HAVE?
ENOUGH TO SAY GOODBYE TO HIS MOTHER.
S.H.I.E.L.D. HOSPITAL, NEW YORK:
THANKS FOR GIVING HER THE CHANCE.
IT WAS THE LEAST WE COULD DO, CAP. FOR BOTH OF YOU.

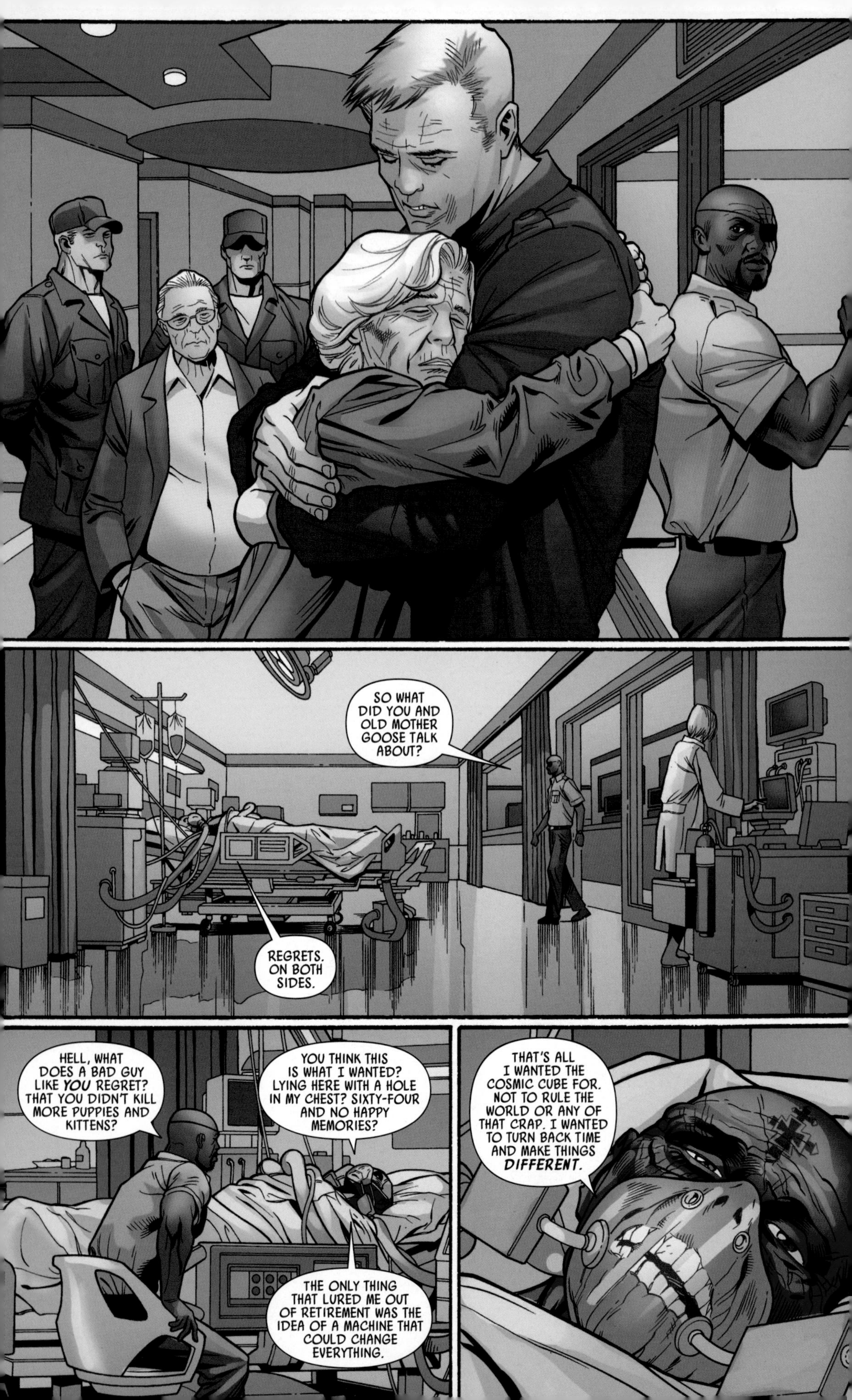
SO WHAT DID YOU AND OLD MOTHER GOOSE TALK ABOUT?
REGRETS. ON BOTH SIDES.
HELL, WHAT DOES A BAD GUY LIKE *YOU* REGRET? THAT YOU DIDN'T KILL MORE PUPPIES AND KITTENS?
YOU THINK THIS IS WHAT I WANTED? LYING HERE WITH A HOLE IN MY CHEST? SIXTY-FOUR AND NO HAPPY MEMORIES?
THE ONLY THING THAT LURED ME OUT OF RETIREMENT WAS THE IDEA OF A MACHINE THAT COULD CHANGE EVERYTHING.
THAT'S ALL I WANTED THE COSMIC CUBE FOR. NOT TO RULE THE WORLD OR ANY OF THAT CRAP. I WANTED TO TURN BACK TIME AND MAKE THINGS ***DIFFERENT***.

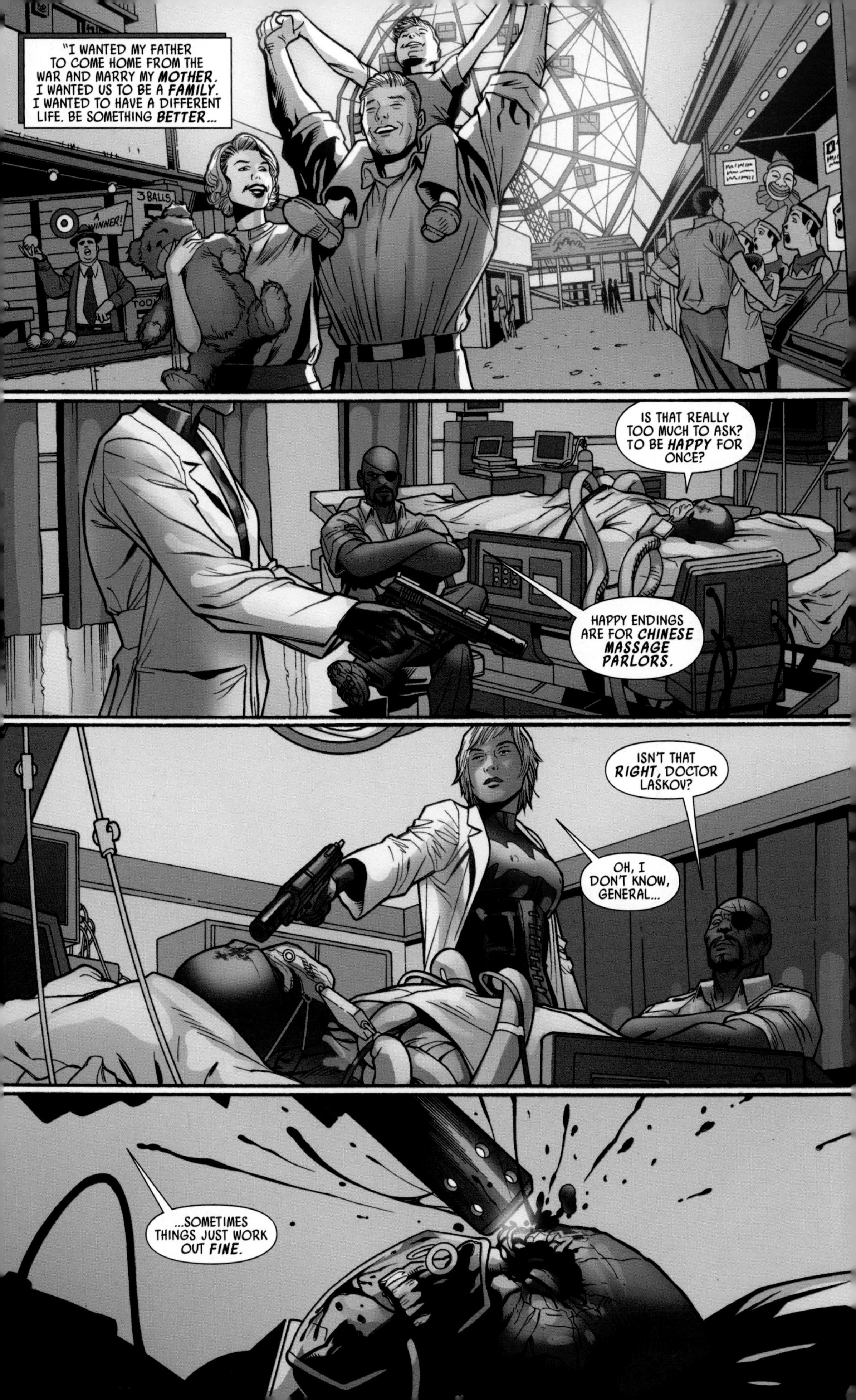
"I WANTED MY FATHER TO COME HOME FROM THE WAR AND MARRY MY MOTHER. I WANTED US TO BE A FAMILY. I WANTED TO HAVE A DIFFERENT LIFE. BE SOMETHING BETTER...
3 BALLS
A WINNER!
IS THAT REALLY TOO MUCH TO ASK? TO BE HAPPY FOR ONCE?
HAPPY ENDINGS ARE FOR CHINESE MASSAGE PARLORS.
ISN'T THAT RIGHT, DOCTOR LASKOV?
OH, I DON'T KNOW, GENERAL...
...SOMETIMES THINGS JUST WORK OUT FINE.

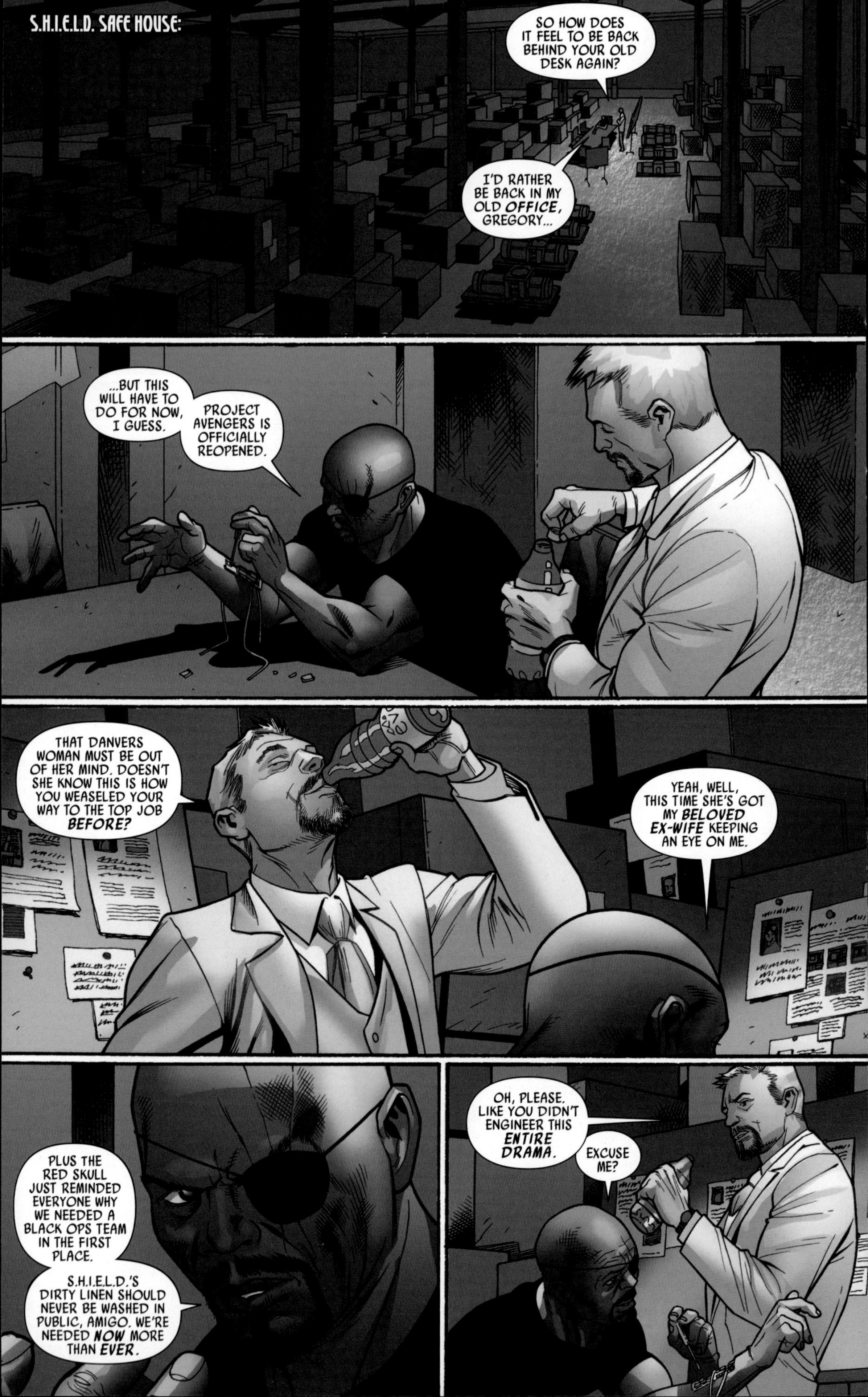
S.H.I.E.L.D. SAFE HOUSE:
SO HOW DOES IT FEEL TO BE BACK BEHIND YOUR OLD DESK AGAIN?
I'D RATHER BE BACK IN MY OLD OFFICE, GREGORY...
...BUT THIS WILL HAVE TO DO FOR NOW, I GUESS.
PROJECT AVENGERS IS OFFICIALLY REOPENED.
THAT DANVERS WOMAN MUST BE OUT OF HER MIND. DOESN'T SHE KNOW THIS IS HOW YOU WEASELED YOUR WAY TO THE TOP JOB BEFORE?
YEAH, WELL, THIS TIME SHE'S GOT MY BELOVED EX-WIFE KEEPING AN EYE ON ME.
PLUS THE RED SKULL JUST REMINDED EVERYONE WHY WE NEEDED A BLACK OPS TEAM IN THE FIRST PLACE.
S.H.I.E.L.D.'S DIRTY LINEN SHOULD NEVER BE WASHED IN PUBLIC, AMIGO. WE'RE NEEDED NOW MORE THAN EVER.
OH, PLEASE. LIKE YOU DIDN'T ENGINEER THIS ENTIRE DRAMA.
EXCUSE ME?

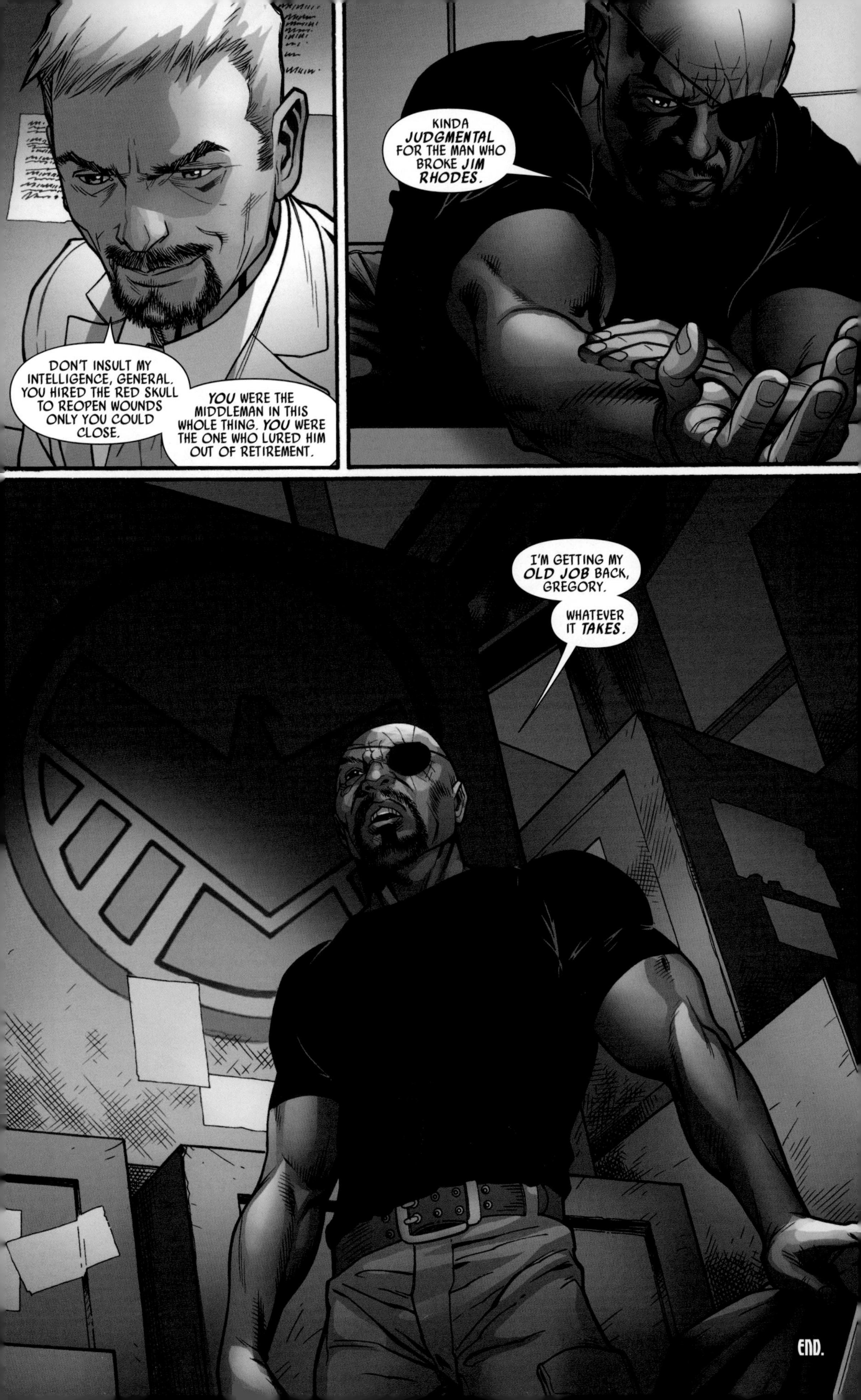
DON'T INSULT MY INTELLIGENCE, GENERAL. YOU HIRED THE RED SKULL TO REOPEN WOUNDS ONLY YOU COULD CLOSE.
YOU WERE THE MIDDLEMAN IN THIS WHOLE THING. YOU WERE THE ONE WHO LURED HIM OUT OF RETIREMENT.
KINDA JUDGMENTAL FOR THE MAN WHO BROKE JIM RHODES.
I'M GETTING MY OLD JOB BACK, GREGORY.
WHATEVER IT TAKES.
END.

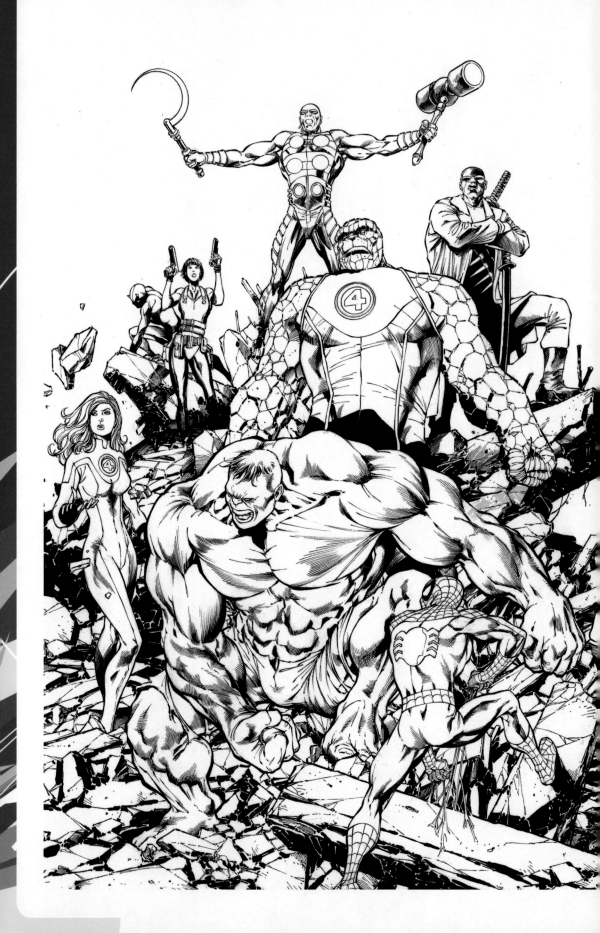

1 SKETCH VARIANT
BY CARLOS PACHECO

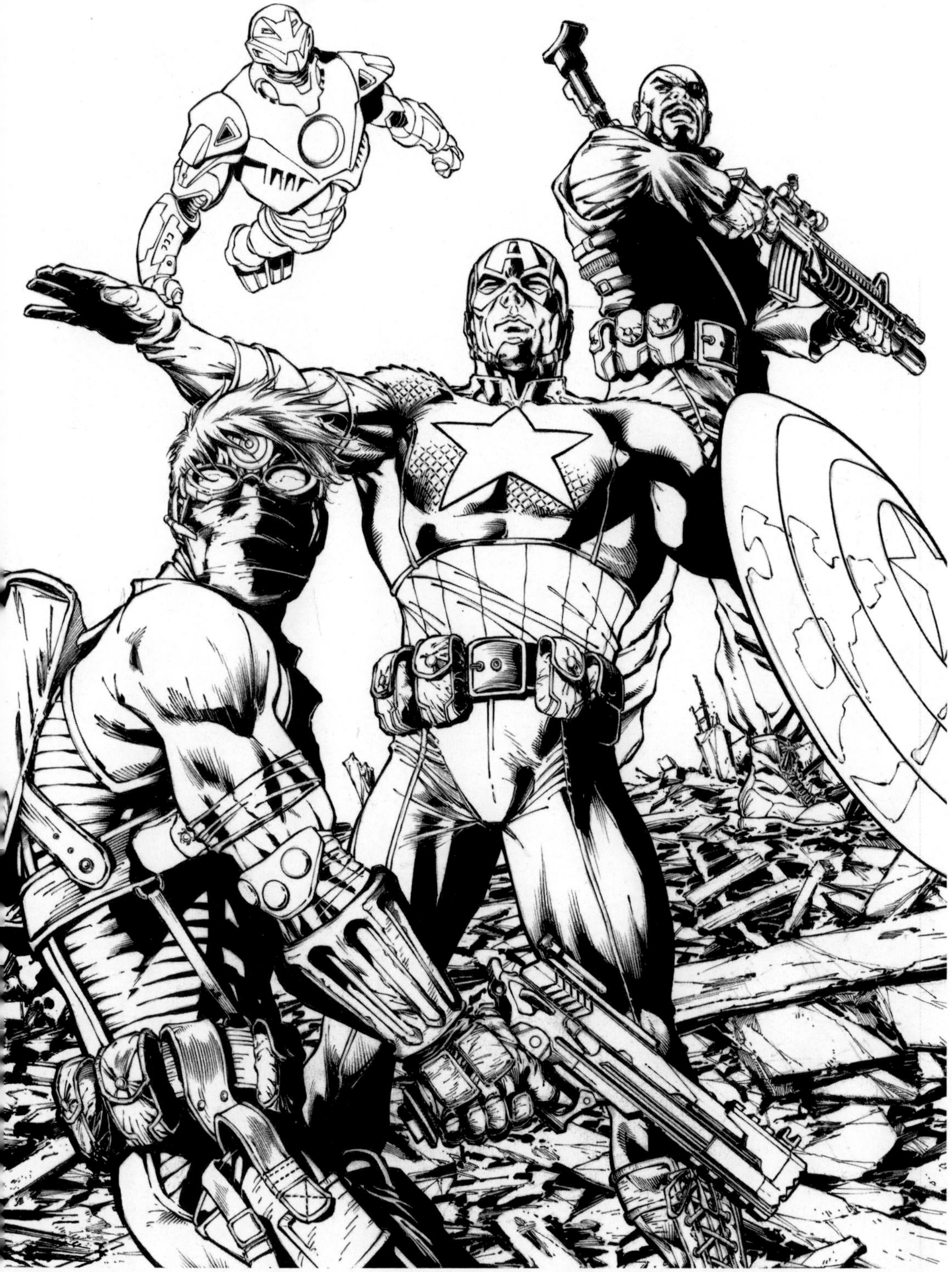

 # 1 VARIANT
BY LEINIL FRANCIS YU

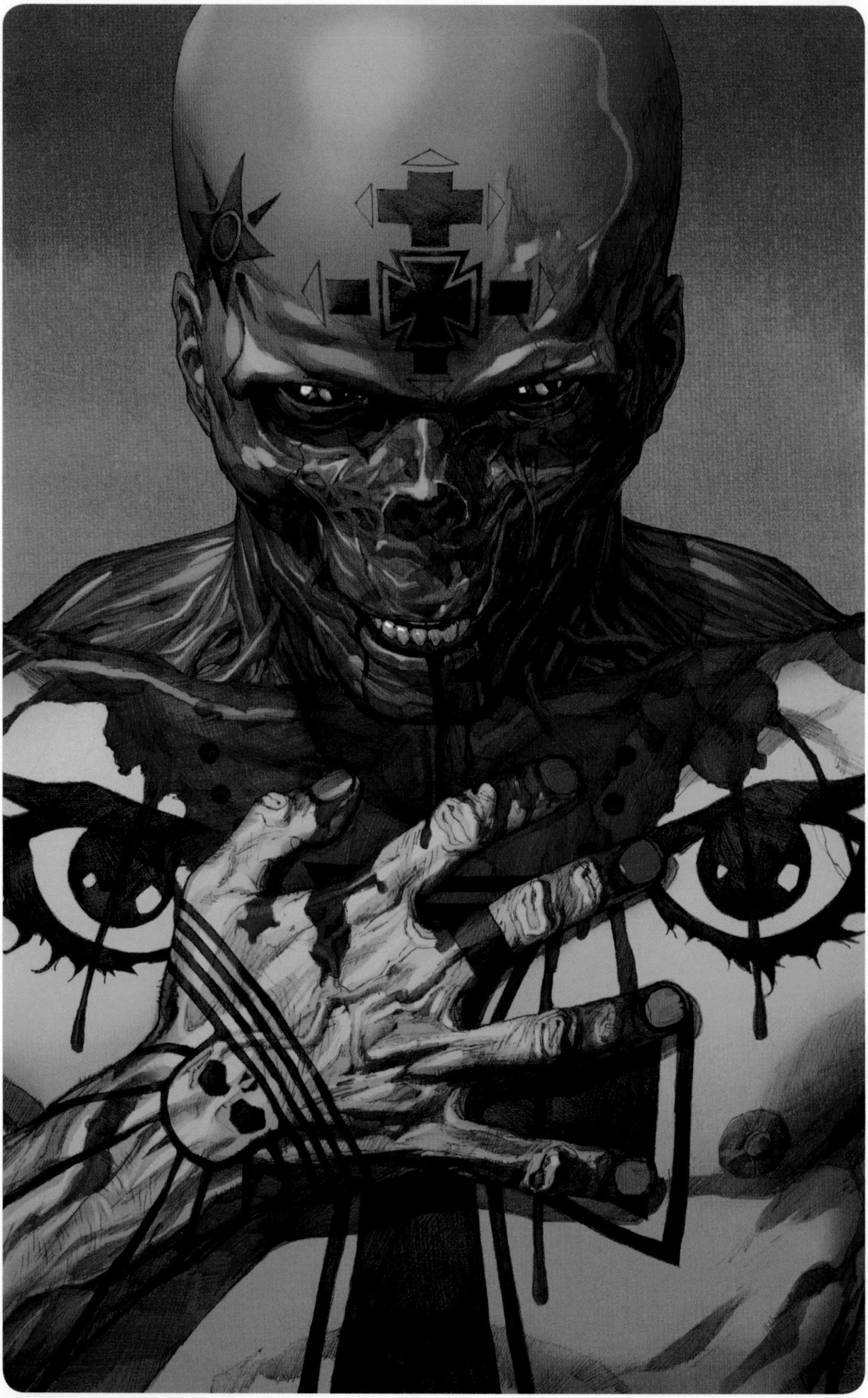

CARLOS PACHECO SKETCHBOOK

BLACK WIDOW

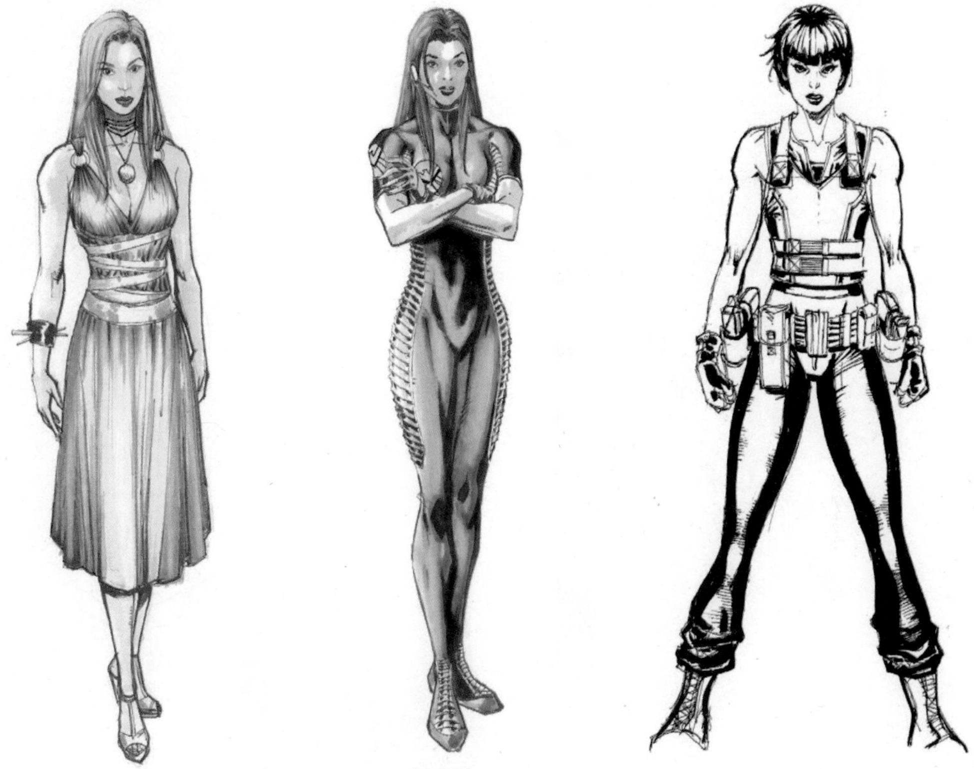

RED WASP

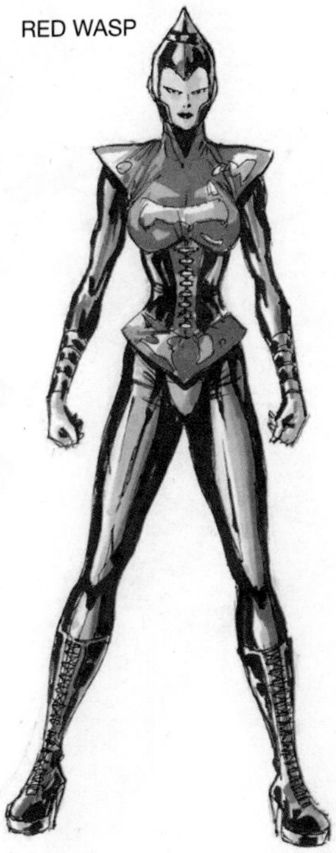

NICK FURY &
BLACK WIDOW

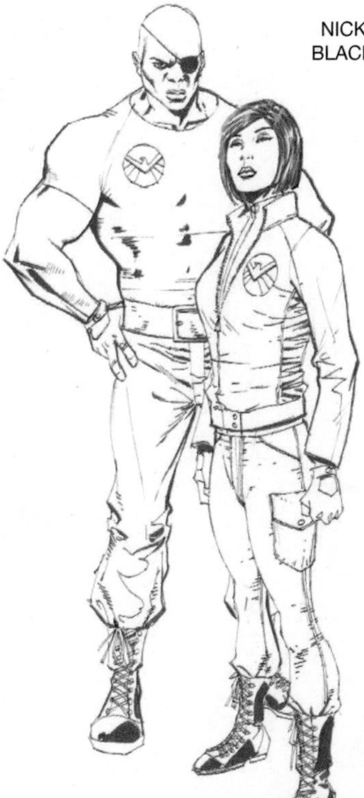

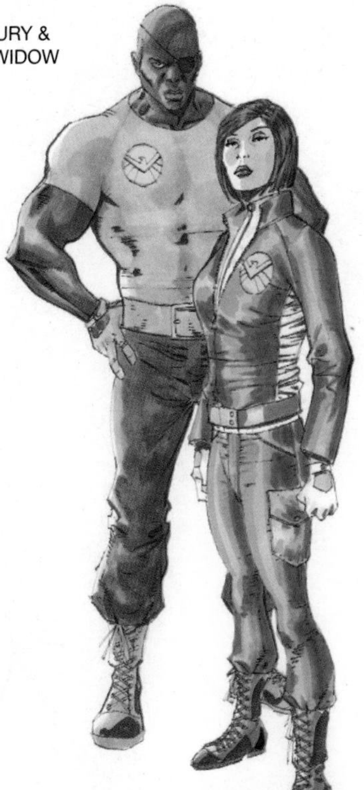

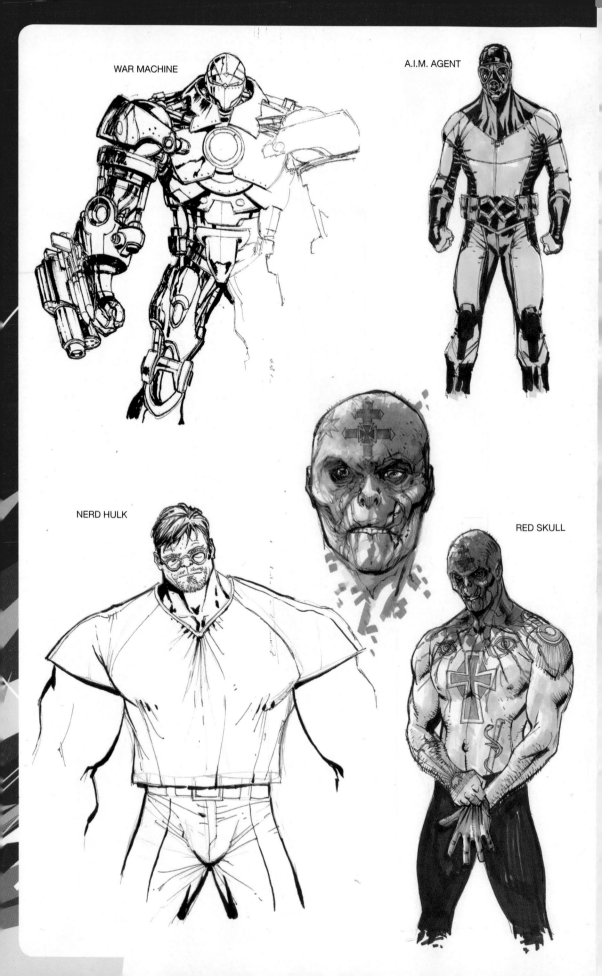

WAR MACHINE

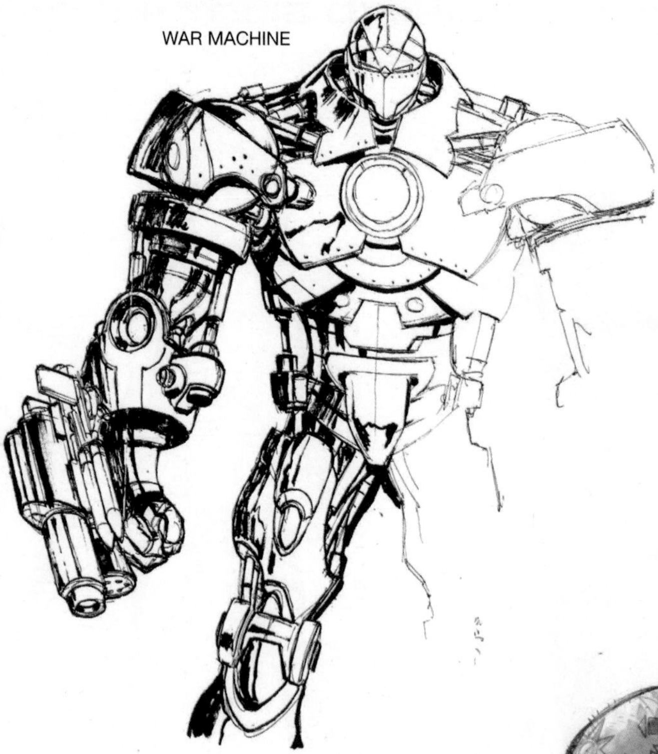

A.I.M. AGENT

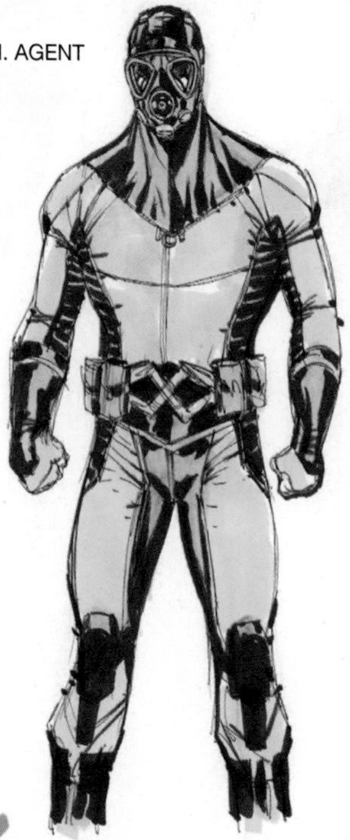

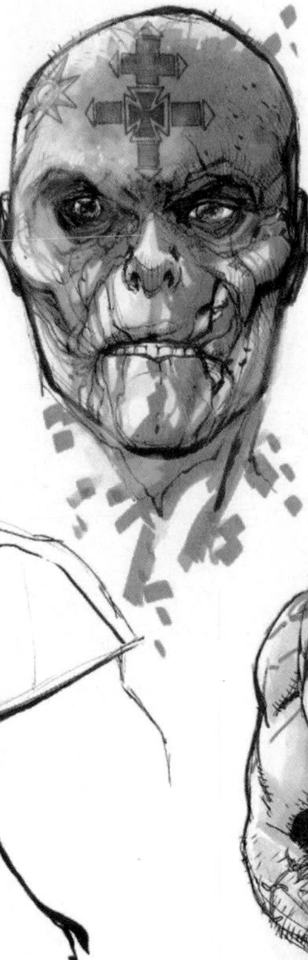

NERD HULK

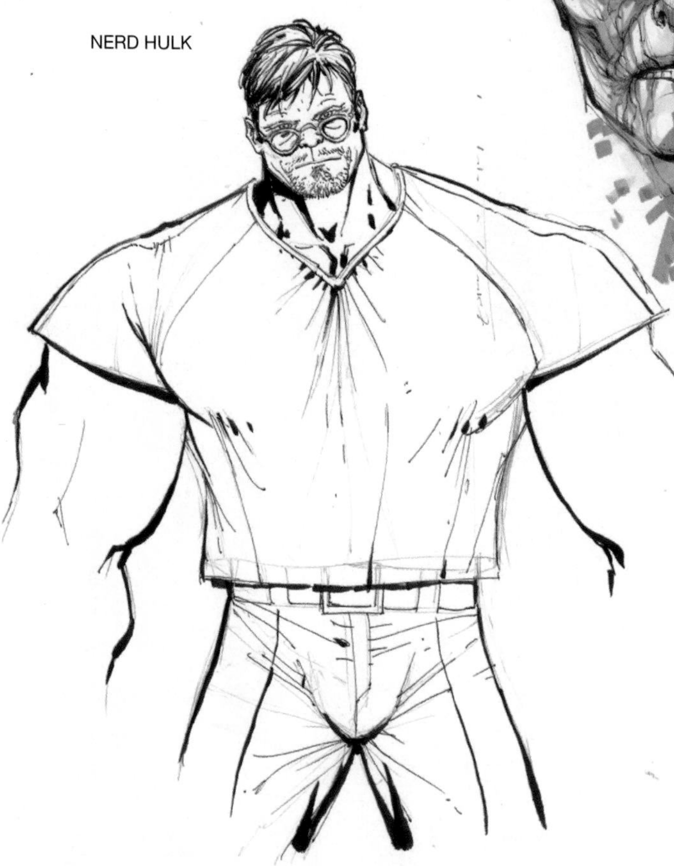

RED SKULL

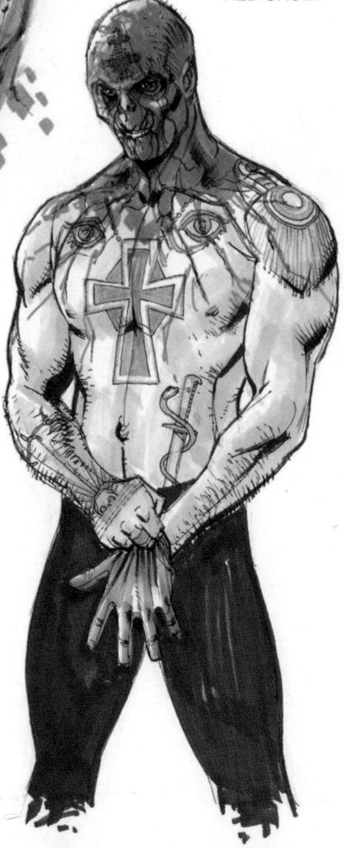